Developing Property Sustainably

Developing Property Sustainably introduces readers to the key issues surrounding sustainable property development in the global marketplace. Pulling together received wisdom and original research, the authors provide a clear and practical overview of the sustainable property development process as well as a critical appraisal of the problems faced by global built environment stakeholders. Throughout, the authors demonstrate how the property development industry could and should respond better to debate on sustainable practices in the built environment by adopting more rigorous measurement techniques and sustainable approaches.

Starting by examining key definitions and stakeholders, the book goes on to explore finance, planning, construction, procurement, occupation, retrofit and life cycle sustainability in order to provide the reader with a detailed understanding of all the issues involved in the delivery of sustainable property development from inception to occupation and beyond. Throughout the book, international case studies are used to demonstrate how sustainable property development is applied in practice around the world. With a logical chapter structure and accessible writing style, *Developing Property Sustainably* would be perfect for use on undergraduate and postgraduate modules and courses in real estate development, property and urban development and other built environment programmes.

Sara J. Wilkinson is Associate Professor at the University of Technology, Sydney, Australia and a Fellow of RICS. She has published widely in the areas of sustainability, building adaptation and property.

Sarah L. Sayce is Emeritus Professor at Kingston University, UK, having previously led the School of Surveying and Planning there for many years. She holds both an initial degree and a PhD from the University of Reading, UK, and is a Chartered Surveyor. In addition to being a well-known academic, author and researcher in the field of sustainability and real estate, she is active in her professional body, for which she is currently an elected member of the International Governing Council.

Pernille H. Christensen is a Senior Lecturer at the University of Technology, Sydney, Australia where she is the Course Director of the Property Economics programme. Her research focuses on decision making related to sustainability in the built environment.

Developing Property Sustainably

Sara J. Wilkinson, Sarah L. Sayce and
Pernille H. Christensen

Routledge
Taylor & Francis Group

LONDON AND NEW YORK

First published 2015
by Routledge
2 Park Square, Milton Park, Abingdon, Oxon OX14 4RN

and by Routledge
711 Third Avenue, New York, NY 10017

Routledge is an imprint of the Taylor & Francis Group, an informa business

British Library Cataloguing-in-Publication Data
A catalogue record for this book is available from the British Library

Library of Congress Cataloging in Publication Data
Developing property sustainably / [edited by] Sara Wilkinson,
Sarah Sayce and Pernille Christensen.
     pages cm
  Includes bibliographical references and index.
  1. Real estate development – Environmental aspects.
  2. Sustainable design. 3. Sustainable construction. I. Wilkinson,
  Sara, 1961– II. Sayce, Sarah, 1950– III. Christensen, Pernille.
  HD1390.D44 2015
  333.73´15–dc23   2014046140

ISBN: 978-0-415-83566-4 (hbk)
ISBN: 978-0-415-83567-1 (pbk)
ISBN: 978-1-315-76482-5 (ebk)

Typeset in Goudy
by HWA Text and Data Management, London

Contents

Figures

Tables

Foreword

My interest in developing buildings to be sustainable started in San Francisco as a mechanical engineer trying to design buildings with air conditioning in a place where power black outs and brown outs were becoming the norm. The fantastic engineers around me at Arup had set their goal to reduce the need for energy in buildings, this had me hooked as it was easy to design a building using all the materials and equipment you had at your disposal, but it was much harder and more fun to design without. I returned to Australia and set about designing a sustainable building at Regatta Point, Canberra, using the lake for cooling and heating through a reverse cycle heat pump, low-level inlets and high-level turrets to naturally ventilate the building, all in the name of creating a better environment for the occupants and reducing energy consumption. The building went on to win the Energy Efficiency Award.

Many years later I returned to this building during a visit to Canberra and enquired about its performance, the feedback was not good but as I asked more questions I found out why: the people did not know how to use it. A motor had broken in the low-level louvres, so they shut it down rather than fix it. Then a drought prevented the heat pump from working as the lake was too low. If they had fixed the motor then during the drought they could have naturally ventilated the space at night cooled the slab and so cooled the building, but this option no longer existed. The learning I took from this is that sustainable development is as much about people as it is about technology: it is not just design and construction – it is the whole life of a building and how it works for its occupants that really matters.

Sustainable development is a key part of the future. Buildings generate a significant environmental and social impact either during design, construction or operation. Buildings are essential to us all: they provide humanity with protection, security, comfort, history and so many more positive things. Therefore sustainable development and ensuring it is done right is intrinsically linked to our future health and wellbeing. Developers have always struggled with 'what is sustainable development'? Some think it is a philanthropy, others simply relate it to the energy consumed or the materials used. In reality it is all that, but so much more. The only way to create a truly sustainable development is through integrated design and holistic thinking. We must never forget that in general buildings are for people. People use energy, create rubbish, design, construct, use buildings.

True sustainable development starts at the start of a project, not half-way through, it must be part of the vision, the concept, the idea! It is also essential that people form part of this early thinking, design inside-out not outside-in. How will the development be used, who will use it, how long for. It is important we remove the short-term thinking and replace it with long-term thinking. Buildings are around for many years.

Interestingly, London has set a carbon emission reduction target of 80 per cent by 2050, and 65 per cent of existing buildings will still be standing in 2050. So as you read this book look around at the buildings nearby and ask will they be able to reduce their consumption by 80 per cent?

With this in mind it always good to be ahead of the game, to be thinking now how will my portfolio deliver the change required. How will the new developments contribute to this change? New developments account for a small percentage of the buildings in a city but they generally lead, they provide the chance to innovate.

This book sets out the importance of integrating sustainability at the start of the process, retaining it through the middle, not value engineering it out, then maintaining it through sustainable property and facilities management. A whole-of-life approach is critical to being able to deliver a sustainable development. Sustainability must not be a bolt-on, rather integrated into the whole development process. As you read this book you note that the authors stress the importance of a holistic approach, ensuring all the time that long-term thinking is taken into account.

To deliver a sustainable development more work is required upfront, but the benefits over the lifetime, or in most cases the period of the first lease (normally ten years), far exceed the initial work. Importantly this book recognizes the importance of post-occupancy evaluations to establish the outcomes of sustainable development.

I once sat in an audience where a tenant advocate was asked if his clients wanted sustainability, he said 'No'. I then asked 'Do they want daylight, extra fresh air, comfort, access to nature, views, breakout spaces, good amenity, lower running costs, etc,' 'Yes'. This is of course sustainability.

This book takes the academic expertise of the authors and overlays real world examples, which is important in demonstrating the solutions. By overlaying an international lens they have managed to identify some of the leading examples notably from the UK and Australia. No country has all the answers but the countries highlighted through this book are definitely leaders on a global scale. I have learnt a tremendous amount working in the USA, UK and Australia, and I know from personal experience the international perspective is critical to getting it right.

This book helps to pull together all parts of the property process into one place and demonstrate how sustainability fits in. Remember, it's all about people and the planet, we need to ensure we do our bit to make certain both are still around and enjoying life.

Paul Edwards
Group General Manager Sustainability
Mirvac Group, Sydney, Australia

Acknowledgements

Writing any book is a journey – and as with any journey that is worthwhile – they tend to take a long while in the planning and often take unexpected turns. This book was no different!

Whilst we had been familiar with each other's work for a long time, we had not actually met until 2012 when we were both presenting at the ERES (European Real Estate Society) Conference in Edinburgh: Sara on 'A conceptual understanding of sustainability in australian property companies' and Sarah on 'Towards a fairplace award: the evolution of a scheme to reward property management which respect people, planet and community'. Also at the conference was Ed Needle from Routledge who brought us together for discussions – and so *Developing Property Sustainably* was conceived as an idea. So thank you Ed for the initial 'matchmaking' and all your subsequent help and encouragement to put it together 'across continents'.

At the time we planned the book, Sarah's then work commitments meant that finding the time to undertake the necessary research and write it on a completely 50/50 basis would be tough – so it was good to have Pernille Christensen join the writing team in 2013 to provide a US perspective. Thank you for taking the drafting lead to Chapters 6 and 9.

Professor Chris Eves also very kindly also agreed to make a contribution. Chris is Professor in Property Economics at Queensland University of Technology and Academic Program Director, Urban Development, but importantly, Chris had worked for many years with the State Bank of NSW and was therefore able to bring an Australian finance perspective to the chapter on Chapter 5. Chris has published widely on topics ranging from valuation methodology to property investment performance and was able to integrate this to the work. Thank you Chris.

Our ambition for the book is that it will help in not only raising awareness of the benefits of a more planetary and socially respectful approach to property development but it will do so in a way that is understanding of, and sympathetic to, the pressures under which development takes place. We hope that we have got that about right – and therefore our thanks to Paul Edwards who in his foreword would suggest that we have! Paul 'walks the sustainability walk' on a daily basis in such a personally and professionally committed way that his endorsement is very much appreciated.

While authors tend to get the glory of their name on a book there are a whole army of people behind the scenes who by their support, encouragement and at times nagging, ensure that the whole does finally come to fruition. Our thanks to you all – without you it would not happen.

Lastly, our thanks to family and friends for all those lost times for coffee and a chat when 'the book' has taken precedence. Sara would like to thank Ted, Ruskin and Lindsay. In Sarah's case – thanks to David, Charlotte and Ed for their understanding that retirement hasn't meant retirement, but merely more time to commit to endeavours such as this.

We hope you, the readers, enjoy it. And if there are any errors please do let us know! They are ours and ours alone.

Sara J. Wilkinson and Sarah L. Sayce
May 2015

1 Introduction to sustainable property development

Sara J. Wilkinson and Sarah L. Sayce

1.0 Introduction

The built environment in general and property development in particular, have significant impacts on all aspects of sustainability, economic, social and environmental. The development process impacts on resource consumption, energy use, biodiversity, water consumption and water course patterns, waste production and the physical design and impact of urban spaces. This book examines the impacts that property development has at each stage of the process and identifies ways in which developers can reduce negative impacts and furthermore, how they can contribute positively to mitigate issues facing society such as climate change.

It is our contention that the concept of sustainable property development is not an absolute. We have only a developing understanding of the terms 'sustainability' and 'sustainable development'; they are still contested and multi-definitional. Therefore it is possible only to speak of *relative* sustainability. That is to say that one building or property may be judged to be *more* or *less* sustainable than another one; but even this judgement is contentious.

With this as a starting point, this chapter seeks to explore some definitions of sustainable development, sustainability and sustainable property development. It illustrates that sustainability is a contested concept and describes what this implies for our conceptual understanding. The characteristics of sustainable property development and sustainable property, we argue, vary from land use to land use, from one time frame to another and also, from location to location. The chapter describes the various stakeholders and their respective roles and abilities to determine the level of sustainability embraced in any property development. Developing property sustainably is an essential goal, if we are to develop a built environment that has the least environmental impact possible and engenders a more equitable and healthy society for all. Whether this aim can be realised remains to be seen, but it should not deter us from trying as the philosopher Emanuel Kant said in the 1750s 'it is often necessary to make decisions on the basis of information sufficient for action, but insufficient for the intellect'. It is on this basis that the strategies for developing property sustainably are posited.

1.1 Definitions of sustainable development, sustainability and sustainable property development – a contested concept

Most modern texts on sustainable development take as their starting point that of the Brundtland Commission (1987: 43) 'development that meets the needs of the present without compromising the ability of future generations to meet their own needs' and it is this definition which has been embraced and is embedded in much legislation – including that concerning property development. However, whilst undoubtedly laudable in ambition, it is difficult to translate into action, and it is action with which this book is concerned. Indeed the problem with the Brundtland definition was neatly summarised by Sir Jonathan Porritt (*Financial Times* 1998) who opined: 'Sustainable development is one of those ideas that everybody supports, but nobody knows what it means.' When trying to define sustainable development, it is clear confusion reigns and that no single definition or interpretation exists or satisfies all (Washington 2015). It follows that if our understanding of sustainable development is flawed or incomplete, efforts to deliver sustainable development may be futile at best, or exacerbate the problem at worst. So, why is sustainable development so difficult to define?

Sustainable development, sustainability and thus sustainable property development have the characteristics of 'contested concepts' (Paton 2010). Gallie (1956) introduced the term to the Aristotelian Society to facilitate understanding of abstract, qualitative concepts such as 'social justice' or 'fairness'. To illustrate how social justice may be interpreted differently depending on one's viewpoint; one only has to consider the saying 'one man's freedom fighter is another man's terrorist'. In essence contested concepts are notions that involve endless disputes about their proper uses on the part of the users and second, cannot be settled by appeal to empirical evidence or logic. The disputes arise from a range of different, though reasonable, interpretations of the concept.

When analysing sustainable development, it is necessary to deconstruct the definitions and explore the interpretations that are possible. Returning to Brundtland, whilst the first part of the definition as set out above is commonly cited, the section goes on to place priorities in terms of the world's poor, which they argued should be prioritised and the need to recognise 'the idea that limitations imposed by the state of technology and social organisation on the environments ability to meet present and future needs' (Brundtland 1987: 43). This latter extension recognises that shifting agendas and technology changes will affect the interpretations of what can or cannot be achieved.

However, frequently these extensions are omitted, which limits the breadth and depth of our understanding of sustainability (Washington 2015). It is easy to say 'that does not apply to me or my circumstances'; sometimes the issues are simply too hard to process and understand. Nowhere is this the case more than with property development, which all would recognise has long-term implications, but about which decisions have to be made with imperfect knowledge and often with a pressing economic priority. The definitions adopted and their interpretations demonstrate the difficulty in applying appropriate relative weights to environmental, economic and social spheres by different groups and how the concepts of impartiality, fairness and future are applied to these spheres. The analysis described below allows a more informed perspective of sustainability and sustainable development to be realised.

1.2   Sustainability from ecocentrism to anthropocentrism

The following section sets out some of the more theoretical aspects of sustainability and whilst, at first read, much of it would appear to be unconnected with the notion of property development, it is not as the philosophical arguments go to the heart of different policy approaches adopted both in the developed and developing parts of the globe.

So, what are the underlying philosophical, economic, social and environmental beliefs or constructs driving perceptions and actions and the executive? It is possible to analyse conceptual understanding within the property sector alone, however this limits the overall understanding of sustainability and sustainable development across all sectors and importantly, how it relates to the rest of the world. Literature shows distinct characteristics and sub-groups that can be de-constructed and ordered to clarify shared and distinct characteristics.

A key division is between ecocentrism and anthropocentrism (Pepper 1984; Dobson 1990; Washington 2015). An ecocentric worldview perceives ecosystems as part of an integrated environmental system with organisms, biological communities and ecosystems creating the mantle of life surrounding the planet. Ecocentrism is advocated by an environmental movement known as Deep Ecology (Naess 1990; Brown 1995), grounded in seeking the common good of the human and non-human world (Purser and Montuori 1996). Ecocentrics are radically egalitarian where animals, humans, rivers, seas and lakes all have equal and intrinsic value. Ecocentrics argue that only when this worldview is adopted will we substitute environmentally destructive policies for more benign policies. Paradoxically, in asking humankind to take responsibility for the whole of the ecosphere, ecocentrics express anthropocentrism. Furthermore, the egalitarian ecocentric world would collapse into nihilism if no distinctions of value are made, where for example the value of a child in a ghetto is equal to that of a family of rats (Brown 1995). Taken to extremes, ecocentrism lends itself to an ideology of domination, where eco police enforce eco policy (Dobson 1990). Whilst reduction in mankind's interference with the ecosphere is desirable, some forms of ecocentrism would lead to the rejection of human rights in favour of the ecosphere, for instance propositions of a human population cull advocated by transpersonal ecologists (Naess 1990). Within social and political systems, ecocentrics tend to dislike centralised systems and materialism and this puts them at odds with current prevailing neo-liberal paradigms.

Ecocentric approaches, although appearing radical, are rapidly gaining credence within governments and organisations at many levels. Hawken *et al*'s (1999) strong call that natural capital should be quantified and fed through into definitions of growth argues strongly that a failure to recognise issues such as resource depletion is completely unsustainable. The United National Environment Programme's World Conservation Monitoring Centre (UNEP-WCMC) is an influential voice developing and supporting work in relation to assessment of the real value of ecosystems to wider economics. As tools are developed and adopted which provide economic data as to the value of natural resources, so they are becoming part of the property development decision framework. For example, within the UK significant work is being undertaken within the National Ecosystems Assessment Project to understand the value of species to both society and the economy (www.uknea.unep-wcmc.org).

Although there is a strong resurgence in ecocentric thinking in the newer guise of ecosystems analysis, the dominant worldview is still anthropocentric, where mankind dominates, only humans possess intrinsic value, and are the rightful 'masters of nature' as well as being the origin and source of all values (Cook and Golton, 1994). As such, anthropocentrism is a very different worldview to ecocentrism (Brown 1995). Within the anthropocentric paradigm resources are extracted without replenishment, and non-reusable materials such as plastics and nuclear waste accumulate. Some argue anthropocentrism is based in the positivist, objective-thinking characteristics in our scientific, mechanistic and technological worldview which emerged from the Enlightenment in the seventeenth century (Paton 2010). Anthropocentrism is perceived by ecocentrics as the root cause of the ecological crisis (Paton 2010). Anthropocentrics believe that mankind can provide a technological fix to the environmental problems; another term for this approach is technocentric (Cook and Golton 1994). However the hegemony of anthropomorphic approaches, whilst still dominating actions, are being tempered by governments who increasingly recognise that to deliver sufficient sustainability to avert overwhelming levels of climate change, it is necessary 'to persuade civil society to break from the anthropocentric perspective where the environment affects and benefits humans' (Salinger 2010).

Even so, it is too simplistic to see a clear divide between ecocentrism and technocentrism, as boundaries are blurred and issues are complex (Washington 2015; Pepper 1984). One issue between an ecocentric worldview as opposed to an anthropocentric one is: where does the line between fair use and abuse lie (Purser and Montuori 1996)? Or where does economic development become exploitative? Furthermore Pearce (1993) and Pepper (1984) perceived sub-groups within ecocentrism and anthropocentrism. Within anthropocentrism, those on the left, known as 'accommodating environmentalists', tend to be gradual reformers believing in careful economic and environmental management but without radical change to social economic and political structures (Cook and Golton 1994). Those on the right, known as 'cornucopian environmentalists', believe in unfettered economic growth and humankind's right to utilise the world's resources as they see fit. Within the ecocentric camp there is a divide between those on the right, 'deep ecologists', who put a greater emphasis on the limits to growth or carrying capacity of the earth, and those on the left, 'moderate ecologists' who believe in decentralised political and social institutions. Deep ecologists believe in compulsory restraints on human population growth and on resource consumption. Sitting between them all, are those responsible for property development who have to make decisions that sit within both their own value sets and the regulatory frameworks devised in the light of the debate.

Economically, anthropocentrics belong to the neo-classical school. Believing growth is always possible and desirable, they tend to reject interventions in the economy by tax or incentives which would promote sustainability; to them it is a 'market' issue. There is evidence that this stance is beginning to change and evolve in capitalist economies with an increased recognition of connection between the natural world and human wellbeing which is resulting in environmental legislation, at least as far as the connection between fossil fuel use, carbon emissions and theorised impacts on climate.[1] Further, this legislation recognises that the built environment is a major source of natural resource depletion and may be a catalyst in climate change through its contribution to carbon emissions. Matters of sustainability are increasingly being aligned in growth economics as related to risk as much as to reward, a phenomenon first put forward in the UK in 2000 by the then Sustainable Construction Task Group (2000).

Therefore even the most free market advocates are now prepared to accept interventions which seek to control carbon and energy use in buildings. For example, in 2010, the disclosure of energy consumption in commercial buildings in Australia became mandatory (Warren and Huston 2011) and in the EU the Energy Performance of Buildings Directive, 2002 (2003/91/EC) introduced by 2009 a mandate for every building (with some exceptions) to declare its asset energy rating (Energy Performance Certificates [EPCs]) upon sale or letting (DirectGov, 2012); further, some public buildings have to display energy usage via a Display Energy Certificate (DEC). More contentious legislation in Australia was the introduction of a carbon pricing mechanism which commenced in July 2012, the notion of 'taxing' carbon pollution met with significant resistance in parliament during 2011. There was concern about the potential impact on the economy and the amount of the carbon price compared to other countries. The Australian Labor government largely offset potential negative political and economic impacts of the carbon tax with generous government assistance to households.

However, when the Liberal coalition government was elected in 2013, they repealed the legislation immediately. Within the UK, the introduction of a mandatory carbon reduction commitment programme affecting larger corporate organisations is effectively providing a taxation regime to encourage reduction in carbon emissions within some property portfolios held in both the public and private sectors.

Overall it is hard to say whether there is a temporary or permanent shift in the neo-liberal economic philosophy adopted by cornucopian environmentalists towards an economic outlook more attuned to accommodating environmentalism. What is of concern, is that within the built environment, improved economic performance through a perceived increase in rental or even capital value is often the main argument used to persuade property owners and investors to adopt sustainability (Eichholtz *et al.* 2009 and 2013; Fuerst and McAllister 2011; Newell 2008; World Green Building Council 2013) and indicates that economic drivers remain paramount.

In summary, a spectrum of ideas and values exist within the concept of sustainability from weak to strong (see for example Costanza and Daly [1992]) which goes from dark green to light green, or as some have suggested to grey; implying that the pursuit of weak sustainability (the cornucopian set of values) does not deliver sustainable outcomes (Söderbaum 2011). The range of standpoints identified in the literature is expressed in Table 1.1. Five distinct groups are identifiable; two are anthropocentric (accommodating and cornucopian environmentalism) and three are ecocentric (transpersonal, deep and moderate ecology). Within the current context in which property development takes place, most frameworks lie within the weak sustainability framing.

Another way of presenting these beliefs and standpoints figuratively is shown in Figure 1.1 as the spectrum of sustainability concepts. Figure 1.1 illustrates the disconnection between transpersonal ecology and environmentalism. Elsewhere there is some overlap between the groups in their value systems and beliefs. There is a broader divide between ecocentrism and anthropocentrism where one is considered to deliver strong sustainability and the other weak sustainability. Current collective practice tends to fall in the environmentalist conceptual framework delivering very weak to weak sustainability. Is weak and very weak sustainability going to deliver sufficient changes for the generations to come and those already here to mitigate environmental damage? Brown (1995) asserts this level of sustainability will fall short of what is needed.

The built environment including property development is responsible for significant environmental impacts. Estimates vary but according to the Energy Savings Trust (www.energysavingstrut.org.uk) and the World Green Building Council (www.worldgbc.org) some 40 per cent of carbon use relates to buildings, significantly more if transport is taken into account. Further, buildings generate some 30 per cent of water use and are a major source of waste; in short they are critical in terms of global resource depletion. Buildings use resources during construction with the extraction of resources; energy and water resources are used in the transport and manufacturing of construction materials and components. Considerable amounts of waste are created at this stage. During the building's operational phase, energy resources are used in lighting, heating and cooling and water is used in building services. Occupant health is affected by the materials used during construction. At the end of the building life cycle, unless materials are reused or recycled, they will be transported to landfill where the resources are lost in perpetuity and further development may be prevented due to contamination.

Within the built environment, property developers are a sub-group who impact on the sustainability of the buildings they construct, design and sometimes operate and in

Table 1.1 Ecocentric and anthropocentric standpoints

Standpoint	Transpersonal ecology	Deep ecology	Moderate ecology	Accommodating environmentalism	Cornucopian environmentalism
Belief system	Religious level of belief	Bio-ethics and intrinsic value	Primary value of ecosystems	Intra and inter-generational equity	Support for traditional ethical reasoning
	Silent			Instrumental value in nature	Rights of humans
	Silent	Accepts 'carrying capacity' of earth argument	Accepts 'carrying capacity' of earth argument	Silent	
	Emotional and irrational			Rational and pro science	
	Silent	Lacks faith in technology			Faith in science and technology
Population	Population cull	Reduce population	Zero population growth	Silent	
Resource consumption	Silent	Extreme preservation	Resource preservation	Resource conservation	Resource exploitation
Worldview	Ecocentric			Anthropocentric	
	Lacks faith in technology				Faith in technology
Waste	Reuse, repair and then recycle			Recycle	

Economic	Capitalism is not sustainable. Rejects consumerism.	Heavily regulated economy. Capitalism is not sustainable. Does not favour overseas trade. 'Eco'nomics. Rejects consumerism. Little overseas trade.	Zero economic growth. Capitalism is not sustainable. Does not favour overseas trade. 'Eco'nomics. Rejects consumerism. Little overseas trade.	Managed growth. Capitalism is sustainable. Consumerism is acceptable. Overseas trade is acceptable.	Maximise growth. Capitalism is sustainable. Substitution theory prevails. Laissez faire economics. Green consumerism is accepted. Promotes consumerism. Promotes foreign trade/agreements.
Energy	Preservation	Preservation	Conservation	Conservation	Nuclear is acceptable, conserve and increase consumption
	Very strong sustainability		*Strong sustainability*	*Weak sustainability*	*Very weak sustainability*

Source: Wilkinson (2012)

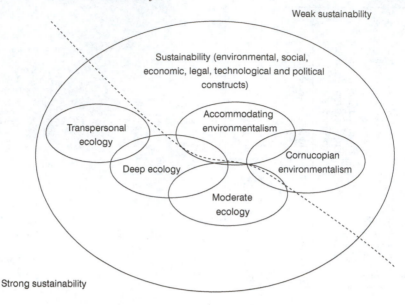

Figure 1.1 The spectrum of sustainability concepts
Source: Wilkinson (2012)

this regard their conceptual understanding of sustainability is extremely important. It has become a current practice for many organisations, and not just property developers, to adopt 'corporate social responsibility' (CSR), or Corporate Responsibility (CR) as a means of organising, structuring, managing and reporting their environmental impact (Wilkinson *et al*. 2004). Indeed over a period of some 20 years the widespread adoption of CR practices has permeated deeply through leading companies and the notion of Responsible Property Investment (RPI) is becoming increasingly embedded (UNEP-FI 2012). A requirement of CSR is to provide information about sustainability targets, policies and strategies, usually on company websites and here one can determine attitudes to and perceptions of sustainability.

Figure 1.2 shows property developers as a subset of the built environment. Other key stakeholders include architects, designers, building users, owners and policy makers and enforcers, all of whom may have divergent conceptual understandings of sustainability but which are important and collectively significant. Currently, within most developed countries which typically operate under a neo-liberal economic paradigm, sustainable property development tends to be applied and realised more in the context of economic goals, though social and environmental goals are noted as significant (Ang and Wilkinson 2008).

1.3   Defining sustainable property development

The Green Building Council of Australia, part of the World Green Building Council movement, defines sustainable property development in the following way:

> The property industry is defined as all those who produce, develop, plan, design, build, alter, or maintain the built environment, and includes building materials manufacturers and suppliers as well as clients and end use occupiers.

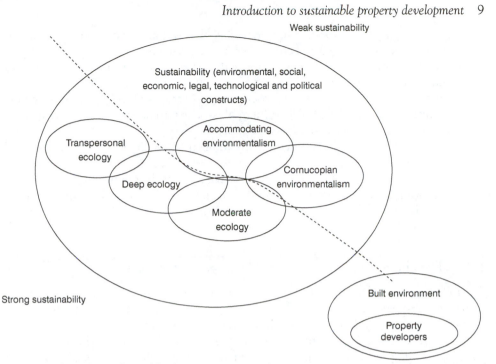

Figure 1.2 The relationship of built environment and property organisations to the spectrum of sustainability concepts
Source: Wilkinson (2012)

> A sustainable property industry will balance environmental, social and economic issues to ensure a viable and valuable industry for future generations.
>
> Building green is an opportunity to use resources efficiently while creating healthier buildings that improve occupant health and wellbeing.
>
> (GBCA 2013)

This definition embraces social aspects such as improving occupier health and wellbeing, and environmental aspects around using resources efficiently, and in the interests of economies, to ensure a 'viable' and 'valuable' industry, though it is acknowledged the terms 'viable' and 'valuable' are broad and capable of various interpretations. *Inter*-generational aspects are covered loosely in the mention of 'future generations' but *intra*-generational equity is omitted. Finally this definition embraces more or less the whole life-cycle of built environment property (the end of life cycle is omitted) in which developers are participants with other stakeholders. In this book 'sustainable property development' is defined as:

- Recognising that the environmental impacts of the sector – including but not restricted to impacts on climate change, potable water availability, resilience to flood and weather events, waste, biodiversity and natural resource depletion – are significant, and that mitigation of those impacts must take a beyond-compliance perspective.
- Accepting the link between property and social infrastructure, including the creation of a sense of place, contribution to social amenity and the inherent relationships between healthy workplaces and increased workforce productivity.

- Acknowledging that business value, including but not limited to economic value, can be created by a committed and comprehensive approach to:
- using resources (such as energy, water and materials) in an efficient manner and sustainably where possible,
- anticipating and managing risks and opportunities across all levels of an organisation,
- recognising that all stakeholders, internal and external, expect improvements in economic, social and environmental performance.

(Department of Environment and Climate Change NSW 2013)

Given the issues described above, it is acknowledged that the definition is not complete and may be wanting in some respects, nevertheless on the basis that 'some considered action is generally better than no action', it provides a framework in which to determine and, where possible, benchmark actions in sustainability.

1.4 The characteristics of sustainable property development

The following set of characteristics is proposed to evaluate whether a property development could be considered 'sustainable'. This section of the chapter briefly introduces those characteristics, noting that developers have varying degrees of control in respect of each development in terms of its contribution to sustainability. They are outlined in order of wider societal impacts to building-related and individual impacts and are explored in more detail in subsequent chapters.

The discussion has been based upon and adapted from many sources but notably the Department of Environment and Climate Change NSW (http://www.environment.nsw. gov.au.htm) *Sustainable Property Guide 2013* and *Sustainable Design and Construction Toolkit*, London Development Authority, prepared by URS Europe 2005, www.lda.gov.uk.

1.4.1 Land use, urban form and urban quality

Urban design/place making: The creation of spaces which inspire individuals and encourage and facilitate safe pedestrian movement and that link logically and respectfully to their contexts, complementing existing features are all qualities which will not only make a development successful economically but which will promote longevity and hence sustainability. Whether a formal master plan process is involved or not, there is now recognition that engagement with local communities can not only speed up approvals but promote better urban design. Whilst community engagement has been promoted by theoreticians for many years, notably Arnstein's seminal ladder of participation (Arnstein 1969), it is only in more recent years that such engagement has been formalised into policy in some countries (see for example the Localism Act 2011 in the UK which increased the rights of local groups and individuals within the planning process).

Attractive site design: Sites should be designed to meet the needs of the end users, with consideration given to how the buildings, infrastructure or open space will be used in practice, while (although subjective) also creating attractive spaces. Depending on local climatic conditions, the orientation of the building within the site will also be critical in both the use of resources and the reaction of both those viewing the building from the exterior and those experiencing it internally.

Reuse of land and buildings: Using a 'brown field' or contaminated site in preference to a 'green field' site is written into planning policy in some countries. Not only does reuse of previously developed land often reduce dependence on transport and promote more compact settlements, it could be seen as protection of important habitats. However, this must be balanced against the other environmental arguments against dense development, including propensity to flood due to increased hard surfacing. It is not just land reuse which is a sustainability consideration; much of current thinking is the promotion of retrofit and refurbishment of buildings. Such solutions can help to maintain a sense of place whilst reducing the creation of waste as well as increasing the period over which embodied carbon is amortised.

Density: Ensuring that a development is designed to a density appropriate for the location is another critical consideration. Whilst high density around transport nodes may be optimal, there are trade-offs in relation to noise, traffic congestion and privacy and, as mentioned above, biodiversity and flooding. Where high density is deemed appropriate, measures such as sustainable urban drainage schemes (SUDS) can be critical.

1.4.2 Environmental protection and enhancement

Supporting biodiversity: As will be discussed in later chapters, considering and conserving ecological values including locally, regionally and nationally important species as well as retaining or improving habitat values is increasingly recognised not just as an environmental concern, but also as an economic matter as methods of quantifying the impact of species loss are developed and accepted politically.

Pollution to air, water and land: Construction and operation of buildings can produce pollutants which are harmful to humans, fauna and flora; some are capable of sterilising land for long periods; therefore for development to be sustainable due consideration must be given to minimising, mitigating or avoiding polluting emissions during construction and operation. Further, there is a strong relationship between energy production and pollution and contamination; for the energy sourcing used within buildings, there is a material consideration in relation to pollution off-site.

Noise abatement: Excessive levels of noise can be detrimental to human health; not only can damage be caused to hearing, but it is associated with hypertension, heart disease, sleep disturbance and loss of academic performance (Passchier-Vermeer and Passchier 2000). In extreme cases, those responsible for excessive noise can be subject to legal action in nuisance, even where the development had been approved in planning terms. Noise has two main connections with sustainable property development. First, the ambient noise of the area or within the site will affect the quality of life and health of the occupants and those that live or work nearby during the construction period; this is something that has to be handled sensitively to mitigate adverse effects. Second, in designing and locating a development the long-term impacts of noise emanating from the use of the facility should be considered as well as the impact on the development of noise levels already prevailing in the area. In both cases, the use of careful mitigation works in terms of screening, orientation of buildings and user controls can be effective in reducing issues. However, there is some research that demonstrates that a low level of background noise can lead to a sense of security; in an uncertain world those who live in urban areas can find a *lack* of nose disturbing, though it tends to be sounds from the natural world, such as birdsong, which promote calmness. Designing for sound is now an important factor and that includes consideration of finishes within a building as these have a significant impact on sound levels.

1.4.3   Location and transport

Location and access: The role of location to successful property development is fundamental. However within the broad heading of location, accessibility is sometimes overlooked. Access via a variety of modes of transport is increasingly important to provide flexibility of use in the future and in the light of planning policies favouring public transport, although this will depend on the type of development and its overall location. For example, a logistics distribution centre must have good access by road, but rail connections are probably not an issue; within an urban setting however, easy walking distance to a public transport node can be key to occupier demand. Accessibility too means due consideration, beyond statutory requirements, to consider the needs of people with disabilities; these include not just mobility issues but can include design to allow access to those with visual or hearing impairment.

Further, access to local amenities will be very important for office workers where the ability to attract a good workforce may be partially determined by proximity to local shops and service facilities, such as restaurants, health and fitness facilities and schools. Some of the issues of proximity to local amenities may be overcome by including these within the scheme, but a lifestyle predicated on spending the entire working day within the confines of a single building is increasingly recognised as unhealthy both physically and mentally. Another recent move is the reuse of redundant office buildings for educational use – ensuring that working parents can overcome issues of picking up children from locations remote from their own workplaces. This again is a further recognition that 'access' is taking on new dimensions.

Active and sustainable transport: There is increasing emphasis on the relationship between sustainable transport means and health and wellbeing. The Urban Land Institute's ten principles for building healthy places (ULI 2013) draws down on an increasing body of research to argue that design at all scales (place to building) which promotes walking and cycling can yield positive health and economic returns. Their principles, explored later in the book, include the need to put people first, create mixed use which encourages interactions and makes it easier to walk than drive. Whilst the ability to design for active transport will depend on the climatic and other conditions, the link between health and levels of physical activity can no longer be ignored by the development community.

1.4.4   Resource use

Energy efficient design: Energy efficiency is perhaps the leading issue in terms of the global agenda of improving the resource use sustainability of buildings. Efficient energy use is a key measure to reduce carbon dioxide emissions; mitigating the impacts of global warming and climate change. Not only are changes to building codes tightening in most countries, so developers can, at little or no extra cost, take advantage of the many technologies available to avoid energy wastage and track energy consumption during occupation. Within the EU, binding targets have been set for a 20 per cent reduction in energy by 2020 although the emphasis is now shifting from energy reduction to carbon reduction.

One of the major concerns, explored later, is that despite the introduction of rating schemes designed to promote good design, there exists a significant gap between the *designed* efficiency of many buildings and their *performance* in energy use terms. For example the work of the Useable Buildings Trust (http://www.usablebuildings.co.uk) has found that buildings can consume between two and five times more energy than originally predicted.

Further, it should be noted that the issue of energy differs between climatic regions, both in terms of scale and in terms of focus – with some areas requiring heating whilst others require cooling. What is of concern to some commentators is the expectation that, within the work environment, internal temperatures should remain almost constant all year round regardless of outdoor conditions. Such an approach leads to further disconnection between people and their environments which can be detrimental to raising awareness of the world around us.

Renewable energy: Of increasing concern is the *source* of energy, as well as its quantum of use. Renewable energy (solar, wind, water, biomass, ground and air source heat pumps) has the dual benefits of being both zero carbon and perpetual, depending on climatic conditions. It can either be captured for use in grid systems for wide distribution or produced on-site, which is generally less efficient. Whilst some countries, such as Iceland, New Zealand and Canada, have abundant sources of renewable energy which have been harnessed within main distribution systems, these are in the minority. The potential for renewables varies depending on climate and topography, but most developed countries have policies and in some cases obligations aimed at increasing the percentage of renewable energy. Within the UK, a 'roadmap' for renewables production of 20 per cent of needs by 2020 (DECC 2011) provides for a coordinated approach based on attracting inward investment for major schemes and financial initiatives (such as the Feed-in-Tariff and the Renewable Heat Incentive scheme) aimed at promoting the use of on-site schemes. The presence or otherwise of such financial schemes can have a profound influence on the design choices of developments.

Water conservation: Whilst too much water can itself present real sustainability issues in the form of flooding, the growth in world population combined with increased per capita use of water associated with increased wealth level, changing lifestyles and increased intensification of agriculture including intensive meat farming and the production of biofuels has placed pressure on potable water supplies. For example, within the UK, from an average consumption of some 20 litres per head in the late nineteenth century, it was estimated that by the early twenty-first century the average UK daily consumption was some 150 litres per head (Aquaterra 2008) compared with less than 110 litres in Belgium. However within the US, estimates put usage as high as 360–400 litres per day (http://water.usgs.gov/edu/qa-home-percapita.html). Not only is this a large occupation cost, it is also unsustainable. Although moves to change designs to capture and use rain, storm and waste water can all help, more drastic solutions are required in many countries, especially in developing countries where potable water systems are a new requirement and in countries where use has been profligate.

In some countries, like Australia, water economy is very important due to drought conditions that frequently prevail and this is often the driver for the introduction of regulatory measures which are becoming more common for both residential and commercial developments in the future. Current expectations focus on water efficient appliances and fittings, while new design ideas, including water sensitive urban design and water efficient technologies, such as composting waterless toilets, are becoming more commonplace.

Low-impact building materials: When developing the design of a building, the environmental impact of the materials used is a consideration. It is estimated that, despite increased awareness of environmental matters, natural resource extraction is 60 billion tonnes a year, an increase of some 50 per cent over that of only 30 years ago and one-third of this relates to construction (SERI/Global 2000, 2009). Therefore the minimisation of finite resources is a sustainability ambition and the substitution of finite resources with materials that can be reused or recycled, thus prolonging the life cycle and reducing the burden on virgin material sources. Further the transport miles of materials should be considered: importing stone half way round the planet is hardly a good option – but it is commonplace. Local sourcing should be the preferred option where possible. Not only is this better environmentally but it can help retain or develop distinctiveness of place and help local employment; it may also be a cheaper option. Finally, when designing, reuse of materials at the end of building life is a consideration as this will improve sustainability.

Minimising waste to landfill: Concerns about the volume of material going to landfill have risen in recent years. This may not be an issue where land is plentiful, but in regions of high density of population such as Northern Europe and cities such as Hong Kong, it is a very significant concern resulting in government action aimed at changing behaviours through pricing mechanisms (see for example DEFRA 2012; Yu *et al.* 2013). Waste can be reduced in the design phase by the specification of material to include reused or recycled materials and thinking ahead to ensure that material can, at life end, be used. The development of Building Information Modelling (BIM) can be used to aid with this. This approach, the cradle to cradle approach, typifies the moves towards a circular, rather than linear, economy and is explored in more detail later in the book. Waste can be also be reduced during the construction phase by good working practices, such as the optimisation of off-site manufacture techniques. Designers can also assist in reducing waste in occupation by ensuring that plans allow for inclusion of waste sorting on-site where appropriate, although this is not always the optimal solution; sometimes collection and expert sorting can lead to greater reuse and recycling.

1.4.5 Business and community characteristics

Local labour and skills: Sustainability is not solely concerned with environmental issues; economic and social concerns may be less well developed as built environment development concepts but are nevertheless important considerations. Within the construction process, consideration of encouraging or giving preference to local labour through the construction process or during the lifetime of the completed development may have the economic and social regenerative effects of stimulating the local economy and increasing the skill base; in the case of controversial schemes it may also help to develop goodwill towards the development thereby easing the course of obtaining consent.

Sustainable and local procurement: Sustainable procurement chains are well established within some industries, notably food where schemes such as FairTrade have had a transformational impact on attitudes of many consumers towards the products they buy; provided that price is not significantly adversely impacted. However, the concept of sustainable procurement is now deeply embedded within many organisations and indeed governments. For example, within the UK public sector policy as long ago as 2006 (Sustainable Procurement Task Force, 2006) makes clear that it is a priority area. Since then Green Procurement Policies (GPP), although they remain voluntary, are advocated strongly by both the EU and the UN (see for example http://ec.europa.eu/environment/gpp/pdf/handbook_summary.pdf). Whilst there is a difference between Green and Sustainable Procurement, the principles related to construction are the same, including: employing consultants with appropriate skills, designing for energy efficiency and renewability, sourcing materials locally, building green capacity, acting fairly and/or through local suppliers with economically viable and fair labour policies. Local procurement goes slightly further by the encouragement of prioritising the use of SMEs (Small and Medium Sized Enterprises) in the award of contracts and within the UK has been given statutory backing (Public Services (Social Value) Act 2012). A study one year on found that adoption of local procurement had produced demonstrable benefits to the local economies.

Green and local procurement is not restricted to the public sector. Many private sector contractors, investing institutions and corporations also adopt such practices so their use within the design and construction process may be an attraction to those financing or buying out the development.

Community involvement/engagement: The case for engaging local communities within the planning and development process has been advocated for many years. From Arnstein (1969) onwards, theorists have promoted the notion that early engagement with local people will result in more sustainable development. Although some developers may still regard local stakeholders as potential impediments to their schemes, engagement is now deeply embedded within statutory processes. Creating interest and preferably buy-in from local stakeholders, achieved in part through community consultation and engagement initiatives over and above those required by the development approval process is now regarded as a normal part of sustainable development.

Community facilities: No developer will wish to provide facilities which will play no role in enhancing the economic value of the development. For this reason within some planning systems, there is statutory provision for developers to be required either to provide some form of community facility on-site as part of the consent or make cash contributions to pay towards community infrastructure. Within the UK two systems prevail: an S.106 agreement whereby a developer must provide, for example, a percentage of 'affordable' housing within a scheme and, in some authority areas the payment of a fixed tariff Community Infrastructure Levy to enable the local authority to provide facilities, such as clinics, schools, roads, parks or other amenities required as a result of overall new developments in the area. Whereas such contributions to community facilities may not be made out of choice, in large developments, economic value may be underpinned by designing in facilities for community or multiple users. This is more likely where the development is commissioned by a landowner who has the intention of long-term ownership.

Designing for community: The point has been made above that early engagement with communities can both aid the speed with which a development is approved; it can also improve the very nature of the design. Bell and Morse (2003), in their work in southern Europe, found that working closely with communities enabled a real sense of belonging to occur and generated a sense of community. This is important. A building is a long-term asset; it should help to foster a sense of place and sit within a compatible context for its users and other stakeholders; in many cases it will help to generate a community and provide space for people to meet socially and accidentally.

Equality and diversity: Many neighbourhoods are characterised by a lack of social and cultural diversity – even though many government policies may seek to foster equality across communities through regeneration or development. However, this can be difficult to achieve – likeminded or culturally connected communities tend to cluster together leading to the development of areas of social exclusion. Whilst property development is not an exercise in social engineering and measures are in place to prevent developments being discriminatory on physical access grounds, having cultural sensitivity within the design process and, for large schemes, ensuring access to amenities required by a range of people, can help to promote equality and diversity actively.

Health and wellbeing: As discussed above the links between health and wellbeing and the physical setting to a building are well documented. The quality of the internal environment is also important in relation to thermal comfort, lighting/daylighting, indoor air quality, ventilation and the presence of pollutants. With high rise buildings, it may not be possible to have natural ventilation, but many air conditioning systems if not well maintained can harbour contaminants or if not producing severe physical conditions may lead to discomfort. Seppanen and Fisk (2006), in an extensive literature review, found strong evidence linking poor indoor environmental quality with physical illness, such as respiratory disease and decline in worker productivity. For developments to be sustainable, due care must be given at the design stage to ensuring that good internal environmental quality is designed in; in many cases natural ventilation will be preferred.

Safety and security: People wish to live, work and play in spaces in which they feel safe. If they do not, then attempts to 'reclaim the streets' and promote walkability will be destined to fail; further areas deemed unsafe or where there is obvious surveillance may lose value. However, achieving both the sense and reality of security can be problematic. It is over half a century since Jacobs (1961) criticised the design of cities based on the car rather than the pedestrian and more than 40 years ago that Newman (1972) developed the notion of 'defensible space' as a set of design principles based on territoriality, visibility/surveillance, image and impression and safe adjoining areas and uses. Compatible though the views of these major authors are with the concept of sustainable development, they are still not universally embraced. However, they are again gaining prominence as recognition grows that developments which are designed to provide safe and well lit environments, accommodate mixed uses, overlook walkways and car parks and encourage ground level walk-through are likely to prove more successful than those which do not.

Accessibility and diversity: Making the development accessible to a diversity of users including the disabled, mothers with young children, visually or aurally impaired and the elderly is important. Whilst some of this is subject to regulation and design codes, notably those with mobility issues, sustainability can be improved through early attention to risks and opportunities during the design process. Further, with aging populations in some countries, it only makes economic sense to cater for the people who may have divergent needs and effective demand capacity. A further social consideration is that of the needs of more ethnically divergent societies. Within the workplace, prayer rooms, private spaces and specially adapted toilet facilities are required. For residential developments, the design needs to consider the nature of the likely occupant community. Whereas the 'standard' western view of a dwelling is based on the concept of exclusivity of occupation, there is a long tradition of shared facilities among many groups that does not appear to be well catered for within many cities. As globalisation sees increasingly mixed communities, so developers will need to adapt their designs.

1.5   Conclusion

This chapter has introduced the concept of sustainable property development sharing Gallie's (1956) attributes of a 'contested concept'; that it is in essence, 'all things to all men'. It is a notion that varies from market to market, location to location, land use to land use, country to country, and of course over time. As such, the best we are able to claim is that one property is, or may be, relatively speaking more sustainable than another; it is impossible to speak of sustainable property development in an absolute sense. In that case, we face the situation stated by Kant in the 1750s that sometimes 'it is necessary to make decisions on information sufficient for action but insufficient to satisfy the intellect'. It is also noted that the philosophical, political, economic and social constructs underpinning our definitions of sustainability are broad and complex. It is shown that in some respects our current application of sustainability in the built environment draws on limited understanding and inclusion of selected and therefore limited aspects of sustainability. In particular when the research and policy agendas are examined they reveal that the preoccupation has been with energy efficiency in buildings, at the expense of other environmental and social concerns. Given that there are concerns about the finite nature of fossil-based fuels and the observations of climate change, this is understandable, but not satisfactory.

It is highly desirable that a narrow perspective is broadened over time as we are in danger, as a sector, of 'hitting the targets but missing the point'. The point being that our planetary resources are finite and our consumption levels, pollution and waste levels and widely accepted contribution to climate change continue to increase. Therefore the struggle politically is to decide how governments can respond. In relation to property development, this has primarily been through policy, fiscal and legislative moves which gradually improve the energy efficiency of new and refurbished buildings and encourage or mandate the use of renewable energy sources. Additionally, the pricing mechanism has been used to steer developments towards the use of less resources, notably water and the reduction of waste, particularly to landfill.

Sustainable development is, however, a much broader philosophical concept than reduction of environmental impacts; it has a strong social agenda aimed at equity both within and across generations (Brundtland 1987). This is harder to relate to sustainable development but there is now growing awareness that for buildings to be sustainable, matters such as health and wellbeing need to form part of the design and development agenda.

The chapter explained briefly the characteristics of sustainable property development from the macro or urban scale to the micro or building scale, noting that geographical location and land use type, among other variables impact on the breadth and depth of sustainability delivered in projects. However, it also highlighted that the very notion of a sustainable development could be considered an oxymoron; therefore debates have arisen around the concept of 'strong, semi-strong and weak sustainability'. Further chapters will draw out in detail the factors, including sustainability factors, that each stakeholder considers in the process.

Note

1 We put theorised in connection with the link between carbon and climate change as it is not the purpose of this book to argue the scientific case for this this. Although the authors are fully accepting of the science as developed and disseminated by the Intergovernmental Panel on Climate Change (IGPCC) (2013).

References

Ang, S.L. and Wilkinson, S.J. (2008). Property developers and sustainability: the Melbourne experience. *Journal of Property Management*. 26(5). http://www.emeraldinsight.com.ezproxy.lib.uts.edu.au/search.htm?st1=Wilkinson+and+Ang+&ct=all&ec=1&bf=1

Aquaterra (2008) *International Comparisons of Domestic Per Capita Consumption*, Bristol: Environment Agency.

Arnstein, S.R. (1969) A ladder of citizen participation, *Journal of the Institute of Planners* 35(4): 216–224.

Bell, S. and Morse, S. (2003) *Measuring Sustainability: Learning by Doing*, London: Earthscan.

Brown, C.S. (1995) Anthropocentrism and ecocentrism: the quest for a new worldview, *The Midwest Quarterly* 36(2): 191.

Brundtland Commission (1987) *Our Common Future: The Report of the World Commission on Environment and Development*, New York: United Nations.

Cook, S.J. and Golton, B. (1994). Sustainable development concepts and practice in the built environment. A UK perspective. CIB TG 16, Sustainable Construction, Tampa FL, 6–9 November 1994.

Costanza, R. and Daly, H. (1992) Natural capital and sustainable development, *Conservation Biology* 6 (1): 37–46.

DEFRA (Department of Environment, Food and Rural Affairs) (2012) *Progress with Delivery of Commitments from the Government's Review of Waste Policy in England (2011)*. Retrieved from https://www.gov.uk/government/uploads/system/uploads/attachment_data/file/69519/pb13738-waste-review-progress.pdf.

Department for Energy and Climate Change (DECC) (2011) UK renewable energy roadmap https://www.gov.uk/government/uploads/system/uploads/attachment_data/file/48128/2167-uk-renewable-energy-roadmap.pdf.

Department of Environment and Climate Change NSW (2013) *Sustainable Property 17 Guide 2013* Retrieved 24 August 2014 from http://www.environment.nsw.gov.au.htm.

DirectGov (2012) Energy Performance Certificates. Retrieved 1 March 2012 from https://www.gov.uk/buy-sell-your-home/energy-performance-certificates.

Dobson, A. (1990) *Green Political Thought: An Introduction*, London: Routledge.

Eichholtz, P., Kok, N., and Quigley, J. M. (2009) *Why Do Companies Rent Green? Real Property And Corporate Social Responsibility. Program On Housing And Urban Policy*. Working Paper No. W09-004. University of California, Berkeley, CA. Retrieved 28 February 2015 from http://ssrn.com/abstract=1521702.

Eichholtz, P., Kok, N., and Quigley, J.M. (2013) The economics of green building, *Review of Economics and Statistics* 95(1): 50–63. Retrieved from http:// www.corporate-engagement. com/files/publication/EKQ_ RESTAT_2013.pdf.

Financial Times (1998) Natural steps to sustainability, *Financial Times*, 7 January.

Fuerst, F. and McAllister, P. (2011) Green noise or green value? Measuring the effects of environmental certification on office values, *Real Estate Economics* 39(1): 45–69.

Gallie, W. B. (1956) Essentially contested concepts, *Proceedings of the Aristotelian Society* 56, 167–198 reprinted in M. Black (ed.) (1962) *The Importance of Language* Englewood Cliffs, NJ: Prentice-Hall Inc.

GBCA Green Building Council of Australia (2013) What is sustainable development? Retrieved 27 April 2013 from http://www.gbca.org.au/resources/fact-sheets/what-is-sustainable-development/27.htm.

Goodchild, R.N and Munton, R.J.C (1985) *Development and the Landowner: An Analysis of the British Experience*, London: Allen and Unwin.

Green Construction Board (2015) Mapping the real estate life cycle for effective policy interventions. Retrieved from http://www.greenconstructionboard.org/images/stories/Valuation_and_Demand/GCB610%20Final%20Report.pdf.

Hawken, P., Lovins, A., and Lovins, H. (1999) *Natural Capitalism: Creating the Next Industrial Revolution*, London: Little Brown and Co.

Jacobs, J. (1961) *The Death and Life of Great American Cities*, New York: Random House.

Naess, A. (1990) *Ecology, Community and Lifestyle: Outline of an Ecosophy*, Cambridge: Cambridge University Press.

Newell, G. (2008) The strategic significance of environmental sustainability by Australian-listed property trusts, *Journal of Property Investment & Finance* 26(6): 522–540.

Newman, O. (1972) *Design Guidelines for Creating Defensible Space*, Basingstoke: Macmillan Publishing.

Passchier-Vermeer, W. and Passchier, W.F. (2000) Noise exposure and public health, *Environmental Health Perspectives* 108, Supplement 1: 123–131.

Paton, G. J. (2010). *Seeking Sustainability: On the prospect of an ecological liberalism*. London: Routledge.

Pearce, D. (1993) Blueprint 3 – Measuring Sustainable Development, London: Earthscan.

Pepper, D. (1984) *The Roots of Modern Environmentalism*, London: Routledge.

Purser, R.E. and Montuori, A. (1996) Ecocentrism is in the eye of the beholder, *The Academy of Management Review* 21(3): 611–613.

Ricardo, D. (1817) *On the Principles of Political Economy and Taxation*, London: John Murray.

RICS (Royal Institution of Chartered Surveyors) (2014) *RICS Valuation – Professional Standards January 2014*, London: RICS.

Salinger, J. (2010). The climate journey over three decades: from childhood to maturity, innocence to knowing, from anthropocentrism to ecocentrism ..., *Climatic Change* 100(1): 49–57.

Seppanen, O.A. and Fisk, W.J. (2006) *Some Quantitative Relations between Indoor Environmental Quality and Work Performance or Health*, Berkeley, CA: Lawrence Berkeley National Laboratory.

SERI (Sustainable Europe Research Institute), Friends of the Earth and Global 2000 (2009) *Overconsumption: Our use of the world's resources*. Retrieved from http://www.foe.co.uk/sites/default/files/downloads/overconsumption.pdf.

Söderbaum, P. (2011) Sustainability economics as a contested concept, *Ecological Economics* 70(6):1019–1020.

Sustainable Construction Task Group (2000) *Risk, Reputation and Reward Building Research Establishment*. Retrieved from http://projects.bre.co.uk/rrr/RRR.pdf.

Sustainable Procurement Task Force (2006) *Procuring the Future* DEFRA. Retrieved from https://www.gov.uk/government/publications/procuring-the-future.

ULI (2013) *Ten Principles for Building Healthy Places*. Retrieved from http://www.uli.org/wp-content/uploads/ULI-Documents/10-Principles-for-Building-Healthy-Places.pdf.

UNEP-FI (United Nations Environment Programme – Finance Initiative – Property Working Group) (2012) *What the Leaders are Doing*, second edn, New York: UNEP-FI.

Warren, C.M.J. and Huston, S. (2011) Promoting energy efficiency in the public sector commercial buildings in Australia. Proceedings of RICS Construction and Property Conference. COBRA: Construction and Building Research Conference, Salford, UK, 12–13 September 2011, pp. 128–134.

Washington, H. (2015) *Demystifying Sustainability. Towards real solutions*. London: Earthscan Routledge.

Wilkinson, S.J. 2012. Conceptual understanding of sustainability in Australian construction firms, CIB Montreal, Canada, June 2012.

Wilkinson, S. J, Pinder, J., and Franks, A. (2004) Conceptual understanding of corporate social responsibility in the UK construction and property sectors. Session T6 Paper 380. CIB Toronto, 2004.

World Green Building Council (2013) *The Business Case for Green Building: A Review of the Costs and Benefits for Developers, Investors and Occupants*. Retrieved from World Green Building Council. http://www.worldgbc.org/files/1513/6608/0674/Business_Case_For_Green_Building_Report_WEB_2013-14.pdf.

Yu, A. T. W., Poon, C.S., Yip, A., and Jaillon, L. (2013) Impact of construction waste disposal charging scheme on work practices at construction sites in Hong Kong, *Waste Management* 13(1): 138–146.

2 Stakeholders through the development process

Sara J. Wilkinson and Sarah L. Sayce

2.0 Introduction

Chapter 1 introduced the concepts of sustainability and sustainable development and concluded that these are contested terms capable of widely differing interpretations depending on the perspective of the individual or organisation. The notion of sustainability, although only embraced widely in the last 30 years, is not new. Ruskin argued in 1849 that:

> the idea of self-denial for the sake of posterity, of practising present economy for the sake of debtors yet unborn, of planting forests that our descendants may live under their shade, or of raising cities for future generations to inhabit, never, I suppose, efficiently takes place among publicly recognised motives of exertion. Yet these are, none the less our duties; nor is our part fitly sustained upon the earth, unless the range of our intended and deliberate usefulness include, not only the companions but the successors of our pilgrimage.
>
> (Ruskin 1849: 171)

To Ruskin, the need to consider future generations was a duty, but to others it is not a matter of responsibility and duty to those who come after us – it is a current risk. Certainly the climate change agenda has been expressed not just as a future environmental impact but, as concluded by Stern (2006), a current economic imperative and a risk mitigation matter. Many companies who have developed Corporate Social Responsibility policies, see sustainability in social and economic terms as well as environmental; to them it is about good business sense, brand recognition and reputation (Sustainable Construction Task Group 2000).

Within the built environment the sustainability agenda has developed in two, initially discrete ways. On one side, fuelled by government-led positions, the *supply-side* of the industry has been in a 'push' position with regulatory frameworks developing, partly due to a lack of perceived movement among *demand-side* players. More recently, the demand-side has moved forward and the fracture between these interests, as elegantly expressed in the so-called 'circle of blame' (see Figure 2.1) has been argued to be converging into a 'virtuous circle' (see Figure 2.2).

Whether such convergence has actually taken place is not the direct argument of this chapter; what is explored are the differing types of stakeholders in the development of the built environment, all of whom have a direct influence on whether the buildings that are achieved are ones that not only fulfil today's occupiers' needs but, in so far as we can predict,

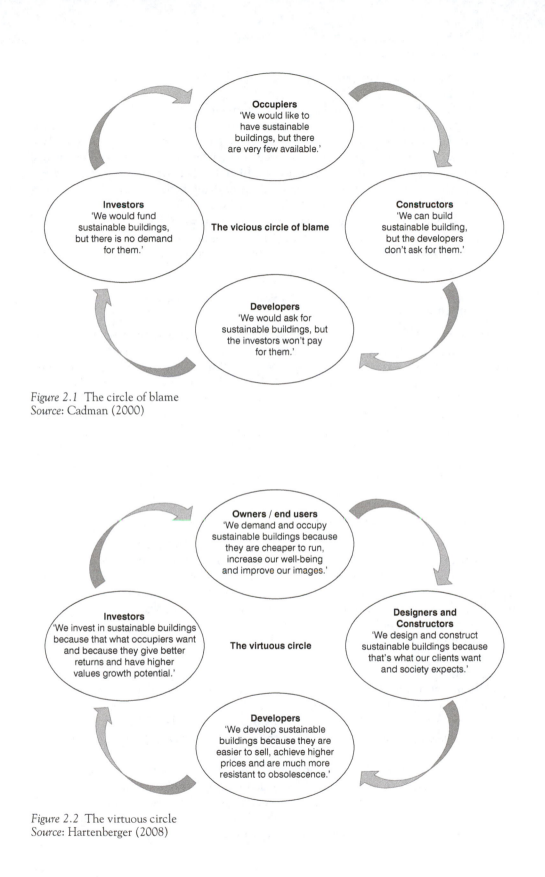

Figure 2.1 The circle of blame
Source: Cadman (2000)

Figure 2.2 The virtuous circle
Source: Hartenberger (2008)

will continue to serve a useful purpose moving forward and not place unnecessary pressures on the environment.

In addition to the plethora of stakeholders, what has to be recognised is that, depending on the power relationships and cultural context, the influences brought to bear at each moment of decision-making throughout the development process will vary and influence the outcome. For example, at times of weak occupational demand, the perspective tenants' view will hold greater sway than when demand is high. Further the influence of banks and institutions that control the flow of funding will be critical: if they require, as a matter of routine, sustainability appraisals for the buildings on which they propose to secure loans, it will shift behaviours. If they do not, opportunities to drive towards sustainable development will be lost. It is therefore vital that stakeholder positions are understood and that they are provided with the knowledge, motivation and influence to support ambitions they may hold towards their own sustainability objectives.

2.1   Stakeholders

With each stage of the development process there are numerous significant stakeholders. Though each stakeholder adds to the outcome of the process, they may have very different viewpoints and expectations; the developer is required to manage the miscellaneous and possibly contradictory objectives of all stakeholders. The significance of the stakeholders fluctuates from project to project and not all feature in every project. Further some stakeholders are transient, for example most consultants and indeed many developers; others have an ongoing interest. Further, although many stakeholders will have a financial interest (we call these internal stakeholders), many do not. External stakeholders, such as visitors to a shopping centre, can also exert significant influence, notably on redevelopment decisions (Walker *et al.* 2004).

2.1.1 *Public sector and government agencies*

In many countries, the public sector and government agencies are the most important developers and, in the wake of the global downturn earlier this century, public sector-led construction activity is proving crucial in stimulating economics. However, much depends on the political persuasion of the government. Currently, the US public sector is undertaking little direct development as a result of their neo-liberal perspective; however the UK, whilst it has shifted away from a direct development role in recent years, preferring to enter into public/private partnering arrangements (Dubben and Williams 2009) is nonetheless not only a powerful stakeholder but, in their role as occupier and funder of private initiatives, an important influencer of markets. Within the UK, there is now a major commitment to public infrastructure development in the form of rail, air and flood management. In other countries, responses differ. For example, in Australia a National Stimulus Plan in the education sector, refurbishing and building schools, was instigated by the Labor government, and aimed to keep some momentum going in the economy as the global financial crisis took hold.

At the sub-national level, local authorities typically develop for their own occupation or community (such as housing) use and, to provide local infrastructure schemes but globally they are often limited by financial resources and their legal powers and requirements to be accountable to their communities. Involvement in development is contingent on whether they want to support or restrict development. Some authorities carry out economic development to promote investment in their area; with more proactive authorities stimulating the process by sometimes supplying land and buildings. Authorities are often owners; maintaining a long-term interest, holding the freehold of developments and signing over long leasehold interests to developers, sharing in rental growth through the ground rent. This has been a prevalent feature of many town centre schemes, in which public ownership provides an assurance of civic society protection. Whatever the level of activity, the public sector undertakes as direct developer, the key aim of their policies and strategies will almost always be consistent with the ambition of long-term sustainability. In making their decisions, the tools used, which include for example Cost Benefit Analyses, are more to take account of *all* stakeholders, internal and external, than private sector developers. This last statement however does not necessarily apply to sovereign wealth funds set up by wealthy nations for the purpose of economic gain and long-term financial stability. The majority of these funds have been formed within the last 15 years (Lipsky 2008) and are estimated currently to control some $6.3 trillion worth of assets (http://www.swfinstitute. org/fund-rankings), 14 per cent of which is estimated by McKinsey to be invested in real estate, excluding infrastructure (http://voices.mckinseyonsociety.com/sovereign-wealth-funds). They tend to act in line with private sector developers and institutions.

For governments, public sector and policy agencies require both good advice and deep internal knowledge to act as effective drivers of sustainable development. In many authorities, this may exist and certainly many governments worldwide are investing heavily in capacity building and knowledge creation. However, for this to be *effective* they also require knowledge of the development industry, something that Adams *et al.* (2012) from an empirical longitudinal study in Scotland saw to be lacking. In their research, they found only limited understanding of what drives the development process or motivates individual developers; yet this, they considered to be a prerequisite to effective urban policy-making.

2.1.2 *Planners*

Planning systems were largely established in developed countries during the mid-twentieth century. The UK planning system has existed in comprehensive form since 1947 and is the major regulator of property development (see Chapter 6). Depending on the jurisdiction it can be nationally or locally led; often it is a combination of two or more tiers of administrative control in both policy-making and practice implementation. Planners can be divided into public sector policy makers/development managers and external private sector consultants (see section 2.1.6.2). The development managers who are regulators, are liable to approve plans brought forward in compliance with government approved local plans; the role of planners is in reality ambiguous as, in many cases, decisions are not undertaken by the professionals but by elected local authority politicians, acting in the light of advice provided by their planners. Recent research within the UK (Green Construction Board 2015), points to the role of planning as a 'negotiated hurdle' in which a process of consultation, often including community groups as well as reports from a wide variety of experts, feeds into the ultimate decision.

Ultimately, most planning systems aim to encourage desirable development with the guidance for determining applications set out in statute and policy guidance notes. Again to quote the UK, the National Planning Policy Framework (DCLG 2012) states that 'the purpose of the planning system is to contribute to the achievement of sustainable development' taking five guiding principles:

- living within the planet's environmental limits;
- ensuring a strong, healthy and just society;
- achieving a sustainable economy;
- promoting good governance; and
- using sound science responsibly.

(DCLG 2012: 2)

Whilst other countries have differing systems, in most developed nations, the aim of planning is to balance the desires of individuals with the deemed best interests of society – both for the present and into the future. Decisions, in theory, in relation to any individual application are made in the context of development plans, written government policy and advice, previous decisions and the application itself. However, such matters are frequently not straightforward and developers often engage planning consultants to advise them in negotiations prior to the application being made; hence the view that planning is a negotiated process – not an absolute one.

A modern feature of the UK planning system is the use of planning agreements and local taxation measures (Community Infrastructure Levy) to offset perceived externalities of the development or support provision of community facilities off site. Where tight public spending controls exist, the use of such devices is a way to ensure that the external costs of the development begin to be borne by those who stand to gain financially from the scheme. In this way, there begins to be a balance towards social goal achievement against economic gain and environment costs.

2.1.3 Owners

As Adams and Tiesdell (2012) argue, landowners may play an active or passive role within the decision to develop and indeed the development process. Owners may actively initiate sustainable property development when they wish to sell and/or improve their land; conversely if they do not initiate the process, they become a barrier to development. Without a willingness to sell their interest or partake in the project (unless compulsory purchase powers are used), no development can take place. Also the owner's motivation may affect their decision to release land for development, and this follows whether they are individuals, corporations, public bodies or charities, a point made strongly by Goodchild and Munton (1985). Further owners may take on the role of the developer, in total or in part. A classification of owners into traditional, industrial or financial produced in 1979 (Massey and Catalano, 1978) remains valid today, although the balance of assets has changed, with the role of the financial institutions and other investors playing a critical role. Notwithstanding this, owner-occupiers still account for some over 50 per cent of commercial property and significantly more in the residential sector.

In the UK the church, landed aristocracy and gentry, and the Crown Estate are regarded as 'traditional' owners and have significant amounts of land area and capital value. Similar institutions exist in other countries. A distinguishing attribute is that they are not being entirely motivated by the economic imperative; which is potentially beneficial in sustainability terms. Overall their purposes for ownership are broader than return on capital and involve environmental, social, political and ideological issues.

Conventionally, financial owners see their proprietorship as an investment and participate if the return on their land is economically optimal. These owners have economic drivers and are often knowledgeable about land values and development or employ consultants with real estate skills. The main group are financial institutions such as insurance companies and pension funds, which hold substantial amounts of land by capital value and invest heavily in property. Financial institutions develop directly or with property developers. Furthermore, major property companies own substantial portfolios and carry out development. To these more recently can be added a growing number of high net worth individuals (HNWIs) who share the characteristics of requiring financial gain at acceptable risk but who act in ways that could be regarded as maverick as they do not tend to follow the established investment theory-driven norms of the institutions. It is this collective group (the financial investors) to whom the notion of sustainable development has been seen as problematic. Driven by the requirement to produce optimal financial gains, they need to see a business case in order to incorporate 'beyond compliance' sustainability features. However, as explored in later chapters, such evidence is increasingly forthcoming (World Green Building Council 2013)

Finally, industrial owners (perhaps now rather a misleading name) hold land for reasons related to their main purpose, some manner of service provision or production. This group includes retailers, manufacturers, industrialists, farmers, extractive industries and service industries. Public authorities that own land might be included in this group. This group is restricted and affected in their mind-set with land as the primary cause of their being, their product. Other constraints may be their legal status that may mean they will not always wish to maximise economic returns on land or property as that may be subservient to their key aim. As a developer group, their incentive will be driven primarily by function and form but increasingly, the requirement to produce a financial advantage over renting space may be a key consideration. Therefore, as a development stakeholder, they tend to operate only where the building they require is unobtainable to purchase as existing stock (for example a specialist production function) or where there are reasons of prestige that encourage them to develop for their own occupation. Where this is the case, there is even the possibility, with the embedding of social responsibility policies into corporate missions, that sustainability will be a key requirement of the specification.

Owners impact considerably on the spatial layout and the type of development constructed, especially in respect of sustainability. Planning regulations may reduce the impact they are able to have on the type of development, but as this is a negotiated process, they have influence over the design as well as location and specification of the development.

2.1.4 Developers

In the private sector, development companies can range from transnational companies employing thousands of people to single person operations. They may operate primarily either as traders or investor-developers. For the majority, their purpose is to make a direct economic profit from the development, although the large organisations will tend to have well developed CSR policies. For example, Land Securities in their commercial 1 million square foot development at Victoria London, are working closely with Westminster City Council to find ways in which the development can assist with solutions to some of the area's most pressing social issues: homelessness, unemployment and opportunities for young people. As a result they have set up long-term partnerships with homelessness charities and local schools which will include volunteering, job shadowing and contributions to affordable housing schemes; they have also set up an endowment model to award grants to a number of local charities and projects (http://www.landsecurities.com/responsibility/news-case-studies/case-studies?id=53).

Although it is fairly self-evident that the big investor-developers have a strong business case to engage with their local communities to underscore underlying confidence and values within areas, there is some evidence that developers, even where they may be developing for trading, are changing in their approach away from a totally single bottom line profit approach. Partly this will be in response to stronger planning and building codes; partly it is a shift in approach. For example, in a survey of Australian developers, Taylor *et al.* (2012) found that, in relation to climate change issues, developers and their interest groups are seeking greater levels of participation and joint decision-making in public-adaptation policy and its implementation.

Most small developers have to sell the properties they develop because they do not have the capital to retain completed schemes; that is their business model and in most countries it is taxed as such. Some larger publicly listed developers trade some of their developments to capitalise on rising rents and values whilst retaining others within an investment portfolio. Trader-developers tend to use debt finance obtained from the banking sector to be repaid when they dispose of completed assets. Whilst such a position can be advantageous during periods of growth, it can lead to excessive borrowing and vulnerability when economic downturns occur because limited assets are inadequate to continue trading.

Developers will turn to bank finance where institutional funding (see below) is not available either due to the type of development or if the developer is either not prepared or unable to provide the required guarantees. Another option is to use debt finance in a period of rising rents and values to maximise the potential profit on completion. There are many means of obtaining finance from the banks for short- and medium-term finance, although this has been restricted following the global financial crisis of the late 2000s. The banks make a financial profit from lending money. Banks lend against a particular development or lend to the development company; using the property assets of the company or the property as security for the loan. Property is attractive as security as it is a large tangible asset with resale value. Banks wish to ensure that the proposed development is well located, the developer is able to deliver the project and the scheme is feasible. Where corporate lending is concerned, the bank reviews the strength of the company, in particular assets, profits and cash-flow. Where a bank is exposed to above normal risk, they may secure an equity stake in the scheme.

The alternative to debt funding from banks is to work with those who will become the long-term investor, through arrangement of pre-sale deals. This reduces their risk and may encourage designs which are better 'future-proofed' in sustainability terms. However, such funders have very specific requirement in terms of what is 'institutionally acceptable'.

Many trader-developers aspire to become investor-developers, where profits are used for investment. Some large companies undertake little new development, managing their portfolio with increasing emphasis on retrofitting and redevelopments. In the residential sector, developers operate mostly as traders as the market is dominated by owner-occupation, however, during the development process many are owners of large tracts of land. Further, when economic gains through the land conversion process are compromised due to uncertain demand for the finished product, developers can deliberately 'land bank', holding back land for development until such time as a developed land supply shortage starts to create 'value push'. Although this is sometimes viewed by governments as an unacceptable tactical position, the reality, as discussed later in the book, is that the value of land is a product of the value of the completed development – not the other way round.

It also follows that the kind of development undertaken varies considerably. For example some companies will specialise in a particular type of development, such as offices or retail, and also in particular geographical locations; whilst others prefer to spread their risk across types and locations and countries. Some remain in a specialist type of development but cover a wide geographical, even international, area. Property companies formulate their policy according to the interest and expertise of their directors and their perception of the prevailing market conditions. Unless they are investor-developers, they may have little fundamental incentive to prioritise sustainability unless there is a proven financial case to do so. In the past this did not exist; now in some sub-markets it may. In terms of the knowledge base, in a study of Malaysian property developers, Zainul Abidin (2010) found that, whilst some did have a good level of knowledge of sustainable construction, many did not, particularly those within small and medium-sized companies. Further, their knowledge was limited to environmental issues, with little cognisance of social matters such as health and wellbeing concerns. Whilst Malaysia is still often regarded as a developing country and doubtless the situation has moved on slightly since this work was undertaken, the level of interest in sustainable development is high and the situation is believed to be similar in many other countries.

2.1.5   Financial institutions

Financial institutions, as sources of finance, have a vital role in the process unless a development is being financed wholly with the developer's own capital or that of a partner. The term usually describes superannuation or pension funds and insurance companies but also includes specialist property investors such as REITs (Real Estate Investment Trusts) and other financial vehicles. Nevertheless, there are many other financial institutions for example clearing and merchant banks (both UK and international) and building societies that finance development, as detailed above.

Financial institutions (pension funds and insurance companies) are motivated by their requirement to meet their fiduciary responsibilities to their stakeholders. Normally this means the pursuit of financial gain at levels of risk that are acceptable given their status. Property is but one of a range of investments and may represent only 5–10 per cent of their full investment portfolio, if that. Unlike most developers, they take a long-term view advised by actuarial calculations in order that their assets and liabilities match. Whilst at times this favours real estate development, more stringent liability modelling and a move from a requirement to invest in growth products for future pensioners, have seen moves towards income performance. Although superannuation, pension, life and investment funds are in theory long-term holders, their managers are assessed on their short-term performance with respect to other forms of investment and to the returns they realise against rival funds, which promotes a short-term approach which may not favour sustainability, but others do recognise its significance (Newell 2008).

Institutions can offer short- and long-term finance to developers through forward-funding where they agree to purchase the development on completion whilst providing finance. Typically, almost all risk is transferred to the developer who usually provides a financial guarantee. Otherwise, institutions may act as developers to create an investment: they bear all the risk but do not have to share any profit. Some purchase completed and let developments only as they see development as too risky.

Whether acting as developer, financier or investor, institutions adopt conservative and largely homogenous policies which typically seek a balanced portfolio of property types, although some investment houses have specialist funds geared towards particular types of opportunities. For example, Igloo, part of the Aviva group, was an early specialist fund seeking regeneration and sustainability opportunities. Furthermore most try for a good geographical spread of investments. They look for properties or developments that fit their specific criteria in terms of location, quality of building and tenant covenant (financial strength). As developers often rely on borrowed funds and have a requirement to be able to sell the eventual scheme, they will need to take account of the requirements of financial institutions in preference to those of users, where the two are in conflict. However, as the drivers for the financial institutions if they wish to buy property with the broadest tenant appeal in uncertain markets, there should be convergence between requirements, especially in markets where short leases prevail. However, some marketing advisors may take a cautious view and propose very high specification in the belief that it will lead to great lettability. Unfortunately sometimes, this can lead to over-specified, and ergo less sustainable, buildings (Cook and English 1997; van de Wetering and Wyatt 2011). Where they do consider the longer term, they can be very sensitive to demand-led factors; further, most of the large institutional investors and investment management houses now have highly developed responsible investment policies. Over the last ten years since the publication of a seminal paper by Pivo and McNamara (2005), they have begun to link this agenda with their property stance.

In the residential sector, developers build housing for owner-occupation, normally utilising short-term bank finance, with their capacity to secure finance based on track record and the value of the development.

In the public sector, the sources for residential development are comparable though more challenging to obtain especially after the financial crisis, with very tight central government controls on public sector borrowing operating in most developed economies. Some authorities may obtain funding through grants for urban regeneration projects in specific geographic areas, from central government sources. In the European Union, so-called European Structural Funds have provided funding previously. However, access to funding is often competitive and sometimes targeted at schemes where partnerships between the community and the private sector exist. Developers may acquire economic support from government agencies in the shape of grants, rental guarantees and equity participation through the provision of land, though they have to prove that the project would not proceed without such assistance and that jobs will be created in the local community. For these reasons, at least in the UK, public sector engagement in the residential sector has almost ceased, with a shift towards third sector providers, many of whom are now entering into partnerships with private sector developers, either by choice or through planning requirements to integrate 'affordable' or 'social' housing within schemes. At best, such arrangements enable a deepening dialogue between different types of organisations which can lead to more inclusive sustainable design; at worst it is a recipe for an uncomfortable alignment of two-tier stock.

2.1.6 Producers

2.1.6.1 Construction firms

The conventional model is for the developer to contract with a construction firm and possibly, through them, a range of sub-contractors, to build the development. This model leads to the potential for disputes as each party pursues their own financial objectives, and any over-arching ambition towards sustainability can be jeopardised as a result. Larger firms with the relevant expertise can act as a management contractor and oversee all the subcontracts for the developer for a fee, to minimise risk to the client. Although some firms are now developing an ethic for sustainability and expertise in sustainable construction methods where the supply chain is fragmented, such an ethic may become diluted or lost. Nonetheless, the impact of disputes is a major issue within the construction industry leading to time and financial loss (E.C. Harris 2013).

However, this is not the only model and many contractual systems for procuring property exist (see Chapter 8). In some cases, developers employ their own contractors whilst larger residential developers or house-builders lean towards in-house expertise. Other, normally commercial, organisations have a contracting division as an independent profit-making centre. Another widely used model is design and build, under which combined control over design and construction aims to reduce the inter-organisational arguments and miscommunications which can increase cost and time and impact negatively on quality (Ng and Price 2010). Whatever model is adopted, a major determinant will be the type of development and the attitude towards risk, notably the liability for any cost increases. Construction firms, such as house-builders, which act as developers, assume the added risks related to development. When a builder is engaged as a contractor alone, the economic profit is related to building cost and the length of contract but where the construction firm is the developer, a larger profit is needed because of the risk.

Construction firms perform a specialist activity within the process, starting when there is maximum developer commitment and risk. A wise developer will vet thoroughly the ability of the construction firms to deliver the development, looking for the optimum balance between time, cost and quality. It is in neither the developer's nor the construction firm's interest to create circumstances where the construction firm is unable to obtain a reasonable profit. It is not in the developer's interest for the construction firm to compromise on quality or to go into liquidation; too frequently this happens.

Public Private Partnerships (PPPs) cover a wide range of different types of contractual and collaborative partnerships, such as the Private Finance Initiative (PFI), the introduction of private sector ownership into state-owned businesses, the sale of government services into wider markets and the generation of commercial activities from public sector assets through, for example, the Wider Markets Initiative. Over two decades, they have become a vital part of many governments' strategies, including the UK, to deliver public infrastructure or buildings such as hospitals and schools. Generally all PPPs have three objectives:

- to deliver significantly improved public services, by contributing to increases in the quality and quantity of investment;
- to release the full potential of public sector assets to provide value for the taxpayer and wider benefits for the economy; and
- to allow stakeholders such as taxpayers and employees to receive an equitable share of the benefits of the PPP.

Thus PPPs bring together a public body and a private company in a long-term (normally 30 + years) joint venture for the delivery of high-quality public services for mutual benefit after which the facility reverts to the public sector. In theory therefore both parties are in the arrangement for the long term which should promote the inclusion of sustainability characteristics in the specification.

The original thinking behind PPP was that the public sector cannot always deliver major investment projects and the private sector could bring perceived benefits such as increased efficiency and innovation, a motivation to invest in high-quality assets to optimise maintenance and running costs, and finally, improved management of the risks in delivering complex investment projects within time cost and quality constraints. PPPs provide additional resources for investment in public sectors and the efficient management of the investment although the benefits have been widely questioned on both cost and quality grounds (see for example, Akintola *et al.* 2003; Bennett and Ioassa 2006). Further, Hamilton and Holcomb (2013) argue that, despite many undoubted successes of PPPs in promoting sustainable development, many international operators are not motivated to make investments in developing regions where the need for social services is greatest.

Thus development is complex and most developers have neither the skills nor the expertise to undertake a major development without interfacing with other expertise. Consequently, developers employ different professionals to advise them at different stages of the process depending on their needs. In this way, other stakeholders can also influence the degree and extent of sustainability included or omitted from projects. These interactions can result in obscurity as to who in the final analysis makes the decision about the final specification of a building, including the approach to sustainability (Green Construction Board 2015).

2.1.6.2 Planning consultants

Planning consultants, acting on behalf of developers or landowners, negotiate with local authorities to obtain the most valuable permission for a development. Where an application is rejected they can act as expert witness to make the case for the developer. In addition planning consultants advise owners to safeguard that their sites are allocated within the development plan to their most valuable or appropriate use. They may negotiate with the local planning authority at plan preparation stage or make representations at an enquiry into the development plan. In this role they can be significant initiators of the process. They can have an impact on urban sustainability in terms of issues such as transport and proximity of residential developments to services such as retail, health, educational, commercial and employment. Whilst they have a contractual obligation to work for their clients, they also have an ethical duty to act in the public interest which now might include an obligation to advise clients as to the implications for sustainability of their proposals. In preparing planning applications, consultants frequently have to employ specialists, such as ecological or sustainability experts to carry out biodiversity or other impact assessments, which can have a negative impact on costs and time.

2.1.6.3 Architects

Developers employ architects to design the form and construction of new buildings or the adaptation of existing buildings; as such they can have a substantial effect on the design and operational sustainability of the development. Architects sometimes administer building contracts on behalf of the developer and certify completion of the works. In the case of adaptation, building surveyors are employed to survey the existing property, advise on alterations and provide contract administration services. Where a planning consultant is not used, architects will obtain planning permission for new builds, whereas with an adaptation the building surveyor will perform this task. They are paid on a fee basis, typically a percentage of the total building contract sum.

The architect is appointed usually at the beginning of a project to ensure all design work is completed when construction begins. Developers look for appropriate experience, reputation, resources and track record as well as the right balance of skills to generate fine architecture that is cost-effective and attractive to users. As this balance is hard to deliver, it is vital for developers to provide a clear brief as issues arise when there is a lack of communication between developer and architect.

Some architects offer project management, engineering and interior design services; however, though this may be effectual on some projects, most developers prefer to compile their own professional team. Finally some developers employ architects and design professionals directly. Architects often are highly skilled in relation to some aspects of sustainability but may take a techno-centric approach to the design at the expense of wider considerations. One such debate is whether sustainable development is better served by the construction of massive structures with high embodied energy but with the ability to retain heating /cooling over lengthy periods and designed for long life, or lightweight flexible structures which have lower embodied energy but may need efficient cooling and heating systems.

2.1.6.4 Valuation surveyors

Valuation surveyors or property economic consultants produce a detailed analysis of the market in terms of supply and demand at the evaluation stage. This information allows the developer to determine the profitability and risks associated with the proposed project. Many financiers, especially the institutions, insist on market analysis when evaluating funding proposals and within the UK, some lenders now require specific mention of sustainability within the valuation report. A major recent review of the business case for going green (World Green Building Council 2013) has shown increasing evidence that within commercial property developments in large city centre locations, sustainability certified buildings may command value differentials over those designed to less sustainable standards. Valuers have been criticised for a lack of awareness and knowledge of sustainability matters (Warren-Myers 2011). This is beginning to change, and a requirement to consider the implications of sustainability within valuations is now explicit within the RICS's global standards to which all their registered valuers must adhere (RICS 2014: VPS 4: 60).

2.1.6.5 Construction economists or quantity surveyors

Construction economists or quantity surveyors (QSs) advise the developer on the probable costs of the total building contract and related costs. Their responsibilities can include costing the architect's designs, tendering the building contract, advising on the form of building contract (procurement), monitoring construction and approving stage payments to the contractor. QSs frequently manage the administration of design and build contracts, where their fee is based on a percentage of the final contract sum. As with the architect, the selection of the QS should be centred on experience and reputation. Furthermore the developer should appoint QSs who work well with architects and other professional team members to deliver cost-effective designs. The QS should be able to offer cost-effective alternatives to those proposed by the architect. With issues around perceptions (if not a reality) of increased costs of developing property sustainably, the QS has a key role in suggesting and facilitating cost-effective sustainability solutions for developers, for example using a Life-Cycle Approach (LCA) to evaluate different options in the design and specification. It is therefore important that they develop skills in terms of methods of evaluating sustainability such as LCA.

2.1.6.6 Engineers

Structural engineers advise on the design of structural components to ensure the stability of the building and they may contribute to supervision of the structural construction; their knowledge of materials' strength, longevity and environmental impacts can influence the final sustainability rating of a building. Civil engineers are engaged where major infrastructure works and/or groundwork are part of the project. On larger or more complicated projects, mechanical and electrical engineers design the building services and can have a significant impact on the sustainability of the design and operational phase of the development but in designing buildings it is critical that they do have a clear understanding of how a building will be occupied or their systems designed to minimise energy use, may simply not work. There is an increasing recognition that sustainability knowledge is a necessary component of the future engineering skill base. Engineers are usually paid a percentage fee based on the value of their element of the building contract.

2.1.6.7 Project managers

Project Managers (PMs) manage the professional team and the contract for the developer; and are particularly engaged for complex or large-scale projects. Typically they have been educated and trained as architects, engineers or surveyors prior to becoming project managers; this initial training and education often influences their style of project management. Developers can act as a PM or they can appoint another member of the professional team to fulfil this role. PMs should be appointed before any of the professional team or the contractor so that they can counsel the developer on the best team for the scheme; as such they are in a position to influence the scope and extent of sustainability. Although their fees are often a percentage of the building contract sum, they can be incentive based for delivering the project on cost and on time. Developers can fulfil the PM role for building users who wish to engage a developer in constructing their own premises.

2.1.6.8 Solicitors

The services of solicitors are required at several points in the process, from the purchase of the site to the preparation of leases and contracts of sale. Furthermore they negotiate legal agreements covering funding arrangements entered into by the developer. When a developer appeals a planning application, solicitors and barristers may represent the developer. Where collateral warranties are demanded by purchasers, solicitors prepare the documentation. Collateral warranties are agreements under which parties with contractual obligations, in connection with the construction or operation of a project, accept liability to the lenders for their performance. With the growth of interest in so-called 'green leases' and the recognition that the owner/occupier interface is critical in promoting sustainability, Brooks (2008) argues that 'lawyers are on the front lines of lease negotiation, and can lead change'. However, to date there is little evidence that, their knowledge base has so widened, with the notable exception of some vanguard experts (Sayce *et al.* 2009).

2.1.6.9 Accountants and financial advisors

On occasion, specialist accountants advise on the complexity of tax and, in the UK, VAT regulations that can have a major cost impact on a project. They may advise on the structure of partnership or financing arrangements. Accountants are not likely to have much impact on the sustainability of the development directly, unless tax advantages exist which benefit developers through the implementation of various sustainability measures. Regretfully, even where tax breaks do exist which can support sustainability objectives, these are not necessarily promoted by financial advisors.

The description of the professionals and specialists above does not completely cover the full range of professional expertise that is engaged in property development or indeed their roles in respect of sustainability within the process. There are many other specialists who may be needed depending on the project and its complexity. Other appropriate professionals may comprise of land surveyors, soil specialists, archaeologists, public relations consultants, highway engineers, landscape architects and marketing consultants.

2.1.7 Marketeers – agents

Real estate agents often exert influence right at the start of the development process by bringing together stakeholders; their skills lie in understanding rental and capital markets and interpreting them. They tend to operate through strong networks of personal contacts among stakeholder groups and are therefore well placed to connect the developer and the end user, unless the developer employs in-house staff to perform this role.

Agents obtain direct financial profit from their fees charged to their client (developer or user). They may play a key role in initiating the development by sourcing a site or advising a landowner to sell a site on account of its development potential. In this way they indirectly influence sustainability. Unless they are retained to find sites for a particular use, agents identify sites for developers. The agent negotiates for the developer and advises on matters relating to feasibility. Agents may receive a fee for finding the site that is often a percentage of the purchase price. Furthermore if the purchase proceeds, they may be appointed to let the development or secure funding for the scheme. When an agent acts for an owner, they may provide professional advice on estimated land value and the likely market for the site; however, whether they can provide value advice will depend on the jurisdiction in which they operate. They therefore have a critical role in understanding how sustainability characteristics are impacting on the demand-side, which in turn can feed back into development decisions.

Frequently agents are not brought in at the concept stage and are only engaged as letting or selling agents. In this case, they may be too late to really influence the depth and breadth of sustainability incorporated in the design; it is therefore preferable that they be appointed from the early stages; it is also important that they develop a real understanding of the complexities surrounding sustainability rather than a superficial knowledge of accreditation and rating schemes. We return to this later in the book.

2.1.8 Consultees

Within most developed countries' planning systems, consultation with external stakeholders is a critical part of the pre-construction process. Such consultees may be statutory (i.e. prescribed in law) or they can be members of organisations or indeed individuals who wish to express views. Within the UK, there are five principal statutory consultees for major schemes. They are English Heritage, the Environment Agency, the Health and Safety Executive, the Highways Agency and Natural England, all of whom have informed voices in terms of sustainability, either social or environmental.

Whereas many consultees will be supportive and offer constructive and useful suggestions, others may object, leading to possible delay and in some cases abandonment of proposed developments. They might comprise self-interested neighbours and as such are often labelled 'NIMBYS' ('not in my back yard'). As such, they can have the potential for negative or positive impacts with regards to sustainability; but where there is a drive for development at almost any cost they can provide an essential counter-balance.

Objectors include some well-organised professional, permanent bodies at local and national level. At local level, they include amenity societies who consider every proposal affecting local environment and heritage, for example, the Victorian and Georgian Societies, the Society for the Protection of Ancient Buildings (SPAB) and the National Trust. They have influence on local planning authorities and are referred to on major applications; they also express views at the policy level.

Of most significance to sustainability are the environmental activists who emerged in the 1990s, usually focused on substantial projects. A good example of environmental protest is the Chinese Three Gorges Project. Protest can be direct such as occupation or passive, for example letter writing or petitioning to administrators. It is anticipated that environmental protests are likely to increase in scale over time as the evidence of environmental degradation increases and the impact of manmade climate change becomes more evident. However it is not just at the development phase that objectors make a difference to the type of buildings that get commissioned. As they gain power and influence over matters as diverse as energy policy and corporate responsibility, so they begin to impact on the actions and policies of those who will become the ultimate building occupiers and owners, and on the government level policy makers.

Developers, therefore, should be cognisant of potential objector/supporter groups and be ready to accommodate or contest their views. If these discussions can be carried out before the planning application is submitted long delays may be avoided. By embracing those with strong causes and significant research behind them, the scheme may prove more successful in the longer term. Over recent years, this message has increasingly found its voice (see for example BPF/LGA 2014a, b).

2.1.9 Building users

Actual or perceived user demand for accommodation is the basic trigger for the development process; it influences land prices and rents, to which developers respond; such is established, though sometimes challenged, Ricardian theory (Ricardo 1817). If the user of a building is the developer or is known prior to design completion, they become a key stakeholder within the process and this is a desirable position as it improves the chances of the building operating successfully over a long period of time. However, it is often not the case. In many residential schemes, and some (though currently less commonly) commercial schemes, developers produce buildings geared primarily to the financiers' short or long-term requirements whilst failing to fully appreciate who might subsequently occupy the building and therefore failing to adequately plan for users' needs. It is recognised now that developers should investigate and understand users' requirements and likely future requirements; so doing will assist in ensuring that the building meets with higher levels of sustainability. It is also likely that the building will be designed with flexibility either within use, or possibly across use, in mind. Building flexibility is regarded as a key criterion of sustainability (Ellison and Sayce 2007) as is discussed later.

When the user is known early, they are the most significant stakeholder, but an uninformed client may be strongly influenced in decision-making by their advisory team. In principle, the property will be designed and built to their needs, which can be specialised, especially for industrial or non-commercial, non-domestic users (e.g. education or health facilities). Where the known future occupier is a lessee and they seek to impose any features which the developer deems may negatively impact on future user demand, the developer will seek to negotiate a compromise to provide a more standard and flexible type of building, so that the investment market for the building is wider in the event of disposal and the value is protected as security for loan purposes. It could be argued that such an approach could better future-proof the building and hence enhance whole life sustainability. The counter argument is that if a building is designed to meet its users' needs, there is less likelihood of it failing functionally or being vacated prematurely.

Non-domestic occupiers mostly perceive the buildings they use as a resource and a necessary overhead cost of fulfilling their activities as service or product providers; they have little sense of their space as an investment asset. Many major occupiers employ in-house property and/or facilities management teams; however, despite strenuous moves to contain costs, many users still do not plan their property requirements pro-actively and expertly resulting in calls for changed behaviours (see for example Haynes 2012; Taylor 2013); they simply react to changes as they happen and this approach can and does affect the whole life cycle sustainability of a development. Inevitably the property requirements of building users are influenced by both the short-term business cycle and long-term structural changes underlying the general economy. The design of property and its rate of development including its inherent sustainability are inevitably affected by this. As such, these attributes influence users at a specific level or across the business sector in which they operate. Their accommodation requirements are affected further by advances in technology impacting physical property needs; and, the move to more sustainable workplace practices.

Building users have been criticised for not knowing what they want, though many companies are gaining more understanding of the role of sustainable property within their businesses and their requirements in terms of specification (see for example, Harrison *et al.* 2004). This is partly demonstrated by the expansion of Facility Management (FM) as a role as well as sustainability rating tools for design and operational phases in the life cycle. As users have divergent needs and concerns, it renders it hard for developers to produce sustainable buildings that meet the needs of as many users as possible. Financial institutions respond by looking for the best quality specification with space plans to suit the widest possible range of users. The result is users may have to lease space that compromises their requirements in terms of location or specification that leads to users stripping out buildings and retrofitting or fitting them out to their requirements. Frequent fit out is inherently unsustainable and there is evidence in some markets which short lease terms lead to fit out and to waste of services, materials, fixtures and fittings (Forsythe and Wilkinson 2015). In response, there is now a widespread movement to understand more fully how buildings can be designed to facilitate sustainable retrofits and refurbishments.

Lease terms highlight another area of divergence between financial institutions and users. Users require flexible lease terms to respond in the short term to changes in their property requirements. In markets such as the UK, institutional investors conventionally prefer longer lease terms with upward-only rent reviews and repair clauses placing liability on the tenant. However when there is excess supply and a downturn in the market, as with the global financial crisis, many will accept shorter lease terms with break clause options if the market is demanding such agreements and the tenant's covenant is strong, albeit that value adjustment may result. In the US and Australian markets it is usual to have shorter lease terms, and within the UK this too has been a structural trend with commercial new lease lengths now being typically between five and 15 years. This could have an impact on the whole life cycle sustainability of property as users typically fit out their space when taking new leases – if tenants relocated every five to seven years or so, the rate of fit out will be high with its attendant high embodied energy, higher rates of waste and landfill and so on (Forsythe and Wilkinson 2015). However, a new lease does not necessarily mean a new tenant, though there is little hard evidence as to the average occupation (as opposed to lease) length.

Another sustainability issue concerns the tendency to over-specify, notably in office developments. Although developers and the financial institutions arguably do consider user needs, in an effort to future-proof their developments against assumed ever greater reliance on technology, many office buildings developed over the last decade have been over-specified with over-use of non-renewable imported materials and are over-reliant on complex air-conditioning with a consequent increase in embodied carbon and also in-use greenhouse gas emissions (van de Wetering and Wyatt 2011). More recently, the trend is moving towards energy efficient buildings which maximise their use of natural ventilation, minimise imported materials and use air-conditioning only where absolutely essential. However, in the interests of true triple bottom line sustainability, such specification changes should not be seen as a trigger to accelerate the pace of building replacement: that in itself becomes an unsustainable approach. In the interests of sustainability, it should be accepted that it takes many years to replace existing stock with new build and that process itself has high social and environmental impacts; therefore it is imperative to improve the existing stock.

In summary, decision-making in property development is complex, more so when the desire or requirement to embed sustainability in all its guises is embedded in the process. Much of this complexity arises from the lack of deep understanding of the issues; but some is the result of the interactions between the many stakeholders all of whom have legitimacy in influencing decisions to varying degrees and at different points in the process (Kincaid 2002). Each stakeholder represents a different interest and has different educational and professional backgrounds that further influence their decisions. Furthermore some stakeholders fulfil more than one role in the process. Table 2.1 provides a summary explanation of some of the relationships detailed above between the stakeholders and their respective roles and responsibilities as well as their influences or impact on sustainability in projects.

2.2   Conclusion

This chapter has described the role of each of the major stakeholder groups that engage with property development and it established that their actions can impact on the eventual level of sustainability achieved within the development. Whilst some groups, such as investors, constructors and developers, have an easily recognised role, it would be too simplistic to ascribe the sustainability or otherwise of a building solely to their actions. Table 2.1 indicates that they do indeed exert differing levels of influence dependent on the type of development.

In 2000, concern in the UK had become so intense that, despite strong encouragement from the government to stimulate 'sustainable buildings', developers were not seeking to go 'beyond compliance' within their schemes. And so was developed the notion of a circle of

Table 2.1 Stakeholders and their influence on decision-making and sustainability in projects

Stakeholders	Description and professional affiliations	Stage in development process where decisions are made	Degree of influence on sustainability/ impact on sustainability
Policy makers	Federal, state and local government departments	Direct influence on potential site supply and use. Indirect effect on decision-making in adaptation at all stages	High to low
Regulators	Local authorities, planners, heritage, building surveyors, fire engineers (Planning Institute of Australia, Institute of Fire Engineers)	During design concept and development stage (and possibly during construction if amendments are made)	High
Owners	Landowners, public and private institutions, individuals	Beginning and throughout if likely to be end user	High to low
Developers	Organisations that combine investment, production and marketing in whole or in part. Professionals from bodies listed in producers above and others	Throughout	High to low
Investors	Pension/superannuation funds, insurance companies, banks, independent investors, professionals who find capital to invest	Beginning/early	Low?
Producers	Professional team – facilities ,anager, quantity surveyor, architects, engineers, contractors, surveyors, suppliers (Royal Institution of Chartered Surveyors, Australian Institute of Architects, Australian Institute of Quantity Surveyors, Australian Institute of Building Surveyors, Australian Institute of Refrigeration, Air Cooling and Heating)	Varies depending on specialism (see above)	High to low
Marketeers	Surveyors, stakeholders, agents, professionals who find users for buildings (Australian Property Institute, Royal Institution of Chartered Surveyors)	During design (if selling off plan) and /or construction stage	High to medium
Objectors	Large institutional owners, individuals, business organisations, local community groups, pressure groups	Beginning/early stand eventual take out	Medium to low
Users – corporate residential	Large institutional owners and users Individuals Business organisations Users	Beginning to late	High to low

Source: Wilkinson 2011

blame in which each major stakeholder group was seen to be in favour in *principle* but lacking a business case to move forward. Since then, market demand pressures have changed; so too have many of the regulatory frameworks which are discussed in later chapters. Undoubtedly, where buildings are commissioned for owner-occupation for the long term, the interests of differing stakeholders can coalesce and aid in the drive towards sustainability. Therefore, perhaps it is understandable that many case studies of sustainable buildings, including the early examples of those certified to the highest rating levels are buildings that lie within the public sector owner-occupation, such as the Wessex Water Building. This building, completed in 2001, achieved the highest ever rating at the time. In commissioning it, the company placed sustainability at the centre of its operational requirements; as a consequence, the project considered environmental, social and economic factors including staff opinions, the relationship with neighbours and the ability of the building to adapt to future change (Heid 2001).

However, what has also become more widely recognised is that there are many stakeholder groups, all of which interface in often complex and non-transparent ways which, subtly or otherwise, impact on the decisions made regarding specification, design and execution of the development. The last decade, which witnessed the world financial crisis and consequent falling rents, caused many stakeholders to appraise both their attitudes and policies. It also coincided with the strengthening of the CSR agenda and the regulatory response to the challenge of climate change. Whilst collectively these pressures on stakeholders may not yet have completely turned the vicious circle into the desired virtuous circle, undoubtedly headway has been made. Further chapters will draw out in detail the factors, including sustainability factors that each stakeholder considers in the process.

References

Adams, D. and Tiesdell, S. (2012) *Shaping Places: Urban Planning, Design and Development*, London: Routledge.

Adams, D., Croudace, R., and Tiesdell, S. (2012). Exploring the 'notional property developer' as a policy construct, *Urban Studies* 49(12): 2577–2596.

Akintola, A., Beck, M., and Hardcastle, C. (2003) *Public Private Partnerships: Managing Risks and Opportunities*, Oxford: Blackwell.

Bennett, J. and Iossa, E. (2006) Building and managing facilities for public services, *Journal of Public Economics* 90: 2143–2160.

British Property Federation (BPF)/Local Government Association (LGA)/Planning Advisory Service (PAS) (2014a) *Ten Commitments for Effective Pre-application Engagement*, BPF/LGA/PAS. Retrieved from www.planning resource.co.uk.

British Property Federation (BPF)/Local Government Association (LGA)/Planning Advisory Service (PAS) (2014b) *Planning Positively through Partnership* BPF/LGA/PAS. Retrieved from www. planning resource.co.uk

Brooks, S.M. (2008) *Green Leases: The Next Step in Greening Commercial Buildings*, Real Property Association of Canada.

Cadman, D. (2000) The vicious circle of blame, in M. Keeping (ed.), *What about Demand? Do Investors Want 'Sustainable Buildings'?*, London: The RICS Research Foundation. Retrieved from: http://www.rics.org/Practiceareas/Builtenvi.

Cook, S.J. and English, C. (1997) Overspecification of speculative UK commercial office building: an international comparison, in P. Stephenson (ed.), 13th Annual ARCOM Conference, 15–17 September 1997, King's College, Cambridge, *Association of Researchers in Construction Management* 1: 183–192.

DCLG (Department of Communities and Local Government) (2012) *The National Planning Policy Framework*. Retrieved from https://www.gov.uk/government/uploads/system/uploads/attachment_data/file/6077/2116950.pdf.

Dubben, N. and Williams, B. (2009). *Partnerships in Urban Property Development*, Chichester: John Wiley & Sons.

E.C. Harris (2013) Global construction disputes: a longer resolution. Available from http://www.echarris.com/pdf/EC%20Harris%20Construction%20Disputes%202013Final.pdf.

Ellison, L. and Sayce, S. (2007) Assessing sustainability in the existing commercial property stock: establishing sustainability criteria relevant for the commercial property investment sector, *Property Management* 25(3): 287–304.

Forsythe, P. and Wilkinson, S. (2015) Measuring office fit-out changes to determine recurring embodied energy in building life cycle assessment, *Facilities* 33(1/2) 262–274.

Fuerst, F. and McAllister, P. (2011) Green noise or green value? Measuring the effects of environmental certification on office values, *Real Estate Economics* 39(1): 45–69.

Goodchild, R.N. and Munton, R.J.C. (1985) *Development and the Landowner: An Analysis of the British Experience*, London: Allen and Unwin.

Green Building Council Australia (GBCA) (2013). Retrieved 27 April 2013 from http://www.gbca.org.au/resources/fact-sheets/what-is-sustainable-development/27.htm .

Green Construction Board (2015) Mapping the real estate life cycle for effective policy interventions. Retrieved from http://www.greenconstructionboard.org/images/stories/Valuation_and_Demand/GCB610%20Final%20Report.pdf.

Hamilton, G. and Holcomb, V. (2013) *Public-private Partnerships for Sustainable Development*. New York: United Nations Economic Commission for Europe (UNECE). Retrieved from http://www.commonwealthministers.com/articles/public-private_partnerships_for_sustainable_development/.

Harrison, A., Wheeler, P., and Whitehead, C (2004) *The Distributed Workplace: Sustainable Work Environments*, New York: Spon.

Hartenberger, U. (2008) *Breaking the Vicious Circle of Blame – Making the Business Case for Sustainable Buildings* FiBRE (Findings in Built and Rural Environments), London: RICS.

Haynes, B.P. (2012) Corporate real estate asset management: aligned vision, *Journal of Corporate Real Estate* 14(4): 244–254.

Heid, D. (2001) Wessex Water Operations Centre – building services strategy, *Facilities* 19(11/12). http://dx.doi.org/10.1108/f.2001.06919kaf.001

Kincaid, D. (2002) *Adapting Buildings for Changing Uses: Guidelines for Change of Use Refurbishment*, London: Routledge.

Lipsky, J. (2008) Sovereign wealth funds: their role and significance. speech at the seminar, *Sovereign Funds: Responsibility with Our Future*, organized by the Ministry of Finance of Chile, Santiago, 3 September 2008. Retrieved from https://www.imf.org/external/np/speeches/2008/090308.htm.

Massey, D.B. and Catalano, A. (1978) *Capital and Land: Landownership by Capital in Great Britain*, London: Edward Arnold.

Newell, G. (2008) The strategic significance of environmental sustainability by Australian-listed property trusts, *Journal of Property Investment & Finance* 26(6): 522–540.

Ng, K.A. and Price, A.D.F. (2010). Causes leading to poor site coordination in building projects. *Organisation, Technology & Management in Construction: An International Journal*, 2: 167–172.

Pivo, G. and McNamara, P. (2005) Responsible property investing, *International Real Estate Review* 8(1): 128–143.

Ricardo, D. (1817). *On the Principles of Political Economy and Taxation*, London: John Murray.

RICS (Royal Institution of Chartered Surveyors) (2014) *RICS Valuation- Professional Standards January 2014*, London: RICS.

Ruskin, J. (1849) *The Seven Lamps of Architecture*, London: Smith, Elder and Co.

Sayce, S., Sundberg, A., Parnell, P., and Cowling, E. (2009) Greening leases: do tenants in the United Kingdom want green leases?, *Journal of Retail & Leisure Property* 8(4): 273–284.

Stern, N. (2006) *Stern Review: The Economics of Climate Change*, London: HM Treasury.

Sustainable Construction Task Group (2000) *Risk, Reputation and Reward*, Building Research Establishment. Retrieved from http://projects.bre.co.uk/rrr/RRR.pdf.

Sustainable Procurement Task Force (2006) *Procuring the Future*, DEFRA. Retrieved from https://www.gov.uk/government/publications/procuring-the-future.

Taylor B.M. (2013) Sustainability and performance measurement: corporate real estate perspectives, *Performance Improvement* 52(6): 36–45.

Taylor, B.M., Harman, B.P., Heyenga, S., and McAllister, R.R. (2012) Property developers and urban adaptation: conceptual and empirical perspectives on governance, *Urban Policy and Research* 30(1): 5–24.

Van de Wetering, J. and Wyatt, P. (2011) Office sustainability: occupier perceptions and implementation of policy, *Journal of European Real Estate Research* 4(1): 29–47.

Walker, A., Sayce, S., and McIntosh, A. (2004) *Building Sustainability in the Balance: Promoting Stakeholder Dialogue*, London: Estates Gazette Ltd.

Warren-Myers, G. (2011) Sustainability – the crucial challenge, *Pacific Rim Property Research Journal* 17(4): 491–510.

Weick, K.E. (1969) *The Social Psychology of Organizing*, Reading, MA: Addison-Wesley.

Wilkinson, S.J. (2011) The relationship between building adaptation and property attributes, PhD thesis, Deakin University. Retrieved from http://hdl.handle.net/10536/DRO/DU:30036710

World Green Building Council (2013) The business case for green building: a review of the costs and benefits for developers, investors and occupants, World Green Building Council. Retrieved from http://www.worldgbc. org/files/1513/6608/0674/ Business_Case_For_Green_ Building_Report_WEB_2013-14.pdf.

Zainul Abidin, N. (2010) Investigating the awareness and application of sustainable construction concept by Malaysian developers. *Habitat International* 34(4): 421–426.

3 Site feasibility

Evaluating the site, commitment and sustainability

Sara J. Wilkinson and Sarah L. Sayce

3.0 Introduction

An evaluation of site feasibility and the purchase of the site are normally the initial stages in any property development, except where land is already held in either a 'land bank' or is held by the owner for prior use which is now redundant. Consequently the decision has a substantial and long lasting impact on the sustainability of any development. Site acquisition is usually the property developer's first major financial commitment to a project. Furthermore initiation, site feasibility and site acquisition are closely related and often occur concurrently. Considerations of sustainability should be embedded throughout the process. Ideally the purchase of the site should be completed after the site feasibility and development evaluation process has taken place, except where already owned prior, as detailed above. This chapter is concerned with the site feasibility, initiation and the acquisition stages of the development process. Initiation is defined as 'Starting a process that can result in the authorisation of a new project' and 'the first, and most critical phase in the project life cycle where the project is defined, a team is assembled, and approval is given to proceed with the project' (PMBOK Guide 2013). Additionally the attributes which enhance sustainability are discussed, including any which might have a negative impact on sustainability, which are highlighted. Legal and political influences on site acquisition are also covered.

Appropriate site selection is fundamental to development success, as it affects the nature of a development. If the site has a location which is not appropriate for the type, scale or specification of the proposed development, or the economics in terms of cost and developed value (see Chapter 4) render it unviable, no amount of good design, promotion or sustainability features can overcome the issues; indeed it will fail in terms of being a sustainable development. Site acquisition can be a frustrating and unpredictable process as many issues can impact on its success. Every site is unique and each project will require consideration of different variables to various degrees; however, it is possible to outline a comprehensive list of considerations for developers (Wilkinson and Reed 2008). Figure 3.1 illustrates the typical sequence of development and where initiation and site acquisition sit with respect to feasibility.

The site feasibility study comprises the business proposal for the development. It establishes the budget for the site acquisition and also the buildings and profit. The study identifies the requirements of the development, defines viable alternatives, analyses alternatives and delivery methods and recommends the preferred solution. The feasibility study is reviewed at times depending on the project circumstances, timelines and external factors such as general economic trends in order to confirm the preferred solution, is still the

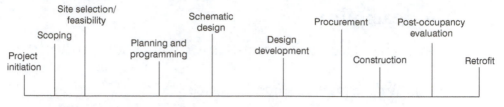

Figure 3.1 The development process: from initiation to retrofit
Source: Author (2014)

optimum. If not, changes will be made as necessary. In extreme cases, development projects may be temporarily or permanently shelved.

Developers need to adopt well-researched site acquisition strategies; however, its achievement, in the time and way originally envisaged, is often beyond the control of the developer. The following preconditions need to be in place for the development process to be initiated through site acquisition:

1 The site owner's readiness to sell the site on terms of agreement and at an agreed sales price which allows a viable development to proceed.
2 Proposed use allowable within the relevant development plan and regulations, or the acquisition of planning permission for the proposed development to proceed (see Chapter 6).
3 The existence of infrastructure and services to support the proposed development.
4 The existence of suitable ground conditions to support the development (if necessary after appropriate treatment at a reasonable cost).
5 The necessary development finance (see Chapter 5).
6 A known end-user or occupier demand for the proposed development (see Chapter 4).

If any of the above preconditions are not in place, either the development will not proceed or the development will present a significant risk to the developer. Local authority involvement and government assistance may be available in relation to compulsory acquisition, provision of infrastructure, site reclamation, finance or occupier/investor incentives depending on the nature of the proposed development and its location. Most importantly, the requirements of occupiers and eventual owners/investors must be at the forefront of any developer's site acquisition strategy.

3.1 Sustainability issues affecting site feasibility

This section describes the characteristics affecting site feasibility in respect of sustainability issues at the macro and micro level. Starting with issues around urbanisation and population growth, the section moves on to look at transport and infrastructure factors and how they can impact on the sustainability of the development. The issues of site contamination or brownfield sites are discussed before covering climate change factors such as flooding.

3.1.1 *Climate issues and development*

Weather patterns are changing in ways consistent with a warming global climate (IPCC 2014) and scientific research points to rainfall patterns changing, in particular by greater intensity and fewer events (Solomon and Qin 2007; Met Office Hadley Centre for Climate Research 2007; IPCC 2014). Although specific extreme events cannot be attributed to climate change, the consensus is that the frequency of intense rainfall events is rising over most site masses (including those where average rainfall is decreasing) and this is likely to continue in some seasons (Solomon and Qin 2007). Intense rainfall events can trigger flash floods, particularly in dense urban areas with low permeability, leading to serious impacts on the affected owners and occupiers. Furthermore areas previously unaffected by flooding may become more flood prone in future. This is a risk developers need to manage increasingly and if they develop and hold their exposure to risk may be greater.

For example, in Australia, the prolonged droughts have been replaced by increased intense rainfall: the estimated cost of building remediation following the 2010/11 floods in the states of Queensland and Victoria varied from A\$9 billion to A\$20 billion (Companies and Markets 2011). The densely populated East Coast area was subjected to severe floods in two consecutive years (Bureau of Meteorology 2012). In the UK, the cost of flash flooding has risen in recent decades: 3.8 million properties in England are estimated to be at risk from surface water flooding alone (Environment Agency 2013). Extreme rainfall events in 2007, 2012 and 2014 caused localised flash flooding in city centres including Glasgow, Hull, Newcastle and York, with substantial damage and disruption and widespread flooding across a large area in the south west of England. The real cost to local economies may be long lasting and difficult to measure, as many businesses fail to recover after suffering flooding (Cumbria Intelligence Observatory 2010; Ingirige and Wedawatta 2011; Wedawatta *et al.* 2011). The flooding was so severe in the UK in 2014 that the authorities in affected areas are now considering whether 'floating' house design, already used in the Netherlands, should be adopted into the building codes for long-term sustainability. Further, developments in potential flood affected areas may become impossible to insure, and therefore in effect potentially unsaleable.

Development contributes to this problem, as the growing damage impacts of increased pluvial flooding are not attributable to changing weather patterns alone: it is exacerbated by increased development pressures and urbanisation (Jha *et al.* 2011). In the UK, for example, there have been effects arising from the policy of redeveloping brownfield sites, together with the popularity of paving green spaces to provide car parking; likewise, in Australia, urban planning has increased the density of development and amount of impermeable surfaces. Stormwater runs swiftly off these surfaces, rather than slowly infiltrating into the ground, as it would have done on open or agricultural site. Furthermore, in many city centres, piped drainage systems were installed when lower density development existed and their design has not been updated to accommodate the increased runoff (French *et al.* 2011). So not only are developers potentially exposed to greater development risks, but they also contribute to the problem with ill-considered development proposals. There are some low-lying coastal locations which, on current predictions, will be inundated with water in the future. This is often now a planning issue (see Chapter 6).

One option developers can adopt is measures designed to restore, or mimic, natural infiltration patterns; by decreasing runoff volumes and attenuating peak flows, the risk of urban flooding is reduced. Within city centres, this could involve the inclusion of green roofs, permeable paving and other surface or near-surface drainage options in developments (Charlesworth and Warwick 2011). Infiltration and storage devices, such as permeable paving, can be employed around commercial premises to reduce runoff, whilst green roofs and rainwater gardens can absorb rainwater, thereby attenuating peak flows. Urban renewal and refurbishment provide an opportunity for such initiatives: in the US this method has been adopted in New York (NYC Environmental Protection 2011, 2012) and Portland.

In Portland, financial incentives were offered to increase the uptake of green roofs and disconnection of downspouts (Environmental Services – City of Portland 2006, 2011). Developers may, in some areas therefore benefit from financial incentives which also enhance sustainability. In other cases, flood risk to an urban site can be mitigated by 'buying' the right to flood elsewhere – for example, by designing flood holding basins upstream.

Other weather events related to a changing climate include intense heat leading to bushfires or wildfires in some regions. Parts of Australia and the US are particularly vulnerable to bushfires during certain periods of the year. With changes to the weather patterns, the bushfire season is variable and months previously not associated with bushfires then became associated with bushfires and the geographical areas experiencing bushfires also change. Developers not only need to be cognisant of local issues and to integrate effective design strategies within their projects, but also to consider whether some areas are suited to development in the long term. This might mean designing buildings which are flexible to later adaptation for a changing climate.

3.1.2 Urbanisation and population growth

Although urban settlements take up only 2.8 per cent of the earth's surface, by 2008 they accommodated more than half of the world's population (El Sioufi 2010). There is an increased rate of urbanisation which is happening fastest in developing countries where a substantial demographic shift has huge implications in respect of poverty, natural resources and the environment. The 'State of the World's Cities Report' (UN-HABITAT 2008) predicated average growth of 5 million new urban inhabitants per month in the developing world. In the next three to four decades, the developing countries will account for 95 per cent of the world's urban population growth. Levels of urbanisation are expected to rise, with the least urbanised regions of Asia and Africa changing from rural to urban societies (El Sioufi 2010). By 2050, the urban population of the developing world is projected to be 5.3 billion; with Asia accommodating 3.3 billion people. More recent predictions indicate that it is unlikely that world populations will stabilize this century (Desa 2013).

Population growth and economic development can cause drastic changes in land use and where this is likely institutional arrangements need to ensure sustainable use of the increasingly scarce land resources. In developed countries, some of the critical issues include accommodating increased densification in urban settlements, accommodating aging populations and different family sizes, together with the impact of inward migration, often from developing countries. Compounding these population and social challenges in our cities and urban settlements are challenges related to climate change and extreme weather events. As noted in Chapter 1, some of the challenges of climate change globally that are predicted to impact the built environment are:

- Increasing threats in coastal areas due to sea water rise and severe weather risk.
- Increasing threats to human settlements in coastal areas and islands, and:
- Increased probability of droughts and erratic rainfall due to climate change.

(IPCC 2013)

The severity of these predictions vary from continent to continent and country to country. There have been warnings that sea levels are rising twice as fast as previously forecast (IPCC 2014), resulting in an increased threat of flooding and water-related crises for people living in low-lying areas, coastal areas, deltas and small island states (IPCC 2014). If sea levels rise by just one metre, many major coastal or tidal river cities will be under threat. This means that Buenos Aires, Rio de Janeiro, Los Angeles, London, New York, Lagos, Alexandria, Mumbai, Kolkata, Dhaka, Shanghai, Osaka-Kobe and Tokyo, are among the major and mega cities that are under imminent threat.

While the threat of sea-level rise to cities is one problem, more extreme weather patterns such as intense storms are another. Tropical cyclones and storms, from 2008 to 2010, affected 120 million people globally, largely in developing countries (El Sioufi 2010). For example, in January and February 2014 extreme weather impacted countries in both the northern and southern hemispheres. In the northern hemisphere, the UK experienced almost unprecedented inland flooding, whilst Canada and North America experienced extreme cold and ice storms. Meanwhile, in the southern hemisphere, Australia suffered intense heat resulting in record-breaking temperatures around the continent. Globally, flooding and drought are occurring in the same place and in the same year more frequently and significantly impacting food security, energy and water supply in these areas.

There are many issues related to climate change that remain unknown. However, what we do know is that our cities will require change and adaptation, renewal and expansion. The question is: *will we have the foresight and will to make the necessary changes to policy and industry practices to mitigate the coming changes to our climate and to accommodate increases in populations?* Some of the changes will be instigated at a policy and regulatory level, whereas others will be the result of the efforts of enlightened and forward thinking property developers and other property industry practitioners. It remains the case that the cumulative actions of individuals lead to the consequences we reap as a society. On a micro level, the issues to consider with individual sustainable property developments are location, transportation and site survey and analysis.

3.2   Location

The oft-quoted mantra for property development is 'location, location, location'; and it is indeed critical to consider location when it comes to selecting development sites. When economies are growing, developers are able to increase their bid price for sites in highly sought after, quality areas; however, when economies contract, properties in prime locations may hold their value better than those in secondary locations which may fail to sell quickly and might therefore diminish in value. Developers may be influenced in their site selection strategy by whether they intend to develop and hold or develop and sell. Some developers may purchase in secondary locations with a longer-term view of developing and then holding the development for some years in anticipation of the area undergoing a renewal. Other developers taking a shorter-term view of develop and sell may prefer safer prime locations despite profit margins potentially being lower in these areas.

Characteristics that affect location are views, proximity to amenities and services (Wilkinson and Reed 2008). Therefore, for residential developments, access to local retailers and schools are important characteristics for the site as are access to recreational activities. For industrial property development, the location factors are different; here proximity to transportation networks for delivery of raw materials and goods that can be shipped to customers is vital. Retailers often seek to cluster, to enable comparison shopping, whilst good office locations increasingly demand access to a wide range of services.

In every case, transport links are critical and the growth of environmental concerns, notably carbon emission, has led to accessibility to public transport nodes being critical in many cases. Indeed, frequently, developers will be required to produce 'green transport plans' and they will estimate the number of vehicle trips generated by the proposed development as part of its environmental impact in order to fully evaluate the location. Location dictates almost everything that follows, from transportation access to environmental impact, to the occupier's involvement with local initiatives and economies to the place, cost and form of the development (Wilkinson and Reed 2008).

For developers looking to develop and hold, some identify sites to be held in land banks until such time as conditions favour proceeding with the development, or to allow them to strategically plan their workloads moving forward. For these organisations, the process is one of periodic review to determine whether the conditions favour development. However, developers, notably house-builders, are often accused of land banking in order to tighten land supply and drive up prices, a practice which research in the UK has refuted (Home Builders Federation 2014).

Typically, volume house-builders operating in UK markets work in this way (Isaacs *et al.* 2010), as do many US developers. However, residential development in countries like Australia tends to be different. Here developers purchase the site and sell off each parcel separately for individuals to develop independently. At times, developers offer packages where purchasers select a suitable house for their site from a range of housing types. Whilst this is uncommon in the UK, Urban Splash is experimenting with customable modular kit homes sold off plan.

Other developers specialise in land uses and will search specifically for sites which meet the criteria they establish (Isaacs *et al.* 2010), such as 'out of town' or 'big box' retail developments. Here criteria such as the population within a certain catchment area are important, as well as the socio-economic characteristics of the area and the supply and vacancy rates for existing retail development. The site selection criteria the developers adopt in their searches relate to their level of risk awareness and risk taking. For example some developers may be prepared to take higher risks for higher profits, whereas others prefer a more risk adverse approach.

There is more room to move when it comes to profit margins in areas that do not have identifiable affordability ceilings. That is, locations that are so highly sought after and desirable that people are willing to pay whatever it takes to secure premium property in that particular locality, even if it comes at a record breaking price tag. Another reason to undertake developments in areas that support higher property values is that the cost of doing a development is much the same whether you are building in a high value or low value area. Many of the costs remain comparable irrespective of the final value of the buildings, such as sand, cement, pipes, cable and plaster. However, high value areas may also be volatile value locations, which increase development risk. Not only that, but the capital tied up in the development pipeline is higher.

As far as predicted climate change is concerned, developers need to consider, especially if they intend to hold a development over the long term, whether there are any risks which might affect the long-term viability and value of the project. For example, development consideration in coastal or low-lying areas must consider the risk of rising sea levels or flooding and evaluate the impact if the development becomes increasingly inundated with water over time. Such risks can deter future purchasers and leases and can therefore negatively affect value. Other climate change effects could be excessive rainfall undermining property developed on cliff locations or properties becoming affected by wildfires or bushfires with increasing temperatures and diminishing rainfall. Prudent developers will be factoring such issues to site feasibility.

3.2.1 Transportation and infrastructure issues

The principles of sustainability require developers and local authorities to consider the emissions associated with transportation. Therefore developments which reduce the need for travel or promote public transport systems, especially transport modes which have low emissions are to be encouraged. Sustainability can be enhanced where sites have good access to public transport networks. Some environmental rating tools, such as BREEAM and LEED, give credits to developments which allow workers or owners to use public transport as a means of travel to and from the development (for more details see Chapter 9). Often too, transport links are planning requirements. The use of public transport systems promotes cleaner air because of the reduction in transport-related emissions. Using existing roads and sewers also saves on resource consumption. However, the targets to reduce emissions and consumptions are only achieved if the public transport system is well developed and used, and this is not captured in the rating tools. Interestingly, the type and amount of parking provision may also be significant, depending on building use, recognising the automobile-centric nature of urban cities.

The provision of supporting infrastructure is vital to site acquisition and local authorities and central governments normally play important roles in its provision, although developers can be required either to directly provide or pay contributions towards it. Infrastructure describes all the services which are necessary to support development, such as roads, sewers, open space and community facilities such as schools, clinics, etc. The existence or proposed provision of roads is critical in evaluating locations for property development. Whilst proposals for a new road will generate pressure for development along its route, new development also creates new traffic pressures on the existing road network. As infrastructure is so critical to the viability of a particular development scheme, it directly influences site values. If the necessary infrastructure does not exist to support a development then a developer will take account of the cost of its provision in the evaluation of the site value or the possibility that other agencies will provide it. Developers may be rewarded by taking such factors into account with higher scores in the environmental rating tools they may adopt for the project (see Chapter 9).

Public authorities are largely responsible for deciding the level of infrastructure required and securing its provision, and they have to determine who is responsible for the cost of its provision. Whilst major schemes will normally be the responsibility of central authorities, local authorities are important at the district level. Using the UK as an example, the assessment of future infrastructure requirements at a strategic level is the responsibility of the county council or the unitary authority (see Chapter 6) as part of the process of preparing development plans and they now have the ability to set and enforce levies (the Community Infrastructure Levy). In most cases, it is the highway authority for the area that is responsible for creating these requirements, although they may delegate some responsibility to district councils. The highway authority will be consulted on all planning applications to establish whether a development can be supported by the existing road infrastructure. The Department for Transport (Highways Agency) is responsible for motorways and trunk roads. Similarly, water companies are responsible for the provision of sewers and the water supply in each area. When the increased demand on the sewer and water supply results directly from a particular development, the cost of increased load on the infrastructure is agreed directly with the developer.

Many authorities embrace an active approach to the provision of infrastructure in recognition that new roads open up sites for development. The site is often assembled in conjunction with the new road so that the authority can benefit from enhanced site values by packaging sites for disposal to the private sector. There is much debate about the pressure for development caused by new roads, particularly in the prosperous and environmentally sensitive areas, and how the cost of provision should be allocated. Again using the UK as an example, developers may be required to enter into Section 278 agreements (under the provisions contained in Sections 106 and 278 of the Town and Country Planning Act 1990) with the relevant highway authority or the Department for Transport, to secure a financial contribution to pay for improvements to existing roads required to accommodate traffic from a particular development proposal. Further, under local agreements (known as S.106 agreements) they can be required to undertake onsite improvements. The UK government wants to reduce car travel by influencing the location of development schemes relative to the existing road network and public transport. They wish to encourage development which is accessible via alternative forms of transport such as walking, cycling and public services. Overall the aim is to encourage local authorities to co-ordinate site use policies and transport infrastructure to achieve a reduction in travel needs and the principles underpinning this are contained in the National Planning Policy Framework (for further details on PPG13 see Chapter 6). In addition, the government reviews major road building projects as evidence suggests that new roads create more traffic congestion. Patently there is a conflict here with accommodating ever more people in urban settlements and sustainability.

Many local authorities promote sustainability through public transportation, for example light railway/tram systems, to ease traffic congestion, for example, the tram systems in Edinburgh and Croydon, both of which have been introduced in recent years. In order to secure the necessary public funding for such transportation systems, UK government regulations stipulate that private sector contributions have to be secured in advance. This may not be the case in all countries however. Often developers and landowners with sites that will benefit from the transport system proposed are approached to make a contribution. However, there is a limit to how much developers can pay, as any contribution will impact on development viability. The same applies to contributions made by developers for road improvements as discussed above.

3.3   Site survey and analysis

A site survey undertaken by qualified land surveyors or geotechnical engineers establishes the extent of the site and whether the boundaries agree with those shown in the legal title deed. This is important where a site is assembled by bringing together various parcels of land in various ownerships. Here the survey has to establish that all the boundaries of the various parcels dovetail together and that the whole of the land is being acquired. It would be devastating if the developer discovered mid-way through a scheme that a small but vital part of the land had not been acquired. The developer would then have to negotiate from a very weak position with that landowner, effectively being held to 'ransom'.

The land survey establishes the site contours and levels. The presence of any waterways, cisterns or underground utilities which might affect development is identified. Geotechnical engineers also comment on the soil type and likelihood of shrinkage or swelling, corrosion, landslides, collapse, creep, seismic activity and liquefaction. Also, if ground water exists on the site, the survey notes the location and depth and makes comments and recommendations on means of controlling groundwater during construction. Where appropriate, recommendations are also made for further exploration and testing. In terms of environmental site issues, developers in some locations will test for the presence of

Table 3.1 Site analysis tasks

- Identify existing conditions and topography
- Identify access, reciprocal and utility easements
- Review site boundary and topographic surveys
- Identify logistical issues with regard to construction and/or operation
- Review parking at proposed site and vehicular, pedestrian, bicycle, mass transit and building service access and safety issues
- Review building orientation
- Review preliminary stormwater management
- Review legal description

Source: Author

methane gas and take necessary action. With some large-scale developments, and with public developments, in some jurisdictions, notably the EU region, Environmental Impact Statements (EIS) and Environmental Assessments (EAs) will be required. Similar provisions exist in the US where they are termed Environmental Impact Assessments (EIAs) and are typically required for all large projects and all public developments. An EA is a document prepared to determine whether an EIS is required. The EA typically describes the need for the development and includes a list of agencies and persons consulted. If the agency reviewing the EA decides a significant impact will result, then an EIS is required. The EIS is a detailed written statement focused on the environmental issues and the alternatives to the proposed action. In this case, the developer will need to engage environmental consultants to identify the environmentally significant features and aspects, and assess the likely impact of the development on them. Where necessary the EIS report will also outline how the developer proposes to minimise harm, mitigate hazards and safeguard the environment.

If any existing buildings on the site are to be retained in a scheme, structural surveys will be required. The legal search of the title deeds should establish responsibility for the maintenance of the boundaries. In addition, the access arrangements to the site need to be checked to ensure that the site boundary abuts the public highway and to identify where access points are allowed. If a public highway exists the solicitor needs to check whether it has been adopted by the local authority and is maintainable at their expense. If access to the site is via a private road, then the ownership and rights over that road need to be established. Table 3.1 identifies tasks related to site analysis.

3.3.1 *Ground investigation*

Unless reliable information exists regarding the state of the ground, a ground investigation needs to be undertaken by appropriate specialists. Ground investigations can vary in cost and extent depending on the proposed scheme and information already known. An investigation usually takes the form of a series of boreholes and trial pits taken at strategic locations on the site. Samples taken from the boreholes and trial pits are analysed in a laboratory to establish the composition of the soil and substrata, the depth of the water table and whether any contamination can be identified in the ground. The issue of contamination will be examined further below as it has an effect on sustainability. The results of the investigation will be given to the structural engineer, architect and quantity surveyor (cost estimator). They analyse the results to establish whether any remedial work is necessary to improve the ground conditions or whether any piled foundations are required, e.g. where the ground is made up with fill material. Both circumstances will have an impact on the cost of the development scheme, which may affect the overall viability and impact on sustainability. Given that increasing percentages of developments are being targeted towards previously developed land (see below) ground investigations may be vital.

3.3.2 *Brownfield sites – contamination*

Sites previously developed for any purpose are generally known as 'brownfield' sites, whereas sites which have no previous development are known as 'greenfield' sites. The US Environmental Protection Act (EPA) defines the term 'brownfield site' as real property, the expansion, redevelopment or reuse of which may be complicated by the presence or potential presence of a hazardous substance, pollutant or contaminant. Successful projects built on brownfield sites can improve water quality, remodel eyesores or restore community character. The fact that a site has been previously developed may, or may not, mean that it has any features which render redevelopment difficult or more expensive than the development of greenfield sites. However, additional cost and delay are often the case, particularly where the previous development has involved industrial use which may have been associated with toxic materials (see below for a list of typical site types that are associated with contamination).

Further developments on brownfield sites may suffer residual value 'stigma' for residential units (see for example McCluskey and Rausser 2003), though as it becomes increasingly common to build on brownfield this is less likely to be the case. Further, in sustainability terms, it has been found that redeveloping contaminated sites can lead to increases in values of properties close by as a positive 'spillover effect', thus providing social sustainability benefits (De Sousa *et al.* 2009).

Property development is about assessing and managing risk; as such the existence of any contamination on a site cannot be ignored due to potential legislation and litigation as well as the physical and value uncertainties it presents. Broadly, similar legislation exists in Australia, the US and the UK with regards to contamination, though readers should refer to local legislation in detail as there is insufficient space here to discuss each in detail. Using the UK as an example, a contaminated site is defined in Part IIA of the Environmental Protection Act 1990 (EPA) section 143 as a 'site which is being or has been put to contaminative use' (and was brought into being by way of section 57 of the Environment Act 1995). The statutory definition of contaminated site (EPA 1990, s 78A (2)) is:

> any site which appears to the local authority in whose area it is situated to be in such a condition, by reason of substances in, on or under the site, that –
> significant harm is being caused or there is a significant possibility of such harm being caused; or
> pollution of controlled waters is being, or is likely to be, caused;

The important inference here is that 'significant harm' is resulting or is likely to result from the contamination, and not that there is possible harm from pollutants on the site. There is much debate about the point at which 'significant harm' ensues as there is a definitive point where this occurs because each site parcel is unique in terms of geology, extent of pollution and so on. Three key factors impact on the amount of harm which can ensue and are:

1   the type of contaminant,
2   the pathway, and;
3   the receptor.

Different contaminants lead to different types of harm and the extent of harm depends on the pathway or way in which the contaminant migrates or moves around the site and in this way the geology of the site has a significant effect. For example, soils which are dense or solid allow less opportunity for pollutants to move around. Receptors vary from being animal, plant or human and different pollutants and concentrations have different effects depending on the receptor. Some pollutants such as zinc can make plant growth verdant and abundant, whereas the effect on human health is adverse and negative. Environmental consultants will examine the relationship between these three variables to establish whether 'significant harm' is likely.

The emphasis of government policy in many jurisdictions on environmental legislation is based on the principle that 'the polluter pays', following the example set by EU legislation (for further information see Beder 2013). Contamination is usually caused by a previous occupier's use of the site, though for many sites the use of contaminants is unrecorded which makes it incumbent on the developer to undertake a detailed investigation particularly of brownfield sites. Occasionally contaminants migrate onto site from other sites and thus pollute the land, clearly such an occurrence can cause complex issues to arise in terms of getting the polluter to pay costs of remediation. Site use types that have led to contamination include:

- Infrastructure sites:
  - cemeteries
  - docks, canals and shipyards
  - quarries
  - railway sites
  - sewerage works
  - petrol stations.
- Industrial storage sites:
  - landfill sites
  - military airfields
  - oil and petroleum refineries and storage sites
  - scrap yards.
- Power generation:
  - gas works
  - nuclear power stations.
- Manufacturing and industry sites:
  - dry cleaners
  - asbestos works and buildings containing asbestos
  - food processing plants
  - metal mines
  - brickworks and potteries
  - chemical works
  - steel works
  - plating works
  - munitions factories and test sites
  - paint works
  - paper and pulping works
  - printing works
  - tanneries
- textile mills.

The emphasis, since 2000, is placed on the condition of the site itself and whether this would be likely to cause 'significant harm'. Earlier policies towards contaminated land had led to some sites being blighted and the UK government subsequently introduced the concept of the 'suitable for use standard' with regards to remediation. Previously, a policy of a total clean up (or gold standard) had been adopted towards remediation; however, the costs of remediating a site to such high standards meant that some development proposals were no longer viable. Some jurisdictions may adopt this 'gold standard' and developers must apprise themselves of local requirements. The 'suitable for use' concept means that any contamination is considered in the context of the use to which the site will be put. So for example a site with a proposal for residential units would have higher remediation standards than a proposal for industrial development on the same site.

Where contamination is present, the cost of ground investigation is much higher and furthermore represents a potentially abortive up-front developer cost. Developers should obtain as much information on the site history before ground investigation is commenced. This is achieved by looking at Ordnance Survey maps, local authority records and other sources of information, such as previous owners. In areas where contamination is widespread, the local authority may have records of contaminated land. In addition, local authorities hold information on waste disposal sites in their area. However, information obtained from records may be limited and will always need to be checked.

The ground investigation comprises taking soil samples down to the water table level, as well as extensive surveys of all underground and surrounding surface water because of the risk of contaminants seeping through water. The results of the ground investigation allow an assessment to be made of the extent and cost of remedial measures. There are many ways of treating contamination including removal, treating in situ or containment either under a blanket of clean earth or a capping. Ongoing measures may be needed after completion of the development, for example, venting methane gases to the surface. If the contamination is restricted to one part of the site it may be possible to design around the problem, for example locating car parking directly over the area. If the ground has to be filled with imported material as part of the process then, depending on the standard of treatment required, deep piled foundations may be required. Nevertheless, once on site, sometimes developers find during construction that, due to the selective nature of ground investigation surveys, contamination is more widespread than first reported. Such circumstances can impact on the economic viability of a project and represent another risk developers have to manage. When a developer is faced with a contaminated site then the remedial measures, typically costing on average in excess of £500,000 per hectare, usually preclude all but the higher value uses. The type of use under contemplation will also determine the level of decontamination required. For example, an industrial use will not require such a rigorous clean up as one to be developed for housing. . However, grant assistance is available in some areas to offset these costs.

In view of the increasing concerns about contaminated land, the move towards urban regeneration, the increased use of brownfield sites, the debate about who should be financially responsible and the implications for sustainability, it is critical that developers spend time to thoroughly assess whether there is any contamination on site before proceeding with the development. Where necessary, the appropriate professionals should undertake a full environmental audit, which can later be presented to potential purchasers, financiers and tenants.

3.3.3 *Utility services*

The site survey ascertains the existence of utility services (water, gas, electricity and drainage). Utility companies should confirm that the services surveyed correspond with each of the companies' records. Furthermore, the capacity and capability of existing utility services to meet the needs of the proposed development should be determined. If the existing services are insufficient, the developer needs to negotiate with the company concerned to establish the cost of upgrading or providing new services, such as a new electricity substation. However, these needs may be offset with sustainable design such as on site power generation from renewables. Where work needs to be carried out by either an electricity or gas company the developer will be charged the full cost of the work, but a partial rebate is usually available once the development is occupied and the company is receiving a minimum level of income. Sometimes the route of a service may need to be diverted to allow the proposed development to take place, and the cost of diversion and the time involved should be established at the earliest possible stage. Furthermore, the legal search of the title deeds will reveal if any adjoining occupiers have rights to connect to or enjoy services crossing the site. The developer may need to renegotiate the benefits of these rights if they affect the development scheme. Increasingly, even where a developer does not set out to be a leader in sustainability terms, planning requirements will place the requirement for a certain percentage of power to be generated on site through the use of renewable technologies; similarly there are moves to reduce pressure on foul drainage by the use of digester units.

3.4   Historic properties

Frequently developments integrate historic sites or heritage buildings and these can serve as examples of reclamation and reuse of cultural historic resources and signal the developer's commitment to historic preservation or conservation, sustainability and local communities (Wilkinson 2011). Such developments also demonstrate the developer's leadership in respect of heritage conservation. The architectural, social and/or cultural attributes of buildings should be considered to ensure projects are undertaken with minimum adverse effect on the qualities that constitute their significance. Developed countries have legislation which protects culturally significant buildings and requires developers to follow guidelines in their proposals. This retention of cultural capital can lead to the award of points under some of the environmental rating tools as retention of the buildings adds to social sustainability. In addition, reuse of historic and heritage buildings reduces the carbon footprint of the development because of the embodied carbon in the existing buildings. However, where the retention or inclusion of historic buildings is included within the scheme, risks are increased and costs can become open-ended. Therefore careful investigation as to the physical constraints they impose on the development need to be evaluated early on in the process. With sustainability in mind, the developer must balance the potential social spillovers of embracing heritage with the economic impacts (positive and negative) and the associated uncertainty.

3.5   Legal title

Developers appoint solicitors to deduce the legal title to be acquired and to carry out all necessary enquiries and searches before contracts are entered into with the landowner. The developer's solicitor will apply to the Site Registry, or equivalent, to examine the official register of the title. If the site to be acquired is leasehold, the register will reveal brief particulars of the lease and the commencement date. Thereafter the developer needs to ascertain the term of the lease, the pattern of the rent reviews and the main provisions of the lease. The provisions have to be checked to ensure the terms are acceptable to the provider of the development finance (see Chapter 5). The solicitor also establishes that the site will be acquired with vacant possession and that there are no unknown tenancies, licences or unauthorised occupancies. The fact that a site or building is unoccupied does not mean that no legal rights of occupancy exist. The register should show if there are any conditions or restrictions affecting the rights of the landowner to sell the site. In addition, all rights and interests adversely affecting the title will be established, such as restrictive covenants, easements, mortgages and registered leases.

Any easements or other legal right may profoundly affect a development scheme. An easement may be positive, such as a public or private right-of-way, or take the form of a negative covenant, such as a right of light for the benefit of an adjoining property. Within the UK, some negative covenants are private but 'run with the land' and are revealed by searches; others such as rights to light are enshrined in statute (Rights of Light Act 1959). If easements exist to the detriment of the proposed scheme, the developer may be able to negotiate removal or modification to allow the scheme to proceed. Rights of light might affect the proposed position of the scheme and the amount of floor space provided and, as they are statutorily protected, may not be able to be overcome through negotiation.

Restrictive covenants may adversely affect a development, for example a covenant prohibiting a specific use of a site. Often it can be challenging to determine who benefits from a covenant, particularly if it was entered into many years previously. If the beneficiary can be found, the developer may negotiate the removal of the restriction. If the beneficiary cannot be found, in the UK the developer can apply to the Lands Tribunal for its discharge, although this is a lengthy process. Another option is for the developer to take out an insurance policy to protect against the beneficiary enforcing the covenant. The insurance cover will compensate against the loss in value caused by any successful enforcement action. However, this latter course of action is not desirable: restrictive covenants were often put in place for good estate management reasons and it is a risk to rely simply on insurance.

Further developments often take place abutting other buildings. In this case, the development may create what is termed a shared or 'party' wall. If this exists before the redevelopment, or will be created as part of the scheme, it is necessary to agree a schedule of condition with the adjoining property owner or make a party wall award of compensation. In the UK, a chartered surveyor with specialist knowledge on party wall matters may need to be appointed by the developer and by the adjoining owner(s).

A solicitor searches the local site charges register maintained by the local authority. This reveals any planning permissions for the site and whether any building on the site is listed as a building of special architectural or historic interest. In addition, enquiries are made of the local authority to establish whether the road providing access to the site is adopted and maintained at public expense. The existence of any proposed road improvement schemes might affect the site, e.g. a strip may be protected at the front of the site for road widening purposes. Enquiries are made of the landowner (vendor) and include standard questions with regards to boundaries and services. Enquiries will disclose whether any over-riding interests (rights and interests that do not appear on the register of the title) or adverse rights (rights of occupiers of the site) exist. Solicitors also make enquiries of the vendor which are particular to the site being acquired.

The developer must aim to acquire the freehold or leasehold title of the development site free from as many encumbrances as possible by renegotiating or removing the restrictions and easements. Financiers, particularly the financial institutions, prefer to acquire their legal interest with the minimum of restrictions which might adversely affect the value of their investment in the future. The developer has to be able to 'sell' the title to purchasers and tenants as quickly as possible without complications.

The worst scenario if legal title mistakes are made could be that the development goes ahead and subsequently has to be demolished – this is not a sustainable solution.

3.6   Site acquisition

The findings of the site survey and analysis investigations should be reflected in site acquisition arrangements. The degree to which developers reduce the risk inherent in the property development process depends partly on the type of transaction agreed at the site acquisition stage. Shrewd developers try to reduce risk to a minimum and site acquisition arrangements are important. If possible, no acquisition is made until all the relevant detailed information has been obtained and all problems resolved. In practice, however, it is almost impossible to remove every element of uncertainty. The degree to which the developer can reduce risk to the site acquisition stage depends on the landowner's method of disposal, the amount of competition and the tenure. It is possible to transfer some risk to the landowner, but this largely depends on the developer's negotiating abilities.

Most site acquisitions are straightforward if executed on a freehold basis but it should be noted that once contracts are exchanged risks pass to the purchaser. The developer reduces the transaction risk through negotiation of the contract terms; for example, contracts can be conditional and payments phased or delayed. If no planning consent exists for the proposed development, it is usual for the developer to negotiate a contract subject to a 'satisfactory planning consent'. If such a condition is acceptable, the vendor tries to ensure that the term 'satisfactory planning consent' is clearly defined. The developer may obtain planning consent which does not reflect the optimum value of the site but satisfies the condition in the contract and then, at a later stage, obtain a better planning consent. It is not uncommon for 'top-up' arrangements to be made whereby the vendor benefits from any improvement created by planning consent obtained by the developer. Developers carefully weigh up the degree of uncertainty in relation to potential planning issues and make a judgment as to whether the risk is acceptable. If the vendor is undertaking to sell the site with vacant possession then the contract should be conditional upon this, for there could be a delay in the occupants of a building vacating.

Whilst the normal period between signing a contract to purchase a site and the completion in the UK is 28 days, developers may be able to negotiate for a delayed completion, e.g. three months. Delays cost money, so the developer should ensure any potential problems revealed by investigations are dealt with before contracts are completed, or the time needed to resolve them is reflected in the evaluation and the price paid for the site.

As an alternative, especially if the planning process is likely to prove contentious, the developer may consider it advantageous to pay for an option to reserve the site. An option involves the developer paying a nominal (or higher) sum to secure the right at a future date to purchase the freehold. There is usually a 'long stop' date after which the vendor is free to sell the site to anyone if the developer has not taken up the option. The option agreement might specify that after certain conditions have been complied with, the developer has to purchase the site. Alternatively, the agreement may allow the developer to call upon the vendor at any time to sell the site after sufficient notice. The developer aims to fix the value of the site at the time the option agreement is entered into but in practice this is difficult to achieve. Conversely, in a rising market, vendors usually try to ensure that the open market value is fixed at the time the developer actually purchases the site.

3.6.1 Finance

No prudent developer, unless there are sufficient internal cash resources, should enter into a commitment to acquire a site without first having secured the necessary finance or development partner to cover the cost of acquisition. This includes consideration of the interest on the acquisition cost while the site is held pending development. The developer should ensure the financial arrangements are completed to coincide with the acquisition of the site. If no financial arrangements are in place then the developer must be satisfied that either the finance will be secured or that the site can be sold on the open market if no funding is forthcoming. The developer must ensure that all investigations have been carried out thoroughly so that any financier or partner has a full and complete picture of the site. Every area of doubt must be removed if at all possible. In recent years, a number of incentives have been established by financiers and local authorities to enhance sustainability through favourable financing mechanisms (see Chapter 4).

3.6.2 Initiation: from theory to practice

Having set up considerations for purchase and formed a strategy as to the type, location and nature of development intended, a developer then needs to search for and identify potential sites. This can be achieved in a number of ways. However, before the various methods of site finding are described, it is important to understand that theory and practice often differ. A developer may have a thoroughly researched site acquisition policy but putting that into practice depends on various factors, many beyond the developer's control. The ability to acquire a site is dependent on the availability of the site at any particular time. Furthermore the availability of the site depends on the state of the market, planning policies and physical factors, any tax regimes affecting land holding and the motives of the particular landowner. The various types of landowners and their motives for owning the site were discussed in Chapter 2. The developer, landowner, agent and public sector are the main stakeholders involved in the initiation process. The landowner may take an active or passive role in the process, depending on whether or not they retain a financial stake. In the case of local authority land ownership, for civic protection reasons, the authority may wish to retain the underlying freehold and grant the developer a long lease (typically 125 years) in order that they can retain some control over the type of development that takes place and its management.

Typically more land is brought forward for development when site values are rising rapidly as landowners are tempted to realise their asset values. The availability of land will be influenced by the land use allocation of sites within a local planning authority's 'development plan' (Australia and UK) or 'land use plan' (US) and the perceived chances of obtaining planning permission. Although a site may be available on the market and is allocated within the development plan for the proposed use, it still might not be suitable for development due to physical factors. For example, a lack of infrastructure such as roads and services might make a development scheme not viable. Also the state of the ground, which might be contaminated or unstable, may prohibit profitable development. The various ways of initiating the site acquisition process are examined below.

3.6.3 *Developer's initiatives*

A developer may employ an in-house team, an agent or a planning consultant to find development sites based on the criteria set out in the site acquisition strategy. Many developers who specialise in certain types of development (e.g. offices) and the large house-builders, employ 'acquisition surveyors' or 'site buyers' whose role is to discover and acquire sites in accordance with the company's strategy. The developer needs a thorough knowledge of the target area and relevant planning policies. Finding sites in this way may incur considerable hard work with no results. Searches commonly used to be made by car or foot to identify potential sites, but increasingly a first step is desk top using digital satellite mapping where this is available. This done, the next step is to ascertain who owns the site and there are various ways to achieve this, including examining the planning register, interrogating the Land Registry (in the UK), asking local agents or literally knocking on the door.

For example, in England all local planning authorities publish online all planning applications and permissions in a particular planning authority's area so a site's full planning history can be obtained via a free desktop search. When a planning application is made, the owner of the site to which the application relates, if they can be traced, must receive a statutory notice from the applicant. Therefore, an examination of the register will normally reveal the owner of a piece of site, provided a planning application has been made. However, the details of the landowner may be out of date. Local authorities hold a register of publicly owned vacant and underused sites which is also available for inspection. The Land Registry, the statutory registry of all legal titles to freehold and leasehold sites in England and Wales, is open to the public with a computerised statutory register of around 15 million properties in England and Wales. Developers can apply to the Site Registry to establish the name and address of the owner of a property, if it is registered, for a fee. However, despite registration having been compulsory for all transactions for very many years, there are still many sites that are unregistered as they have simply not changed ownership.

A developer may employ a planning consultant to carry out a strategic study of a particular area and identify suitable sites which are likely to achieve an appropriate planning consent taking full account of the policy context and analysing them against their planning history and the client's requirements, including any sustainability considerations.

The report will normally include sites that have not been allocated but where there is a good chance of obtaining planning consent by negotiation or on appeal. The best time to undertake this study is when the development plan is in the draft or review stage; at this time there is an opportunity to influence the plan by presenting evidence at any public inquiry. Therefore, it is crucial that developers are fully cognizant of the plans in their area and take opportunities to influence as and when the possibility arises. Whilst local authorities will normally make every endeavour to include sustainability considerations within their plans, a responsible developer can also help to ensure that this is the case.

Alternatively a developer may retain an agent(s) to find sites in a particular area. The agent is briefed as to the requirements in terms of the nature and size of sites, and should have a good knowledge of the area and its planning policies. The developer should also cultivate contacts with a number of non-retained agents as it is important to develop good relationships. If the agent is retained directly by the developer, a fee will be payable if the latter is successful in acquiring a site identified by the agent and this is often negotiated based on the agent's subsequent involvement in the development, letting and funding of the development scheme. Through their knowledge of the area, they can often anticipate whether a site may come onto the market and with occupied buildings they may know when leases will expire and thus when possible redevelopment opportunities might arise.

The early identification of sites gives the developer the opportunity to negotiate directly with the landowner and secure the site before it goes on the market. A developer's ability to acquire sites off the market depends both on their negotiating abilities and the state of the market.

Developers can also identify sites in less obvious ways, for example by acquiring a company as a means of securing a site or an entire portfolio of properties which fit in with their acquisition strategy. Where a company is bought, the developer retains ownership of property assets and either sells the operating part of the business or ceases trading. Developers also may acquire individual properties or entire portfolios through direct approaches to other developers or property investment companies.

Any developer seeking to establish a reputation for sustainability should exercise caution in purchasing trading companies for the purpose of closing the operation as this could be viewed as socially irresponsible.

3.6.4 Agents' introductions

Agents may introduce prospects to developers directly. The opportunity may be a site already on the market or a site that is likely to come on to the market shortly. If the introduction leads to a site acquisition, then the agent will obtain a fee from the developer, unless they are retained and instructed by the landowner. The agent will look at the experience of development companies and their financial status before making an introduction as they want the best possibility that the sale will proceed.

A development company, depending on its size and financial status, may receive introductions on a daily basis when market conditions are favourable. Therefore, a large development company may need to set up a record system so that they know which agent made the introduction in order to avoid any issues about who gets the introduction fee.

When introducing a site, the agent should provide enough details to enable an initial decision to be made by the developer as to whether to pursue the opportunity or not. Ideally, the particulars should include a site plan, location plan, planning details and details of the asking price and terms.

The introducing agent is responsible for assisting the developers throughout the acquisition. The agent should advise on the local property market and rental values to help the developer in the evaluation process. Information on existing and proposed schemes of a similar nature is also vital. The agent will often negotiate the site price on behalf of the developer. This method is a two-way process. The developer must establish and maintain a good relationship and regular contact with local and national agents. It is important to provide those agents with details of site requirements to avoid a situation where site opportunities are continually rejected and the agent gives up and goes to a rival developer. Agents should provide a good service to their developer clients as there may be chances that other instructions, such as lettings, will flow from the initial introduction. Other property professionals such as solicitors, planning consultants, architects and quantity surveyors may introduce opportunities to developers.

Where an agent is a member of a professional body, they will normally be bound by standards and best practice guidance (for example the RICS has commercial agency and brokerage standards to which agents are expected to adhere (RICS 2014)).

3.6.5 *Landowner initiation*

A landowner may initiate the development process by deciding to sell their site or enter into partnership with a developer. A source for identifying development sites for sale is advertisements, whether in the media, internet, on a site board or via direct mail. Most countries carry property publications (e.g. *Estates Gazette*), but increasingly the use of internet is important as a means of connecting with possible buyers or their agents.

The property press carries advertisements each week for sites and development opportunities. Developers may receive particulars of a site for sale from a landowner or agent. Where a site is advertised on the open market the developer will be competing for the site. The degree of competition depends on how the site is offered to the market. There are various methods, including informal tender, formal tender, competitions involving one or several short listings and, finally, auctions. The method of disposal depends on market conditions and the motives of the landowner. The developer may be in competition with any number of others or there may be a selective list of bidders.

3.7   Methods of sale

There are several methods commonly in use to bring property to market. The choice will depend on the market conditions, the size and specification of the property and the likely buyer profile. Each is considered briefly below. At all times, the method used should be carefully discussed with the vendor as the method chosen can have a significant bearing on the terms finally achieved.

3.7.1 *Informal tenders and invitations to offer*

Informal tenders or invitations to offer involve inviting interested parties to submit their highest and best bids within a timescale. This usually involves all parties who have expressed an interest in the site and the invitation may include an indication of the minimum price acceptable. For example, it might state that offers of over £5,000,000 are invited and indicate what conditions attached to the bid may or may not be acceptable to the landowner. The important point from the developer's perspective is that the bid made is subject to any necessary conditions. After a bid has been accepted by the landowner, the developer has the ability to renegotiate the price if there is some justification to do so before contracts are exchanged, though there is always a risk that the landowner may not accept a revised price and may go to another party who made a bid.

Private treaty informal arrangements as set out above tend to be the most common and preferred choice as they allow bids to be made on the developer's own terms. However, the more conditions a developer attaches to a bid, the less likely it is that the bid will be acceptable, even if it is the highest received. The landowner generally accepts the highest bid unless the conditions are unacceptable or the developer's financial standing is questionable; however, where the vendor is seeking to ensure that the site is developed to high sustainability standards, they do have the ability to choose a bidder who they consider will reflect their standards. However, to impose this is difficult unless adjoining land is retained and a covenant imposed or the disposal is by way of long lease rather than by freehold.

After receiving the bids, the landowner may negotiate with several of the parties before making a decision in an attempt to vary conditions or the level of the bids. It is within this process that a developer can show their sustainability characteristics most clearly and thereby possibly seek an advantage over other potential buyers.

3.7.2 Formal tender

A formal tender binds both parties to the terms and conditions set out in the tender documentation, subject only to contract. It involves an invitation to interested parties to submit their highest and best bids by a deadline. The invitation sets out the conditions applicable. The document will usually state that the landowner is not bound to accept the highest bid. This method may or may not involve a selection of the interested parties. Generally developers do not prefer formal tenders as it reduces flexibility and increases risk. It also requires them to bid to their highest point, for risk of losing the site. The only time when developers are normally prepared to enter a tender is a situation in which all the possible unknowns have been eliminated, e.g. where a detailed acceptable planning consent was in place, a full ground and site survey had taken place and the site was being sold with full vacant possession. Tenders are used in strong market conditions or where the level of value is very hard to determine. In this method, it is the vendor who can drive sustainability by placing requirements on the purchaser.

3.7.3 Competitions

Competitions are used by landowners when financial considerations are not the only criteria for disposal of the site. For example, competitions are used by local authorities and other public bodies seeking a developer to implement a major scheme. They are used more informally by other landowners seeking development partners, for example, a landowner may want to obtain planning permission before disposing of the site and, therefore, the developer may be selected on the basis of planning expertise and track record. Alternatively, the landowner may not wish to dispose of the land and will seek a developer to project manage the scheme for a profit share.

As most competitions involve local authorities and other public bodies, this discussion is confined to public authority competitions. Local authorities and public bodies invite competitive bids on a tender basis, whether formal or informal, and the bids will normally be judged on a financial and/or a design basis. As a first step, the authority will usually advertise their intention to set up a competition and invite expressions of interest. Alternatively, the authority may choose the developers to enter the competition. If the former method is adopted, developers are usually invited to express their interest. They will be asked to provide details of relevant experience and track record, financial status (usually a copy of their company report and accounts), the professional team if appointed and any other relevant information. Relevant information could be that the developer may own an adjoining site to the competition site or that the developer has been involved with the subject site for some considerable time.

The public authority will assess the expressions of interest and compile a shortlist to enter the competition. This may or may not be the final selection process, and bids may be invited from those shortlisted in order to compile a final shortlist. The number of steps in the selection process will depend largely on the numbers of interested parties and the complexity of the competition. If the authority is asking developers to submit both financial and design bids, and the design submission requested needs to be fairly detailed, then the number of developers shortlisted for the final process should be no more than three to five, due to the costs involved by the bidder. Competitions for public bodies and local authorities are likely to have a greater emphasis on sustainability considerations in the development proposals and are usually adopted when the *quality* and social and *economic regenerative impacts* of the scheme are deemed critical to the owning authority .

It is important that a development brief is prepared to provide guidelines for the competition, including a statement outlining the basis of the competition and details related to the criteria by which the developer will be selected. The development brief will set out the design requirements of the public authority with regard to such matters as total floor space, pedestrian and vehicular access, car parking provision, landscaping and any facilities which the authority considers desirable in planning terms. The public authority may include a sketch layout or outline sketch drawings illustrating the development required, but in the majority of cases it is the developer's responsibility to bring forward design solutions, so the developer will normally be working with a design team. The brief should state how flexible the authority will be in assessing whether the bid meets its requirements. The developer needs to find out whether they will be penalised for not strictly adhering to the brief. Generally developers who follow the guidelines in the brief will be looked upon favourably, unless a developer proposes a better solution than that outlined in the brief. It may be that, through their ability and expertise, a developer may produce a higher financial bid by proposing a higher density scheme than that envisaged in the brief whilst still producing a sustainable and sensitive design. Every competition is different and it pays the developer to study the development brief in depth and look at all possible angles that can be used to advantage. Competitions are the least attractive method of acquiring development sites as the process demands time and expense in the preparation of drawings and financial bids, which are abortive if the developer loses; however they bring prestige and publicity which can be very positive.

3.7.4 Auctions

The trigger to choose a sale by auction is often that the site is unusual and difficult to value, therefore it is a case of what potential buyers see in the proposition. For example, a rail company may use auctions to dispose of disused railway embankments and sites with no, or limited, access. Other types of assets that are auctioned are secondary or short-life investments and properties in a dilapidated condition. Developers regularly look through auction catalogues for opportunities. At auction, the highest bid secures the site, providing that the reserve price has been exceeded. The landowner instructs the auctioneer of the reserve price which is the lowest price acceptable. If the reserve price is not reached through the bidding then the lot is withdrawn or negotiations are made with the highest bidder in an attempt to meet the reserve price. The auction sets out the standard conditions of sale and special conditions of sale relating to each lot. Once a bid is accepted, the successful bidder exchanges contracts at that point by handing over the deposit and details of their solicitor. If a developer acquires a site at auction a thorough evaluation and all other preparatory work should have been carried out beforehand. Another option is to acquire the lot prior to auction by direct negotiation with the landowner.

When market conditions are favourable, competitions and tenders are often the vendors' preferred approach to sales, though developers prefer to obtain a site off the market, thereby avoiding competition. If a developer enters a number of competitions and tender situations, they could all be lost, or all or some could be won. There is no certainty and the developer may become very frustrated, wasting much time and money. Success is based on the developer's ability to judge the right opportunities to pursue and the right level at which to submit a financial bid. However, in many instances it may be a case of luck and being in the right place at the right time. The site acquisition process is very competitive and it must be realised that even the best thought out acquisition strategy may not be achieved in the way, and in the timescale, first envisaged.

3.8   Conclusion

This chapter has traced the steps that have to be undertaken to establish feasibility of a site, excluding considerations of planning or financial appraisal. Prior to that, it has linked the issues of climate change and environmental and social concerns to the choice, location and characteristics of the site. As a result, it is argued that site feasibility, selection and acquisition have a significant impact on sustainability and viability of any development.

A commitment to sustainability begins with site location – avoiding inappropriate sites, reducing the environmental impact of building on a site, channelling development to areas of existing infrastructure and locating near to alternative forms of transportation. Site issues should be considered early in the development process and should be investigated prior to purchase as they will impact on price (see Chapter 4). Site selection involves a series of data collection and assessment tasks that become more specific over time as the development proposal moves from the realms of uncertainty to that of certainty.

The steps that developers have to take in order to reduce their exposure to risk are also outlined. Considerations of sustainability should be embedded throughout the process and this is highlighted throughout the chapter. This chapter examined the site feasibility, initiation and the acquisition stages of the development process. Furthermore, attributes which have a negative impact on sustainability are highlighted with suggestions for minimisation and mitigation of developer risk.

The site evaluation informs the feasibility study which comprises the business proposal for the development. Here sustainability issues related to the site should be identified and the strategy and proposals for site sustainability set out, along with building sustainability. It establishes the budget for the site acquisition and also the buildings and profit. The study identifies the requirements of the development, defines viable alternatives, analyses alternatives and delivery methods and recommends the preferred solution. The feasibility study is reviewed at times depending on the project circumstances, timelines and external factors such as general economic trends in order to confirm the preferred solution is still the optimum.

Finally, it is often not acknowledged that the way in which a property or site is brought to market, can be instrumental in determining the extent to which sustainability features are included within the final scheme. By choosing a method of sale which allows either or both parties to insist on sustainable solutions being part of the scheme, both landowner and developer can move the process forward.

References

Beder, S. (2013) *Environmental Principles and Policies: An Interdisciplinary Introduction*, London: Routledge.

Bureau of Meteorology (2012) Heavy rain and flooding. Retrieved 9 July 2012 from http://www.bom.gov.au/wa/sevwx/perth/floods.shtml.

Charlesworth, S. and Warwick, F. (2011) Adapting to and mitigating floods using sustainable urban drainage systems, in J.E. Lamond, D.G. Proverbs, C.A. Booth and F.N. Hammond (eds), *Flood Hazards, Impacts and Responses for the Built Environment*, New York: Taylor CRC Press.

Companies and Markets (2011) *Australian Flood Damage Reconstruction Likely to Cost Billions*. Retrieved 12 July 2012 from http://www.companiesandmarkets.com/News/Construction/Australian-Flood-Damage-Reconstruction-Likely-to-Cost-Billions/NI1713.

Cumbria Intelligence Observatory (2010) *Cumbria Floods November 2009: An Impact Assessment*, Carlisle: Cumbria County Council.

DESA (2013) World Population Prospects, 2012 Revision. New York: Department for Economic and Social Affairs.

De Sousa, C.A., Wu, C., and Westphal, L.M. (2009) Assessing the effect of publicly assisted brownfield redevelopment on surrounding property values, *Economic Development Quarterly* 23: 95–110.

El Sioufi, M. (2010) Climate change and sustainable cities: major challenges facing cities and urban settlements in the coming decades. Nairobi: UN-HABITAT. Retrieved from https://www.fig.net/pub/monthly_articles/june_2010/june_2010_el-sioufi.pdf.

Environment Agency (2013) *Flooding in England – A National Assessment of Flood Risk*. Retrieved 21 June 2013 from http://www.environment-agency.gov.uk/research/library/publications/108660.aspx.

Environmental Services – City of Portland (2006) *Downspout Disconnection.*, 2013 Portsite, OR: City of Portland.

Environmental Services – City of Portland (2011) *Portland's Ecoroof Program*. Retrieved 21 June 2013 from http://www.portsiteoregon.gov/bes/article/261074.

Environmental Services – City of Portland (no date) *Downspout Disconnection Program*. Retrieved 21 June 2013 from http://www.portsiteoregon.gov/bes/5465.

French, L., Samwinga, V., and Proverbs, D. (2011) The UK sewer network: perceptions of its condition and role in flood risk, in J.E. Lamond, D.G. Proverbs, C.A. Booth, and F.N. Hammond (eds), *Flood Hazards, Impacts and Responses for the Built Environment*, New York: Taylor CRC Press.

Home Builders Federation (2014) *Permission to Land: De-bunking the Myths about House Builders and Land Banking*. Retrieved from http://www.hbf.co.uk/fileadmin/documents/research/HBF_Report_-_Landbanking_May.pdf.

Ingirige, B. and Wedawatta, G. (2011) Impacts of flood hazard on small and medium sized companies: strategies for property level protection and business continuity, in J.E. Lamond, D.G. Proverbs, C.A. Booth, and F.N. Hammond (eds), *Flood Hazards, Impacts and Responses for the Built Environment*, New York: Taylor CRC Press.

IPCC (Intergovernmental Panel on Climate Change) (2013) *Climate Change 2013: The Physical Science Basis: Summary for Policy Makers*. Retrieved from http://www.climatechange2013.org/images/report/WG1AR5_SPM_FINAL.pdf

IPCC (Intergovernmental Panel on Climate Change) (2014) *Climate Change 2014: Impacts, Adaptation and Vulnerability*. Retrieved 21 June 2013 from http://ipcc-wg2.gov/AR5/report/.

Isaacs, D., O'Leary, J., and Daley, M. (2010) *Property Development Appraisal and Finance*, second edition. Basingstoke: Palgrave Macmillan.

Jha, A., Lamond, J., Bloch, R., Bhattacharya, N., Lopez, A., Papachristodoulou, N., Bird, A., Proverbs, D., Davies, J., and Barker, R. (2011) *Five Feet High and Rising – Cities and Flooding in the 21st Century*, Washington, DC: The World Bank.

Lamond, J. and Proverbs, D. (2009) Resilience to flooding: learning the lessons from an international comparison of the barriers to implementation, *Urban Design and Planning* 162(2): 63–70.

McCluskey, J.J. and Rausser, G.C. (2003).Stigmatized asset value: is it temporary or long-term? *Review of Economics and Statistics* 85(2): 276–285.

Met Office Hadley Centre for Climate Research (2007) *Climate Research at the Met Office Hadley Centre – Informing Government Policy into the Future*. Retrieved 2 June 2013 from http://www.metoffice.gov.uk/research/hadleycentre/pubs/brochures/clim_res_had_fut_pol.pdf.

NYC Environmental Protection (2011) *NYC Green Infrastructure Plan, 2011 Update*, New York: New York City Department of Environmental Protection/New York City Department of Buildings.

NYC Environmental Protection (2012) *Guidelines for the Design and Construction of Stormwater Management Systems*, New York: New York City Department of Environmental Protection/New York City Department of Buildings.

PMBOK Guide (2013) *A Guide to the Project Management Body of Knowledge* (PMBOK Guide) fifth edition. Newtown Square, PA: Project Management Institute.

RICS (2014) *Real Estate Agency and Brokerage Guidance* Second Edition. London: RICS.

Solomon, S. and Qin, D. (2007) *Climate Change 2007: The Physical Science Basis. Contribution of Working Group 1 to the Fourth Assessment Report of the Intergovernmental Panel on Climate Change*, Cambridge and New York: Cambridge University Press.

UN-Habitat (2008) *The State of the World's Cities 2008/2009 Hatmonious Cities*. London: Earthscan Retrieved from http://mirror.unhabitat.org/pmss/listItemDetails.aspx?publicationID=2562&Aspx AutoDetectCookieSupport=1.

Wedawatta, G., Ingirige, B., Jones, K., and Proverbs, D. (2011) Extreme weather events and construction SMEs: vulnerability, impacts and responses. *Structural Survey* 29(2): 106–119.

Wilkinson,S.J. (2011) The relatrionship between building adaptation and property attributes, PhD thesis, Deakin University. Retrieved from http://hdl.handle.net/10536/DRO/DU:30036710

Wilkinson, S. (2012) Back to the future: heritage Buildings, sustainability and adaptation in the Melbourne Central Business District. *Historic Environment (A)*. 24(2) 7–13.

Wilkinson, S. and Reed, R. 2008. *Property Development* fifth edition. London: Taylor and Francis.

Wilkinson, S.J. and Reed, R. (2009) Green roof retrofit potential in the central business district. *Property Management* 27(5): 284–301.

Wilkinson, S.J., Reed, R., and Jailani, J. (2011) Tenant satisfaction in sustainable buildings. *Pacific Rim Real Estate Conference*, Gold Coast, Australia 16–19 January 2011.

Wilkinson, S., Rose, C., Glenis, V., and Lamond, J. (2014) Modelling green roof retrofit in the Melbourne Central Business District. *Flood Recovery Innovation and Response IV*, Poznan, Posite, 18–20 June 2014.

4 Project appraisal and the triple bottom line

Sarah L. Sayce

4.0 Introduction

Whenever a development is under contemplation, a project appraisal will be required to establish whether or not the scheme is worth undertaking. Many of the criteria upon which such decisions are taken have been detailed in Chapter 3 (site feasibility). Within this chapter, the discussion revolves around what a project is 'worth' at the end of the process so we extend the concept of feasibility to that of viability. Within private sector schemes, this will hinge primarily on the likelihood that the developer will be able to obtain a satisfactory profit or return on their investment from undertaking the scheme at an acceptable level of risk and given their financing (see Chapter 5). In turn, this is dependent upon the eventual likely sale price or investment value of the scheme.

Therefore convention dictates that this is based upon the single bottom line of economic merit. However, as key stakeholders begin to consider the impact of their schemes in relation to the so-called 'triple bottom line' (Elkington 1997), so the traditional notion of economic viability begins to be questioned. A development that, seemingly, provides the highest market value, may not meet the requirements of planning authorities or indeed be resilient in the face of climate change and rapid social change. Whilst the developer who is purchasing land with a view to building speculatively for sale is likely to be concerned only with short-term gains and may still view the appraisal solely through the economic lens, those who are building to hold or who have a wider social remit are likely to undertake appraisals which at least consider to some extent the impact of the development in a wider context. Indeed, even where the development is focused on short-term gain, a developer will need to consider their own reputation; therefore if this begins to be associated with buildings which pay scant attention to sustainability characteristics it may have negative economic repercussions for the developer especially if they subsequently seek to undertake schemes in partnership with those espousing corporate responsibility or with public or third sector organisations.

Although the focus of this book is primarily on private sector development, it is important to consider development appraisals from the viewpoint of public sector and public/private sector schemes. Indeed as sustainability criteria begin to be more deeply embedded both in the principles adopted by the key stakeholders and the regulatory framework so there has been a tendency for the notions of 'public' and 'private' sectors to coalesce. This can be witnessed, for example, in UK housing schemes in which developers are required to provide 'affordable housing' for management by third sector organisations as part of the consent process. In undertaking the appraisal, the appraiser needs skill and expertise in valuing such units (RICS 2010).

Although the main purpose of undertaking an appraisal is to determine levels of viability given the requirements of the developer and the conditions prevailing in the marketplace, it is important to recognise that development appraisals take different forms and are often carried out as part of an iterative process. For example, the appraisal may be carried out to determine whether a site, either a 'greenfield' undeveloped proposition or an existing building ripe for redevelopment or refurbishment, is worth purchasing. Alternatively it may be undertaken after purchase to determine whether a scheme is worth pursuing.

The methods used to establish viability will depend both on the stage at which the appraisal is undertaken and on the client requirements. With the exception of the comparative method they all require an evaluation of the worth or value which will be realised (expressed as the Gross Development Value in standard appraisals) with deductions for costs and the time value of the development period.

In complex schemes, each element will be subject to many considerations. Therefore one of the criticisms made of development appraisals is that they involve so many variables that they are not reliable and it is for this reason that they are conducted iteratively. In terms of building sustainability into the process, this has been seen as a barrier in the past (Cadman 2000) with the notion of a 'circle of blame' inhibiting sustainable development decisions. To many, it still is so perceived but changing attitudes of stakeholders are beginning to change perceptions (Lorenz and Lützkendorf 2008; World Green Building Council 2013). If a development's costs escalate due to incorporating sustainability criteria, then this may reduce viability – unless the eventual value of the scheme is enhanced by its sustainability characteristics. It is not the role of this chapter to rehearse the characteristics that mark out one building as being more sustainable than another; however, in this chapter we rehearse some of the evidence that market values of completed developments are influenced by their environmental and social credentials – normally viewed in terms of accreditations.

The methods most frequently used to assist decision-making and which are considered are:

- comparability
- residual valuation
- discounted cashflow (DCF) approach
- cost-benefit analysis
- revealed and stated preference theories
- ecosystems analysis.

In and of themselves none provide a solution to what decision should be made: they are indicators against which decisions can be made. Within private sector development schemes, the normal approaches are comparability, residual valuation and discounted cash flows. It is only within public or third sector schemes that other methods are normally undertaken.

At its simplest, anyone seeking to undertake development will only do so if they obtain a satisfactory financial return at an acceptable level of risk which, as demonstrated in earlier chapters, is likely to be significant, as the number of variables which will determine the outcome are many. Indeed, at the time that a decision to proceed is taken, the level of uncertainty is high but steadily decreases as time progresses. This is illustrated diagrammatically in Figure 4.1.

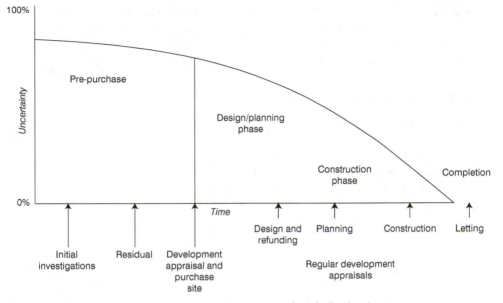

Figure 4.1 The relationship between risk and uncertainty though the development process
Source: Adapted from Dubben (2008)

4.1   Standard methods of appraisal

The following standard methods of appraisal are detailed on the basis of a private sector scheme which is not complex or phased in nature. Where a phased scheme is contemplated, a Discounted Cash Flow is almost always undertaken. It should be pointed out at this early stage that all methods of financial appraisal are prone to inaccuracy – they are not an exact science or as Beaman (2014) puts it 'the magic lies in the quality of the information on which the appraisal is based'. It is also important to stress that both the comparative and residual approaches outlined below seek to arrive at a 'likely transaction price'. However, any developer wishing to purchase a site of development land will also undertake a calculation in terms of what the opportunity affords to them given their own standpoint. This is in effect a calculation of 'worth' as opposed to 'value' and is considered later in the chapter.

4.1.1 Comparative approach

Where the site or redevelopment opportunity to be appraised is similar in size, characteristics and development potential to other recently transacted sites in the vicinity, the normal way to arrive at an appraisal is by use of the comparative method of valuation. Under this method, an analysis of the price achieved for sites with broadly similar development characteristics is undertaken primarily in relation to size. Whilst it is argued that this methodology is essentially objective and therefore to be preferred, in practice it may not be possible to adopt. RICS (2008: 7) argue that it is 'only reliable if evidence of sales can be found and analysed on a common unit basis, such as site area, developable area or habitable room'. Except where development sites abound, possibly in an area newly identified for development and in which recent transactions take place, this is not likely. It may be useful as a check method or to establish parameters of value but, as the RICS (2008) point out, values may differ considerably within a small geographical area and conditions and scheme intention can vary making such an approach inaccurate. For these reasons, the comparative approach is seldom used in isolation. It is also not helpful in differentiating between evaluating projects with different levels of sustainability.

4.1.2 Residual valuations

The residual valuation approach is that which is employed as standard to determine how much a developer should/could bid for a site. The information used within a residual valuation is also used to establish the likely profitability of a scheme where the land has already been acquired. The residual method requires the use of a large range of data. As RICS (2008) argues whilst some of these data sets may be capable of a high level of certainty, others are not and assumptions have to be built into the process. This leads to potential inaccuracies that cumulatively can lead to large changes in the land value or profit.

The starting point of any residual valuation is the establishment of the development potential of the site, taking full account of planning matters and market demand. Having established this, the appraisal needs to enumerate site considerations, costs of development, development finance, timing of the scheme and consideration of risk. This produces, in schematic form, calculations such as set out below (Figures 4.2 and 4.3).

In Figure 4.2, the output is the bid price; in Figure 4.3, the development profit assumes the site already lies in the developer's landholding. This calculation is now considered on an elemental basis.

4.1.3 Gross Development Value

The Gross Development Value (GDV) is normally taken to be the market value, as defined in the RICS Red Book (RICS 2014: 9) on the assumption that the development has been completed i.e. taking the market conditions and levels of value prevailing at the time of calculation – not the projected value at the likely date of completion. This figure does not include an allowance for purchaser's costs which would normally be taken into account if a sale were subsequently to be undertaken. The extent to which the sustainability characteristics of the development are reflected will depend entirely on the market evidence. Therefore fundamental to driving the development industry towards higher engagement with sustainability is that the *market* recognises these characteristics within transaction values.

The World Green Building Council's review of evidence (WGBC 2013) concluded that there exists a convincing case for developing to higher than compliance standards, even if extra costs are involved. They concluded that as investors and occupants become sensitised to and concerned about the environmental and social impacts of their buildings, so buildings with better sustainability credentials are easier to market and may command differentially higher transaction prices (WGBC 2013). Figure 4.4 is taken from their findings and illustrates the variations reported in a series of academic projects.

The evidence base from which this chart was compiled included studies conducted primarily in the major developed countries (see for example Das *et al.* 2011; Eichholtz *et al.* 2013; Fuerst *et al.* 2013a; Chegut *et al.* (2013) and showed a marked change in evidence from that available only three years before (see for example Sayce *et al.* 2010). However whilst the WGBC report does suggest that buildings with sustainability ratings achieve higher rents and lower yields, such findings must be viewed with caution. As WGBC

Gross Development Value (Market Value or Worth)
Less
Total Development Costs including:

- Construction costs
- All fees including planning contributions
- Minimum required level of profit
- Contingency

Equals
The 'residue'
which represents the offer price for the land plust the holding cost and any tax on purchase

Figure 4.2 Schematic of residual to establish land value
Source: Authors

Gross Development Value (Market Value or Worth)
Less
Total Development Costs including:

- Construction costs
- All fees including planning contributions
- Finance costs plus any interest payments
- Site cost (assumes site purchased)
- Contingency

Equals
The scheme profit

Figure 4.3 Schematic of residual to establish scheme viability
Source: Authors

admits, the reasons for the differences are not yet clear (WGBC 2013: 44). The studies are concentrated primarily in the CBDs of major centres primarily in the US but also Australia and some parts of Europe. They are almost exclusively large office buildings and further the studies do not differentiate between the rating grade of the sample buildings or the date of certification. Both these factors can significantly impact on achieved standard, and no account is taken as to the grade of the rating or the date it was given. For these reasons, the findings have to be treated with caution. Further studies relating to residential properties also show some differential values in some countries. For example Fuerst *et al.* (2013b) found a positive relationship between residential values and EPC ratings; however Cajias and Piazolo (2013), in their work in the US, call for caution in interpreting a relationship between Energy Star ratings and house prices. Further, Walls *et al.* (2013) in finding a link between house prices and the existence of Energy Star ratings, discovered that in some cases it appeared that prices moved more than the level of anticipated energy savings

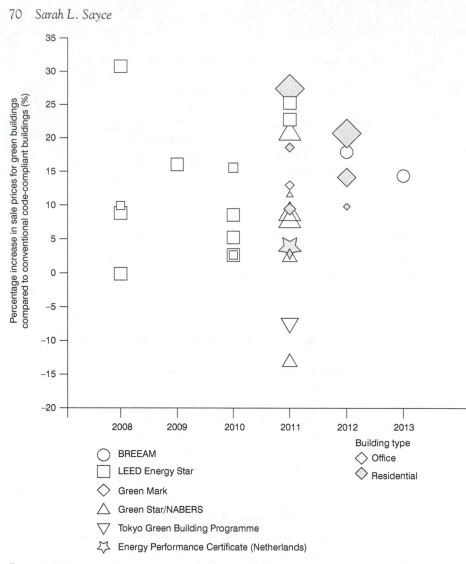

Figure 4.4 Asset price premiums reported by World Green Building Council (2013: 37)

leading to the possibility that other factors were at play. They also found that the link to a price 'premium' only existed in older houses: in new stock as building regulations have tightened so purchaser expectations are for an energy efficient unit and Energy Star was not a noticeable price determinant.

The nature of property is that it is heterogeneous and to conclude that the narrow range of characteristics embedded in rating schemes can be a clear indication of value is probably misleading. Whilst it is clear that a rating scheme can present a clear marketing advantage and anecdotal evidence would suggest that for prime office stock the presence of a rating is regarded as a 'norm', it is not a simple algorithm to assess what sustainability characteristics feed through into value.

In part, this may be due to the lack of relevant data that is or can be obtained by valuers, but it is suggested that it depends on the profile of the likely tenant or purchaser and the sub-market conditions. In respect of the former, the RICS have now built into their mandatory valuation professional standards (colloquially known as the Red Book (RICS 2014)) a requirement, accompanied by guidance for valuers of commercial properties to gather sustainability data insofar as they can when conducting a valuation (RICS 2013) with the intention of stimulating changes in market behaviours. Similar, earlier guidance was issued in relation to residential property valuation informing valuers of the ways in which it was recommended that include consideration of sustainability within their valuations (RICS 2011). From the above discussion, it can be seen that the notion of sustainability is not separate from that of market value – it is simply embedded in value if that is what the market recognises.

4.1.4 *Establishing market value*

The next question to consider is how to establish market value. Market value, as defined by the International Valuation Standards and incorporated in the RICS Red Book (2014), is:

> The estimated amount for which an asset or liability should exchange on the valuation date between a willing buyer and a willing seller in an arm's length transaction after proper marketing and where the parties had each acted knowledgeably, prudently and without compulsion.

When establishing the market value of a commercial property, the most common method adopted is the investment method. The theory and practice of this is covered comprehensively in many textbooks (see for example Sayce *et al.* 2006; Blackledge 2009; Baum *et al.* 2011; Isaac and O'Leary 2013). For the purposes of this book it is only necessary to cover the key principles. For any investment valuation calculation, there are two key elements: the rental value and the investment yield (or multiplier). Therefore, in establishing market value it is critical to understand both occupational demand, as expressed by rent, and investment price, as expressed as a capital value.

Finding rental value is the first part of an investment valuation. It relies on finding suitable comparable evidence and then breaking this down into 'units' (RICS 2010). Whilst this sounds very easy in theory, the difficulty in finding rental value for a residual calculation is that evidence is inevitably obtained from already built stock whereas what it being estimated is that which has not yet been built. Whilst for some stock the age of the property may not have a significant effect, the impact of changing building regulation requirements, notably relating to environmental issues, may mean that the specification of new stock will be very different from anything already constructed and transacted.

Often one of the most difficult adjustments relates to the terms of the lease. Although most countries will have standard leases, in reality most leases are individually negotiated and the terms may not be strictly comparable. Further, unless market conditions at the time of the grant are very buoyant, rent-free periods and other concessions may impact on the rent that is agreed and this may not always be publicly available information.

In relation to sustainability, there has been a move in recent years towards the introduction of so-called green leases, in which tenants and landlords agree to work together to promote good environmental management of the building. First developed in Australia as a tenants' initiative (Power 2004), they range from 'light green', relying primarily on non-enforceable memoranda of understanding to 'deep green', involving responsibilities and penalties (Hinnells *et al.* 2008). Whilst advocated widely in, for example, Australia, the US, Canada and Europe (Oberle and Sloboda 2010; Roussac and Bright 2012), take-up has met barriers (Sayce *et al.* 2009a). However, given that one country (France) has taken statutory measures in an attempt to gain traction (Brigstocke 2013) it is possible that they may become more commonplace. The issue then in terms of establishing rental value is whether they are seen as an *enhancement* due to a 'good' landlord or a downwards negotiating 'chip' as they may place extra burdens on the tenant or, in the case of a multi-let building, increased service charges. In summary the role of the appraiser is to make all necessary and appropriate adjustments to rental evidence and establish, with as much accuracy as possible, the rental value of the development at today's prevailing level of values.

Having established the most likely rental value, it is necessary to convert this projected income flow into a capital value by multiplying the rental value by a years' purchase (YP) figure that is basically a multiplier. It is the expression of the number of years it will take to recoup the initial capital invested. So, if the multiplier is 10, it will take 10 years before the money is recouped; if it is 20 it would take 20 years, etc. The reciprocal of the multiplier (or YP) is the investment yield. Taking a very simplistic example:

Rent (or rental value)	£1,000
Multiplier (YP) (yield 10%)	10
Capital value	**£10,000**

Or if the valuer decides a 20 YP (5 per cent yield) is appropriate:

Rent (or rental value)	£1,000
Multiplier (YP) (yield 5%)	20
Capital value	**£20,000**

Although this is an overly simplistic example, it demonstrates that the choice of multiplier is absolutely critical to value. The yield adopted is again taken from evidence of investment sales and will reflect market conditions, as well as perceptions relating to risk, likely levels of future rental growth, resilience to obsolescence, building type and specification, usage, location and so on.

The GDV of commercial property is extremely sensitive to slight alterations in the yield pattern and this is the single most problematic area in an appraisal. Yield 'shift', both upwards and downwards can take place very quickly and a yield that might have appeared fully justified by evidence at a pre-purchase point leading to a decision to go ahead, can render the scheme lacking in viability just a few months later. For example in a market in which demand significantly exceeds supply, yields may be driven down as low at 3.5 per cent for the best prime retail investments; whereas in a weaker market that same property might transact at 5.5 per cent even 6 per cent. This means a multiplier to income which can potentially half, or double! Whilst rental values will also change consequent on economic patterns it is yield shift which tends to have the most significant effect on value.

The investment method is only used for commercial private sector assets; for non-commercial developments that are undertaken for the 'public good' different evaluations are undertaken that are discussed below.

For residential property that does not fall under the heading of 'affordable housing', the normal method applied is a simple analysis of transaction prices achieved recently, decomposed for size, location, amenities and condition. Again the appraisal will assume no major change in market conditions during the period until completion/sale. However, although there are many occasions when a residential scheme comprises exclusively properties for sale or rent at market values, it is commonplace in the UK and some other countries that the consent to develop will contain a requirement for a percentage of the housing provided to be 'affordable'.

There are many types of 'affordable housing' ranging from equity share schemes to social rented properties, often to be held within public or third sector organisations. What is common to them all is that the process of calculating the GDV for affordable housing is more complex (RICS 2010) than for standard developments, as it contains two components as follows:

- Rental and capital receipts (usually below market value – typically 75–80per cent)
- Subsidies and grants.

The exact nature of reductions and grants and subsidies varies according to jurisdiction and over time, but due to the complexity, appraisals containing affordable housing are typically undertaken using DCF techniques.

One further consideration under GDV is whether the scheme is phased or not and the length of time until income/sale is achieved. In the event of rent frees or phasing where receipts are likely to be spread over a period of time, a DCF may be required.

Once the GDV less costs or likely *net* receipts have been estimated, the costs involved in development must be calculated and the principles for these are now discussed.

4.1.5 Development costs

4.1.5.1 Pre-construction costs

In Chapter 3 we considered matters related to site feasibility, including issues of contamination, topography, flood risk assessments, etc., and in Chapter 6 we consider the planning issues. All these processes cost money and time and due allowance must be made for them within the calculation. As sustainability and environmental issues have risen up the agenda of both developers and planners, so pre-construction costs have tended to rise both in relation to statutory requirements and out of a desire to create a more sustainable, resilient product. In particular if a decision is made to design to achieve a sustainability rating, the costs of these consultants must be factored in to the calculation. In terms of sustainability, there is generally encouragement to develop 'brownfield' sites, but it should be recognised that such sites not only may be more expensive to develop, they may need specialist land audits or investigations in order to establish the extent of remediation that may be required.

4.1.5.2 Construction costs

After the GDV to which both profit and land value are extremely 'sensitive', the build cost is one of the items that will have most influence on the residual calculation. Depending on the jurisdiction, practice varies as to the ways in which buildings are measured for the purpose of establishing costs. Within the UK, this is gross internal area (GIA) as currently defined in the RICS Code of Measuring Practice (RICS 2007), whereas *value* is normally determined in relation to net internal areas, except in the case of industrial units. However, the way in which buildings are measured varies from country to country leading to a multi-agency initiative (for further details see http://ipmsc.org/) of some 44 organisations to establish a global consensus, this is viewed as an increasing requirement as global investors seek to compare opportunities in a meaningful way.

From a sustainability viewpoint, it is also critical that that good comparative cost data is available in order that decisions are taken which promote environmental and economic ambitions. Whether the appraiser assumes an added cost to building sustainably will depend on circumstances, but it is increasingly unlikely. Davis Langdon (2007), writing in an Australian context, concluded that there is no significant difference in average cost for green buildings as compared to non-green buildings. However, this will not always be the case and a range of other sources considered by the World Green Building Council (2013) concludes that the additional costs of achieving the highest certification ratings could be up to 12.5 per cent – 15 per cent.

In assessing build costs key issues to consider are:

- *The specification required, which should be commensurate with the market requirements.* In every case, the locational context and sub-market at which the building is targeted will impact on specification and hence build cost. In the UK when developing residentially where a requirement may have been placed on incorporating an element of 'affordable housing', it will be usual practice to adjust costs for the affordable element to reflect that the internal specification (for example kitchen fitments) may be to a lower standard. Whilst it could be argued that such approach to specification is lacking in ethicality, the appraiser must, in the interests of arriving at a viable land value or profit calculation, take the line that others in the market will take.
- *The impact of design on cost.* The challenge for those wishing to build 'beyond compliance' and to high environmental and social standards is that not only is the market value differential potentially difficult to assess, but also the comparability of other build costs from which to establish the cost element may be more difficult. Although there is a rapidly increasing knowledge base of the cost levels for builds which have strong sustainability design features, the reliability of the data may be less than with standard builds. It should also be recognised that, whilst the inclusion of some items associated with 'sustainable' builds might increase costs significantly (for example, a Triple A roof structure and the use of some type of high insulation glass or renewable heating/cooling systems can be costly), other items if incorporated at design stage do not have a significant effect.

Normally when undertaking an appraisal, especially if it is prior to land purchase, the build costs will not be known and the appraiser therefore has to make an estimate as to the likely impact. Put simply: the appraiser is taking a rough estimate, not a detailed costing. If the appraisal is being undertaken later in the process, exact costings may be capable of being substituted.

The source of cost information for standard developments is often found with reference to textbooks, websites and industry-developed pricing books. However, not only are they very generalised, they may be inapplicable to the scheme particularly when it contains new technologies or in some way departs from a traditional build. Within the UK, the *Green Guide to Specification* (http://www.bre.co.uk/greenguide/podpage.jsp?id=2126) enables the environmental impact of individual components to be evaluated. For complex schemes it will not normally be possible to rely on generalised building cost indices, although for the purposes of appraisal undertaken for prospective purchase there will be little or no opportunity to have accurate costings, although RICS (2008) does advocate the use of a quantity surveyor (QS) or other appropriate expert adviser.

If standard building cost books are used, it will be important to ensure that costs are appropriately adjusted for any specific site characteristics or the requirement, possibly through planning, to retain heritage features and the extent to which sustainability characteristics are built in to the assumptions for GDV. Furthermore, as noted in Chapter 8 the choice of procurement route may influence the building cost. It is therefore important that the assumptions made about the planned procurement route (if not fixed by the date of the appraisal) are stated explicitly.

One of the perceived barriers to developing sustainably has been that it increases costs (World Green Building Council 2013); an argument that used to be countered by the longer-term benefits of lower running costs (Kats 2003; Edwards and Naboni 2013). However, whilst such arguments might be tenable where property is being developed for owner-occupation by the owner, it is irrelevant if the developer is either seeking to complete and sell on or hold as investment, unless the sustainability characteristics are appropriately reflected in the market value, the initial rent or the prospects for future growth. As noted earlier in this chapter, this may be the case. Within the construction cost element, added additional costs such as security and insurance which can be considerable particularly where expensive items are held on site should also be considered.

4.1.5.3 Tax relief and grants

Of importance in many cases is the presence (or absence) of tax reliefs and grants. It is in this area in which building compliance may have significant advantage. Clearly it will depend on the jurisdiction but increasingly incentives or tax breaks are being introduced at state or even regional level to encourage sustainable construction. This may include enhanced capital allowances, zero rating on certain materials deemed to be sustainable or subsidies and grants for the inclusion of certain technologies, such as renewable energy schemes. Further, in some locations, notably old industrial areas in which contamination of sites has acted as a negative to development, grant schemes and tax breaks are frequently used as stimuli. Whilst consideration of such matters is contained in Chapter 3, from a development appraisal viewpoint, it is important that the appraiser does need to take cognisance of the availability or otherwise of such funds and their potential longevity as sometimes they can be withdrawn or reduced at short notice. An example of this is within the UK, where a scheme, known as the Feed In Tariff Scheme (FITs) was introduced. Under this scheme, building owners installing photovoltaic panels (PVs) can sell their surplus energy production back to the national grid. The level of payment was so advantageous initially that not only was domestic take-up, for which it had been designed, extremely good, but it set off a series of proposals for commercial PV 'farms'. Subsequent significant reductions in tariff rates have reduced the attractiveness of such technologies domestically but have continued to stimulate applications to change conventional farmland into solar farms. For current details see www.fitariffs.co.uk.

4.1.5.4 Fees

The incidence of fees and expenses will vary according to the size, complexity and aspirations of the scheme. In the case of large house builders developing a standard product using primarily in-house expertise, the actual fee burden will be low in percentage terms.

However, for commercial or more complex schemes, the fees, which are normally written into the appraisal on a percentage of build cost basis, will rise to anywhere from around 15 per cent to 18 per cent. As the need for more investigation expands, and the range of consultants increases, so will the fees. This can be an issue where a client is seeking to build in additional sustainability criteria and will need to pay for sustainability consultants and accreditation organisations.

Among the normal consultant team for a major scheme, all of whose costs should be factored in to the appraisal are:

- designers,
- project managers,
- planning consultants,
- engineers,
- landscape architects,
- letting and sales agents; and,
- the legal team.

Added to which, in the case of some notably more ambitious schemes, in sustainability terms, should be:

- acoustic engineers,
- traffic engineers; and,
- environmental consultants.

Further, where a scheme is being designed to achieve accreditation, among the additional costs to be factored in may be monitoring of performance in the first three years. This is an increasing trend aimed at countering the 'performance gap' between design and operation (Menezes *et al.* 2012).

4.1.5.5 *Finance*

The approach to financing a scheme taken within an appraisal will vary and there are no set rules, just local practice and consideration of the financial context. Conventionally, the appraiser will work on the assumption that the project is to be 100 per cent debt funded with finance costs rolled up until completion when the money will be recouped either through sale or the arrangement of long-term finance. In practice, especially where property is being developed for and by an owner-occupier, the opportunity cost will be far less if internal funds are used. Nonetheless to establish viability or market value borrowing is normally assumed. In the case of post-purchase appraisal, where market value is not the unknown to be established, the actual projected costs are more commonly adopted.

It is also normally assumed that money will be borrowed in stages at a fairly standard commercial rate with an average (simplifying) assumption that half the money is borrowed at any one time – or that the whole of the costs are borrowed for half of the development period but the calculation is based on the assumption that borrowing costs will be compounded quarterly or annually (see for example RICS 2008). Such an approach is known as a straight-line approach. However, where the scheme is more complex and a DCF approach is adopted, it is increasingly common to use an S-Curve in which finance (and build costs) is weighted according to the most likely scenario. For example, where a development is taking place on a heavily contaminated site or is a structure with great mass, the costs are likely to be front loaded; conversely where the building (such as a retail scheme or high grade office) is dependent on extensive internal fit out and external landscaping, the costs may be back ended. In the view of the RICS, S-curves whilst they are 'sophisticated and specialised' if used without the necessary expertise, are not likely to lead to greater accuracy (RICS 2008: 13).

However, as explained in Chapter 5 funding is never that simple – it depends on four main variables:

1   the nature and size of the scheme which will impact on the risk profile;
2   the market context at the time of the appraisal;
3   the track record of the borrower; and
4   the source of funding.

From a sustainability perspective therefore, the question to be asked is: does the fact that the scheme is being built to advanced environmental and social standards impact on either the cost or availability of funding or increase the type of funder willing to support the development? Chapter 5 has considered the availability of different types of incentives and funding for sustainable developments. Whilst this will vary by jurisdiction, type of development and over time, the appraiser should be cognisant of the possibility that the scheme might achieve preferential funding or an increased range of funders.

Within the UK, some finance schemes are now beginning to take the view within the residential sector that lending against sustainable property might be less risky. For example there is a move towards mortgage lenders judging their loans against the total overall outgoings of the borrower; if a property is cheaper to run by, for example, its energy credentials, the amount that can be borrowed will increase. Whilst this will not currently affect the cost of borrowing, it is a trend that is likely to emerge over time.

4.1.5.6 Approach to risk – the developer's profit

Under the paradigm of conventional project appraisal, the assumption is made that the object of carrying out development is to achieve a 'single bottom line' profit. No account is taken of external costs of the development carried by the community or other stakeholders, other than is required in the form of levies and taxes imposed by government, such as development taxes. Currently in the UK a Community Infrastructure Levy is a local tax that may apply to developments which increase overall floor space or the requirement to provide social benefits as an integral part of the scheme. Therefore, where the appraisal is being undertaken in order to establish a bid price or market value, the addition to the build and other costs of an allowance for profit is fundamental to the appraisal. Alternatively, where the appraisal is being undertaken for viability purposes *after* purchase, the profit will in effect be the residual element after all costs including land holding are established and accounted for.

The conventional way of expressing the amount of profit that is required is as a percentage of the development cost; alternatively a percentage of GDV is taken but, according to the RICS (2008) this is less common as an approach and there is no 'hard and fast' rule; it depends on the prevailing practice in the market for the sector and the buoyancy of the market (in a strong market profit margins will fall as developers seek to outbid each other) and on the risks perceived in the scheme.

Increasingly, however, when a scheme is to be undertaken for a long-term 'hold', a DCF approach is undertaken in which costs and cash flows are annualised in real (i.e. projected) terms and discounted back to the current time using a discount rate that is deemed appropriate based on the cost of money and the risk. If using the discount rate the result is positive (that is the net present value (NPV) is greater than zero) the scheme is deemed viable. The higher the risk the greater the discount rate adjusted and the less likely this will be the case. Alternatively, using Excel or any other spreadsheet package it is possible to calculate the discount rate at which the NPV is exactly zero. This discount rate (the Internal rate of Return (IRR)) is then considered against what is deemed a fair and acceptable return for the level of risk inherent in the entire appraisal. The question of the discount rate adopted is referred to in more detail below as it has fundamental implications for any holistic understanding of sustainability.

4.1.5.7 Contingency

Although again there is no set rule, it is usual for a development appraisal to make allowance in the calculation for contingencies, given that uncertainty is associated with each element of cost and value. However, in allowing for contingency costs it is important to check that this has not been double counted – i.e. within the QS assessed build cost estimate and as a 'stand-alone' add-on.

Referring back to Figure 4.1, the degree of uncertainty decreases as the plans progress so any contingency should, in theory, be decreased in line with cost elements. Typical ranges for contingency are between 0–5 per cent on new build, with 'greenfield sites' being at the lower end. For refurbishment schemes or developments on previously developed land, depending on the nature of the scheme, contingency levels are likely to be higher, typically at between 5–10 per cent of build costs.

4.1.6   From residue to land value

Once the total projected costs of the scheme have been deducted from the GDV, what is left is a 'residue'. This represents the amount of the site value – as a proportion of the completed building. As such, it is a figure in the future and must be 'brought back' to the current time. It also includes any tax or other costs on the land purchase. Conventionally, therefore, the residue is reduced by the holding costs taken at a borrowing rate on the assumption that the scheme is 100 per cent debt financed, even though this will be seldom, if ever, the case (Dubben 2008). The resultant netted down figure represents the current land value.

4.2   From purchase appraisal to subsequent assessment

The analysis above illustrates the complexity of assumptions that will be built into any appraisal of land undertaken prior to purchase. However, as indicated above, frequently land is held within a portfolio waiting viability *before* a scheme is started. Whilst, within an operational estate, timing might be dictated by the needs of the business, where it is held by a commercial developer, this scenario can lead to 'land banking', where land is held pending the 'right time' to develop. Such practices have been advocated as positive in sustainability terms by providing a reserve of potential resources to aid economic growth, community developments and strengthening markets by helping to keep a supply/demand balance (Alexander and Housing 2011). This view is supported in the analysis conducted by van der Krabben and Jacobs (2013) in relation to public sector land assembly in the Netherlands. However, within the UK, land banking has more frequently been associated with notions that developers have deliberately assembled land and held it in an attempt to distort supply, push up GDV and hence increase profitability. However, as the Home Builders Federation point out within a UK context (Home Builders Federation 2014) developers normally acquire land in order to develop; land held undeveloped represents unrealised profit. Their review of previous reports including the Barker Review (Barker 2004), the Office of Fair Trading Report (2008) and the Molior Report (Craine 2012) confirmed that, contrary to some widely held belief, the evidence pointed to the fact that land was generally only held undeveloped where to develop would incur a loss or the land was held by a non-developer (normally an owner-occupier). Nonetheless, the failure of land to come forward for development during times of housing shortage has been a perennial issue within the UK and one with social consequences in terms of pressure on existing stock challenging affordability. However, in relation to commercial developments, whilst the same scenario may prevail, the results are not normally regarded in such an adverse light, except where small parcelling has occurred as a speculative endeavour (Land Registry 2012) against both the spirit and practice of social sustainability.

4.3   Development appraisals using Discounted Cash Flow

Where a development appraisal is undertaken after purchase, it is commonly conducted by a Discounted Cash Flow (DCF) in which the projected cash in and cash out sums are entered and then brought back to the present time using a pre-determined discount rate chosen to reflect both the cost of capital and the perceived level of risk inherent in the cash flows (both in and out). The higher the discount rate, the less likely the scheme is to be viable as future cash flows have increasingly less value. Where the NPV at the allocated discount rate is positive, the scheme is deemed viable to proceed; where it is not, development should not take place. Alternatively the calculation can be set up to calculate the projected rate of return (IRR) that will be achieved against any cash flow scenario. Where the IRR is above the target rate or allows a margin against the cost of money, the result is acceptable.

It follows from the above that the choice of discount rate (or the level of acceptability of any IRR) is a critical decision factor; it is also one with sustainability implications. Given that, under the Brundtland paradigm (WCED 1987), the very notion of sustainable development is that future needs are anticipated and accommodated, any level of interest effectively places the needs of today above those of tomorrow. The higher the discount rate adopted, the greater impact initial costs will have and the less future receipts are valued, as illustrated simply in Table 4.1 in which a proposition offering cash receipts of 1.2 million in two years' time is evaluated against costs today of 1 million.

Although Table 4.1 is very simplistic, it serves to illustrate what a profound impact the discount rate has. If a development opportunity is to be assessed against high discount rates, innately there will be less likelihood that decisions will be taken that recognise the long term over the short.

For development appraisals it is unusual that the period over which cash flows are evaluated will take account of any time-scale *post* construction and occupation, as the in-built assumption is that the property will be sold. Therefore the discount period concludes at a point of presumed sale. This produces, in effect, a disconnect between development viability appraisals and investment appraisals, which reinforces a silo between these stages of the life cycle: silos that work against any notion of sustainability. However, there are calls

Table 4.1 The impact of discount rate choice

Discount rate	0%	5%	20%
Initial outlay	1,000,000	1,000,000	1,000,000
Receipts after 2 years	1,200,000,	1,200,000,	1,200,000,
Discount factor (1/1+discount rate)$^{discount\ period}$	1	0.907	0.694
Discounted future receipts	1,200,000– 1,000,000	1,200,000 ×.907 =1,088,400	1,200,000 ×.694 =832,800
Profitability (NPV of cash flow measured as discounted receipts less initial outlay)	200,000	111,600	(167,200)

Source: Author

for whole life cycle approaches to be employed even at the viability stage (GVA Grimley 2009). Where a development is undertaken for owner-occupation, this disconnect, which acts as serious impediment to sustainable practices, is less likely to occur as the whole life cycle of the building and its components are likely to form an ongoing part of discussions.

The choice of discount rate chosen will depend on market factors and on risk (see 4.3.1 below). Logically it could be assumed that discount rates are set in relation primarily to the cost of capital or borrowing rates. However Coleman et al. (2013) conclude that this is not the case with discount rates chosen for a wide range of reasons.

4.3.1 Building in risk through scenarios and other means

However much a commercial developer is committed to the promotion of sustainability, if funding, long-term or short-term, is from an institution or bank, the needs of the shareholders must be considered as a contractual and/or fiduciary relationship will exist and fulfilling these duties is paramount (Pivo and McNamara 2005). Return is a key consideration but so too is risk and consideration of risk is critical to any appraisal.

The most elementary method to reflect risks is the application of a risk-adjusted discount rate (see for example Sayce et al. 2009b; Baum and Hartzell. 2012). However, as demonstrated above, to simply adjust the discount rate upwards results in a decision skewed towards a very short-term, and hence essentially unsustainable, viewpoint. Nonetheless, from a purchaser viewpoint, this is often the approach taken and is the approach adopted within a residual valuation.

Increasingly risk is also built into appraisal with the use of sensitivity analysis, scenarios or a multi-variate risk model such as Monte Carlo simulation (Figure 4.5). Sensitivity analysis (see Table 4.2) works on the assumption that a single variable (e.g. rent or yield) will not be as predicted, but all other inputs remain unchanged. In reality, although, for example, rents might be fixed through pre-let arrangements, most variables are interlinked. Sensitivity analysis can be used to model the impact of a percentage change in one variable to measure the impact on profitability; alternatively it can be used to assess what change would throw the scheme out of viability. As a tool, it provides useful information to give comfort to the appraisal and, for this reason, it is commonly adopted practice. Such an approach has the advantage of concentrating research activity on those items that are likely to have the biggest impact on the outturn in financial terms. In most cases, as shown in simple terms, the yield and rent are the items to which profit is most sensitive, with cost less so.

Table 4.2 Simplified example of sensitivity analysis (changed assumptions are in bold)

	Most likely outturn	Assuming rental down 10%	Assuming yield up 10%	Assume build costs up 10%
Rent	1,000,000	**900,000**	1,000,000	1,000,000
YP at yield 7%	14.28	14.28	**12.98**	14.28
GDV	14,280,000	12,852,000	12,980,000	14,280,000
Less				
Build costs	10,000,000	10,000,000	10,000,000	**11,000,000**
Other costs (including site purchase and holding)	2,000,000	2,000,000	2,000,000	2,000,000
Total costs	12,000,000	12,000,000	12,000,000	13,000,000
Predicted profit	2,280,000	852,000	980,000	1,280,000
Effect of change	0	Down 63%	Down 57%	Down 46%

Source: Adapted from Dubben (2009)

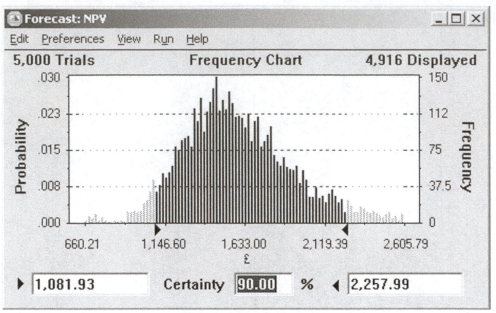

Figure 4.5 Screen shot showing results of running a Monte Carlo simulation using random numbers

This reinforces the point that unless, and until, sustainability is reflected in market rents and yields, it will not be a driver for developers if costs are pushed upwards due to changes in specification to achieve higher levels of sustainability. Whether this is the case in both value and cost terms will depend on the particular locality and sub-market (World Green Building Council 2013).

Scenarios are simply that – a succession of different appraisals based normally on most likely, pessimistic and optimistic assumptions in relation to each variable. Whilst not always undertaken, it is also common practice to weight the likelihood of each scenario in order to obtain an estimated net present value, based on the identified risks and the likelihood that they will occur. A more sophisticated approach to the assessment of risk within the development is by use of Monte Carlo simulation, which is built in to several industry standard software packages, such as Microsoft Project[1] or as the Solver add-in to Excel[2]. There are many variants of Monte Carlo, but in simple terms it relaxes the assumption that only one variable is involved in the appraisal changes and instead assumes that each can vary within prescribed parameters. Then, using random numbers, it generates through computational iteration a frequency table from which probability can be calculated. However, it does not guarantee that any project will or will not be viable – it is only an aid to decision-making.

4.3.2 *Summary and examples*

In order to illustrate the principles that have been set out above, two examples are given: one of a simple redevelopment of a single dwelling into a small block of flats; the other of cash flow analysis of commercial property.

EXAMPLE 4.1

A residual valuation for a site on which a large outmoded house stands that has a capital value of say £700,000 as a single dwelling. Due to planning policies and the requirement for a more dense form of development in the area to promote walking, the developer can get permission to build a block of eight executive flats each of which would sell for £350,000 on a standard specification. There is no requirement to supply any element of affordable housing given the small scale of the development. The developer considers the evidence that a higher sales price per unit could be achieved by providing a higher standard of specification incorporating greater energy efficiency and water-saving measures which would enable certification to be obtained.

The residual calculations set out below indicate that, if the increase in sales price can be achieved with only a limited increase in build cost, the overall residual value of the land increases. Whether the developer would have to bid up to this increased figure would depend on the assumptions made by others in the market who might be bidding for the site.

Example 4.1

Standard residual valuation block of flats (calculation 1)			
Completed value of 8 flats (£350,000 × 8)		2,800,000	
Less costs of sale (agents, legal fees, etc. – say 5%)	140,000		
Net sale proceeds		**2,660,000**	
Less costs:			
Pre-construction costs (planning, etc.)	20,000		
Demolition/construction @ approx £120,000 per flat	960,000		
Fees, etc. (based on build cost) @15%		144,000	
Interest on build costs @ 8%			76,800
Contingency @ 5%			55,200
Reward for risk @ 17.5% of build cost	180,120		
Total costs anticipated		**1,436,120**	
Balance available (residue)		**1,223,880**	
Less holding costs and purchase costs		112,918	
Assume 7% purchase costs and 1 year until sale completion discounted at 8%			
Available for land purchase		**1,110,963**	
Site value as % of GDV		40%	

Sustainability residual valuation block of flats (calculation 2)				
Completed value of 8 flats (£370,000 × 8)		2,960,000		
Less costs of sale (agents, legal fees, etc. – say 5%)	148,000			
Net sale proceeds			2,812,000	
Less costs:				
Pre-construction costs (planning, etc.)		20,000		
Demolition/construction @ approx £130,000 per flat		1,040,000		
Fees, etc. (based on build cost) @15%			156,000	
Interest on build costs @ 8%				83,200
Contingency @ 5%				59,800
Reward for risk @ 17.5% of build cost		194,880		
Total costs anticipated			1,553,880	
Balance available (residue)			1,258,120	
Less holding costs and purchase costs			116,077	
Assume 7% purchase costs and 1 year until sale completion discounted at 8%				
Available for land purchase			1,142,043	
Site value as % of GDV			39%	

EXAMPLE 4.2

A developer has the opportunity to purchase for the sum of £30,000,000 a site with a likely planning consent for 8,000 square metres (net internal area) of offices over eight retail units. There is no anticipated problem in gaining consent and the development is likely to let at £375 per square metre for offices and £125,000 per unit for the retail space. The likely yield profile is 5.25 per cent for the offices and 5 per cent for the shops. The developer wishes to calculate the likely return.

Example 4.2 calculations

Costs

Development	Office	Initial costs	
Letting area NIA	8,000 sq m	Planning	£20,000
Rent	£375 per sq m	Statutory	£1,250,000
Yield	5.25%	Building regulations	£20,000
Purchase costs	5.800%	Site investigation	£60,000
	Retail	Topographical	£10,000
Retail units	8	Environmental assessment	£125,000
Market rent per unit	£125,000	Gas	£15,000
Yield	5.00%	Electricity	£0
		BT	£25,000
		Water	£0
Site			
Site costs	£30,000,000		
Land agents fee	1.00%	**Letting and disposal fees**	
Stamp duty	4.00%	Legals and letting	12.00%
Legal fees	1.00%	Residential agents	1.00%
Construction costs		Marketing	£150,000
Offices		Sales fee	2%
Construction area	9,600 sq m	**Finance**	
Construction costs	£1,750 per sq m	Interest	6.50% p.a
Retail units		Quarterly	1.59%
Construction area GIA	150 sq m	Valuation fee	£10,000
Construction costs	£1,400 per sq m	Bank initial fee	1%
		Bank legals	£20,000
		Monitoring fee	£25,000
Contingency	5.00%	Land holding	27 months
Demolition	£80,000	Estimated development length (months)	24 months
Construction fees			
Initial fee	£300,000	Estimated void period (months)	3 months
Architect	4.00%		
Quantity surveyor	2.00%		
Project manager	2.00%		
Engineers	3.50%		
Total fees	**11.50%**		

Development value			
Gross development value			
Offices		Retail	
Market rent	£3,000,000	Market rent	£1,000,000
YP in perpetuity @5.25%	19.0476	YP in perpetuity @5%	20.0000
Capital value	£57,142,857	Capital value	£20,000,000
Total GDV	£77,142,857		
NDV (reflecting costs)	£72,913,854		

Source: Author, but based on Smith (2013)

Placing the calculations in Figure 4.7 into a cash flow (see Table 4.3) shows a most likely IRR of approximately 15.3 per cent per annum over the holding period and a profit (NPV) of just over £7.5 million which, even allowing for risk, is an acceptable return given the rate of opportunity cost of money.

If the developer is considering developing to a higher specification, to go beyond compliance to obtain either a LEED or BREEAM certification, costs are likely to be affected. However, the development value may or may not change. In every case, a full appraisal should be undertaken to see what the impact is on the eventual bottom line. As the commonly perceived cost addition for a more sustainable specification erodes, but rental values of yields are positively impacted, so developing to higher sustainability standards should become simple good business sense.

In the example above, were there to be a rent premium and the rents achievable to £375 per square metre for the offices and £145,000 per unit for the shops, with yields shaded downwards to 5.2 per cent and 4.9 per cent respectively, then even if costs per square metre rose to £2,200 there would be a positive impact on both the NPV and the IRR. The NPV would rise to £12,267,101 with IRRs of 4.64 per cent per quarter or 19.91 per cent per annum.

4.3.3 Building in sustainability

Building sustainability into the appraisal should in theory not be required as an explicit exercise: it should be embedded within a standard approach. However, that is not the typical practice yet, even though it does not require fresh modelling if the intention is simply to consider sustainability within the process as a matter of changed specification and influences on costs and the eventual value line. As markets sensitise, so the inputs to appraisal will adjust. However, it is noted that such approaches are not truly triple bottom line as they still undertake the appraisal through the lens of the commercial or financial stakeholder, be they a developer and investor or a commissioning owner-occupier.

4.4   Considering other stakeholders

Sayce et al. (2004) in their consideration of redevelopment/refurbishment decision-making, considered whether a much wider approach should be adopted and developed a matrix approach in which they advocated that decisions should be informed by the

Table 4.3 Cashflow calculations

Item	Quarter 1	Quarter 2	Quarter 3	Quarter 4	Quarter 5	Quarter 6	Quarter 7	Quarter 8	Quarter 9
Site cost	(30,000,000)								
Land agents fee	(300,000)								
Stamp duty	(1,200,000)								
legal fees	(300,000)								
Construction costs									
Offices		(1,176,000)	(1,680,000)	(2,856.000)	(5,376,000)	(2,856,000)	(1,680.000)	(1,176,000)	
Retail units		(117,600)	(168,000)	(285,600)	(537,600)	(285,600)	(168,000)	(117,600)	
Fees	(300,000)	(161,700)	(231,000)	(393,700)	(739,200)	(392,700)	(231,000)	(161,700)	
Contingency									
Additional costs (totalled)	(1,410,000)								
Services installation		(40,000)							
Legal and letting								(480,000)	
Marketing sales						(75,000)		(75,000)	
Sales fee									(1,458,277)
Finance and valuation fee, etc.	(610,145)								
NDV									72,913,854
Net cash flows	(34,255,145)	(1,568,065)	(2,182,950)	(3,711,015)	(6,985,440)	(3,786,015)	(2,182,950)	(2,083,065)	71,913,854
PV factor @7.5% p.a.	0.9844	0.9690	0.9539	0.9390	0.9243	0.9099	0.8956	0.8517	0.8679
PV'ed value	(33,720,065)	(1,519,460)	(2,082,244)	(3484,521)	(6,456,643)	(3,444,752)	(1,955.159)	(1,836,554)	62,015,394
NPV	7,515,998								
IRR per quarter	3.62%								
IRR p.a.	15.3%								

environmental, social and economic impacts on both 'internal or financial' stakeholders, such as investors and tenants and external stakeholders such as visitors and the community. Their conclusions were that developers should consider the wider negative and positive impacts of developments on all parties if sustainability objectives are truly to be achieved. There is some evidence that such thinking is being built into the views of leading investors, but not across the general markets. Evidence comes for the responsible property investment movement (UNEP FI 2009: 4), which advocates that when investing in development, decision-making should relate to:

- *Energy conservation*: conservation retrofitting, green power generation and purchasing, energy efficient design.
- *Environmental protection*: water conservation, solid waste recycling, habitat protection.
- *Voluntary certifications*: green building certification, certified sustainable wood finishes.
- *Public transport oriented developments*: transit oriented development, walkable communities, mixed-use development.
- *Urban revitalisation and adaptability*: infill development, flexible interiors, brownfield redevelopment.
- *Health and safety*: site security, avoidance of natural hazards, first aid readiness.
- *Worker wellbeing*: plazas, childcare facilities on the premises, indoor environmental quality, barrier-free design.
- *Corporate citizenship*: regulatory compliance, sustainability disclosure and reporting, independent boards, adoption of voluntary codes of ethical conduct, stakeholder engagement.
- *Social equity and community development*: fair labour practices, affordable/social housing, community hiring and training.
- *Local citizenship*: quality design, minimum neighbourhood impacts, considerate construction, community outreach, historic preservation, no undue influence on local governments.

It must be stressed that such decision-making criteria tends to be within the remit of only the largest investment houses. Whilst the criteria have been developed as qualitative measures and align well to the Global Reporting Initiative (GRI) reporting framework, it is difficult to place a single bottom line value on many of them but increasingly this is being attempted, primarily through the use of the Delphi research technique (see for example Pivo 2008; Barzilay *et al.* 2012) or even 'fuzzy' Delphi (Damigos and Anyfantis 2011). This evidence shows that, possibly over a longer term, a development that builds in more walkability and better design is more likely to achieve long-term success. Delphi research methodologies were originally developed in the 1970s by Linstone and Turoff (1975) and are increasingly adopted where uncertainty levels are high and forecasting is required. There are different variants but essentially they work through an iterative series of anonymous surveys of experts from differing knowledge bases in which, through iteration, consensus views are derived. Okoli and Pawlowski (2004) argue that Delphi offers four attributes which make it useful for forecasting; these include that the Delphi:

1   assists in establishing parameters and variables;
2   provides a means by which the specific can be generalised;

3   helps to determine causal relationships; and,
4   constructs validity.

Given the uncertainly that surrounds each element contained in a standard appraisal, Delphi does provide a non-statistically based approach by which large-scale development schemes could be evaluated and, as such, Delphi offers potential as an aid to sustainable property development decisions, encompassing as they can a full range of environmental, social and economic expertise. However, Delphi investigations are slow and potentially expensive and unless skilfully undertaken can be difficult to interpret. To date therefore, their use is not widespread and, within commercial development, approaches to inclusion of sustainability considerations are still primarily restricted to environmental matters, such as energy waste and water and to design and construction. Little evidence has been found of longer-term sustainability management issues pervading private sector development appraisal decision-making.

4.5   Pigouvian taxation

The other prime method used to encourage greater sustainability through private sector developments is through the use of taxation or incentives to mitigate or eliminate the socially or environmentally harmful costs of development that create so-called 'spillover' costs on society. These impacts or externalities are taken into account in the private sector only through consideration of social responsibility principles or priced in (internalised) through regulation or taxation. For example, as explored through Chapter 5, the costs to society are often imposed on developers through a development tax or levy.

Such taxes, known as Pigouvian taxes, after the economist who first promoted them in the eighteenth century (see for example Anderson 1993; Panayotou 2013), can help promote sustainability by:

* incentivising more sustainable behaviour which reduces the externality;
* minimising the social cost; and,
* providing the funding for mitigation.

However, social costs can be difficult to measure accurately: they may be possible to evade and can have collection costs outweighing the revenue. Burge and Ihlanfeldt (2013), arguing for impact (Pigouvian) local taxes, summarise the types of externalities that they argue are most appropriately addressed through the imposition of local impact taxes. These are:

* *Non-conforming land uses.* Sometimes these can lead to value reduction in the locality. A typical example of this might be the siting of an anaerobic digester or a waste incinerator linked to fuel generation, which in itself could be argued to be sustainable developments but which could lead to potentially reduced property prices in the vicinity.
* *Destruction of open space amenity.* Whilst in many counties there is a requirement to prioritise redevelopment of previously developed land, inevitably many new developments result in the loss of 'greenfield' land with negative impacts on people's health and wellbeing and potential loss in biodiversity terms.
* *Congestion.* Perhaps one of the first externalities to be recognised, traffic congestion can have serious economic, environmental and social impacts. Largely controlled through

regulation, congestion charges, such as that introduced in London, have had positive effects on air quality and travel times. Within development, the imposition of 'green travel plans' seeks to minimise external dis-benefits.

- *Compromised public infrastructure.* With new development, particularly residential, comes increased pressure on infrastructure such as schools, clinics and other local amenities. Local taxes, such as the UK's Community Infrastructures Levy (see below), provide mechanisms to ensure local facilities are enhanced.
- *Degradation of environmental quality.* Development inevitably has environmental impacts, whether this be in terms of increasing local flood risk, increasingly climatic 'urban heat island' effects or the destruction of vegetation with carbon consequences. Good design and the incorporation of e.g. green roofs and rain gardens can help but adaptation schemes may be required at high cost.

Within the UK, two principal processes are in place to assist in mitigating the externalities of development. The first are Planning Obligation agreements entered into under the Town and Country Planning Act 1990 (as amended), commonly known as s106 agreements, or developer's contributions. They relate to site specific mitigation, often in relation to biodiversity measures and the inclusion on site of affordable housing and provide a mechanism to make a development acceptable where it would otherwise not be so. Community Infrastructure Levy (CIL), introduced as a discretionary charge under the UK's Localism Act (2011), enables local authorities to establish a levy on developments, through a process of independent scrutiny, the cost of infrastructure requirements necessitated by private and public sector development, including social facilities, transport infrastructure and including local training and skills development. A special feature of CIL is that it enables communities at a local level to determine what type of development they wish to encourage (by a zero or low charge) and those which they deem place a higher burden but produce greater developers' profit (by a higher charge). As such, both internalise the external cost to society and, arguably, promote sustainability.

More generally, a range of carbon related taxes are employed through the development process in many countries, such as the Carbon Reduction Commitment in the UK, and the EU Emissions Trading Scheme all aimed at offsetting the negative externalities of development (see carbontax.org for information on various tax structures). In the US, there is no national carbon tax, though it does exist in some states. A carbon tax was introduced in Australia in 2012 but repealed in 2014, since when it has been reported in the Pitt and Sherry CEDEX index that emissions have started to rise again (http://www.pittsh.com.au/assets/files/Cedex/CEDEX%20Report%20Sept%202014.pdf).

However, the measures outlined above, whilst they represent costs to developers will not necessarily change commercial decision-making; they will only do this if mindsets change or compliance costs escalate or new, social value oriented techniques are adopted. Within developed countries, standard commercial developments do not tend to undertake social evaluation. However, within large complex schemes in developing countries, this is commonly undertaken, partly due to requirements of funders who wish to fully appreciate the risks involved; partly because such schemes are frequently partially public sector financed. For example, the International Finance Corporation has since 2003, been advocating the inclusion of social impact criteria on development decisions (IFC 2003). However, it tends to only be in the public sector where appraisal techniques that embrace a true triple bottom line are most commonly to be found as a routine approach.

4.6   Public sector methodologies

Public sector developments have long been required to take a much wider perspective as the public interest is of paramount concern. As Van Hagen (2006, but quoted in Ergas and Robson 2009) states 'The core of public finance is that some people spend other people's money'. This means that governments are required to take a responsible attitude and consider all stakeholders within the project appraisal process. It therefore requires them to consider spillover costs and ensure that such externalities are fully accounted for in the appraisal.

Within the UK, there is a commitment that where public monies are to be used they 'should be subject to comprehensive but proportionate assessment, wherever it is practicable, so as best to promote the public interest' (HM Treasury 2003: 1). Other countries also espouse these principles though whether they succeed is a far less settled point. Indeed, Ergas and Robson (2009), writing in relation to major infrastructure projects in Australia, concluded that such projects were sometimes undertaken without rigorous assessment and without the transparency that, they argue, should underpin decisions and would indeed be required to fulfil any serious notion of social sustainability.

4.6.1 Cost-benefit analysis

The most widely utilised approach to development appraisal is cost-benefit analysis (CBA) (Prest and Turvey, 1965). In essence, as Mishan and Quah (2007: 5) state, cost-benefit analysis does not ask different questions from those posed in the private sector: what it does do is ask them on behalf of society and it asks them more searchingly. For profit, social benefit is substituted and direct costs are augmented to include the opportunity costs imposed by the development. However, simple though this may appear in principle, benefits and costs are seldom distributed evenly and whilst, using the *pareto principle* of uneven inputs/outputs to obtain optimal net benefit, a project may appear viable, for individuals who suffer costs outweighing benefits, compensation may be appropriate. For example a new rail or airport scheme may bring economic benefits to a country and social benefits in terms of ease of travel for many people, but those living under the flight path or alongside the track may suffer noise and other pollution issues. Frequently, compensation to such people has either not been forthcoming or has been inadequate to provide full recompense. Despite attempts to deal with this, even in countries where codification is advanced, such as the UK, whilst those who are dispossessed *may* receive adequate compensation, those who are adversely affected but who have no land taken, may not be adequately treated (see for example Denyer-Green 2013). Even when land is taken, the ability to provide appropriate and adequate compensation rests on the ability to provide a fair market value (for an illustration of some of the issues involved see for example Kalbro and Lind 2007).

From the above, it can be seen that the calculation of costs imposed by a scheme can be extremely difficult. Calculating benefits can be equally challenging. For example a scheme may have the estimated benefit that it will reduce poverty in an area or improve public health. The questions are, by how much and over what period of time? The benefit of better health may be measurable in terms of reduction in costs to medical facilities and the prolongation of life, but that could increase the cost of pensions or other social support.

It follows that CBA is not an exact science and a methodology or group of methodologies has to be exercised with caution. However, possibly the most difficult issue surrounding CBA, is in the treatment of the discount rate (Almansa and Martínez-Paz 2011;Pearce *et al.* 2013). The theoretical arguments surrounding the choice of discount rate are complex and result in widely differing approaches. In essence, if the aim of sustainable development is that the needs of future generations are considered within decision-making, the question is should their quantified needs, which inevitably have uncertainty attached to them, carry the same weight as those of current populations? If it is concluded that they should be given equal weight then, in equity, no discounting should be applied. However, such an approach is hardly practical and fails to pick up the issue of uncertainty so even Stern (2007), who veered towards such an approach in his analysis of the economics of climate change, worked on a discount rate of 1.4 per cent. Such an approach has been challenged (Nordhaus 2007) and, for example, there is a school of thought that promotes use of financial discount rates, even though it is acknowledged that they may be flawed (Beckerman and Hepburn 2007).

Freeman and Groom (2013) in their useful case study of biodiversity valuations, calculate the significance of adoption of different discount rate approaches and conclude that, for schemes which involve long-term environmental considerations, financially based discount rates, such as those advocated through the UK Treasury's Green Book (HM Treasury 2003) are inappropriate for the following reasons:

• The implications of the decision are long-term but financial bond rates are essentially short-term. As they argue, applying a 30-year bond rate to a 300 year forestry scheme is clearly problematic.
• Financial rates are determined by only the wealthiest in society, not society at large; and,
• Financial rates relate to private sector profit motives, not to community benefit.

For some schemes this is undoubtedly the case; however, for many infrastructure projects where technology or social trends will impose a shorter life, a more commercially driven discount rate could be considered appropriate, but only if the costs of restoration of the facility are fully accounted for.

4.6.2 Preference theory

The value of a cost-benefit analysis depends on the accuracy of the individual cost and benefit estimates; however, this is often not the case (Adler and Posner 1999; Ackerman and Heinzerling 2002) and where objective costs/benefits cannot be obtained, more subjective approaches have to be undertaken. Key among the approaches taken are preference theories.

The most widely used of these within the development appraisal decision process is stated preference or contingent valuation. This technique, developed over half a century ago, relies on survey methodology in which people are asked the value to them of assets which lack a readily established market value, such as the value of an historic landscape. Such surveys work in one of two ways: either the willingness to pay (WTP) (i.e. the benefit) for something, such as a new road or the preservation of a right of way or a willingness to accept being deprived of something. Contingent valuation methods have been widely adopted for schemes that have spillover effects. However, whilst in theory they are laudable and may be the only practical approach, they are not without difficulty, not least in the construction of an appropriate questionnaire and in achieving a good, unbiased sample. There is also the simple issue of human behaviour: what people actually *do* is frequently not the same as what they *say* they will do. For example, a WTP analysis may show that there would be a reluctance to pay for car-parking in an area previously open to public access; however, the reality if the scheme goes ahead may be quite different with pricing proving to demonstrate an inelastic demand. Whilst such techniques have been widely used as part of CBA, their use has been developed into the field of compensation following the adoption of the technique in the case of the Exxon Valdez oil spill (Carson *et al.* 2003) which was an unprecedented environmental disaster.

The challenges and frequent lack of accuracy of WTP techniques have given credence to the alternative approach: revealed preference. First developed by Samuelson (Samuelson 1938 reviewed by Wong 2006; Varian 2006) revealed preference works in retrospect, using what people *actually* pay as an indicator of its value. However, Beshears *et al.* (2008) argue that both revealed and stated preferences may differ from each other and be less than reliable as decision-making tools as they: involve passive choice (i.e. they are not immediately affected), complexity, may be based on limited personal experience/knowledge, may be subject to third-party marketing pressure and, importantly to the notion of sustainable development, involve inter-temporal choice. Notwithstanding these criticisms, the whole notion of public sector projects that have long timespans and significant triple bottom line impacts is difficult. A further development of preference theory application is to use both stated and implied together (Whitehead *et al.* 2012). Whilst preference theories do not present ideal or comprehensive answers they are a part of the armoury of the analyst.

As stated above, CBA and the methods that lie behind it are primarily a public sector approach. However, with the wider adoption of triple bottom line principles and the growth of public private partnership developments and the increased use of 'green' taxation measures, the over-arching principles and methods are increasingly required of those working with private sector schemes.

4.7   Ecosystems appraisal

No consideration of sustainable development appraisal would be complete without mention of ecosystem services as their analysis and appraisal is now increasing in national and international importance and in many ways is an application of and extension to CBA (Wegner and Pascual 2011). Ecosystem services (ESS) are those services currently or potentially provided by nature whose presence, in single bottom line terms, may have little value, but in terms of wider implications has significant value in terms of environmental protection. A commonly quoted example, studied by Barbier (2007), concerns mangrove swamps in Thailand. Due to development pressures and the greater economic value that can be obtained by draining them for use as shrimp farms, the area of land occupied by swamps has fallen significantly (Spalding *et al.* 2010). However, the development appraisals which have supported the change of use to what would be termed by valuers as 'highest and best use' (Corps 2007) has led to environmental damage and risk as mangrove swamps are extremely effective as coastal protection measures, including protection from tsunamis (Alongi 2008). The argument is therefore powerful that although to an *individual* the value of a swamp is low and likely to be enhanced by drainage and change of use to intensive farming, in terms of the national economy this is simply not the case. More recently issues relating to the extraction of shale gas have been linked with similar ecosystem concerns (Phillips and Goldberg 2013).

As awareness of the value of ecosystems to protect and enhance the environment grows so the issue of payment for ecosystem services (PES) has developed. For example if a residential or commercial development leads to greater surface run-off putting pressure on drainage systems and increasing the possibility of flooding, so land which can act as a flood plain should be valued as a holistic part of the development. Some version of PES has been introduced in more than 25 countries around the world including Australia, Germany and the US (DEFRA 2013a). It is currently considered 'best practice' in the UK but is not compulsory (DEFRA 2013b). The concept of PES is shown diagrammatically in Figure 4.6.

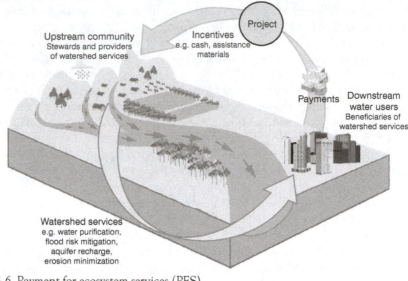

Figure 4.6 Payment for ecosystem services (PES)
Source: DEFRA (2013: 13)

If a PES process is introduced, the buyers are those who are the beneficiaries – those who are willing to pay for the ecosystem services to be safeguarded, enhanced or restored – and sellers are land and resource managers/owners whose actions can potentially secure supply of the beneficial service. This would mean that the market value of the previously low value land (such as the mangrove swamp or river flood plain) would accrue a higher value within its existing use, thus both facilitating development elsewhere and acting as a protection against future development. This approach, the beneficiary pays principle, in the form of biodiversity offsetting, could be regarded as a natural furtherance of the long-established 'polluter pays principle'. Whilst undoubtedly PES may well be regarded as yet another brake on the ambitions of developers, if it results in a slowing down or reversal of environmental degradation, it will reap long-term benefits to investors and occupiers alike.

4.8   Conclusion

Appraisal is a fundamental part of the development decision-making process, but like any other property valuation it is not a certain science. Essentially development will only take place if those commissioning the scheme will extract economic or/and social value from it sufficient to cover the costs, allowing for risks inherent in the process. As approaches towards the analysis of risk/return have become more sophisticated so there has been a tendency for appraisals to be undertaken by use of DCF approaches as well as through conventional residual approaches.

Within the private sector, owner-occupiers may not be looking for a profit: their concern is to produce a property that meets their needs. Non-domestic owner-occupiers will be mindful of the eventual market value – except where the development is of a type not normally sold in the market such as a specialised manufacturing plant, an educational or research facility, etc., where there is no choice but to build in order to carry out their function. However, in the domestic sector, the value may lie in personal aspiration or fulfilment, and viability in conventional terms may be a secondary consideration.

For most private sector developers, however, the profit motivation is critical. In conventional development appraisal practice there is no one standard model in terms of how this is calculated; much will depend on the strength of competition for the development opportunity and on the appetite for risk. To some developers, building to higher sustainability standards is seen as a market opportunity and the possibility of extracting a higher development value; however, the evidence of price differential based on the level of sustainability may or may not support any differential in costs. Arguments flow in both directions: both the cost premium and the value differentiation. Perhaps, the best conclusion to draw from this is to refer back to the fact that property is a heterogeneous product whose pricing will always be difficult to predict and which can change significantly over the development period if the economic environment changes.

Over time, building standards are changing, as the planning and the regulatory framework as well as public opinion and the knowledge base of clients and their advisory teams change. Therefore the current 'sustainable' building label will increasingly become the norm. However, sustainable property development is a far wider concept than building materials and production. It relates to its context and importantly to the impact of the building on its wider setting, through the imposition of external costs and benefits. These have not conventionally been included within the concept of development appraisal except insofar as Pigouvian and other taxes are imposed to transfer community losses resulting from the development back to the development, which should, in theory, result in decreasing land values as development costs rise. The challenge to this is that, if taxation or the transfer of external costs reduce either, or both, profitability or land values, the incentive to develop is reduced, this is turn can lead to a lack of new supply and demand-led pressures.

In the public sector, development appraisals are normally undertaken using cost-benefit analysis and related techniques such as preference theory. The challenge here is that the schemes undertaken require justification in social terms, tend to be large-scale and long-term. Therefore the prediction of both costs and benefits are problematic.

Most recently, wider considerations of sustainability are under debate, notably in the shape of ecosystems appraisal which seeks a new way to consider externalities and allow reconsideration of development schemes which might yield short-term benefits but have long-term ecological damage. Whilst such a 'beneficiary pays' approach as it is sometimes regarded could act as a further brake on development by increasing costs and time, if deeper levels of sustainability are to be achieved, it will be required.

Notes

1 See for example http://www.projectsmart.co.uk/docs/monte-carlo-simulation.pdf.
2 http://www.solver.com/risk-solver.

References

Ackerman, F. and Heinzerling, L. (2002) Pricing the priceless: cost-benefit analysis of environmental protection, *University of Pennsylvania Law Review*, 5: 1553–1584.

Adler, M.D. and Posner, E.A. (1999) Rethinking cost-benefit analysis, *Yale Law Journal*, 109(2): 165–247.

Alexander, F.S. and Housing, A. (2011) Land banks and land banking, *Center for Community Progress* 18.

Almansa, C. and Martínez-Paz, J.M. (2011) What weight should be assigned to future environmental impacts? A probabilistic cost-benefit analysis using recent advances on discounting, *Science of the Total Environment* 409(7): 1305–1314.

Alongi, D.M. (2008) Mangrove forests: resilience, protection from tsunamis, and responses to global climate change, *Estuarine, Coastal and Shelf Science* 76(1): 1–13.

Anderson, J.E. (1993) Land development, externalities, and Pigouvian taxes, *Journal of Urban Economics* 33(1): 1–9.

Barbier, E.B. (2007) Valuing ecosystem services as productive inputs, *Economic Policy* 22(49): 177–229.

Barker, K. (2004) *The Barker Review: Supply of Land: Securing our Future*, London: HM Treasury.

Barzilay, B., Schnell, I., and Portnov, B.A. (2012) Estimating the effect of location externalities on real estate values using the Delphi method, *Territorio Italia, Rivista dell'Agenzia del Territorio* 2012(2): 22–35. Retrieved from http://www.agenziaentrate.gov.it/wps/file/Nsilib/Nsi/Documentazione/Archivio/Territorio+Italia/Archivio+Territorio+Italia+-+English+version/Territorio+Italia+2+2012/metodo+Delphi/eng_Estimating+the+Effect+of+Location.pdf.

Baum, A.E. and Hartzell, D. (2012) *Global Property Investment: Strategies, Structures, Decisions*, Hoboken, NJ: John Wiley & Sons.

Baum, A., Mackmin, D., and Nunnington, N. (2011) *The Income Approach to Property Valuation*, Abingdon: Taylor & Francis.

Beaman, M (2014) *Development, Viability and Planning*. Retrieved from http://www.regenerate.co.uk/Viability%20&%20Planning.pdf.

Beckerman, W. and Hepburn, C. (2007) Ethics of the discount rate in the Stern Review on the economics of climate change, *World Economics* 8(1): 187.

Beshears, J., Choi, J.J., Laibson, D., and Madrian, B.C. (2008) How are preferences revealed?, *Journal of Public Economics* 92(8): 1787–1794.

Blackledge, M (2009) *Introducing Property Valuation*, London: Routledge.

Brigstocke, C. (2013) *Time for a French Lesson*. Retrieved from http://www.squiresanders.com/green-leases-time-for-a-french-lesson.

Burge, G.S., and Ihlanfeldt, K.R. (2013) Promoting sustainable land development patterns through impact fee programs, *Cityscape*, 15(1): 83–105.

Cadman, D. (2000) The vicious circle of blame, in M. Keeping (ed.), *What about Demand? Do Investors Want 'Sustainable Buildings'*, London: RICS.

Cajias, M. and Piazolo, D. (2013) Green performs better: energy efficiency and financial return on buildings, *Journal of Corporate Real Estate* 15(1): 53–72.

Carson, R.T., Mitchell, R.C., Hanemann, M., Kopp, R.J., Presser, S., and Ruud, P.A. (2003) Contingent valuation and lost passive use: damages from the Exxon Valdez oil spill, *Environmental and Resource Economics* 25(3): 257–286.

Chegut, A., Eichholtz, P., and Kok, N. (2013) Supply, demand and the value of green buildings, *Urban Studies*, doi: 0042098013484526.

Coleman, C., Crosby, N., McAllister, P., and Wyatt, P. (2013) Development appraisal in practice: some evidence from the planning system, *Journal of Property Research* 30(2): 144–165.

Corps, C. (2007) *Mangrove Conservation vs. Shrimp Farming in Thailand: A Case Study*. Retrieved from http://vancouveraccord.org/media/2261/vva_case_study_2.pdf.

Craine, T. (2012) *Barriers to Housing Development: What Are the Market-perceived Barriers to Residential Development in London? The Molior Report for the Greater London Council*. Retrieved from https://www.google.co.uk/#q=Molior+report+on+Barriers+to+Housing+Delivery+in++London+(2012).

Damigos, D. and Anyfantis, F. (2011) The value of view through the eyes of real estate experts: a fuzzy Delphi approach, *Landscape and Urban Planning* 101(2): 171–178.

Das, P., Tidwell, A., and Ziobrowski, A. (2011) Dynamics of green rentals over market cycles: evidence from commercial office properties in San Francisco and Washington DC, *Journal of Sustainable Real Estate* 3(1): 1–22.

Davis Langdon (2007) *The Cost and Benefit of Achieving Green Buildings*, Sydney: Davis Langdon.

Denyer-Green, B. (2013) *Compulsory Purchase and Compensation*, Abingdon: Taylor & Francis.

Department of Environment, Food and Rural Affairs (DEFRA) (2013a) *Payments for Ecosystem Services: A Best Practice Guide.* Retrieved from https://www.gov.uk/government/uploads/system/uploads/attachment_data/file/200920/pb13932-pes-bestpractice-20130522.pdf.

Department of Environment, Food and Rural Affairs (DEFRA) (2013b) *Biodiversity Offsetting in England: A Green Paper.* Retrieved from https://consult.defra.gov.uk/biodiversity/biodiversity_offsetting/supporting_documents/20130903Biodiversity%20offsetting%20green%20paper.pdf.

Dubben, N. (2008) unpublished lecture material.

Dubben, N. (2009) Development properties, in R. Haywar (ed.), *Valuation: Principles into Practice*, London: Estates Gazette.

Edwards, B.W. and Naboni, E. (2013) *Green Buildings Pay: Design, Productivity and Ecology*, London: Routledge.

Eichholtz, P., Kok, N., and Quigley, J.M. (2013) The economics of green building, *Review of Economics and Statistics* 95(1): 50–63.

Elkington, J. (1997) Cannibals with forks. *The Triple Bottom Line of 21st Century.* Chichester: Capstone Publishing.

Ergas, H. and Robson, A. (2009) The social losses from inefficient infrastructure projects: recent Australian experience, *Productivity Commission Round Table on Strengthening Evidence-Based Policy in the Australian Federation (August)*.

Freeman, M.C. and Groom, B. (2013) Biodiversity valuation and the discount rate problem. *Accounting, Auditing & Accountability Journal* 26(5): 715–745.

Fuerst, F., Van de Wetering, J., and Wyatt, P. (2013a) Is intrinsic energy efficiency reflected in the pricing of office leases? *Building Research & Information* 41(4): 373–383.

Fuerst, F., McAllister, P., Nanda, A., and Wyatt, P. (2013b) Is energy efficiency priced in the housing market? Some evidence from the United Kingdom. Retrieved from http://centaur.reading.ac.uk/31737/1/wp0113.pdf.

GVA Grimley (2009) *UK Offices: Refurbishment vs. Redevelopment.* Retrieved from http://www.propertyweek.com/Journals/Builder_Group/Property_Week/12_February_2010/attachments/Research%20Refurb%20v%20Rebuild%20FINAL.pdf.

HM Treasury (2003) *The Green Book: Appraisal and Evaluation in Central Government*, London: HM Treasury available from https://www.gov.uk/government/uploads/system/uploads/attachment_data/file/220541/green_book_complete.pdf.

Hinnells, M., Bright, S., Langley, A., Woodford, L., Schiellerup, P., and Bosteels, T. (2008) The greening of commercial lease, *Journal of Property Investment & Finance* 26(6): 541–551.

Home Builders Federation (2014) *Permissions to Land: Busting the Myths about House Builders and 'Land Banking'.* Retrieved from http://www.hbf.co.uk/fileadmin/documents/research/HBF_Report_-_Landbanking_May.pdf.

International Finance Corporation (IFC) (2003) *Good Practice Note 3: Addressing the Social Dimensions of Private Sector Projects.* Retrieved from www.apho.org.uk/resource/view.aspx?RID=93782.

Isaac D. and O'Leary, J. (2013) *Property Valuation Techniques*, Basingstoke: Palgrave-Macmillan.

Kalbro, T. and Lind, H. (2007) Compulsory purchase–reasonable and fair compensation, *Nordic Journal of Surveying and Real Estate Research* 4(1): 7–22.

Kats, G. (2003) *Green Building Costs and Financial Benefits*, Boston, MA: Massachusetts Technology Collaborative, p. 1.

Keeping, M. (2000, September) What about demand? Do investors want 'sustainable buildings'?, in *Proceedings of Cutting Edge 2000 Conference*, pp. 6–8.

Land Registry (2012) *Public Guide 21 – Land Banking Schemes – Warning – Plots of Land in England and Wales Offered for Sale Claimed to Have Development or Investment Potential.* Retrieved from http://www.landregistry.gov.uk/public/guides/public-guide-21#sthash.8uCG4RtN.dpuf.

Linstone, H.A. and Turoff, M. (eds) (1975) *The Delphi Method: Techniques and Applications*, Vol. 29, Reading, MA: Addison-Wesley.

Lorenz, D. and Lützkendorf, T. (2008). Sustainability in property valuation: theory and practice, *Journal of Property Investment & Finance*, 26(6): 482–521.

Lützkendorf, T. and Habil, D. (2010) How to break the vicious circle of blame? The contribution of different stakeholders to a more sustainable built environment, in *Abstract Book of Sustainable Building 2012 Brazil Conference*, Hoboken, NJ: John Wiley and Sons.

Menezes, A.C., Cripps, A., Bouchlaghem, D., and Buswell, R. (2012) Predicted vs. actual energy performance of non-domestic buildings: using post-occupancy evaluation data to reduce the performance gap, *Applied Energy* 97: 355–364.

Mishan, E. J., and Quah, E. (2007). *Cost Benefit Analysis*, London: Routledge.

Nordhaus, W.D. (2007) A Review of the 'Stern Review on the Economics of Climate Change', *Journal of Economic Literature*, 45(3): 686–702.

Oberle, K. and Sloboda, M. (2010) The importance of 'greening' your commercial lease, *Real Estate Issues* 35(1): 32.

Office of Fair Trading (2008) *Homebuilding in the UK: A Market Study*, London: The Office of Fair Trading.

Okoli, C. and Pawlowski, S.D. (2004) The Delphi method as a research tool: an example, design considerations and applications, *Information & Management* 42(1): 15–29.

Panayotou, T. (2013) *Instruments of Change: Motivating and Financing Sustainable Development*, London: Routledge.

Pearce, D., Barbier, E., and Markandya, A. (2013) *Sustainable Development: Economics and Environment in the Third World*, London: Routledge.

Phillips, S.K. and Goldberg, M.S. (2013) *Natural Gas Development: Extracting Externalities-Towards Precaution-Based Decision-Making*. Retrieved from http://www.mcgill.ca/jsdlp/sites/mcgill.ca.jsdlp/files/jsdlp_2013_volume_8_issue_2_151_204.pdf.

Pivo, G. (2008) Responsible property investment criteria developed using the Delphi Method, *Building Research & Information* 36(1): 20–36.

Pivo, G. and McNamara, P. (2005). Responsible property investing. *International Real Estate Review*, 8(1): 128–143.

Power, T. (2004) *Lease Arrangements for Green Commercial Buildings*, Freehills. Retrieved from http://www.freehills.com.au/1917.

Prest, A.R. and Turvey, R. (1965) Cost-benefit analysis: a survey, *The Economic Journal*, 37(300): 683–735.

RICS (2007) *Code of Measuring Practice*, sixth edn, Coventry: RICS Books.

RICS (2008) *The Valuation of Development Land*, Valuation Information Paper 12, London: RICS.

RICS (2010) *The Valuation of Land for Affordable Housing: A Guidance Note*, GN 59/2012, first edn, London: RICS.

RICS (2011) *Sustainability and residential property valuation*, information paper, RICS Practice Standards, London: RICS.

RICS (2012) *Comparable Evidence in Property Valuation: A Guidance Note*, IP 26/2012, first edn, London: RICS.

RICS (2013) *Sustainability and Commercial Property Valuation*, London: RICS.

RICS (2014) *RICS Valuation – Professional Standards January 2014*, London: RICS.

Roussac, A.C. and Bright, S. (2012) Improving environmental performance through innovative commercial leasing: an Australian case study. *International Journal of Law in the Built Environment* 4(1): 6–22.

Samuelson P.A.A. (1938) Note on the pure theory of consumer's behaviour, *Economica* 5: 61–71.

Sayce, S., Walker, A., and MacIntosh, A (2004) *Building Sustainability in the Balance: Promoting Stakeholder Dialogue*, London: Estates Gazette.

Sayce, S., Smith, J., Cooper, R., and Venmore-Rowland, P. (2006) *Real Estate Appraisal: From Value to Worth*. Chichester: John Wiley & Sons.

Sayce, S., Sundberg, A., Parnell, P., and Cowling, E. (2009a) Greening leases: do tenants in the United Kingdom want green leases?, *Journal of Retail & Leisure Property* 8(4): 273–284.

Sayce, S., Smith, J., Cooper, R., and Venmore-Rowland, P. (2009b) *Real Estate Appraisal: From Value to Worth*, Hoboken, NJ: John Wiley & Sons.

Sayce, S., Sundberg, A., and Clements, B. (2010) *Is Sustainability Reflected in Commercial Property Prices: An Analysis of the Evidence Base*, London: RICS

Smith, P. J. (2013) The valuation of property investments. unpublished material.

Spalding, M., Spalding, M., Kainuma, M., and Collins, L. (2010) *World Atlas of Mangroves*, London: Earthscan.

Stern, N. (ed.) (2007) *The Economics of Climate Change: The Stern Review*, Cambridge: Cambridge University Press.

UNEP FI (2009) *Responsible Property Investing: What the Leaders are Doing*. Retrieved from http://www.unepfi.org/fileadmin/documents/responsible_property_investing_01.pdf.

Van der Krabben, E. and Jacobs, H.M. (2013) Public land development as a strategic tool for redevelopment: reflections on the Dutch experience, *Land Use Policy* 30(1): 774–783.

Van Hagen, J. (2006) Political economy of fiscal institutions, in B.R. Weingast and D.A. Wittman (eds), *The Oxford Handbook of Political Economy*, New York: Oxford University Press.

Varian, H.R. (2006) Revealed preference, in M. Szenberg, L.B. Ramrattan, and A. Gottesman (eds), *Samuelsonian Economics and the Twenty-first Century*, Oxford: Oxford University Press.

Walls, M., Palmer, K. L., and Gerarden, T. (2013). Is energy efficiency capitalized into home prices? Evidence from three US cities. Resources for the Future Discussion Paper 13–18. Retrieved from http://www.rff.org/RFF/Documents/RFF-DP-13-18.pdf.

WCED (World Commission on Environment and Development) (1987) *Our Common Future*. Retrieved from http://www.un-documents.net/our-common-future.pdf

Wegner, G. and Pascual, U. (2011) Cost-benefit analysis in the context of ecosystem services for human well-being: a multidisciplinary critique, *Global Environmental Change* 21(2): 492–504.

Whitehead, J., Haab, T., and Huang, J.C. (ed.) (2012) *Preference Data for Environmental Valuation: Combining Revealed and Stated Approaches*, Vol. 31, London: Routledge.

Wong, S. (2006) *Foundations of Paul Samuelson's Revealed Preference Theory: A Study by the Method of Rational Reconstruction*, London: Routledge.

World Green Building Council (WGBC) (2013) *The Business Case for Green Buildings*. Retrieved from http://www.worldgbc.org/files/1513/6608/0674/Business_Case_For_Green_Building_Report_WEB_2013-04-11.pdf.

5 Financing the project

Economic incentives promoting sustainable property development

Chris Eves, Sara J. Wilkinson and Sarah L. Sayce

5.0 Introduction

This chapter is focused on the various financial instruments and incentives that have been implemented in a range of countries to encourage sustainable developments in all property sectors. It is an area that has undergone substantial change globally since 2008. Sustainable property development has been impacted by the Global Financial Crisis, particularly with regard to the availability of private sector funding and the requirements of funders who now have a more cautious approach to risk. Sustainability, and sometimes a lack of it, is increasingly viewed as a risk in some markets; it is also seen as an area in which governments, through creation of markets and through the use of fiscal instruments can seek to speed up the pace at which the economics of sustainable development makes good business sense. However, it is not just governments that provide the incentive for sustainability – or the disincentive for non-sustainable behaviours. Private sector funding too has a role to play, although it currently remains the case that public sector finance and government policies are the real core to achieving sustainability. This can be delivered directly, through public sector funding (for example housing finance), joint venture (JV) or Public Private Partnership (PPP) schemes. Alternatively it can be delivered through reverse funding for public sector development through Private Finance Initiative (PFI). Each approach is discussed in the chapter.

In recognition of the need to pump prime sustainability behaviours many governments have introduced incentive schemes to encourage voluntary high sustainability standards in property developments, or to stimulate refurbishments; either in, or out, of cycle. Panayotou (2013) details comprehensively the ways in which governments can change behaviours through economic measures. These can be summarised by:

- the creation of market-based instruments such as tradable emissions or tradable water schemes;
- the use of fiscal measures which either reward good behaviours (grants for installation of renewables) or penalise bad behaviours (carbon taxes for example);
- simple charging schemes such as landfill taxes;
- outright bans on certain products (such as CFCs, building controls over materials use and building standards).

In reality, governments will normally choose to do a combination and additionally will aim that the private sector will respond proactively. It is outside the scope of this book to provide a comprehensive and detailed analysis of the current schemes and funding mechanisms which are available to developers. However, some of the major routes to development finance and the incentives to changed behaviours are covered, together with the principles of conventional property development finance.

The level of sustainable development in the built environment is still minute compared to the overall building stock. The percentage of 'green' buildings among recent developments in mature property markets has increased though it is restricted to small sectors of the stock, primarily to those developed for government, institutional or major corporate clients all of whom have a heightened awareness of the issue and whose legislation and incentive regimes are providing 'nudges' towards more sustainable behaviours. This chapter explores how, if at all, the financing of developments is shifting in line with occupational and investment awareness.

5.1   Principles of funding property development

5.1.1 *Historic and global perspective*

Property development is cyclical and driven by the demand for property in particular sectors (Chinloy 1996; Barras 2005). The level of development is influenced by the current economic climate for that particular property type and is tied to a property cycle. During periods of higher economic activity when demand is anticipated to increase, if there is sufficient money supply to fund development, activity will increase. There is extensive literature on the property cycle, with most authors considering that cycles are discernible, inevitable and of extreme significance.

The point about finance is critical – the supply must be there and the lending criteria sufficiently flexible to embrace development risk. Lenders have differing risk profiles. The most important source of lending for development traditionally is bank debt. Banks normally undertake first-tier lending, that is, lending that is sourced from money that the bank already has in its reserves to support all the risks it takes. If first-tier lending is not available or is insufficient, developers will be required to obtain second-tier debt, i.e. debt obtained from slightly less secure sources, often at a higher rate of interest. During periods of boom, lenders can often be tempted to breach their own prudence rules by increasing the loan to value (LTV) ratios that they normally observe, in attempts to gain the lending business, thus sowing seeds for inflated pricing and potential busts. Davis and Zhu (2011) in their work on cross-country influences on property prices concluded that GDP and bank credit play an important role in the determination of property prices. Ellis *et al.* (2012), in their analysis of the global crash of 2012 argue that the distress which follows a 'bust' is caused to a large extent, not by falls in value *per se*, but by the credit constraints which are normally put in place, thus restricting the ability to trade on assets.

While the demand for property in a sector remains strong, development finance is readily available encouraging inexperienced participants to enter into property development. When the increased supply of the property type coincides with a decrease in demand, the sector enters a plateau or decline stage in the property cycle. Generally at this stage, there is a correction in property prices to encourage sales. This decrease in property prices reduces the overall asset value of the property, reduces the potential profit from the development and, in serious cases, an overall negative value in the property development. Once a development is worth less than the finance used to purchase and develop the site, the lender will take action under their mortgage to recoup the funds borrowed. Whenever a financier suffers a significant loss in the property development sector, they will reassess their lending policies to reduce further risk in that particular property sector.

The most recent property cycle downturn is evidenced in the Global Financial Crisis (GFC) that commenced in late 2007 and is still impacting on a number of property markets globally. During the GFC, the impact on Australian property was across all property sectors, especially the development sector, with funding criteria for property development tightened to levels that had not been applied to this sector previously. Most developed countries experienced similar conditions to a lesser or greater extent.

5.1.2 *Differentiation: debt and equity finance*

Financing property development is different from financing property investment. With a property investment, the loan and subsequent interest will be repaid in full or part from the rental income that is being received for that property. At the time of financing, the lender has prior knowledge of the current rent that is being paid or the potential rental figure based on current lease rentals for that property type. Although this rent is not guaranteed, it represents a lower risk for the lender compared to a property development application. The main focus for the property lender is the repayment of the interest associated with the loans as well as the principal loan amount. To ensure that both interest and principal are met, the lender assesses the risk of the loan application and will accept or refuse the application and if the application is accepted the risk profile will also determine the pricing for the loan (Bryant 2012; Rowland 1997; and Bailey 1988). This higher risk profile for development projects leads to higher interest costs for the borrower and increased loan fees.

Although a property development loan will have similar risk assessment criteria as the property investment loan, the major difference is that the property development loan is assessed on the basis that the repayment of the loan and subsequent interest charges will be met from the sale or lease of the property at some point in the future. On this basis, a property development loan is similar to a project loan, with the determination of risk also considering aspects of the project itself, not just the economy and property cycle (Bryant 2012). The additional risks associated with property development finance include the:

- risk of whether the developer has the skills and expertise to complete the project;
- risk of time delays in the development process due to issues such as weather, labour force and trade union aspects;
- changes in input types and costs; and,
- legal and consumer issues associated with interest and environmental groups.

Based on the assessment of these risks the financier will accept or reject the finance application. In periods of uncertain property markets, excessive property supply, low demand for property, high interest rates and limited availability of finance, the potential to gain funding for property development becomes more difficult.

Lending to any industry is based on a number of key aspects, and this is very applicable to the property development sector. Lending institutions will assess a property development loan based on the integrity of the borrower, the financial strength of the borrower, their capacity to repay the loan, the level of security they can provide both in respect to real estate and personal guarantees and the various risk factors that apply to the development.

The actual source of funds for a development can be divided into senior debt or junior debt. Using Australia as an example, senior debt refers to funding supplied by the major

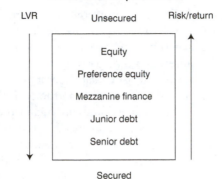

Figure 5.1 The relationship between total development costs, risk/return and funding requirements (Bryant 2009)

trading banks (that is the Commonwealth Bank of Australia, the National Australia Bank, Westpac and the Australia New Zealand Bank). Provided the that the developer can show that the development is feasible, the development risks can be minimised and adequate security for the funds is available, this senior debt will be the most cost effective finance for the developer. The amount of security that the senior lender will approve is subject to their lending guidelines and the loan to value ratio (LVR). The senior lender usually requires the property developer to provide equity for the development and in the majority of property development cases, and if available, will be provided by junior debt. This is also referred to as mezzanine finance. The lender for the junior debt has to give priority to the senior debt provider and the additional risk associated with lending over and above that issued by the senior lender is reflected in the higher interest rate and fees charged by the junior lender. Bryant (2009) has demonstrated the relationship between total development costs, risk/return and funding requirements in Figure 5.1.

Senior debt is the most secure for the lender, with the development secured by a first mortgage over the development site. The junior debt is generally secured by a second mortgage, with priority of the principal amount and the equivalent of 12 months interest to the first mortgager. This level of priority also applies to any mezzanine finance.

The least secure funding from the property developer's perspective is the owner's equity that has contributed to the property development. Equity is the first funding to go into the development (prior to loan funds being made available) and it is not until all loans are repaid and preferential equity is addressed that the developer can achieve their profit in the development. This diagram also shows that the lowest risk and return is for the providers of senior and junior debt (this return is the difference between the lender's cost of funds and the interest rate charged on the loan). At the corporate level this difference can range from 1.5 per cent to 3 per cent and must also cover the administration costs of the funding. Mezzanine finance providers charge a higher rate of interest compared to the senior debt providers: with this return being up to 5 per cent to 8 per cent depending on the debt provider, but also at an increased risk. Equity has the highest proportion of risk but also has the potential for the highest rate of return if the development is successful and meets the internal rate of return assessed in the initial feasibility study.

5.1.3   The impact of gearing

From any property development lender's perspective the more funds (equity) that are provided by the borrower (developer) the less risk to the lender. However, the property developer prefers to accept as little risk to their equity capital as possible and would prefer 100 per cent financing of the project and is prepared to accept the additional cost of this development funding structure. Gearing is a major factor that the property developer considers when assessing a property development opportunity. If the developer's equity is limited, a decision has to be made if all equity funds are included in one project or spread across a range of projects. This decision is also influenced by the interest rate the developer can access for borrowed funds. The higher the interest rate and the greater the percentage of funds borrowed for the development the lower the overall return for that development. In developments during high interest rate periods, the increased interest costs associated with increased borrowing will have a negative impact on the overall profitability of the development and therefore the developer's return on equity. Therefore, if the developer's cost of funds are greater than the expected total return on the development, increased equity into the development project will increase overall profitability, but exposes the developer to greater risk for these equity funds.

5.1.4   Lending criteria and the impact of the sustainability agenda

Credit providers view a lower risk profile in a property development favourably and a development with lower risk will also attract a greater loan to value ratio and lower interest and fee charges. Over the past decade, there is empirical evidence in some markets that sustainable, green and energy-efficient property developments have shown to be more readily saleable on completion, offer the investor/owner a greater yield/return on their investment, have lower vacancy rates on completion and attract a higher lease rental (World Green Building Council 2013). All these factors increase the feasibility of the development and as a consequence lower the development risk for both the financier and the developer.

With the increasing number and market acceptance of sustainable property developments, it is most likely that these developments in the future will not so much attract a lower lending risk; but, property developments that are not sustainable will either attract a significant lending penalty or not even be considered by lenders for development funding. Indeed even those major banks lending against domestic properties are, in some parts of the world, such as the UK, beginning to ask questions about the sustainability criteria of the asset offered as security.

5.2   Traditional methods of sustainable property development finance

Funding for property development and the source of funds depend on the prevailing economic and property market conditions. Market trends play a significant role in who is funding property development, the type of development being funded and the ease of access to development funds. It is important to understand the traditional methods of funding property development to appreciate the incentives and funding models that are now being employed or offered to attract a more sustainable property development sector. The funding types available for a property development proposal include a range of funding vehicles that are available depending on the structure, size and history of the developer and include financial institutions including banks and building societies, equity and preference equity, mezzanine finance, joint venture partnerships, REITs, overseas investors, private individuals, venture capitalists and charities.

5.2.1 Equity

Equity refers to funding that is provided by the developer and can include savings, profit from previous developments or the liquidation of other assets. If the property developer self-funds the development from their own equity they retain all profits and as such the full return from the project; however, they also take on the full risk of the project. The equity injected into the project is not always from the developer alone. They may introduce a development partner also willing to invest funds into the development on the basis of sharing the profit at the end of the development. If this is a formal arrangement, it would be a form of joint venture or preferential equity, discussed below. Equity participation in a property development implies a share of the profit from the development but does not guarantee a return from the development. If the sale of the property at the end of the development does not cover acquisition, legal and marketing costs, as well as the taxation and other holding costs then an equity holder will receive no return from the investment.

5.2.2 Preference equity

Preferred equity is similar to the equity injection, with one major difference. In the case of a formal preference equity agreement for a development, the equity provider can be guaranteed a specific return for their investment and/or a specific share of the profit on completion of the project and this would be disbursed prior to the developer receiving their final profit from the development. If the development fails, the preferred equity partner would not have the initial invested capital repaid and as such receive no return from the development. Preference equity is subordinate to any debt and is often used in cases where the senior debt provided restricts the developer from obtaining funds through junior debt providers or mezzanine finance. Depending on the amount that the preference equity partner provides and the agreement reached, the preference equity holder may have a formal or informal role in the development company and the development process.

5.2.3 Banks and building societies and mortgage finance

The traditional method of financing property investment is by way of funds from a senior or junior debt provider. In Australia, senior debt providers have been the traditional big four banks and the larger second-tier building societies. These second-tier lenders are generally active in the smaller-sized residential property developments and not the larger-scale development projects. In the UK, building societies also lend to property developers in much the same way as the banks. The main lender assesses the feasibility of the development and to determine:

- If they consider the development feasible in the current and future property market.
- The amount that they are prepared to lend on the project (LVR).
- The fees and interest margin that would apply.

- The type of loan instrument that will be provided (commercial bills, variable interest rate loan, fixed interest rate loan).
- The repayment schedule, terms and conditions for the loan (including capitalisation of the interest).

Although mortgage financing attracts an additional interest cost for the developer, it results in the developer including all their funds into the project, or if there is insufficient equity, a loan will allow the project to be undertaken. A mortgage finance arrangement does not involve a share of the profit that is generated from the development, only an interest cost on the funds borrowed. As such, this is a cheaper form of funding compared to the injection of equity from another source, where the potential cost is not capped as a return on the invested funds but a percentage of the overall profit generated from the development.

The funds borrowed from the debt provider have to be repaid regardless of whether the development project succeeds or fails. The senior debt provider ensures this by only lending a percentage of the final value of the developed property (LVR) and establishing a priority on the first mortgage if secondary finance from a junior debt provider is obtained by the developer (again it is stressed that the senior debt provider can lend on the condition that no junior debt is obtained). Senior debt is repaid first, followed by junior (mezzanine finance), preference equity and last; equity.

5.2.4 *Mezzanine finance*

Mezzanine finance is a form of junior debt, used by property developers to bridge the funding gap between the cost of the project and the funds that are approved by the senior debt provider. The mezzanine finance institution accepts a secondary position in respect to both the payment of interest and capital, but has a priority over equity holders and preference equity holders. The increased risk to the mezzanine finance provider is reflected in the higher interest rate charged compared to the senior debt provider. Mezzanine finance allows the developer to reduce the amount of owners or preference equity that needs to be provided for the development. The funds obtained through mezzanine finance make up the difference between the amount that can be borrowed from the senior debt provider and the development costs.

5.2.5 *Joint venture partnerships*

Property developers can also participate in a range of equity participation and joint venture (JV) schemes to fund their developments. This is undertaken when finance from senior or junior debt providers is not available or, the cost is too high for the developer to undertake the project. Although the participation of additional equity partners reduces the potential return on the development, it is often the only way a developer can obtain the funds to undertake the development. A senior or junior debt provider may also fund the project on a joint venture basis. As compensation for a share of future profits from the development, the debt provider may increase the LVR to provide full funding, apply a more favourable interest rate or both. This shifts the overall risk of the venture away from the developer and is shared by the debt provider.

A joint venture is a collaboration of two or more investors who mutually agree to undertake an investment strategy or project. There is an agreement to determine the level of commitment and profit for each party and an outline of the tasks (if any) for each party to provide towards the venture. JV structures can be simple or complicated depending on the project and the requirements of the investors. In all instances the agreement must be clearly defined and understood by all involved and independent legal and/or financial advice should always be sought. A JV should be structured so that all parties benefit. ISPT, an industry superannuation (pension) fund in Australia, is a good example of a company who use JV to finance developments (ISPT 2014). ISPT consider the five following factors when evaluating a JV:

1   financial metrics of the proposal;
2   reputation, track record and expertise of the proponent;
3   fair and reasonable allocation of risk and rewards;
4   level of demand from existing funds or individual investors for the opportunity;
5   an investment structure that optimises risk and returns for our investors.

(ISPT 2014)

Property syndicates are another form of equity participation, particularly if the end property development is to be retained by the developer. In these cases, the developer will promote the development to individual investors and raise the full development costs through these investors. The property syndicate members participate in both the income generated from the completed property and any capital gain on sale.

5.2.6 *Real estate investment trusts (REITs)*

REITs give investors access to property assets with the main benefit being that they can provide access to assets that may be otherwise out of reach of individual investors, for example as large commercial properties. Furthermore their investment is also highly liquid, which appeals to some investors (ASX 2014). REITs appeal to investors seeking to diversify their portfolio into property with the advantage of having a regular and consistent income stream. REITs generate wealth by providing exposure to the value of the real estate assets that the trust owns and the accompanying capital growth, as well as rental income. The fund manager chooses the investment properties and is responsible for administration, improvements, maintenance and rental. Although each REIT has its own attributes, the properties in the portfolio are usually diversified across locations, regions, lease duration and tenancy types. Some concentrate on particular sectors, and typically fall into one of the following groups:

- Industrial trusts invest in warehouses, factories and industrial parks.
- Office trusts include medium-to-large office buildings in and around major cities.
- Hotel and leisure trusts invest in hotels, cinemas and theme parks.
- Retail trusts invest in shopping centres and similar assets.
- Diversified trusts invest in a mixture of offices, hotels, industrial and retail property.

Some REITs in Australia adopt hybrid structures called 'stapled securities' funds which provide investors with exposure to a funds management and/or a property development company, as well as a real estate portfolio (ASX 2014). A share in a stapled securities fund usually consists of one trust unit and one share in the funds management company. These securities are 'stapled' so cannot be traded separately. The REIT holds the portfolio of assets, while the related company carries out the fund's management functions and/or manages any development opportunities (ASX 2014).

The funding sources for both traditional and sustainable property development are varied and based on the size and type of development. Smaller developments are generally funded by banks and building societies, which have specialist departments that lend on these developments. Larger property developments are often funded by a joint venture partner or with the larger purpose built properties funding is often organised through a national or international REIT. In such cases, the developer is required to have a secure long-term lease in place prior to the REIT funding approval.

5.2.7 Property companies

Whilst many large property companies have been re-structured to form REITs, many have not. Where they have not, they normally operate as public limited companies, or indeed small private companies. Their role in development cannot be overstated. The smaller companies tend to operate to individualised objectives; they can be 'fleet of foot' in terms of decision-making and entrepreneurial in attitude. Cunningham in a study of decision-making among small- and large-scale developers concluded that large companies invest resources in cycle watching and utilise equity in order to 'land bank' early in the cycle whereas the smaller, independent developer has neither the equity nor the business model to support this approach (Cunningham 2014). Typically smaller property companies may have to resort to tier-two finance to back their schemes, as they lack the ability to give lenders the comfort that tier-one lenders require.

In terms of sustainability, there is a clear divide between the big companies, who may have sophisticated policies for CSR in place and the small organisations that will not. However, in terms of their *product*, the same may not be true with some smaller organisations seeking a niche positioning based on a differentiated offer, whereas larger developers, notably in the residential sector, are developing similar products on almost production line methods, which makes innovation more difficult. Within the commercial sector this is not likely to be the case as each development tends to be unique in terms of specification and design. In essence there is no reason why property companies should, or should not, be innovators in sustainability; however, as their business model depends on reputation they tend to place high importance on being at the vanguard of ideas. Conversely, when they rely significantly on borrowed funds, as is the normal scenario, the constraints of their funding may require them to adhere to proven formulae.

5.2.8 Overseas investors

Overseas investment has been a result of relaxation of foreign exchange rules. Until the mid-1980s it was almost unknown for countries to allow overseas money to flow into their economies and buy property; today it is the reverse. Whilst some countries do prevent the purchase of assets by those from outside their own economics or may place limits on the percentage that can be owned, frequently leading to the setting up of joint venture partnerships, most developed countries allow the flow of capital both in and out of their countries.

The money provided by organisations from other countries, has been transformational, although more of this tends to flow to the investment created, rather than the provision of capital funds to build. A report by the British Property Federation (BPF) (2014) claimed that up to 80 per cent of commercial property purchases in central London in 2013 was financed by overseas investment money, and some 15 per cent of all residential property, mainly new builds or off plan, went to overseas buyers.

The presence of overseas investment money can be critical when domestic demand and credit is limited; however, such money is volatile and overseas investors will be influenced by what is happening in their home markets as well as in the country of investment. Further factors such as exchange rates will impact on their decision-making and a sudden withdrawal of funds could potentially destabilise values very quickly.

5.2.9 Private individuals

Private individuals are normally more influential within residential development than commercial, both due to matters of scale and to inclination. If a private individual wishes to become a property developer, they will normally operate through a company structure for tax reasons as much as any other driver. Within the residential markets, where a private individual is developing for their own occupation, they can be influential as drivers of sustainability, through adopting a motivated and informed client role which places pressure on their advisory team to embrace sustainable solutions and technologies. Like any other type of developer however, they vary in their funding. Where they are using solely equity and cost is not a major consideration, they are more likely to be able to drive innovation, but if money is constrained, as with any other developer, design compromise may follow.

5.2.10 Venture capitalists

Venture capitalists are third-tier funders. They normally supply money to start-up companies who are unable to access more established traditional sources of funds, normally in return for an equity stake in the development. They raise their money through attracting the funds of individuals, companies and institutions, and then collectively seek out high return equity investments. As their business model is predicated on risk, they are prepared to place money into schemes which are at the cutting edge and they make their returns by being prepared to undertake speculative positions. They may or may not take a stance towards sustainability, but where they do, they tend to be ambitious both in order to attract funds to their companies, and to pursue opportunities which will yield high returns. Some 30 years ago, private equity and venture capitalist organisations were virtually unknown. Now, they attract institutional monies, and, within the UK according to their representative body, the British Private Equity and Venture Capital Association (BVCA), they have produced superior returns for their investors over both the short and longer term (www.bvca.co.uk). Typically such investors will fund a start-up such as a property development, hold for a period of up to five years then exit the scheme. It could be argued that such an approach will normally run counter to the interests of sustainable development; in many cases this is so, but as sustainability bites ever more deeply into occupational and investment demand, so over their usual investment horizon it becomes appropriate business modelling. Indeed a recent report from BVCA (BVCA 2014) claims that awareness levels are high and rising.

5.2.11 Charities

Charities come in many forms. Whilst many are very small and therefore property development funders, large charities are influential developers with extensive portfolios and may act as their own developer or enter joint venture arrangements with property companies, using their equity to fund the development. Although many charities are engaged with commercial or educational development, it is in the housing sector where they are most important, with organisations such as the Peabody Trust in London, which acts both as its own developer and as partner with private sector organisations. Some charities also act as grant aid organisations providing funds for other organisations but this tends not to be their core business model. Where charities are involved with funding developments, either for their own investment purposes or for other developers, the principles of sustainability are often deeply embedded as most charities take a long-term view towards funding and this will tend to help decision makers gravitate towards decisions which take 'the long view'.

5.3   Public sector finance

Public funding of sustainable property development can be directed towards any sector of the property market. The availability of schemes and initiatives varies with different governments and also within sectors of government. The UK has a primarily two-tier system of government; at local and national level. Australia on the other hand has three levels of government; at Federal, State and Local level. This fragmentation of governance has meant that the availability of incentives can vary considerably, within sectors and within countries. In Australia to date, incentives have focused mainly on the commercial, education and housing sectors rather than the retail and industrial sectors. However, education and housing insulation programmes, introduced in the late 2000s, have been terminated by the national liberal coalition government elected in 2013. In essence, public sector finance can comprise direct government assistance or come in the shape of private finance initiative (PFI) and public private partnerships (PPP). Within the UK, finance for development is predominantly at the national level.

5.3.1   Public private partnerships (PPPs)

A public private partnership (PPP) is defined as a 'business relationship between a private sector company and a government agency for the purpose of completing a project that will serve the public' (World Bank 2014). PPP refers to arrangements, typically medium to long term, between the public and private sectors whereby some of the services that fall under the responsibilities of the public sector are provided by the private sector, with clear agreement on shared objectives for delivery of public infrastructure and/or public services. PPPs typically do not include service contracts or turnkey construction contracts, which are categorised as public procurement projects, or the privatisation of utilities, where there is a limited ongoing role for the public sector. Often the public sector will be motivated by sustainability objectives and use their influence to ensure certain levels of sustainability are delivered in the projects.

5.3.2   Private finance initiative (PFI)

PFI projects are typically long-term contracts for services that include the provision of associated facilities or properties. Under the contract, a private sector party will have responsibility for designing and constructing the building or facility and maintaining and servicing it throughout the contract term (Davies and Fairbrother 2003). There are a variety of slightly different forms of PFI such as Design Build Finance Operate (DBFO) which is the most common. However, different combinations of the construction, operation, and finance responsibilities appear in the various options and there are also often different patterns of ownership. In theory, PFI funded schemes should promote developments in which effective management is key, given that the developer is responsible for managing the asset typically for more than 30 years. However, PFI has had many critics and Dubben and Williams (2009) concluded that the chief beneficiaries of PFI tend to be the private sector investors, who after initial risk taking provide a sound investment. However, their research pointed to strong economic and practical issues with the concept but that it remained a committed policy position, at least in the UK.

5.3.3   Community generation funds

Within the UK a new type of government fund has recently been set up – the Community Generation Fund, whose aim is to 'provide a catalyst for the widespread development of community-owned renewable energy infrastructure' (http://www.thefsegroup.com/social-impact-funding/community generation fund). The fund provides finance for:

- *Development loans*: to help communities achieve planning and upfront design and environmental costs; and,
- *Construction loans*: to cover all or part of the construction and commissioning costs.

The finance may be freestanding or work alongside other sources of finance. The critical factor with community loans is that the development has to take place in an area of high social deprivation, thus having real regenerative and social impact goals.

5.3.4   Green loans

When any developer is planning a scheme the cost of money will normally be a major consideration. Funders want certainty, a track record and a product which they trust. Very often developments which are pushing at the bounds of conventional technologies are not attractive to funders, as they can be perceived as risky.

Over recent years, there have been many attempts to enable individuals and organisations to access funds for environmental projects. Some, such as those run by the Energy Savings Trust in the UK are primarily about small-scale upscaling; others are geared towards major renewables schemes. Indeed organisations such as the Green Investment Bank (www.greeninvestmentbank.com) have been set up with the sole aim to fund 'green schemes'. However, their emphasis tends to be infrastructure projects, not individual building schemes. So whilst they have importance for large developments which incorporate, for example, biomass generation, or link to associated wind farms, they are not the normal source of funding for individual buildings. At a smaller scale, providers such as Kiva (www.kiva.org) bring together individual lenders and borrowers to invest in technology at the local level in developing countries such as solar schemes in Africa. Indeed, the move towards small syndicated lending or facilitated direct private lending is beginning to be effective in creating change.

Within the UK, the government has set up another loan scheme aimed at individual buildings, the Green Deal, and that is considered below. To date, the Green Deal is focused on the residential sector but is designed also for the commercial sector. In time it is anticipated that commercial green loans may decline as investment in sustainable projects becomes mainstream activity. However, schemes which push the bounds in technological terms are in reality likely to meet funding resistance.

5.4   Incentivising sustainable property development

Most schemes that incentive sustainability within property development have been voluntary rather than mandatory, normally because governments have taken a 'nudge' approach to encourage a greater awareness and participation in sustainable and energy-efficient housing, thereby avoiding a backlash politically if legislation is seen to be too harsh – or result in unacceptable expense. However, some aspects of sustainability are mandated in Building Regulations or Building Codes, notably by setting minimum standards in respect of energy and water in construction, but it should be noted that these seldom permeate to operational use. Design controls also go some way towards addressing other aspects – or examples – in relation to design for disabilities but even here it does not address the needs of other than a few of the more obvious issues such as the needs of wheelchair users. It has therefore often been the private sector that has taken a lead in the development of more holistic measures through rating schemes, such as those considered in Chapter 9. As market demand moves towards greater awareness so such schemes have increasing influence.

Schemes currently running in Australia to incentivise sustainability include Environmental Upgrade Agreements (EUAs) in Victoria and New South Wales, which cover commercial property and encourage sustainable retrofit during the property life cycle. Within the UK, the two main government financial initiatives promoting sustainability are Feed-in Tariffs and the Green Deal, although other schemes such as the Renewable Heat Incentive are gaining importance. As with Australia these incentives are focused on upgrading or retrofitting properties; for new build the approach of government has been towards control through Building Regulations and conditions on planning consents. Whilst these are primarily development standards, their influence is now feeding through to the in-use phase, largely driven by the EU (for example Energy Performance Certificates and Display Energy Certificates). Further incentivisation takes place through adding to costs of non-sustainable practices, such as the landfill tax on waste. This tax, the cost of which escalates each year, has been key to waste to landfill halving over a single decade (Tavri *et al.* 2014). If there are penalties on poor environmental behaviours, it provides a strong incentive to improve. In the UK, the situation is relatively severe given the shortage of land for landfill and this has been a driver behind the introduction of a rapidly increasing tax. Within the in-use phase, the Carbon Reduction Tax, which presents a real cost to large companies if they do not reduce their carbon emissions year on year has again led to changed behaviours.

Perhaps almost more importantly it has led to the embedding of monitoring technologies so that occupiers can see at a glance what their emissions and consumption are. And in words often attributed to Peter Drucker 'What gets measured gets managed.' So as buildings begin to be developed with the systems that enable good resources *measurement* so good management will follow. Whilst monitoring can be seen to be an occupational, not a development, issue, as we have seen elsewhere, developers are far more attuned to the needs of eventual occupiers than was previously the case.

5.4.1   Environmental upgrade agreements

EUAs were developed and adopted in Victoria in 2008 to promote and encourage retrofit to improve commercial building performance (CEFC 2014). In 2011, the NSW government (NSW Government 2011) followed suit and introduced EUAs to encourage the sustainable retrofit of existing buildings. An EUA is an agreement where:

- an owner agrees to carry out environmental upgrade works to improve the energy, water efficiency or sustainability of the building, and;
- a finance provider agrees to advance funds to the building owner to finance those environmental upgrade works, and;
- the council agrees to levy a charge on the relevant land for the purpose of repaying the advance to the finance provider.

The parties to these EUAs are the building owner, the finance provider and the local government authority (council) see Figure 5.2. Each has specific duties under the agreements. The owner is responsible for implementing the environmental upgrade works, and paying environmental upgrade charges imposed on the building. The owner may pass on all or part of the payment of charges to lessees if the lease allows. The owner remains liable to pay any environmental upgrade charges levied on the building by the due date, regardless of any payment by lessees or other third parties. The finance provider advances funds to the owner (including, for example, through an agent such as an engineering company) subject to the payment milestones in the EUA. The council forwards payments (including any late interest) towards environmental upgrade charges received from the owner to the finance provider, aside from a portion retained as service fees under the agreement. The finance provider advances the funds to the owner, or to the energy services or contractor implementing the works. If the owner is the occupier they will receive a notice to pay the environmental upgrade charge by the local government authority. If the building is leased, the owner still receives the notice to pay the environmental upgrade charge but may be in the position to levy this payment from the lessees.

The local authority collects the charge and then the council refunds this amount to the finance provider and the council is not liable to pay the finance provider until they have actually received the funds from the building owner. These agreements are a charge

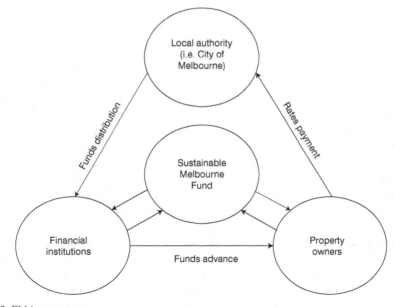

Figure 5.2 EUA structure
Source: Authors

against the land and the debt remains with the land. On sale of the property the outstanding payments can be repaid in full by the original borrower or can be transferred to the new owner. Acceptable upgrade works that can be funded under this scheme include:

- increasing the efficiency of energy or water consumption,
- reducing energy or water consumption,
- preventing or reducing pollution,
- eliminating or reducing the discharge of wastes,
- reducing the use of materials,
- enabling the recovery or recycling of materials,
- enabling the monitoring of environmental quality,
- reducing greenhouse gas emissions,
- encouraging or facilitating alternative methods of transportation (such as walking and cycling).

Examples of acceptable environmental works include reducing greenhouse gas emissions by replacing existing equipment with low emissions or more efficient alternatives, or replacing air conditioning and heating systems with new systems with improved efficiency. A Melbourne hotel reduced its energy consumption by 50 per cent though an upgrade and a Sydney office reduced its lighting energy by 70 per cent, both projects financed by EUAs (CEFC 2014). Overall however, despite the financial incentives available, the uptake of EUAs has been disappointingly low and shows that voluntary schemes only have limited market penetration (Wilkinson 2014). Over the past 20 years, there has been a greater awareness of the benefits of sustainable commercial property development globally, with Newell *et al.* (2011) and Eichholtz *et al.* (2010) finding a positive correlation between increased value and highly rated NABERS commercial office stock. Where GDV is increased, as Newell *et al.* (2011) and Eichholtz *et al.* (2010) suggest then risk to funders is reduced.

5.4.2 The Green Deal

The Green Deal is the UK government's current 'flagship' scheme to encourage upgrading of existing buildings. It is not a development incentive. The scheme is operational for domestic properties and in advanced planning for non-domestic ones. Under the Green Deal, the customer (energy user) does not pay for the installation of energy-saving measures on installation but on cost savings subsequently. It was brought in as there was a belief that the upfront costs of making improvements were a barrier to such works being undertaken. Under the scheme, (for details see http://www.eesy.uk.com/data/The%20Green%20Deal%20 Science%20and%20the%20Environment.pdf) a list of works is approved as appropriate.

These include works, such as condensing boilers and insulation which will undoubtedly help to reduce energy use, but exclude, some other more radical interventions. If a proposal falls out of scope the scheme will not apply. The process starts with an assessment by an approved 'Green Deal assessor' who will identify the recommended measures, after which an application is made for finance and installation to a Green Deal provider. The resultant Green Deal plan details the repayments, which are taken as a charge through the electricity bill. The cost of the installation includes interest on the borrowed sum. One of the concerns of anyone taking out a Green Deal is the possibility that the repayment will be more than the savings achieved. To overcome this, a Golden Rule applies which states that any charge must be less than the 'expected' savings. If a property changes hands after a Green Deal is in place, it stays as a charge against the property with the purchaser having to take over the repayments.

Whilst this sounds attractive the Green Deal has met with a lack of demand from domestic consumers and significant criticism although it is regarded as genuinely innovative and likely to retain government backing (Guertler *et al.* 2012); it is also viewed favourably in comparison with moves in other EU countries such as Germany (Rosenow *et al.* 2013). It is also pertinent to note that the UK Green Building Council (UK Green Building Council, 2013) consider that this incentive alone will not be sufficient to achieve these emission targets and that additional incentives are required for owners of current non-sustainable or energy-efficient homes to take action to improve the energy efficiency of their properties.

Within the commercial arena, the Green Deal has met some significant design difficulty, much of which is based around the issues between the landlord and tenant: the tenant pays the bill and would take the Green Deal – but the asset belongs to the freeholder. Additionally, for many landlords, the works are better undertaken during a regular refurbishment point, and not at the time of the tenant's choosing. As at the time of writing, the Green Deal for non-domestic properties has not turned into a reality.

A further complication of the Green Deal is the link that government have made between this and the requirements of the Energy Act 2011, which places an obligation on all landlords from 2018 to let only those properties which meet minimum energy performance standards (MEPS); however, if a property cannot be made MEPS compliant through Green Deal measures which meet the Golden Rule, the requirement falls away (see Green Construction Board 2014 for a full report on this). Whilst the impact of MEPS may be to stimulate Green Deal take up, this is still far from certain.

5.4.3 Feed-in tariffs

Feed-in tariffs (FITS) are not new and have been in use in some European countries, such as Germany and Spain, for a considerable number of years where they have been claimed to be responsible for uptake of renewable technologies (Ragwitz and Huber 2005). They were introduced in the UK in 2010 and, under a FIT agreement, the property owner installs energy generating capacity, domestically normally in the form of a solar photovoltaic array, and any energy generated is taken back into the national grid with a payment being made to the owner of the installation. Unlike the Green Deal, UK FITS have proved so successful in uptake that it caused the government to reduce the size of the stimulus significantly after only one year and this is now kept under regular review (for details see http://www.fitariffs.co.uk/). Further concerns have been expressed that the original intent to shift from fossil fuel to renewable energy consumption and to energy efficiency has led to domestic consumers viewing it as a commercial opportunity without a reduction in household energy consumption (Cherrington *et al.* 2013).

Commercially, energy can be produced by PV, anaerobic digestion, wind, hydro, and combined heat and power (CHP) schemes. As with domestic take up, the commercial take up is high as the returns have been attractive. This has led to a rapid growth in commercial exploitations in terms of increased applications for wind and solar farms which, although meeting some local resistance on aesthetic grounds, is helping change minds towards the adoption of renewable technologies. By scaling up, some of the issues of unsuitable installations on individual dwellings are avoided and over time it's leading to a new form of property development; such schemes are also enhancing the value of agricultural units which are well placed to diversify into renewables.

5.4.4 Enhanced capital allowances for energy-saving technologies

In the UK the Enhanced Capital Allowance (ECA) scheme enables businesses to claim a 100 per cent first year capital allowance on investments in certain energy-saving equipment, against the taxable profits of the period of investment (The Carbon Trust 2014). Capital allowances enable businesses to write off the capital cost of purchasing new plant or machinery (e.g. boilers, motors), against their taxable profits. The Carbon Trust Guide (2014) gives an example where the general rate of capital allowances is 18 per cent a year on a reducing balance basis. Some technologies supported by the ECA Scheme (e.g. boilers, lighting) are included in a special capital allowances pool where the general rate of capital allowances is 8 per cent. For example, if a business spent £1,000 on a new electric motor, claimed a standard capital allowance at the 18 per cent rate and paid 21 per cent corporation tax then the tax relief would be £37.80 in the first year. Further tax relief could be claimed in subsequent years. If, however, the business invested in a higher efficiency motor listed on the Energy Technology List then it could claim an Enhanced Capital Allowance, giving a one-off 100 per cent tax relief of £210. Additional benefits of purchasing ECA qualifying energy-efficient technologies could include: improved cash flow, lower energy bills, reduction in Climate Change Levy or carbon reduction commitment (CRC) payment. This is another example of a measure to incentivise the stakeholders including developers and install energy-efficient technologies into property developments.

5.4.5 Carbon reduction commitment

The carbon reduction commitment scheme is not a development incentive, but a simple tax on the annual carbon consumption of a small number of large portfolio holders, be they investors or occupiers. Under a reducing annual allowance scheme, companies are presented with a real incentive either to manage their properties in ways which reduce their carbon emissions, or to change the nature of their properties owned or occupied, either through a disposal and acquisition strategy or development programme, to one that reduces their tax burden. Already this has had an impact in terms of the selection process; in terms of specification of new buildings, it may take a little longer.

5.4.6 Other incentives

Trenouth and Mead (2007) highlighted the need to develop a more sustainable residential property sector in New Zealand. They stressed that it is just as important to improve the sustainability of the existing residential property stock is to provide sustainability measures in the new building codes and conditions incorporated into district plans. Trenouth and Mead (2007) stated most of New Zealand's 1.5 million homes were poorly insulated, damp and consumed high levels of energy and water. To address these sustainability issues in New Zealand a number of incentives had to be provided to the general public and incorporated into district plans (Trenouth and Mead 2007). To overcome perceived barriers and improve incentives for sustainable residential property development, better information on sustainability and energy efficiency was needed, recognition of sustainability benefits in the policies, rules and assessment criteria of district plans and the provison of better assessment tools, and training and up-skilling of staff.

In the EU, Germany has set a goal that by 2020 buildings should be operating without fossil fuel. Mandatory disclosure of home energy usage at the time of sale or lease came into effect on 1 July 2008. Two types of Energy Certificates are required: a) a Demand Certificate applies to the building's thermal efficiency, rating aspects of energy efficiency such as the walls, roof, windows and furnace; and b) a Usage Certificate based on the actual energy use of the property over the past three years (Deutsche Energie-Agentur 2010). France introduced thermal regulations in 2000 and 2005 that defined performance levels for new buildings. From 2012, all buildings are to be low consumption (heating, domestic hot water (DHW), cooling, ventilation and lighting). By 2020, all buildings are to be energy-positive by balancing their low consumption by the production of renewable energy (Lenoir *et al.* 2010, French Environment and Energy Management Agency 2010) whilst in the UK, new public and social sector housing will have to be low carbon by 2016 with the private sector following a few years later. Following Europe's lead, legislative sustainability targets for housing, and in particular energy usage in homes, have been introduced in a number of other countries around the world including the US, Canada, Malaysia and New Zealand (Bryant and Eves 2012).

5.5   Traditional methods of sustainable property development finance

Earlier in the chapter we considered the types of funding that may be available and some of the grants and other incentive schemes aimed at encouraging sustainable behaviours. In this section we briefly consider the position of the major types of legal structures used to set up funding arrangements.

5.5.1 Forward-funding with an institution

Every development bears risks and consequently developers will seek to reduce that risk where possible. One way of so doing is to ensure the 'exit' to the scheme by having arranged either a forward sale (i.e. the developer effectively acts as a construction manager for the eventual purchaser) or, if the property is to be retained within the portfolio, a forward-funding deal for the long-term finance of the scheme. In such cases, the institution can be regarded as a partner in the scheme (Dubben and Williams 2009) as effectively the risk is shared. The actual arrangements will vary with each scheme but the funding partner can be expected to have a real negotiable interest in the shape of the scheme and the build quality. As financial institutions have developed their corporate responsibility agendas so they are beginning to build such policies into their approach to investment with the principles of 'responsible property investment' (RPI) now being embedded in major concerns (UNEP FI 2012).

5.5.2 Secured lending

An introduction to debt funding has been given earlier in this chapter. During periods when it is expected that capital values and rents are likely to rise, secured lending will normally be available to support developments. However, particularly since the global financial crash, banks and other organisations that enter into lending arrangements using property as security have become much more cautious in their approach, with loan to value (LTVs) being far lower, to guard against potential downturns in the market. Development finance will always be both more expensive and lower in LTV terms than finance for a completed scheme but much will depend on the track record of the developer. As indicated above, lenders are now asking pertinent questions about environmental considerations – including flood risk – when assessing the loan request. Further, valuers acting for lenders who are RICS members are now required to collect sustainability data, where available, on all the properties they inspect in order that they are in a better position to advise clients on the degree to which such matters are now penetrating notions of market value. Whilst secured lending is not specifically tied to sustainable buildings, we are moving into an environment in which the specifics of the building may impact loan terms. However, as discussed earlier, green loans and community funding may have to fill funding gaps as some schemes in socially deprived areas are seen to present higher than average risk profiles.

5.5.3   Corporate finance

Where a company wishes to develop for their own occupation, or a developer does not or cannot obtain sufficient debt, they will use their own corporate structure as the funding source. This will be done either through use of retained profits or, more likely, by a rights issue, a stock market listing, in the case of a company going public, or the issue of debenture stock. Often the financing arrangements are complex and a mixture of arrangements, including setting up special vehicles (SVs), may be used to keep the funding separate from the main company which can be protected by use of non-recourse loans to the SV company. In essence, such arrangements are neutral in sustainability terms.

5.5.4   Securitisation

Since the financial crash, the very word securitisation has acquired very negative connotations as some of the 'packaged deals' of property loans (commercial mortgage-backed securities) went to the heart of what caused the problem. Essentially securitisation is simply a process of lending on a bundle of fairly illiquid assets (such as real estate) which are grouped together and financially' engineered' to form a financial instrument which can be readily traded. Whilst this may help lenders by enabling them to retain their liquidity whilst entering into long-term funding arrangements, the critical factor is the sustainable value of the underlying assets. As long as values of the underlying assets are maintained the system works but, as demonstrated so strongly in 2007–2008 when they did not, the consequences can be very far-reaching. In the crash of 2008, it was the failure of mortgage debts on the US sub-prime market that triggered a whole series of events as those in possession of the paper investments sought to divest themselves of what they perceived to offer unacceptable risks (see for example Covitz *et al.* 2013). Even now, some six years later, many underperforming bundles of assets are being carefully unbundled but at large losses to the original lenders. As the process works out, analysis may show that certain more sustainable assets withstood the crash better than other properties, but frequently at a portfolio level this will be difficult to unpick.

What is probably the case is that the use of such vehicles inevitably separates the investor of the packed product from the underlying asset – so almost inevitably it will not be a driver towards a more sustainable product.

5.6   The future

In terms of moving forward, it is likely that some schemes in place will be removed, whilst others will take their place as governments begin to place differing environmental and social matters up the political agenda. The UK Green Building Council (UK Green Building

Council 2013), in their report on retrofitting domestic properties, suggested a range of possible incentives such as:

1   cashbacks and grants;
2   variable property taxes and rebates, including a variable transfer tax;
3   minimum standards for the owner-occupied housing sector;
4   low interest loans for retrofits;
5   reduced VAT for energy efficiency measures; and an
6   energy efficiency feed-in tariff.

These ideas are not new and some have been advocated for well over a decade (see for example ERM Economics and ERM Planning 2002) which additionally advocated tax free savings for sustainable home mortgages. Both organisations considered that reducing VAT, transfer tax and subsidies were suitable incentives to improve the sustainability and energy efficiency of both new and established residential property. All these are possible ways forward but possibly two of the most likely trends to encompass commercial and residential property are those discussed below.

5.6.1 Disclosure statements

The old adage that to be managed something must first be measured has long been adopted in many contexts. Recent years have seen the development in Australia of a national scheme for the mandatory disclosure of residential building energy, greenhouse and water efficiency performance at the time of sale or lease (Council of Australian Government (COAG) 2009). The scheme was based on the conclusion, drawn from research, that there is a developing relationship between house prices and energy ratings (National Framework for Energy Efficiency 2008) as the transparency would enable home buyers to forecast future energy savings into home purchase prices.

A similar energy efficiency and sustainability disclosure scheme for the sale of residential property was introduced in Queensland in 2009. This mandated disclosure of sustainability features through the introduction of the Building and Other Legislation Amendment Bill 2009. This initiative was designed to provide potential buyers with a realistic overview of the sustainable features that were included in the house. However, research by Bryant and Eves (2012) found widespread disengagement with the process from sellers and buyers with 98 per cent of buyers not even asking for a copy of the Sustainability Declaration and, consequently, had almost no impact on the purchase decision.

The EPC (Energy Performance Certificate) in Europe is based on the same premise but, as it is an asset rating, it is hard to make real connections between energy costs and ratings. However, over time, mandatory disclosures by companies and individuals will enable more informed decisions and this in turn will provide valuable information for funders; indeed already RIC, through its Red Book (RICS 2014), is requiring its valuers to collect sustainability data where this is available as another nudge to market behaviours.

5.6.2 Carbon taxation and emissions trading

Carbon taxes have been introduced in several parts of the globe already, so in reality they are not a thing of the future. Indeed, the Carbon Reduction Commitment Energy Efficiency Scheme in the UK was introduced in 2010, initially as a tax neutral incentive scheme, but now effectively a levy. Further the EU has operated a carbon trading scheme for some years. However, it is likely that the scale and impact of such taxes will inevitably increase, but it depends on political will and this can change quickly, as the example below from Australia clearly demonstrates.

The Australian Carbon Tax was legislated and introduced in 2012 and aimed to deliver a 5 per cent cut in emissions by 2020. It was targeted at large emitters with a flat rate charge from 2012 based on tonnes of emissions, with the levies raised being reinvested into clean energy technology and renewable energy projects; further development funds were to be established to concentrate on biodiversity, low carbon agriculture, small business grants and indigenous communities. The government pledged also to compensate 90 per cent of households for any increase in energy bills via tax cuts or increases to family benefits.

To complement the tax, Carbon Farming Initiative (CFI) legislation was passed in August 2011 as a carbon offsets programme under which farmers and landholders would be able to trade off carbon credits by first earning credits by storing carbon or reducing greenhouse gas (GHG) emissions on their land and selling them to companies or individuals wanting to offset their carbon emissions. The intention was that by 2015 a full emissions trading scheme would be in operation. However, although these taxes would have brought Australia very much in line with Europe, following a change of government in September 2013, the Carbon Tax was repealed in July 2014 amidst great controversy, as it means that Australia is now out of step with much of the rest of the world; further, it has produced consternation as early indications were that the legislation was proving effective (The Conversation 2014). At the time of writing, alternative proposals are under consideration including penalties for polluters, but it does illustrate just how short-term political imperatives, especially in times when economies are weak, can undermine the resolve to become more sustainable. With the world economies being fragile, the moves to financially incentive carbon reduction are under pressure, but are seen as inevitable.

5.6.3   *It will not just be carbon*

Undoubtedly carbon and energy efficiency are the key issues in terms of financial incentives and penalties, but they are not the only ones. The UK has an escalator landfill tax which has successfully impacted on waste management behaviours, and in many countries, the pricing mechanism is being used to incentivise the design of water managemen. In due time, the fiscal systems, combined in some cases with grants, will increasingly form policy to change market behaviours in ways which will complement legislation and regulation. As this happens so developers will see an increased business case to design buildings which go 'beyond base line compliance' in order that they are financially resilient over time.

5.7   Conclusions

Financing sustainable property developments normally follows conventional financing methods. Any financier is essentially interested in supporting, through equity involvement, schemes which have the greatest likelihood of succeeding. They are also influenced by the track record of the developer. Some two decades ago, many so-called 'green' buildings were regarded as risky in terms of their technologies, expensive to build, whilst not having any additional attraction to occupiers; they were therefore difficult to finance and this led some credence to the notion of the 'circle of blame' (Sustainable Construction Task Group, 2000) standing in the way of the development of more sustainable buildings. However, with market changes and growing awareness of sustainability, helped by rating tools, combined with greater acceptance of new technologies, so financing of greener buildings is mainstreaming. They are now often seen as less, rather than more, risky in the longer term, as they are less likely to suffer premature obsolescence. Research, detailed in Chapter 4, demonstrates that, in some property sub-sectors, additional build cost may be compensated by ease of sale, and rental and capital values obtainable, thus ensuring such buildings are economic from the financier's viewpoint.

Many governments, at all levels, acknowledge the importance of sustainable property developments and provide fiscal incentives to 'nudge' market participants towards incorporating sustainability features into their developments, as well as using mandatory measures incrementally to raise minimum standards and imposing financial penalties, such as the landfill tax, to increase the costs of non-sustainable development practices. But it is not just through fiscal and grant manipulation of demand that governments drive sustainability in development. Direct use of public sector finance is used to further the aim, through funding of housing schemes, joint venture (JV) or public private partnership (PPP) schemes. Alternatively it can be delivered through reverse funding for public sector development through Private Finance Initiative (PFI).

With a growing recognition of the very slow rate at which the global building stock is totally redeveloped, retrofit is also a critical part of sustainable development. Therefore in addition to gearing financial measures towards new build, governments are increasingly focused on incentivising building upgrades, through a range of schemes such as, Feed-in Tariffs and the Green Deal in the UK and the Environmental Upgrade Agreements in parts of Australia. Other initiatives, such as Carbon Taxes, provide a simultaneous penalty approach. The issue with all such schemes is that they may prove transient, dependent as they are on political will and expediency.

What is certain is that the environment of funding combined with government schemes will inevitably provide a push towards the specification of more environmentally friendly buildings. However, funding for social improvement may be harder to achieve. The rise of community grants schemes such as that introduced in the UK are a start, but only a start.

References

Australian Building Codes Board (2009) Building Code of Australia. Canberra: Australian Building Codes Board.

Australian Bureau of Statistics (2008) *Environmental Issues: Energy Use and Conservation*, March 2008 (Cat. 4602.0.55.001).

ASX Australian Stock Exchange (2014) Managed Funds A-REITs. Retrieved 26 October 2014 from http://www.asx.com.au/products/managed-funds/areits.htm.

Bailey, A. (1988) *How To Be A Property Developer*, London: Mercury Books.

Barras, R. (2005). A building cycle model for an imperfect world, *Journal of Property Research* 22(2–3): 63–96.

Better Buildings Partnership (2013) *Green Lease Toolkit*. Retrieved from http://www.betterbuildingspartnership.co.uk/download/bbp-gltk-2013.pdf.

British Private Equity and Venture Capital Association (2014) *Responsible Investment: A Guide to Private Equity and Venture Capital Firms*, London: BCVA.

British Property Federation (BPF) (2014) *Property Data Report 2014*, London: British Property Federation.

Bryant, L. (2009). Property finance – current issues. Udb341 property finance. Paper from Queensland University of Technology.

Bryant, L. (2012) An assessment of development funding for new housing post GFC in Queensland, Australia, *International Journal of Housing Markets and Analysis* 5(2): 118–133.

Bryant, L. and Eves, C. (2012) Home sustainability policy and mandatory disclosure. A survey of buyer and seller participation and awareness in Queensland, *Property Management* 30(1): 29–51.

Carbon Trust, The (2014) The enhanced capital allowance scheme for energy-saving technologies. Retrieved on 28 October 2014 from https://etl.decc.gov.uk/etl/site/about.html.

Chartered Institute of Building (CIOB) (2013) Submission to the All Party Parliamentary Group for Excellence in the Built Environment on inquiry into Sustainable Construction and the Green Deal 4 January 2013. Retrieved March 2014 from http://www.ciob.org/sites/default/files/Sustainable%20Construction%20and%20the%20Green%20Deal.pdf.

Cherrington, R., Goodship, V., Longfield, A., and Kirwan, K. (2013) The feed-in tariff in the UK: a case study focus on domestic photovoltaic systems. *Renewable Energy* 50(42): 1–426.

Chinloy, P. (1996) Real estate cycles: theory and empirical evidence, *Journal of Housing Research*, 7,:173–190.

Clean Energy Finance Corporation (2014) CEFC finance transforms buildings through Environmental Upgrade Agreements: fact sheet. Retrieved from http://www.cleanenergyfinancecorp.com.au/media/63412/cefc_factsheet_euas_lr.pdf.

Conversation, The (2014) Carbon tax repealed: experts respond. Retrieved 20 October 2014 from http://theconversation.com/carbon-tax-repealed-experts-respond-29154.

Council of Australian Government (COAG) (2009) National Strategy on Energy Efficiency. Retrieved from http://www.coag.gov.au/coag_meeting_outcomes/2009-07-02/docs/Energy_efficiency_measures_table.pdf.

Covitz, D., Liang, N., and Suarez, G.A. (2013) The evolution of a financial crisis: collapse of the asset-backed commercial paper market, *The Journal of Finance* 68(3): 815–848.

Cunningham, K. (2014) London Calling: David versus Goliath in developer decision making & performance: an examination of how development decisions are made by distinct developer types and how this impacts performance. Unpublished MSc Thesis, Kingston University.

Davies, S. and Fairbrother, P. (2003) *Private Finance Initiative (PFI) and Public Private Partnerships (PPPs): Definitions and Sources*. Cardiff University School of Social Sciences Working Paper 39. Retrieved from http://www.cardiff.ac.uk/socsi/resources/wrkgpaper39.pdf

Davis, E.P. and Zhu, H. (2011) Bank lending and commercial property cycles: some cross-country evidence, *Journal of International Money and Finance* 30(1): 1–21.

Department of Climate Change and Energy Efficiency (2012) Tenant's Guide to Green Leases August 2012. Retrieved 28 October 2014 from http://www.industry.gov.au/Energy/EnergyEfficiency/Non-residentialBuildings/Documents/glsTenantsGuide.pdf.

Department of Sustainability and Environment (DSE) (Victoria)(2010)*Understanding Climate Change*. Retrieved 22 October 2010 from http://www.climatechange.vic.gov.au/greenhouse-gas-emissions/residential-energy-use.

Deutsche Energie-Agentur (2010) *Energy Performance Certificates for Buildings*. Retrieved 8 October 2014 from http://www.zukunft-haus.info/index.php?id=9632.

Dubben, N. and Williams, B. (2009) *Partnerships in Urban Property Development*, Hoboken, NJ: John Wiley & Sons.

Eichholtz, P., Kok, N., and Quigley, J.M. (2010) Doing well by doing good? Green office buildings, *The American Economic Review* 100(December): 2492–2509.

Ellis L., Kulish, M., and Wallace, S. (2012), Property market cycles as paths to financial distress, in Heath A., Packer, F., and Windsor, C. (eds), *Property Markets and Financial Stability*, Sydney: Reserve Bank of Australia.

ERM Economics and ERM Planning (2002) *Fiscal Incentives for Sustainable Homes: a report for WWK-UK*. Retrieved from http://www.wwf.org.uk/filelibrary/pdf/sustainablehomes.pdf.

Eves, C. (2013) Does sustainable housing construction provide the home owner with a greater investment return?, in Kajewski, S., Manley, K., and Hampson, K. (eds), *Proceedings of the 19th CIB World Building Congress*, Brisbane 2013: Construction and Society, Brisbane, Australia.

Eves, C and Kippes, S. (2010) Public awareness of green and energy efficient residential property: an emprical survey based on data from New Zealand, *Property Management* 28(3): 193–208.

French Environment and Energy Management Agency (2010) Buildings. Retrieved from http://www2.ademe.fr/servlet/KBaseShow?sort=-1&cid=96&m=3&catid=17778.

Green Building Council Australia (GBCA) (2012) *The Green Lease Handbook*. Retrieved on 28 October 2014 from http://www.gbca.org.au/gbc_scripts/js/tiny_mce/plugins/filemanager/Green-Lease-Handbook-20120907-PDF.pdf.

Green Construction Board (2014) *Mapping the Impacts of Minimum Energy Efficiency Standards for Commercial Real Estate Final Report*. Valuation and Demand Working Group: Project GCB630. Retrieved from http://www.greenconstructionboard.org/images/stories/Valuation_and_Demand/GCB%20630%20final%20report.pdf.

Green Leasing (2014) National Green Leasing Policy. Retrieved on 28 October 2014 from http://www.apcc.gov.au/ALLAPCC/GPG%20-%20National%20Green%20Leasing%20Policy.pdf.

Guertler, P., Robson, D., and Royston, S. (2013) Somewhere between 'A comedy of errors' and 'As you like it'? A brief history of Britain's 'Green Deal' so far, in *ECEEE Summer Study Proceedings*.

Hinnells, M., Bright, S., Langley, A., Woodford, L., Schiellerup, P., and Bosteels, T. (2008) The greening of commercial leases, *Journal of Property Investment & Finance* 26(6): 941–991.

ISPT (2014) Joint Venture and Development Partners. Retrieved 26 October 2014 from http://ispt.net.au/your-ispt/joint-venture-and-development-partners.

Kippes, S. and Eves, C. (2010) The attitudes of tenants, home buyers, vendors, concerning environmental questions – an empirical survey based on residential properties. Unpublished conference paper. European Real Estate Society Conference, Milan, Italy, June 2010.

Lenoir, A., Garde, F., Ottenwelter, E., Bornarel, A., and Wurtz, E. (2010) Net zero energy building in France: from design studies to energy monitoring. A state of the art review. Retrieved from http://www.researchgate.net/publication/267691406_Net_zero_energy_building_in_France_from_design_studies_to_energy_monitoring._A_state_of_the_art_review.

Morrissey, J. and Horne, R.E. (2011) Life cycle cost implications of energy efficiency measures in new residential buildings, *Energy and Buildings* 43(4): 915–924.

National Framework for Energy Efficiency (2008) Energy efficiency rating and house prices in the ACT. Canberra: Australian Government: Department of the Environment, Water, Heritage and the Arts. Retrieved from http://greengurus.com.au/wp-content/uploads/2011/03/Effect-Energy-Efficiency-has-on-House-Price_ACT-study.pdf.

Newell, G., MacFarlane, J., and Kok, N. (2011) *Building Better Returns – A Study of the Financial Performance of Green Office Buildings in Australia*, Deakin: Australian Property Institute.

NSW Government (2011) Guidelines for Environmental Upgrade Agreements. *NSW Government Gazette* No. 16.

Panayotou, T. (2013) *Instruments of Change: Motivating and Financing Sustainable Development*, London: Routledge.

Power, T. (2004) *Lease Arrangements for Green Commercial Buildings*, Freehills. Retrieved from http://www.freehills.com.au/1917.aspx.

Ragwitz, M. and Huber, C. (2005) Feed-in systems in Germany and Spain and a comparison, Report of the Fraunhofer Institut für Systemtechnik und Innovationsforschung (ISI). Karlruhe: Fraunhofer Institut.

REALpac (Real Property Association of Canada) (2008) *National Standard Green Office Lease for Single Building Projects*, Toronto: REALpac.

Rosenow, J., Eyre, N., Bürger, V., and Rohde, C. (2013) Overcoming the upfront investment barrier – comparing the German CO_2 Building Rehabilitation Programme and the British Green Deal, *Energy & Environment* 24(1): 83–104.

Rowland, P.J. (1997) *Property Investments and Their Financing*, second edn, North Ryde, NSW: Law Book Company.

Royal Institution of Chartered Surveyors (RICS) (2104) *RICS Valuation – Professional Standards*, London: RICS.

Sustainable Construction Task Group (2000) *Reputation, Risk and Reward: The Business Case for Sustainability in the UK Property Sector*, London: RICS.

Tavri, P., Sayce, S., and Hands, V. (2014) *Developing a Theoretical Framework for Waste and Idenitfiying its Association with UK industry Evidence on Waste Re-Use*. Southampton: WIT Press.

Trenouth, C. and Mead, D. (2007) *District Plan Barriers and Incentives to Sustainable Residential Building: Case Studies*. Report PR201/3 for Beacon Pathway Limited, Auckland: Beacon Pathway Ltd.

UK Green Building Council (2013) *Retrofit Incentives: Boosting Take-up of Energy Efficiency Measures in Domestic Properties: A Task Group Report*. Retrieved from http://www.ukgbc.org/resources/publication/uk-gbc-task-group-report-retrofit-incentives.

United Nations Environment Programme – Finance Initiative (UNEP FI) (2012) *Responsible Property Investment: What the Leaders Are Doing*, second edn. Retrieved from http://www.unepfi.org/fileadmin/documents/Responsible_Property_Investment_2_01.pdf.

US Congress (2009) Energy Efficiency in Housing Act of 2009. Retrieved from http://frwebgate.access.gpo.gov/cgi-bin/getdoc.cgi?dbname=111_cong_bills&docid=f:s1379is.txt.pdf.

Victoria Government (2010) Climate Change Act 2010, No. 54 of 2010, Victoria Government.

Wilkinson, S.J. (2014) Office building adaptations and the growing significance of environmental attributes, *Journal of Corporate Real Estate* 16(4): 252–265.

World Bank (2014) PPPs. Retrieved 28 October 2014 from http://ppp.worldbank.org/public-private-partnership/overview/what-are-public-private-partnerships.

World Green Building Council (2013) *The Business Case for Green Buildings*. Retrieved from http://www.worldgbc.org/files/1513/6608/0674/Business_Case_For_Green_Building_Report_WEB_2013-04-11.pdf.

6 Planning and regulatory issues impacting sustainable property development

Pernille H. Christensen and Sarah L. Sayce

6.0 Introduction

The property development process actively contributes to the built environment in which we live. Planning and regulatory intervention are the public means of managing property development so that the resultant built environment is shaped by policy developed for protection and enhancement of the public interest, rather than mere market forces which promote private interests. They have the ability to speed up or to inhibit property development. To be effective, planners and policymakers must understand the property development process, the risks and rewards that drive property developers and investors, and the impact that planning instruments have on the decision-making process of property developers and investors. The International Society of City and Regional Planners (ISOCARP 2001) has identified five basic elements of a planning system:

- source(s) of power (for planning intervention), articulated through national, state, regional, local or equivalent levels of government and legislation;
- a balance of strategic policies underpinned by incentives to encourage preferred development, and controls to constrain undesirable impacts;
- regulation: the need for consent to carry out change;
- legal rights for public consultation, including rights to object to a plan or decision; and,
- financial arrangements for public infrastructure and for planning administration.

(ISOCARP 2001)

Globally, there have been many changes at each of the power levels of planning in an effort to acknowledge and accommodate the need to create more sustainable urban areas. This chapter highlights what is happening worldwide, sets out the rationale for the direction of policy travel changes and analyses how these changes impact the property development process and, in particular, how they can promote more sustainable developments. Whilst the very nature of planning is that it differs between geographic regions and countries, there are overarching principal issues that provide common threads; these are explored within the chapter so that readers are able to place the practice within their own jurisdiction within a wider context. There are three main instruments through which planning authorities can impact the development process; these include strategic or detailed development plans, development controls and incentives.

Development plans provide the context for control decisions by detailing strategies and principles for planning authorities to implement when managing land use, spatial planning, environmental and other development issues. Planning authorities also use development plans to indicate where they would like to encourage development (e.g. by identifying land for specific uses in some areas), direct development (e.g. allowing some development uses/scales in the CBD but not residential) or prevent development (e.g. by identifying park space). As such, development plans offer guidance for the property market, helping landowners, developers and investors better understand what type of property development is likely to be accepted on the land.

Development controls are the administrative mechanisms that enable planning authorities to make decisions related to specific development proposals. Often, the development controls offer additional details related to the type and location of development and design guidelines related to development (such as scale and appearance, and urban design principles) such as setbacks and sidewalks. Planning authorities are able to use development controls to uphold the development plan, but also to exercise discretion and offer exceptions to the plan. Likewise, landowners, developers and investors can utilise development controls in a community to challenge the strategies and principles of the local development plan.

Development incentives are tools utilised by planning authorities to help stimulate property development and investment within their communities. In many ways, development incentives may be the most effective instrument that planning authorities have at their disposal to promote sustainable property development. Among other things, development incentives can be used to promote and market specific areas within a city, to make land available for development, provide subsidies and/or streamline the approval process. Many cities, councils and organisations have commenced implementing sustainability initiatives, however, few are maximising engagement with their stakeholders on their initiatives. Community and stakeholder engagement is key in reaping the rewards from implementing sustainable projects, gaining stakeholder buy-in, motivating behaviour change and in ensuring that sustainability continues to remain a key strategic driver for change. The issue of community engagement is covered as a separate section.

This chapter will discuss each of the development plans, controls and incentives utilised by planners in Australia, the UK and the US in more detail. However, it should be noted that the scope of this topic and the relationship between development plans, controls, and incentives is too much to examine in detail in a single chapter. As such, the research as presented in this chapter identifies specific statutory plans and controls which have a higher degree of impact on sustainable property development applications, appeals and enforcement. In addition, development incentives, which have shown to have a positive impact on promoting sustainable property development, are also discussed. Last, a case study of the Bullitt Centre in Seattle, and the Living Building Ordinance, developed by the city of Seattle as a demonstration ordinance, that enabled the Bullitt Centre to achieve full Living Building Challenge certification.

6.1   Global planning and policy trends impacting sustainable property development

Historically, local planning laws in middle Europe were guided by sustainability concerns through the eighteenth century. Their approach centred around the land-use systems known as 'allmende' (German) and 'commons' (UK) (Bosselmann 2013). The underpinning concerns of *allmende* were governed by ethics different from those informing modern property rights. The human–nature relationship was one of stewardship in that land could only be owned in so far as it was managed in an ecologically sustainable manner. Humans were users of land; it was a privilege, not a right. Common interests of the community took preference over individual property rights, thereby resulting in the principle of optimisation over maximisation (Bosselmann 2013). However, over the course of the nineteenth century, public environmental law virtually disappeared in some parts of Europe.

The Industrial Revolution dramatically transformed the way land and other natural resources were utilised. This was seen in three aspects: 1) the pressures of population growth caused the agricultural system to expand beyond its natural boundaries; 2) there was a philosophical change which resulted in natural resource exploitation being favoured over ecological sustainability; and, 3) the use of fossil fuels replaced renewable resources as the main producers of energy. Public land law reflected this change in the modern economy; short-term, free enterprise development became favoured over long-term, sustainable development. Private law and absolute property rights emerged as the reigning legal frameworks and largely ignored environmental protection and sustainability issues (Bosselmann 2013).

In many countries it was not until the mid-twentieth century that governments realised the need for environmental safeguards to protect natural resources. However, this was not the case in the UK which had introduced land-use planning provisions much earlier with the first specific planning act dating back to 1909 which outlawed back-to-back housing, and urban sprawl was effectively curtailed through the 1935 Control of Ribbon Development Act. By 1947 in the UK a comprehensive system of land-use controls, based on recognition of the needs to rebuild after the Second World War, had laid out a combined tax/compensation regime to work alongside what was effectively a nationalisation of all rights to develop land. Whilst the tax regime was short-lived, the notion of development rights belonging to the state and administered by local authorities in the public interest has not been seriously challenged and laid down a fundamental framework within which subsequent moves towards recognition of sustainability concerns could become embedded. For a detailed examination of the role of planning see Rydin (2011).

In response to the environmental movement of the 1960s and 1970s, environmental monitoring and regulatory targets related to emissions and other pollutants began to be introduced, and clean-up operations of brownfield sites began to be required (Christensen 2012; Simons *et al.* 2001). Although similar legislative efforts have occurred since then, Bosselmann notes that even until today, 'environmental law has remained a poor cousin of property and commercial law, only able to promote "insufficient measures at the periphery"' (Bosselmann 1995: 10, 2013: 16). Many of the important land-use legal cases and regulations have been more related to property rights, in that they merely added social (e.g. low-cost housing requirements in *Southern Burlington Country NAACP v. Mt. Laurel Township*, 336 A2d 713, New Jersey, 1975) or environmental duties (e.g. the Comprehensive environmental Response, Compensation, and Liability Act (CERCLA), 1980, US – commonly known as *Superfund*) to otherwise unrestricted property rights.

In recent decades, the need to combat environmental degradation caused by the depletion of natural resources, pollution, global warming and the growing urban sprawl in the outskirts of some cities has resulted in environmental issues becoming national priorities in many countries as they prepare for further population growth. Even businesses are expressing concern over the economic impacts of sprawl (Ohm 2000). Whilst sprawl has been a major issue within the US, in the UK the green belts have proved on balance to be highly successful as a containment strategy (Amati *et al.* 2006), although this has not been without its challenges (Amati 2012). Green Belt policies are not just a UK phenomenon; they have been utilised in countries as diverse as for example China (Zhao 2011). Apart from the use of tight policies such as green belts, smart growth, compact cities, new urbanism and liveable communities have emerged as some of the potential alternative policy solutions to sprawl. More recently, in some areas, such as the US, the transformation beyond an industrial economy has presented the pressure of de-population with its attendant social issues reflected in the condition and economic sustainability of real estate leading to calls for increased green infrastructure and community engagement. (Schilling and Logan 2008).

Thus, planning strategies influence development plans and controls (e.g. form- and performance-based codes) as well as the types of incentives offered for sustainable property development (e.g. streamlined approval for 'green' property development; match to tax regimes). As such, discussions related to the economic viability, character of place and actual level of sustainability of these alternative planning strategies have entered the debate. It should be noted, that 'green', 'environmental' and 'sustainable' development are often used interchangeably within these and other urban planning strategies and the instruments which will plan, control and incentivise them. This chapter does not make judgments about the level of sustainability of the various instruments, but focuses on the strategies they take to encourage and promote sustainable property development in their communities.

6.2   Development plans and controls

There are normally two key stages in the urban planning process: 1) forward planning – which defines strategic objectives and policies to achieve them, and 2) development control or management, which assesses development proposals against planning policies. Some countries place greater emphasis on one stage of the planning process than the other. Although strategic planning and development assessment should in theory be two sides of a single coin, in practice there is often a greater emphasis placed on development control/management in part because the resources and expertise of many planning authorities are limited leading to an incomplete policy framework . In other instances, it can be caused by the locus of decision-making lying in the hands of elected lay committee members, rather than planning professionals. It could also be argued that it is this lack of emphasis on strategic planning which has caused some of the urban challenges related to sustainability which many of our cities face today.

To legitimise the development planning and control functions of a planning system the relevant source of power (see ISOCARP above) must be identified through legislation or, in some cases, from several pieces of legislation (Gurran 2011). Different countries assign the source of power either in a top-down or a bottom-up manner. The source of power assigned to a given planning legislation is often tied to the government's philosophy related to property rights (Bosselmann 2013).

For example, Australia and the United States have limited national involvement in planning and policy development, and have a strong emphasis on individual property rights. In these countries, states are responsible for enacting their own legislation related to land-use planning systems while local governments are responsible for the detailed responsibilities related to preparing plans and assessing property developments. In contrast, the planning system in the United Kingdom assigns responsibility to the local planning authorities for enforcing the plan-making and development assessment policies outlined at the national planning policy level, although there have been recent moves to reduce the types of development requiring explicit consent.

Planning controls support development plans by explaining the standards and restrictions for a new development in more detail. Controls can be created for multiple locations and scales (e.g. suburb, street or single lot), types of development (e.g. residential, commercial or industrial) or for particular components of the development (e.g. provision of car parking, control of storm water).

Some planning authorities argue that stringent development plans and controls cannot be justified in areas of economic decline (Hall 2011). Hall's response offers clear direction to tentative planning authorities and offers a case for implementing planning designs and policy. He explains that areas experiencing economic decline should not shy away from pressing developers to achieve high design standards as such profits are most often more profitable. Additionally, high quality developments also add value by promoting regeneration in the community. He notes that 'Reluctance on behalf of both parties to pursue higher standards is more in the mind than in the pocket' (Hall 2011: 90–91).

In the sections that follow, the development plans and controls for Australia, the UK and the US will be discussed, and the impacts of each planning system on sustainable property development will be highlighted. Table 6.1 shows an overview of the planning instruments for each country. This will be followed by a discussion of the development incentives used by planning authorities to promote sustainable development.

6.2.1 Australia

The national government in Australia has minimal impact on the planning process at the state and local levels. There are two exceptions. The Environment Protection and Biodiversity Conservation Act 1999 establishes a framework for assessing impacts of urban planning decisions on, among other considerations, threatened species, World Heritage and National Heritage sites. The national urban policy, released by the Minister of Infrastructure in May 2011, presents a national approach to urban development and offers overarching goals for the nation's cities as well as an approach for addressing the inherent challenges Australian cities must address to become more productive, sustainable and liveable. It identifies 14 key Australian government initiatives and sets short-, medium- and long-term targets and goals for each initiative (DIT 2011).

At the state/territory level, each of the six states and two territories in Australia have their own planning laws and procedures resulting in different systems for land-use management and planning. As such, there is no unified planning system for Australia. Although there are many similarities in the overall approach, each state has their own planning system which operates independently of other states. In order to discuss state and local-level planning systems of Australia in more detail, the discussion below has focused on the planning system in New South Wales. Gurran (2011) offers an excellent assessment of the breadth of issues and challenges related to the Australian urban land-use planning principles, systems and practices.

The primary planning instruments used in New South Wales are the Environment Planning and Assessment Act (EP&A Act) of 1979 and the Environmental Planning and Assessment Regulation 2000. The plan-making system in NSW is explained in Part 3 of the EP&A Act, while the majority of development proposals in New South Wales are assessed under Part 4. It should be noted that the EP&A Act includes a revision for the public to participate in planning decisions impacting the future development of their communities. In addition, environmental planning instruments (SEPPs and LEPs, discussed below) are described as 'legal documents that regulate land use and development' (NSW 2014a).

In New South Wales (NSW) Local Environmental Plans (LEPs) guide planning decisions for local government areas. Area councils use zoning and development controls to regulate

Table 6.1 Planning instruments

	Australia	United Kingdom	United States
Local	Standard instrument local environmental plan Development control plan Local planning study	Local development plans Supplemental planning documents such as site specific/area action plans Adopted proposals map Simplified planning zones	Comprehensive plan Zoning plan Land use plan Design guidelines
Regional	Now governed at the state level		Not enforceable; local planning authorities sign voluntary agreements to accomplish regional goals
State	NSW Environmental Planning and Assessment Act 1979 Environmental Planning and Assessment Regulation 2000 State Environmental Planning Policy (SEPP) Affordable Rental Housing Policy	N/A	Set local planning requirements (e.g. comprehensive plan requirements)
National	Environment Protection and Biodiversity Conservation Act 1999 National Urban Policy, 2011	Planning Policy Acts (e.g. Town and Country Planning Act 1990; Planning Act 2008; Localism Act 2011; Growth and Infrastructure Act 2013) National Planning Policy Framework (NPPF) 2012 Planning Policy Guidance (currently under revision)	CERCLA 1980 Standard State Zoning Enabling Act, 1924

how land is used. Development Controls Plans (DCPs) supplement the LEP and provide specific, comprehensive requirements for types and locations of future development or locations. 'LEPs are the primary planning tool to shape the future of communities and also oversee the estimated $20 billion worth of local [property] development that is determined each year' (NSW 2014b).

Most property development proposals in NSW require lodgement of a development application with the local council. As noted above, the EP&A Act allows for public participation in decision-making related to future development. As such, depending on local council policy, the council will exhibit the development application and accept public comments before making a decision on the development application (DA). Figure 6.1 illustrates the development application process for New South Wales under the Standard Instrument LEP Programme. Minor modifications may still apply in some communities.

However, some development may qualify for a fast-tracked review process for complying development (e.g. home extensions, shop fit-outs) if the development type is specifically covered in the local council or NSW state codes. In this case, the complying development must be certified within ten days. Large developments also have the ability to by-pass local

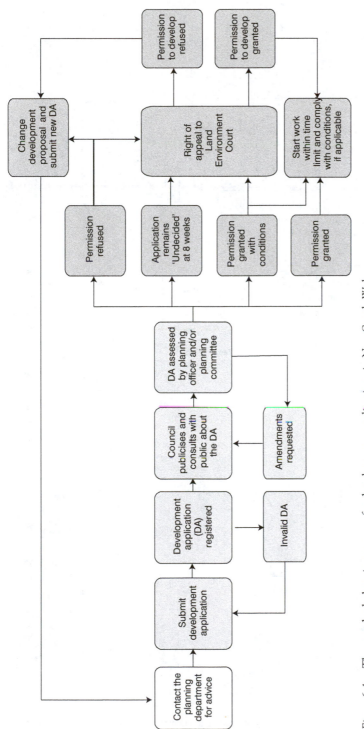

Figure 6.1 a The standard planning process for development applications in New South Wales
Source: Authors

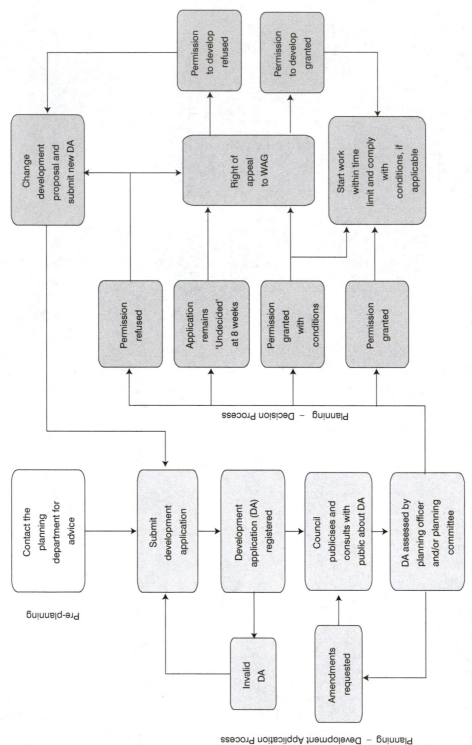

Figure 6.1 b The standard planning process for development applications in New South Wales
Source: Authors

councils if they meet the requirements to be a state significant development (SSD). These developments have a certain capital investment value (CIV), are over a certain size, are located in a sensitive environmental area or in a precinct identified as important by the NSW government. The requirements for developments and sites to qualify for SSD status are found in Schedules 1 and 2 of the State and Regional Development SEPP. Alternatively, the Minister for Planning can declare a project as a SSD after consulting with the Planning Assessment Commission (PAC) on the state/regional significance of the development.

For development applications that are denied or approved with conditions, property developers have the option to appeal against the council's decision in the Land and Environment Court (LEC). The LEC was established by the Land and Environment Court Act 1979 as part of the EP&A Act and as such deals with issues related to public law (i.e. citizens protecting their rights against the government). The court hears both merit and judicial appeals. A merit appeal involves examination and assessment of development application. For planning and building merit appeals related to Class 1 (environmental planning and protection appeals), Class 2 (local government and miscellaneous appeals), or Class 3 (land tenure, valuation, rating compensation) the court examines the development application afresh, *de novo*, rather than reviewing the council's decision. In such cases, the court is concerned with, wheteras a matter of merit, the proposed development is 'good' or 'bad'. In contrast, a judicial review by the court only determines whether the council's decision was made in accordance with the law and is legally valid.

In 2006, The Standard Instrument LEP (SILEP) Programme was rolled out by the New South Wales government in an effort to create a standardised format and content for LEPs. The aim of the programme was to simplify and streamline development plan and control formats so that they might be more easily understood by planners, property developers and investors, and community members. Prior to this initiative, 'there were approximately 5,500 local planning instruments across the State, containing some 3,100 different land-use zones and 1,700 land-use definitions' (NSW 2014b). With such diversity, it is easy to understand NSW's aim of reducing this complexity to a single LEP used by all local government areas. Furthermore, the SILEP Programme standardises the language of the development plans by providing a standard suite of 35 land-use zones and approximately 250 land-use definitions (NSW 2014b). However, even local government areas who have adopted the SILEP still have additional planning instruments. For example, the following additional planning instruments apply to property development within the city of Sydney local area: Sydney Local Environmental Plan 2012 and Sydney Local Environmental Plan 2005 (applies to the Frasers Broadway, the former Carlton and United Breweries site only; this will remain active until the completion of the Central Park development, which is currently ongoing at the time of writing).

For those engaged with property development, the implementation of the Standard Instrument LEP Programme enables more efficient decisions to be made related to the planning process as local development plans are more easily assessed for content related to land use and planning requirements and exclusions. Key outcomes of implementing the Standard Instrument LEP Programme include:

- a consistent way of reflecting recent strategic land-use planning undertaken by councils and the NSW government;
- provision of an adequate supply of land for housing and employment;
- effective management of natural, environmental and cultural resources.

(NSW 2014b)

To further simplify the state's planning system, Regional Environmental Plans (REPs) were eliminated from the hierarchy of environmental planning instruments in NSW in July 2009. All existing REPs are now deemed State Environmental Planning Policies (SEPPs). SEPPs deal with issues significant to each individual state within Australia. Generally, SEPPs are created by the Governor upon the recommendation of the Minister for Planning and his team. Before being finalised as a legal document, SEPPs are first publicly exhibited in draft form for public feedback. During this time, community members, including property developers, are encouraged to submit letters of response to the government related to the proposed planning policy. This could change, however, if the new Planning Bill gets passed into law.

New South Wales has been undergoing the community engagement process since its review of the EP&A Act by an independent review board was completed in 2011. The green paper, a new planning system for NSW was exhibited for public feedback in July 2012. In response to public feedback the white paper and associated draft planning legislation was created and exhibited for public feedback from April–June 2013. At the time of this writing, the proposed Planning Bill has been deferred by the Lower House (28 November 2013). Among the concerns of Lower House representatives are the change in structure of community consultation and the lack of emphasis on sustainable property development. The Planning Bill as written at the time of this writing emphasises community involvement early in the planning process, during the development of the Local Environmental Plan, rather than at the development approval stage, as is currently available. This would enable compliant development applications to be streamlined without input from community members. This has raised considerable debate in the media and concerns about the Planning Bill being 'pro-developer' and excluding community members from the decision-making process. On the other side of the debate are governmental officials supporting the bill. They highlight how this method of community consultation enables community members to influence the LEP which oversees the enforcement of requirements for development applications, and that compliant development should therefore be something community members would support. By streamlining development approvals, communities are more apt to attract new development and investment. A summary list of New South Wales SEPPS and regional planning policies can be found at: www.legislation.nsw.gov.au.

6.2.2 United Kingdom

In contrast to the Australian and American planning systems, the UK's current planning system takes a top-down source of authority approach, but with significant local variation still permitted, due to an increasing emphasis on community engagement (for a discussion see Holam and Rydin 2013). Planning in the UK has a long history, as outlined above and the introduction of a country-wide approach through a unified system in 1947 (Town and Country Planning Act (TPCA) 1947) was one of the earliest comprehensive approaches to land-use planning to be introduced anywhere in the world. It is controlled both through legislation and policy instruments and in recent years the notion of sustainable development has been placed at the heart of policy and statutory developments.

6.2.2.1 The policy framework

From the early days of comprehensive planning systems, there has existed a tiered policy system combined with development control (now called management). The policy environment requires local authorities to produce strategic documents which require consultation and national approval. The system by which policy has been set and plans produced has varied over time, normally being a two-tier system, sometimes three tier. In creating plans at the local level, the influence of central government has waxed and waned depending on the government of the day. In recent years it has become increasingly centralised as there have been moves from central 'guidance' notes to policy 'statements'.

However since 2011, with the enactment of the Localism Act, there has been a complete reform of the UK policy environment. Now, in terms of both setting out the government's intent for planning and their articulation of their understanding of sustainable development, the National Planning Policy Framework (NPPF) published in 2012 (CLG 2012) is the key controlling document. This sets out specifically that '*the purpose of the planning system is to contribute to the achievement of sustainable development*' (NPPF: 3). When it was introduced it produced controversy as it also states that development means growth, which was argued by some to be a developer's charter which would damage rural interests (Brearley 2012). The NPPF provides the framework of principles within which all local planning authorities are charged with developing their own local plans and supplementary documents. At first reading, the principles are ones which promote sustainability, for example, the protection of the natural environment and heritage assets, the promotion of good design and the requirement that planning should assist in the moves to a low carbon economy. Where it has been seen as more difficult in sustainability terms is the *presumption* in favour of granting consent for development that is 'sustainable'. This places pressure on the interpretation of just what *is* or is *not* sustainable. Whilst the document is very clear that sustainable development embraces economic, social and environmental criteria, in practice there is a danger that the need to create job opportunities and increase the old and insufficient housing stock will outweigh environmental considerations, with planning authorities simply taking an accredited rating system attached to a building proposal (such as BREEAM) as sufficient evidence of the development being sustainable.

The introduction of the NPPF required all local planning authorities to revise their planning framework documents to incorporate the principles of the new framework; where this has not taken place there now exists the presumption that developments will be allowed unless there is good reason that they be rejected. Given the pressure that authorities have been under to do this in times of restricted budgets it is perhaps not surprising that as at the time of writing almost half of all local planning authorities have not achieved the required approved revised plans. This is disadvantageous in sustainability terms as the new plans all need to address specifically what is required in their areas to achieve for example biodiversity gains, reduced CO_2 emissions, etc. One feature that is prevalent in most new documentation is a requirement to develop statutory code levels in terms of carbon emissions and reduction in energy use.

The other main UK planning policy initiative that is geared towards sustainability is the so-called shift from big government to big society; as movement set out through the Localism Act (2011) aimed at promoting the right of local people to shape the places in which they live and work. Whilst much of the Localism movement is geared towards local financing, it also embeds planning by giving greater rights to local communities to shape the plan process and determine the nature of developments. In some cases, it also gives such groups the right to develop without the need for express consent but whether these moves to increase democratisation will work is open to debate (see for example Allmendinger and Haughton 2014).

Whilst UK planning is essentially 'plan-led', in many areas there is a gap in up-to-date plans and decisions are therefore taken with reference only to outmoded plans and to the NPPF and to established case law. The actual development management process is set out in the Town and Country Planning Act (1990) as amended by the Planning and Compulsory Purchase Act (PCPA) 2004 and a raft of subsequent legislation including the Planning and Infrastructure Act 2013.

In summary, the UK's policy framework places high importance on sustainability principles lying at the heart of strategic planning; however, progress towards embedding these principles at the local level is slower and, in any event, there is still such ambiguity over the interpretation of the principles (Paterson 2012) that it will take some time before it is seen to bring about the desired change in emphasis (Betts 2011).

6.2.2.2 *Development rights and managing community costs*

As stated above, under UK legislation, effectively all development rights are vested in the state with consent to undertake development being subject to consent (for a full explanation of the law see Duxbury 2012). When this principle was first introduced in 1947, a compensation system was set up to run alongside the act so that any development value pre-dating the planning system remained in the hands of the landowner, whilst any new development value arising was subject to taxation. In principle, this could be viewed as an equitable situation and a means of ensuring that value arising from community action (namely the grant of consent) was returned to the community by way of taxation. However, this system did not persist and within a few years development taxation was abolished and successive attempts to tax the land conversion process have been fraught with political difficulty and have largely proved unsuccessful. As at the time of writing, two systems to recoup for the community the value of planning and offset the negative externalities that result from development exist. These are planning obligations (or S.106 agreements as they are properly known) which require contributions on-site normally in the form of affordable housing and/or biodiversity and other environmental benefits and Community Infrastructure Levy (CIL) which is a discretionary local tax based on a floor area basis the proceeds of which are retained locally to supply the infrastructure demands occasioned by the development, such as clinics, parks and other facilities.

Both planning obligations and CIL are essentially measures which place additional costs on development and can act as a brake on demand for land by potentially decreasing profitability. On the other end of the scale, where authorities wish to drive up the speed of development take-up, incentives can be introduced such as Simplified Planning Zones which reduce the need for specific consent for development but do not provide any financial assistance. Whilst some have been introduced in areas where there is perceived to be a local need to increase the rate of development, they are not common.

6.2.2.3 *The development application process*

Consent is required for any action that constitutes development as defined in S.55 of the 1990 Town and Country Planning Act. Development includes:

- building operations (e.g. structural alterations, construction, rebuilding, most demolition);
- material changes of use of land and buildings;

- engineering operations (e.g. groundworks);
- mining operations;
- other operations normally undertaken by a person carrying out a business as a builder;
- subdivision of a building (including any part it) used as a dwelling for use as two or more separate dwellings.

However, not all development requires explicit consent. First, some categories of work are specifically excluded from the definition, such as works to the interior of a non-listed building. Second, to reduce bureaucracy, by regulation (the General Permitted Development Order), many categories of small works are given a 'deemed' consent, which is capable of rescinding by the authority, albeit with possible compensation attached. Whilst the use of permitted development is important, both logistically and in common-sense terms, recent blanket consents including changes of use from offices to residential can have large impact on the cohesion and vitality of a central area and hence potentially negative social outcomes.

If the nature of the proposed scheme does not fall into one of the exclusions, it will require explicit consent. The development application process is managed by the local authority and Figure 6.2 below sets out in a flow diagram the normal process through which an application moves. Three important elements of the process from a sustainability perspective are:

- the pre-application process;
- the consultations required; and
- the documentation.

Following the implementation of the Planning Act 2008, there has been a requirement for all those seeking to make a planning application above prescribed threshold limits to enter into pre-application negotiations with the planning officers to establish the principles of the scheme. Whilst there was initial resistance by some developers to this process, which was viewed as an added expense and possible time delay (see the Killian and Pretty 2008), in reality this is not always the case and whilst it has been identified as a process capable of improvement it has been found to reduce the likelihood of conditions and appeals (Cambridge Centre for Housing and Planning Research 2014). It is therefore likely that the pre-application stage is one which, used constructively, can aid sustainable development. Although the 2008 Act envisaged only certain large applications requiring pre-application negotiations, the process is now spreading with the Localism Act empowering the use of pre-application advertisement if the authority so wishes. This is now being taken up by some authorities for small sensitive schemes such as solar arrays and wind turbines.

Once an application is lodged, depending on its size and level of contention (for example whether it is a departure from the local plan or is likely to have much opposition), there is normally a requirement to consult not only with statutory consultees, such as parish councils and utilities, but also with the public. As in the US, there is a move towards genuine engagement with stakeholders as realisation has grown that to include the views of local inhabitants and businesses which the development will impact over a long term, is likely to lead to a more appropriate scheme. It is also likely to reduce opposition, speed up the process and reduce the need to appeal against any conditions or indeed receive a refusal. Again the consultation process offers the opportunity for sustainability features to be more carefully considered and appropriately incorporated.

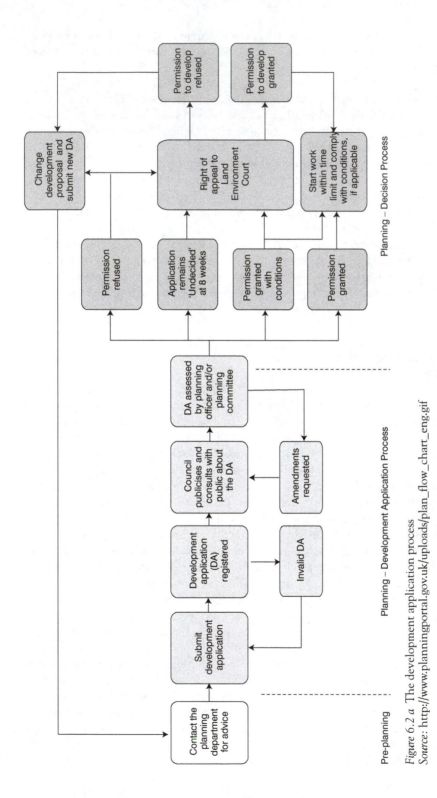

Pre-planning   Planning – Development Application Process   Planning – Decision Process

Figure 6.2 a The development application process
Source: http://www.planningportal.gov.uk/uploads/plan_flow_chart_eng.gif

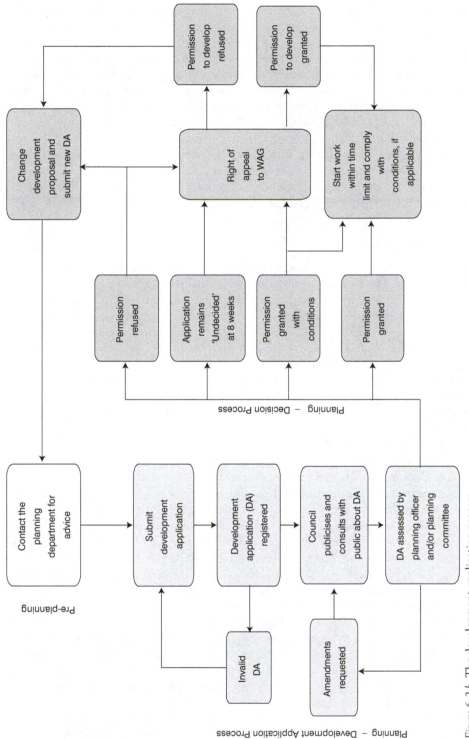

Pre-planning

Planning – Development Application Process

Contact the planning department for advice

Submit development application

Development application (DA) registered

Invalid DA

Council publicises and consults with public about DA

Amendments requested

DA assessed by planning officer and/or planning committee

Planning – Decision Process

Permission refused

Application remains "Undecided" at 8 weeks

Permission granted with conditions

Permission granted

Change development proposal and submit new DA

Right of appeal to WAG

Start work within time limit and comply with conditions, if applicable

Permission to develop refused

Permission to develop granted

Figure 6.2 b The development application process
Source: http://www.planningportal.gov.uk/uploads/plan_flow_chart_eng.gif

Finally, the nature of the documentation required will have an impact on the level of sustainability incorporated. It is here that EU requirements may increase the burden on developers and their teams by the need for an Environmental Impact or indeed full Sustainability Assessment to be undertaken. Even if these are not required, a scheme of any local significance will now almost certainly require a design and access statement which will need to address matters such as the use of sustainable materials, flood risk prevention, travel plans, biodiversity measures and on-site energy generation. Whilst this may increase the initial costs of preparing the application it does ensure that constructive consideration is now routinely built into the planning process by all stakeholders; this should lead to more thoughtful and longer-lived developments which respect their local context and the wider environment.

In summary, the UK process has now embedded sustainability through both national policy and local implementation. Whilst there are still undoubtedly flaws in the systems, it bodes well moving forward. The biggest risk is yet another change in legislative direction before this has been able to bed in and the results become visible in the town and cityscape.

6.2.3 The United States

The planning system in the US has many similarities with the Australian system. Like the Australian system, the federal government has limited responsibilities related to urban planning, although in both countries the federal government is able to influence the state and local planning efforts indirectly through legislation (e.g. environmental impact laws) and funding stipulations. Individual states are responsible for managing the land-use planning system. States develop enabling legislation and policy guidelines to establish local planning parameters (Gurran 2011); however, the ability for states to intervene in local planning policy decisions varies from state to state as a result of differing state constitution provisions for state intervention in local policy matters. This means that any drive to use planning as a mechanism to increase sustainable development is not deeply embedded.

For states mandating the adoption of a comprehensive plan at the local level, required elements most often include land use and transportation elements, but may also include: housing, utilities, natural and cultural resources, economic development or other elements deemed important by the legislators. Examples of this state requirement include the Oregon Department of Land Conservation and Development's Key Elements Of The Comprehensive Plan document (2000) and the Wisconsin comprehensive planning and smart growth law (1999 Wisconsin Act 9 as amended by Act 148). Ohm (2010) breaks down each element of the Wisconsin law in detail. Where states do not mandate the adoption of comprehensive plans, local jurisdictions have more freedom in establishing development plans and controls, although they must still conform to relevant state and federal legislation. As a result of this planning system, there are vast differences in land-use planning and policy approaches across the US not only at the state level, but even more so at the local level. A typical development application process is illustrated in Figure 6.3. Note there will be some variation in implementation as a result of the varying local planning and policy approaches in different local communities. Note also the community consultation process in the US is more extensive than in either the Australian or UK planning systems. Participatory planning plays a major role in the American planning system and can be very influential in the development approval process; indeed the very notion of participatory planning owes its origin to the work of Arnstein whose seminal work promoted the now

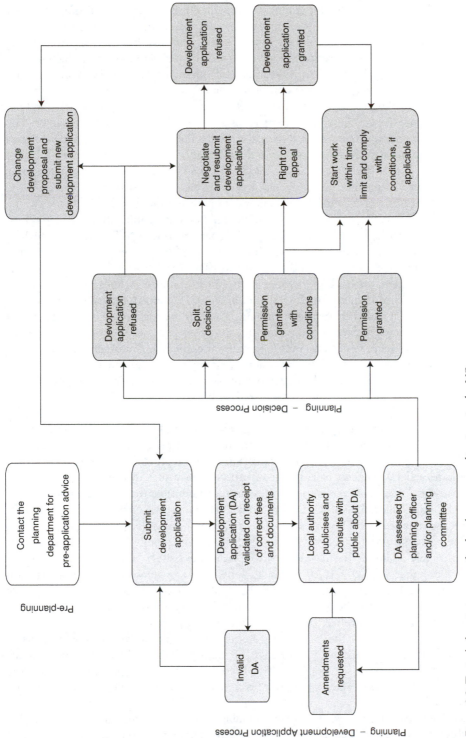

Figure 6.3 Typical planning process for development applications in the US
Source: Authors

well-known 'ladder of participation' (Arnstein 1969). For this reason it is advised that property developers engaged with the participatory planning process begin by building 'buy-in' among the various stakeholder groups which will be influenced by their project; better still they engage them actively as participants in the design journey.

A key driver of the planning process in the United States is that the planning process 'links an upfront public policy making process to a wide variety of follow-on implementation process' (Beckner 2010: 6). This process was laid out in its modern form in the early twentieth century but has undergone significant changes since its inception. The Standard State Zoning Enabling Act was published in 1924 as a model to facilitate orderly land-use development, provide certainty for property investors and protect individual property rights. As a result of the strong emphasis on zoning in American planning practice, the courts have had a significant role in the development of the US planning process. In 1926, in *Village of Euclid, Ohio* v. *Amber Realty Company* (272 US 365), the US Supreme Court upheld zoning as a valid form of regulation and police power. This case had a strong influence on the Euclidean Zoning practices being used in many communities throughout the US today. The 1930s saw land-use zoning, building setbacks and public housing initiatives used to address issues related to the spread of diseases in urban tenement housing. The 1950s brought a series of initiatives for urban renewal which were followed by a series of new programmes focusing on environmental issues in the 1960s and 1970s (e.g. water pollution control, air-quality improvement, wetlands protection, environmental impacts). Current efforts by the American Planning Association (APA), the International Council for Local Environmental Initiatives (ICLEI) and the US Green Building Council include policy guides for 'Smart Growth' and 'Complete Streets' strategies to assist states and local communities in their efforts to achieve more compact, environmentally friendly and sustainable development. Beckner (2010) offers an excellent discussion of emerging trends in planning sustainable communities in the US. Below, the development plans and controls impacting sustainable property development in the United States are highlighted.

- *National-level planning policies:* Among the national-level policies influencing sustainable development is the National Environmental Policy Act (NEPA) 1969, which established a broad national framework for protecting the environment. NEPA requires federal agencies to consider environmental values in their decision-making process and assures that all branches of government consider the environmental impact of any and all major federal actions. Environmental impact statement (EIS) requirements are also detailed by NEPA. In addition, the Comprehensive Environmental Response, Compensation, and Liability Act (CERCLA, or as commonly known, Superfund) specifically addresses the development of brownfield sites. Enacted by Congress on 11 December 1980, CERCLA includes long-term site remediation and short-term removal of hazardous materials. CERCLA collected over US$1.6 billion in taxes from petroleum and chemical industries that went into a trust fund for cleaning up abandoned or uncontrolled hazardous waste sites. For property developers interested in infrastructure projects, the Air Quality Act of 1990 essentially merged comprehensive transportation and land-use planning at the metropolitan level with the regional air-quality planning process. All federally assisted transportation improvements (highway and transit systems) in metropolitan areas were required to attain particular air-quality standards.
- *Local-level planning policies:* A growing number of states require comprehensive plans, which aim to establish guidelines for future growth in a given community. It is a formal

document including goals and policies, maps and guidelines that may be either advisory in nature or adopted into law by the local authority. The comprehensive plan acts as a policy guide for the future community on decisions related to infrastructure systems as well as the quality, location and amount of property development for a 10–20 year time frame. Zoning Ordinances are the most widely used land-use regulation instrument and include written requirements and standards related to the use of land. In recent years, there have been a number of innovative approaches to zoning which increase flexibility for developers and in many cases also promote sustainable property development. Examples of these include: cluster zoning, incentive zoning, inclusionary zoning and flexible zoning.

6.3 Development incentives

In the US, there have been several series of cutbacks from the federal government which limit the ability for communities to use federal aid dollars to incentivise property development projects. This scenario is similar to the challenges faced by communities in many other countries as well. In order to continue supporting projects, local communities have had to increasingly rely on local incentive schemes such as: tax increment financing, special assessment districts, tax abatements, land swaps, lease/purchase agreements, capital improvements, and value creating trade-offs based on zoning bonuses. In exchange for absorbing some of the development risk, the local community often takes a direct financial stake in the property development project through participatory leases and/or profit-sharing agreements. Often the profit-sharing revenues offer minimum profit to the local community during the initial years, however, the profit-sharing structure offers the city other non-financial benefits. In part, they offer political protection to city councils vulnerable to charges that they are giving away too much because 'a financial agreement to share returns is perceived as a sign that the city is acting responsibly and effectively'.

There are essentially two methods by which regulatory and financial incentives can promote the sustainable property development in their communities, carrots and sticks. 'Carrots' include incentives for 'doing the right thing'; some might say these positive incentives are offsetting externalities that could otherwise be considered negative externalities by the developer to create a balanced score sheet. Example of positive incentives include rebates and grants (e.g. Photovoltaic Rebate Program and the Greenhouse Gas Abatement Grant in Australia), carbon credit trading (allowed by the Kyoto Protocol), and streamlining the development application process among others. Another option is by allowing alternative compliance tracks to prescriptive development plans and controls. One example is Queensland's Sustainable Planning Act 2009, which allows developers to choose between a traditional 'code assessable' track or an 'impact assessable' option that offers a potentially more flexible compliance track whereby more interpretive criteria must be demonstrated.

'Sticks' promote sustainable property development through regulatory means; some might say they are a means of preventing negative externalities. Examples include local building codes, taxes and levies (e.g. landfill levies), mandated renewable energy certificates (e.g. the Australian Renewable Energy Act 2000) and slower processing times for development applications. Clark (2003) offers a thorough discussion of the various incentive programmes available in Australia. A report by the American Institute of Architects (AIA) and the National Association of Counties (NACo) (AIA and NACo 2012) outlines state and local government green building incentives and a discussion of how to select which incentives will best meet the needs of both local governments and property developers.

In an interview with Denis Hayes, President and CEO of the Bullitt Foundation, he notes that one of the primary concerns for property developers is time. Most property developers do not have the benefit of the holding period to recoup their costs for developing a sustainable manner. Although market demands may drive sustainable property development in some markets, this is not the case for all urban areas let alone rural areas. As such, local planning authorities looking to influence developers to develop property in a sustainable manner need to consider the planning aspects which they control that might impact a developer's bottom line. Hayes worked with the city of Seattle to develop a Living Building and Deep Green Pilot ordinance to promote sustainable property development. A key aspect of the city of Seattle approach includes the Priority Green Facilitated Pilot programme which shortens review time. As time equals money for most developers, being able to process the development application quicker is a significant incentive for many developers in Seattle. A more detailed discussion of financial incentives can be found in Chapter 5.

6.4   Conclusion

Understanding the purpose and application of development planning policy, controls and incentives enables property developers to understand specific planning local systems within which they aim to achieve sustainable property development. As noted in this chapter, there are different levels at which planning policies and strategies are developed; these include national, state, regional, local, precinct and site level. At all of these levels, planning systems ultimately reflect the strategic goals for property development and aim to prevent negative impacts from development on their communities.

Taxation and incentives, such as relaxed planning zones, can be used to encourage positive outcomes consistent with their strategic plans and local land-use plans. Ultimately, all property development initiates interaction with the planning system upon submission of the development application for a particular project. All property development must work within the confines of the relevant planning controls and regulations at all levels of government, but may find that developing property in a sustainable manner can help streamline the process and reduce the review; indeed in some jurisdictions the principles of sustainability are now being systematically and progressively embedded within policy and control practice. The examples of the varying structures of planning systems in Australia, the UK and the US exemplify the difference in approaches property developers must take to make their projects a reality. As already noted, the trend in Australia is towards greater standardisation and codification of routine development types, while still providing greater flexibility for more significant proposals; in the UK a centralised system is being combined with a loosening of controls at the local level. This dichotomy at times raises other challenges and concerns. The US employs more prescriptive approaches through the use of zoning and development standards, although new strategies such as Smart Codes, smart growth and form-based codes are gaining traction.

Brain argues that policymakers strive to 'achieve an end with means that are never neutral in themselves. In the context of the urban landscape, every design and planning decision is a value proposition, and a proposition that has to do with social and political relationships' (Brain 2005: 233). Brain's contention is that value propositions and value positions cannot be ignored when considering the relationship between the means and ends;

the means being the instruments and the ends discussed in this chapter being sustainable property development. If we truly aim to develop property in a more sustainable manner we must begin to assert these values in the property development process. The planning stage is an ideal opportunity to capture the value propositions and positions in a manner that has the opportunity to influence the development plans and controls; this is being government led in countries such as the UK; elsewhere the state is less interventionist in promoting sustainability. Only by doing so, can we begin to make real progress beyond the few developers who either truly believe in 'doing the right thing and leading the charge' or they believe in the economic proposition and see an opportunity for added value in developing sustainably.

References

AIA and NACo (American Institute of Architects and the National Association of Counties) (2012) Local leaders in sustainability: green building incentive trends – strengthening communities, building green economies. Retrieved 28 April 28 2014 from http://www.aia.org/aiaucmp/groups/aia/documents/pdf/aiab093472.pdf.

Allmendinger, P. and Haughton, G. (2014) Post-political regimes in English planning, *Planning Against the Political: Democratic Deficits in European Territorial Governance* 37(1): 89–103..

Amati, M. (ed.) (2012) *Urban Green Belts in the Twenty-first Century*, Farnham: Ashgate.

Amati, M. and Yokohari, M. (2006) Temporal changes and local variations in the functions of London's green belt, *Landscape and Urban Planning* 75(1): 125–142.

Arnstein, S.R. (1969) A ladder of citizen participation, *Journal of the American Institute of Planners* 35(4): 216–224.

Barker, Kate (2006) *Barker Review of Land Use Planning: Final Report – Recommendations*, London: The Stationery Office.

Beckner, Chrisanne (ed.) (2010) Planning infrastructure to sustain America: next-generation concepts to guide community, design and infrastructure professions. American Society of Civil Engineers (ASCE) Practice, Education and Research for Sustainable Infrastructure (PERSI) Task Committee on Planning for Sustainable Infrastructure. Retrieved 14 May 2014 from http://www.asce.org/uploadedFiles/Sustainability_-_New/Resources/PLANNING%20INFRASTRUCTURE%20TO%20SUSTAIN%20AMERICA%20100915-2.pdf.

Betts, C. (2011) *The National Planning Policy Framework: Eighth Report of Session 2010–12, Vol. 1: Report, Together with Formal Minutes, Oral and Written Evidence*, Vol. 1, London: The Stationery Office.

Bosselmann, Klaus (1995). *When Two Worlds Collide: Society and Ecology.*, Auckland: RSVP Publishers.

Bosselmann, Klaus (2013) *The Principle of Sustainability: Transforming Law and Governance*, Farnham: Ashgate.

Brain, David (2005) From good neighbourhoods to sustainable cities: social science and the social agenda of the New Urbanism, *International Regional Science Review* 28(2): 217–238.

Brearley, J.S. (2012) What's wrong with planning? – and is it about to be fixed? – a cri de coeur, *Journal of Planning and Environment Law* (5): 534.

Cambridge Centre for Housing and Planning Research (2014) *The Nature of Planning Constraints: Report to the House of Commons Communities and Local Government Committee*, Cambridge: University of Cambridge.

Christensen, Pernille. (2012) Key strategies of sustainable real estate decision-making in the United States: a Delphi study of the stakeholders. Dissertation, Clemson University.

Clark, D. (2003) Incentives for sustainable buildings in Australia – a designer's perspective, *Sinclair Knight Merz Technical Paper*, Melbourne, Vic: Sinclair Knight.

CLG (Communities and Local Government) (2012) *The National Planning Policy Framework*. Retrieved from https://www.gov.uk/government/publications/national-planning-policy-framework--2.

Department of Infrastructure and Transport (DIT) (2011) Our cities, our future: a national urban policy for productive, sustainable and liveable future. Retrieved 1 May 2014 from http://www. infrastructure.gov.au/infrastructure/pab/urbanpolicy/.

Duxbury, R. (2012) *Telling and Duxbury's Planning Law and Procedure*, Oxford: Oxford University Press.

Gurran, N. (2011) *Australian Urban Land Use Planning: Principles, Systems and Practice*, second edn, Sydney: Sydney University Press.

Hall, A.C. (2008) The form-based development plan: bridging the gap between theory and practice in urban morphology, *Urban Morphology* 12(2): 77–95.

Hall, T. (2011) Proactive engagement in urban design – the case of Chelmsford, in S. Tiesdell and D. Adams (eds), *Real Estate Issues: Urban Design in the Real Estate Development Process*, Oxford: Wiley-Blackwell, pp. 74–91.

Hayes, Denis (2014) Personal Interview by author, 8 May.

Holman, N. and Rydin, Y. (2013) What can social capital tell us about planning under localism?, *Local Government Studies* 39(1): 71–88.

ISOCARP (International Society of City and Regional Planners) (2001) *International Manual Planning Practice*, fourth edn. The Netherlands: ISOCARP, UNESCO, Ministry of Housing, Spatial Planning and the Environment.

Killian, J. and Pretty, D. (2008) *Planning Applications: A Faster and More Responsive System, Final Report*, London: DCLG.

NSW (New South Wales Department of Planning & Environment (DPE)) (2014a) Legislation. Retrieved 21 May 3 2014 from http://www.planning.nsw.gov.au/en-au/policyandlegislation/legislationandplanninginstruments.aspx.

NSW Department of Planning & Environment (DPE) (2014b) Standard Instrument Local Environmental Plan (LEP) Program. Retrieved 21 May 2014 from http://www.planning.nsw.gov.au/en-us/planningyourlocalarea/standardinstrument.aspx.

Ohm, Brian W. (2000) Reforming land planning legislation at the dawn of the 21st century: the emerging influence of smart growth and liveable communities, *The Urban Lawyer* 32(2): 181–210.

Ohm, Brian W. (2010) Required elements of the local comprehensive plan. Retrieved 12 May 2014 from http://oconto.uwex.edu/files/2010/08/required_elements_of_a_local_comprehensive_plan.pdf

Oregon Department of Land Conservation and Development (2000) *Planning for Natural Hazards: Key Elements of a Comprehensive Plan in Oregon's Statewide Land Use Planning Program*. Retrieved 3 May 2014 from http://www.oregon.gov/LCD/HAZ/docs/landslides/02_elements.pdf.

Paterson, E. (2012) Urban design and the national planning policy framework for England, *Urban Design International* 17(2): 144–155.

Rydin, Y. (2011) *The Purpose of Planning: Creating Sustainable Towns and Cities*, Bristol: Policy Press.

Schilling, J. and Logan, J. (2008) Greening the rust belt: a green infrastructure model for right sizing America's shrinking cities, *Journal of the American Planning Association* 74(4): 451–466.

Sepp, K. (2011) *The Estonian Green Belt*, Tallinn: Estonian University of Life Sciences.

Simons, L., Slob, A., Holswilder, H., and Tukker, A. (2001) A fourth generation: new strategies call for new eco-indicators, *Environmental Quality Management* 11(2): 51–61.

Tiesdell, Steve and Adams, David (eds) *Real Estate Issues: Urban Design in the Real Estate Development Process*, Oxford: Wiley-Blackwell, 2011. Retrieved from site.ebrary.com/lib/utslibrary/Doc?id=10510477&ppg=311.

Zhao, P. (2011) Managing urban growth in a transforming China: evidence from Beijing, *Land Use Policy* 28(1): 96–109.

7   Sustainable construction issues

Sara J. Wilkinson

7.0   Introduction

Apart from land acquisition, arguably design and construction will have more impact on the long-term sustainability of a development than other stages in the initial process. Although building operation and management through the in-use phase has a far larger environmental impact, they are not part of the property development process as such. As far as priorities are concerned, the UK Building Research Establishment (BRE) (2002) promotes a balanced approach that takes account of economic goals, but not at the expense of the environment or society's needs. Sustainability then is concerned with protecting environmental quality, enhancing social prosperity and improving economic performance (Addis and Talbot 2001; Medineckiene *et al.* 2010); however, even as recently as 2011, taking the UK government's Sustainable Construction strategy (UK Government 2008) as an example, the tendency is to consider it primarily in environmental and energy terms.

There is an important distinction between sustainability and sustainable construction. Sustainable construction is a process whereby, over time, sustainability is achieved (Parkin 2000); hence sustainability is an objective. This chapter recognises the importance of the construction phase within development and presents best practice in design and references useful design guides. Global, macro and micro influences, such as climate for example, are considered to demonstrate how sustainable design and construction in one area might not be deemed sustainable design and construction in another geographical area. It is a significant phase in development where the traditional mantra has been to build a quality property to the project deadline that performs well in use, within cost; in essence, 'time, quality and cost' is embedded in the paradigm of sustainable design and construction.

7.1   The impact of construction on sustainability

The built environment is estimated by many to be the single biggest source of environmental impacts, notably in terms of the use of non-renewable resources and the energy and carbon emitted both through production and use. Whilst there is significant debate about the consequences of excess consumption of resources (for a detailed discussion see Hawken *et al.*2010; Stern 2006) one of the most compelling arguments to ensure that the construction process is as 'light a touch' on the planet as it can be is the argument professed notably by Desai (2009) that all development activity should be guided by ten principles including three of which are key to construction, namely zero carbon, zero waste and sustainable materials. Clearly the design affects the way in which the development is built and the materials used. In this section, the key impacts of construction are discussed in order that design impacts may be more clearly comprehended. These impacts can be classified as environmental, social and economic.

7.1.1 Environmental impact

Construction related environmental impacts include energy and water use, pollution and diversity, creation of waste, reuse and recycling.

7.1.1.1 Energy and carbon

The issues of carbon and energy are intertwined but separate. Currently there is recognition that most buildings are not efficient in their use of energy, either during the build or in use. It is therefore important (and increasingly the subject of regulation) that buildings are designed and constructed for maximum efficiency. However, the matter of how that energy is *sourced* is also critical. Many of the newer technologies that provide non-carbon-based power, such as solar, wind, air and ground sources, are much easier to incorporate at the stage of original design and construction than they are once the development is completed. However, progress towards the introduction of renewables has been patchy in many developed countries; it is also more feasible in some geographic areas than others.

The built environment is responsible for large percentages of both energy and carbon, but over recent years; a combination of private and public sector initiatives has seen progress. Edwards (2002) estimated that within the UK, 50 per cent of the total UK energy consumption could be broken down as follows; 45 per cent to heat, light and ventilate buildings and 5 per cent to construct them. More recently, as the emphasis has shifted from energy to carbon, according to the UK's Technology Strategy Board that figure has fallen by 2013 to around 45 per cent of total UK carbon emissions which comprises 18 per cent from non-domestic stock and 27 per cent from domestic stock. Most of these emissions are derived from space heating and hot water provision (https://wwwinnovateuk.org). The US has similar figures to the UK, however, Australia assembles its statistics differently and determined that only 25 per cent of energy is building related, as it accounts for the energy used in industrial buildings or manufacturing emissions separately. The UK government has set a target to achieve 80 per cent reduction in carbon emissions by 2050 (https://www.gov.uk) through a series of voluntary and mandatory measures and other countries have adopted targets to reduce energy use. Reductions are achievable as in 2000. A typical US office building consumed 300 kWh/m^2/year. By 2013, that figure, for high performing buildings, had decreased to 100 kWh/m^2/year, although in Germany that figure is even lower at 50 kWh/m^2/year (Kibert 2013).

As stated above, the emphasis has begun to shift from energy to carbon as it is the latter which has been linked with climate change specifically. Too much energy may put a drain on non-renewable resources but it is the impact on climate that is currently the driving concern. In response, numerous cities around the world have set targets to become carbon neutral such as Sydney and Melbourne by 2030 and 2020 respectively with energy performance in the built environment a key part of the strategies. However, the existence of policies does not mean that targets are met or that progress is universal but in the UK the government now has bound itself to statutory targets under the Climate Change Act 2008. In part, this more stringent environment is in response to criticism (see for example

RICS 2006) that earlier policy initiatives were failing to achieve their targets. Recently many developers are cognisant of the targets and are endeavouring to design and construct buildings with low embodied and low operating carbon (Zalejska-Jonsson 2013). Properties with airtight construction leak less air and consume less energy. Other design measures include high thermal mass, passive design and high levels of insulation to the building fabric. In addition, energy-efficient services within buildings can reduce the energy loads to heat or cool the property; however, the way in which occupants use the building can affect energy usage and there is concern that there exists a large performance gap between design and performance. In part, this is because users are wasteful or profligate in their usage, but also it is a failure through the construction process.

There has been an understandable focus on operational energy use in buildings and reducing carbon emissions through improved design and efficiencies in lighting, mechanical ventilation, heating and air conditioning systems. However, as more buildings are built and refurbished to higher environmental standards the relative importance of carbon emissions will increasingly shift from operational emissions to embodied or embedded carbon, thus having particular resonance with the construction phase (RICS 2012). Embodied carbon is the carbon associated with extraction, mining, transportation and construction as well as demolition and disposal. It is possible to calculate the emissions associated with product manufacture in property development based on the quantity of materials that make up the building. After operational carbon emissions this is the most significant area of carbon emission from the whole life cycle of a property. Some UK local authorities such as Brighton and Hove City Council have made cradle to gate assessment of carbon a mandatory component of the planning process (RICS 2012). Cradle to gate emissions are those generated from the earth i.e. the 'cradle' up to the factory 'gate' and include mining and extraction of raw materials, processing and manufacturing.

Other terminology associated with embodied carbon measurement is 'cradle to site emissions' which add the transportation and delivery emissions plus the cradle to gate emissions. Cradle to end of construction adds in the construction and assembly emissions to the cradle to site emissions. Cradle to grave emissions add maintenance, retrofit and demolition, waste treatment and disposal (i.e. the grave) (see Figure 7.1). RICS have produced an information paper setting out a metholodogy to calculate embodied carbon of materials and this is another useful tool for the developers' design team to adopt in the quest for a sustainable development (RICS 2012). Developers should note that the embodied carbon of any material in one country varies from that of another country.

7.1.1.2 Water use

There are many pressures on the supplies of potable water around the world. Recent statistics issued by UN Water (http://www.unwater.org/) revealed that some 2.5 billion people do not have access to sanitation, and more than 0.75 billion have no clean drinking water. When these statistics are considered combined with the fact that 85 per cent of the world population lives in the driest half of the planet and that changing lifestyles including diet are putting pressure on water, it is easy to see that in many ways the issue of water is perhaps more challenging than that of energy and carbon. Put bluntly, without water, people die. In some regions, such as Australia, a variable supply means that authorities have to manage excessive supplies and drought conditions within short time frames. Overall consumption and population is increasing. In the UK, for example, water usage increased by 70 per cent in the last three decades of the twentieth century (Brownhill and Yates 2001)

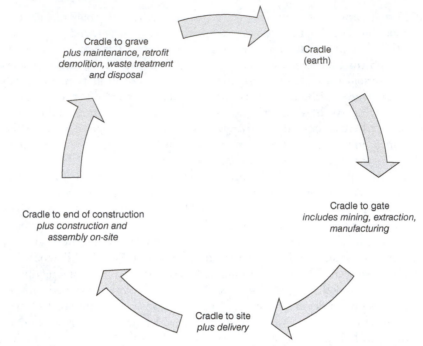

Figure 7.1 Cradle to grave carbon emissions in property development

although it is now decreasing slightly, UK consumption per head is still very significantly above countries such as the Netherlands, but below the US. Changing patterns of usage is increasing consumption further and these factors collectively have a big impact on the water supply (Edwards 2002). Population growth adds further pressures to water supply; globally the population has increased from 5.2 billion in 1990 to 7.5 billion in 2013 (Kibert 2013).

During the design and construction phase of property development there is excellent potential to implement water conservation techniques into the design to encourage reduced consumption. A decade ago calls began to be made for designers to specify water efficient technology, such as low-water flush toilet sand domestic appliances, and reduced flow taps which it was estimated could deliver around 20 per cent efficiency (Better Buildings Summit 2003). A decade later, as technologies have improved, including the increasingly widespread use of waterless toilets and urinals, the savings can be as much as 25 per cent according to Kibert (2013). Even before this, Woking Borough Council in England were able to report that one local authority has succeeded in reducing their water use by more than 40 per cent due to a combination of technologies and the identification of leakages through the system (Sustainable Construction Task Force 2006). Typical measures that may be introduced include, vacuum or pressure operated WCs, waterless or composting toilets, urinal flushing devices and waterless urinals, rainwater harvesting and reuse of waste or black-water recycling. Furthermore adopting construction design and methods that use lower amounts of water is another way of reducing overall usage, as it should be remembered that the choice of building material will impact on water use (Kibert 2013); for example both steel and concrete use significant quantities of water in their production, although a study of MIT campus found steel to have a greater polluting effect on water (http://www.archinode.com/lcasteel.html). However the widespread introduction of mandatory water metering makes water a direct economic good, whereas in previous times it was either paid for at a flat rate or regarded as a free good.

7.1.1.3 Pollution and biodiversity

Pollution from construction is an environmental issue as particles, noise, vibration and vaporous discharges arising from the process need to be identified and then minimised (Kukadia *et al.* 2003; OGC 2005). It has recently been estimated that the construction process is responsible for 4 per cent of particulate emissions, more water pollution incidents than any other industry, and thousands of noise complaints every year. Although construction activities also pollute the soil, the main areas of concern are: air, water and noise pollution (http://www.sustainablebuild.co.uk). Clearly different designs, specification, materials choice and construction methods will lead to different levels of and types of pollutants (Kibert 2013). For this reason, if no other, issues of pollution are included in many building certification schemes.

It is also the case that protection of and, in some cases, enhancing of biodiversity is an obligation in sustainable property developments in terms of good design and landscaping (Kibert 2013; OGC 2005). One way of enhancing biodiversity is to adopt more green space into the design of the development such as green walls and green roofs (Wilkinson *et al.* 2013). Wide scale adoption of green roofs is believed to reduce urban pollution and improve air quality through the absorption of airborne pollutants by plants and some cities have implemented green roof legislation on this basis. Furthermore it is possible to reduce the urban heat island (UHI) effect whereby city centre temperatures can be up to five degrees higher than surrounding suburbs with widespread adoption of green roof technology (Williams *et al.* 2010: 60). For larger schemes, the inclusion of 'green corridors' has long been recognised as important to ensure that animals can connect across their habitat sites and that flora is maintained (Naiman *et al.* 1993; Vergnes *et al.* 2012). Guidance published in the UK in 2012 (Town and Country Planning Association 2012) sets out principles for good practice in including green infrastructure in development; similarly the RICS has issued an information paper (RICS 2011) whilst Hostetler *et al.* (2011) have called for a systematic and strategic approach to green infrastructure. Within the construction process examples of reduction of pollution would be to specify methods that use less mechanical equipment and/or to ensure machinery used on-site operates within acceptable noise levels and does not emit particles or vaporous discharges as well as ensuring that during the construction process animal movement corridors are protected.

7.1.1.4 Waste creation

This is a significant environmental impact during the construction phase of property development. The UK construction industry has been estimated to produce 40 per cent of all UK waste (including greenhouse gas emissions) (RICS 2005). Of the 43.8 million tonnes of waste generated in Australia during 2006–2007, 38 per cent, a similar percentage to the UK, was derived from the construction and demolition sector (ABS 2013a). Between 2001 and 2007, the volume of waste deposited into Australian landfill increased markedly. In 2001, 19 million tonnes of waste were disposed to landfill, and by 2007 this figure had had increased by 12 per cent to 21.3 million tonnes (ABS 2013b). The UK government projected that their landfill capacity would be reached by 2017, and a Landfill Tax and Aggregate Levy was introduced to drive the reduction and minimisation of waste because of increased costs associated with waste disposal (OECD 2006), This escalated each year to a level in 2014 of £80 per tonne; this financial cost has produced very significant change and incentivised the industry to make savings and reduce landfill (Pitt *et al.* 2009). As a result of the levy, most major contractors now have waste management policies and practices in place (Pitt *et al.* 2009); further the amount of waste to landfill has fallen significantly, but it is still just over 30 per cent (ONS 2013). There is now a very strong financial case to reduce the amount of waste through the construction process with Waste and Resources Action Program (WRAP) who estimate that waste management and disposal cost the construction industry the equivalent of 30 per cent of pre-tax profits. However the issue of waste is not merely one of reducing its creation to avoid taxation costs. It is also a matter of compliance at super-national level, at least within the EU where all countries have to comply with the Waste Framework Directive (Directive 2008/98/EC) (European Union 2008). This Directive, under Article 1 calls for member states to take 'measures to protect the environment and human health by preventing or reducing the adverse impacts of the generation and management of waste and by reducing overall impacts of resource use and improving the efficiency of such use' and within Article 4 sets out a five-step hierarchy to be applied as a priority in this order in terms of waste prevention and management legislation and policy:

a. prevention;
b. preparing for reuse;
c. recycling;
d. other recovery, e.g. energy recovery; and
e. disposal.

Within the UK, the government, working closely with its funder partner WRAP, has developed a 13-point action plan against which it reports progress towards the ambitious target of a zero waste economy. However, due to funding restrictions, it was announced that in terms of construction waste, the government will be looking to the private sector to support initiatives (Rogerson 2013). Therefore, for the government to succeed they will require the construction industry to take a leading role.

A further development of waste strategies is the development of a circular economy. Under the notion of a circular economy the old paradigm of make-use-dispose as a linear activity is transposed into a make-use-remake scenario as visualised in Figure 7.3. Although the term is relatively new, the concept is not new. According to the Ellen MacArthur Foundation (http://www.ellenmacarthurfoundation.org/) which was set up to promote it, its origins are unknown but it has gained momentum since the late 1970s led by a small number of academics, thought-leaders and businesses. This momentum has now been taken up, not just at a national level, but also by the European Commission who, through their Online Resource Efficiency Platform (http://ec.europa.eu/environment/resource_efficiency/index_en.htm), are promoting and tracking comparative progress against resource user targets across all EU nation states against a number of priorities including what they call the 'bioeconomy'. However, it is not just the EU countries that are embracing the circularity concept. As Mathews and Tan report (2011) China is making significant progress with the pursuit of the circular economy being enshrined by law as a developmental goal.

Clearly, high population density countries like the UK, Hong Kong and the Netherlands have more pressing concerns with regards to waste, compared to Australia and other less densely populated places; however, waste reduction and elimination is now not just a matter

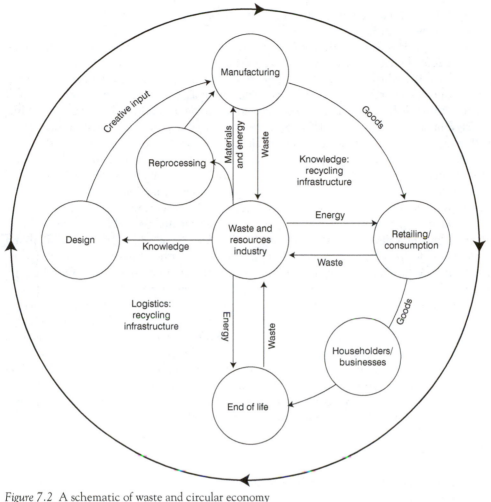

Figure 7.2 A schematic of waste and circular economy
Source: ESA 2013

of environmental protection; it is a social and political issue increasingly being enshrined in policy and regulations as well as a purely financial cost one. Consequently, design and construction methods predicated on the minimisation of waste are an essential component of developing property sustainably.

7.1.1.5 Reuse and recycling

It has long been argued that there should be a systematic approach at an operational level which should include recycling construction materials, and using renewable and recyclable materials in the construction design and process to enhance sustainability (Zhang *et al.* 2000). Factor 4, factor 5 and factor 10 are different ways of comparing design options and evaluating building performance. Factor 4 (Weiszacker *et al.* in Kibert 2013) suggests that for humankind to live sustainably today resource consumption has to reduce to one quarter of its current levels. In a similar study, Schmidt-Bleek (in Kibert 2013) posited that reduction in consumption to one tenth of current levels (factor 10) is required for long-term sustainability. With our current adherence to neo-classical economic paradigms it is hard to see such targets being achieved.

However, as it is the case that as 87 per cent of existing UK building stock will still be in use in 2050, better management and refurbishment of property is required (Kelly 2008). Research by BRE which compared the level of sustainability of retrofit and redevelopment of offices concluded retrofit is the more sustainable option as it is 'lower both in environmental impact and whole life costs than comparative redevelopment solutions' (Anderson and Mills 2002). Embodied energy, the total energy invested in product and materials production as well as transportation to the site and installation, accounts for 20 per cent of the total life cycle energy of the development (Kibert 2013). However, retrofit has a higher risk and uncertainty (Egbu 1995) due to unknown problems that may not be apparent at the commencement of a project. This has led to calls for a better modelling of risks associated with retrofit especially in respect of energy (Lee *et al.* 2014). Wherever possible in property development, consideration should be given to reusing materials and structures; if this is not possible then developers should consider deconstruction and separation of building components for recycling. It is the case that most existing buildings were not built with deconstruction in mind and separation of components and materials can be prohibitively expensive. Going forward however the specification of some recycled or, preferably, reused materials in new developments will reduce their overall environmental footprint. Design with a view to deconstruction and reduced consumption of materials and components is essential for any development to be considered; however, the issue as to whether it is better to redevelop or refurbish is a complex one that should involve a life cycle analysis (Dong *et al.* 2005) and wider social and economic considerations (Sayce *et al.* 2004). The move towards reuse rather than recycling is gaining traction; for example in the UK the most recent waste strategy places firm emphasis on moving *up* the scale from recovery and recycling to preparing for reuse and reduction (Tavri *et al.* 2013).

7.1.2 Social impact

The social impact of construction is substantial as the performance, quality and design of the property development, as well as access to services and recreation, can directly affect the quality of life, promotion of healthy living and cohesiveness of society. Sustainable office buildings, for example, not only benefit from lower operational energy costs but they are perceived to be healthier, which can reduce user absenteeism (Edwards and Naboni 2013; World Green Building Council 2013)). Furthermore, there is evidence that a good environment supports staff retention and recruitment and the overall image and brand of the organisation can be enhanced (Kibert 2013). However, the delivery of a good internal environment is not straightforward or easy, partly because it frequently involves a combination of factors, which are more difficult to measure in monetary values. For example the cost of design measures are evaluated against intangible benefits of 'happier' occupants. In spite of this, methods of measurement are being developed and further evidence is emerging in favour of social sustainability measures which enable property developers to incorporate such measures into their developments. Furthermore some studies have found a link between the inclusion of social sustainability measures and enhanced value (Newell *et al.* 2013; Fuerst and McAllister 2011a; Fuerst and McAllister 2011b) which should reassure office developers that there is a positive return to be made on investment in social sustainability features in a development, although the case is less developed for other types of commercial development.

7.2.2.1 Design impact

Developers should be cognisant that optimum design can lead to optimised performance on the construction site. Design has a pivotal role in sustainability whereby designers work within the client's brief. If the brief is one that is not specific in terms of the required site performance in terms of sustainability criteria, it is unlikely that the building will achieve its design statements. Building contractors are not involved in the decision on how sustainable a building project may be, unless the property is procured under a Design and Build contract. Regardless of their level of involvement in design, however, best construction practices can reduce costs, improve health and safety and improve image (Yates 2003d) thereby delivering on economic and social sustainability goals. Materials selection has demonstrable and significant energy and greenhouse gas emission implications (Treloar *et al.* 2001). Greater involvement and constructive interaction from the demand side will improve best practice ideas, drawing closer relationships to the supply side and, subsequently, in the provision of improved sustainable construction.

7.1.2.2 Site safety

One of the key ways in which social sustainability can be delivered through the construction process is through improvement in working conditions and practices on-site. The construction industry is still one of the most dangerous of workplaces. Despite tightening legislation in many countries and the introduction of, for example, the Considerate Contractors' Scheme in the UK, the track record is still poor and construction is still one of the most dangerous sectors in which to work at the operatives' level. For example, in the UK, the Health and Safety Executive, which holds details of all mandatorily reported incidents stated that in 2011/12 there were 148 fatalities, with 78, 000 other injuries to employees resulting in the loss of some 27 million working days. For 2010/11, they estimated that the cost to society of construction workplace injuries and ill health (excluding cancer) was some **£13.8 billion** (http://www.hse.gov.uk/statistics).

Weeks (2011) categorises the health and safety issues relating to construction under four headings:

- *Chemical*, of which perhaps asbestosis is the best known example, but which includes many airborne and contact hazards and contact materials which result in a range of dermatology and respiratory conditions.
- *Physical*, resulting from unsafe structures, unprotected machinery, noise, extreme heat and cold and poor adherence to safety rules all collectively leading to falls, musculo-skeletal damage and too frequently, death.
- *Biological*, which is less of an issue but can nevertheless be very real. Many naturally occurring materials such as some types of wood can produce allergic reaction whilst working in the open air and sites which disturb habitats can result in attacks from insects and small animals; and finally
- *Social*, due to the frequently intermittent nature of construction work resulting in periods of long hours (which may lead to mistakes) combined with periods of no work with consequent anxiety, stress and social deprivation.

Whilst it is perhaps inevitable that construction activity will always be, at least to some degree, cyclical depending on economic conditions, there are many ways in which working practices can be improved which will yield sustainability dividends. One of the best ways in which improvement can be gained is by greater adoption of off-site manufacturing. Taylor (2009), in a report for the Health and Safety Executive, found through a series of care studies that off-site manufacture delivered a number of benefits including reduction of health and safety risks due to the controlled environment. Similar findings resulted from a review of housing construction by Miles and Whitehouse (2013) for the Construction Industry Council.

Socially responsible investment (SRI), can help demonstrate faster and/or better investment returns, increased flexibility, reduced investment risks, reduced cost, increased market appeal and improved image (Yates, 2003c). According to the *Financial Times* (2013), SRI is:

> an investment strategy which seeks to generate both financial and sustainable value. It consists of a set of investment approaches that integrate environmental, social and governance (ESG) and ethical issues into financial analysis and decision-making.

Responsible investment goes by many names – it is variously referred to as socially responsible investing (SRI), ethical investing, sustainable investing, triple-bottom-line investing, green investing – but underlying these differing names is a common theme focused on long-term value creation. Value in this context refers not only to economic value, but to the broader values of fairness, justice, and environmental sustainability.

7.1.3 Economic impact

The construction industry is the fourth largest contributor to Gross Domestic Product (GDP) in the Australian economy and plays a major role in determining economic growth. Despite the negative impact of the global financial crisis of 2008–2010, which saw a large fall back in confidence to undertake building works and in some countries became a drag on the economy, the construction industry accounted for 7.7 per cent of GDP in Australia in 2010–2011 (ABS 2013a); approximately 10 per cent in the US in 2012 (http://www.bbvaresearch.com/) and some 7.6 per cent in the UK (http://www.ons.gov.uk/ons/). The UK suffered particular issues during the crisis but of greater importance is that volatility in this sector can have very significant impacts on not just GDP but employment and hence social wellbeing. When construction suffers, so do many people. Construction activity, therefore, is often seen as an indicator of general economic activity. In addition, developers actively pursuing sustainable property developments will create opportunities for new or existing businesses to innovate and diversify into sustainability, thereby increasing economic activity.

7.2 Drivers of sustainable construction

Given the importance of improving the adoption of sustainability principles within construction, it is critical to understand what the drivers are towards improving sustainable practices. As detailed in Chapter 2, this has been a vexed question since the so-called 'circle of blame' was articulated in 2000 (The Sustainable Construction Task Group, 2000). At that time, the stakeholders identified were constructors, developers, occupiers and investors. However, within the construction phase, perhaps legislators and policy makers should be identified as important. Whilst many perceive clients as driving sustainable construction, some have questioned if clients know enough to brief effectively (Abidin and Pasquire 2005); however, in the view of Khalfan and Maqsood (2011) economic and social drivers factors will be more important than environmental ones, adding weight to the argument that, after legislation, it is more likely to be client, rather than contractor led.

The environmental consequences of poorly managed construction are significant and for this impact to be minimised, increasing client awareness is vital to transition from the dominance of financial decision-making. Abidin and Pasquire (2005) found those who adopted value management (VM) were more able to minimise environmental and social damage as they were able to define elements of the design such as energy efficiency, waste minimisation, indoor environment quality (IEQ), operating costs and user comfort. VM is mostly 'concerned with ensuring that the client's needs are clearly defined and that a true scope of work is produced for the project' (Facilities Society 2013) with the key aim of attaining a shared understanding of the design problem, identifying design objectives and synthesising agreement about the comparative advantages of various actions. VM is applied at various stages in a project's life with diverse tools and techniques used at different stages to meet the requirements of that stage. As such, VM can deliver good economic returns, accountability and excellence in social and environmental performance, and in this way support sustainability. Some organisations and authorities around the world have development best practice guides and checklists to assist in decision-making during the design briefing and tendering stages to ensure sustainability issues are addressed comprehensively and in a structured way (Department of Environment and Climate Change NSW 2013).

Corporate organisations need to attract investment and being focused on sustainability has been a way of achieving this since the mid-2000s. In the UK, the perception that a company is 'sustainable' enhances company profile and improves relationships with stakeholders (The Sustainable Construction Task Group 2003). Similar experiences are replicated in North America and Australia. The growth in companies adopting strategic Corporate Social Responsibility (CSR) is reflected in the increase of socially responsible investment (SRI) (Pivo 2008; Pitt *et al.* 2009; World Green Building Council 2013). This theme and the reasons for the growth in SRI are explored in Chapter 5. Increasingly, throughout the property life cycle, including the construction phase, incorporating sustainability within the decision criteria is viewed as good for business rather than an added cost.

After allowing for client requirements, the factors which encourage contractors to increase construction sustainability are typically economic or regulatory. Economic factors include direct economic impacts such as the increasing costs of landfill and waste disposal in the UK and elsewhere (Pitt *et al.* 2009); other economic impacts are felt through fiscal incentives. For example, the carbon tax introduced in Australia penalised companies with high greenhouse gas emissions through higher taxes. However, the government elected in September 2013 has repealed the law. The aim was to replace the carbon tax with a system of incentives for Australian businesses to adopt practices which would reduce greenhouse gas emissions: carbon emissions were reduced during the brief time the carbon tax was implemented in Australia. In the UK a climate change levy exists as a tax on the use of energy by businesses, though it is criticised as being not sufficiently stringent to change behaviours (RICS 2006). More effective on those impacted is the carbon reduction commitment, which imposes reducing carbon emission targets on major companies. The knowledge of these taxes, which directly affect only some contractors, has begun to influence some clients' requirements when commissioning buildings, but only some.

Whilst some countries have very regulatory specific performance requirements, such as those imposed by building regulations, or the requirements to build to sustainability certified standards, such as in Malaysia, in other countries the regulatory position is less well established. Regulation may therefore dictate minimums but it is not normally aspirational. In summary there is a 'direction of travel' in terms of legislative pressures on construction but the overall regime could be described as ' fragile', in that it is either not sufficiently strong to make a difference or, it may be repealed.

On the regulatory side, many jurisdictions rely on increasing minimum standards set out in building regulations and codes to drive increasing levels of sustainability in construction. However, building regulations are minimum requirements and typically most of the property developed and constructed merely adopts these minimum levels of efficiency, and they become de facto accepted benchmarks in the marketplace. Furthermore a number of enquiries have established that the minimum standards in the regulations are not always built, in other words 'as designed approved' and as built is not the same thing (Arup 2013). With the enforcement of building regulations being inconsistent and patchy, even in developed countries, the situation in developing countries is possibly more inconsistent. At least building codes apply to all new buildings and many refurbishments also trigger these minimum standards.

A more recent regulatory development in some sectors of the property market has been Energy Performance Certificates (EPCs) in the European Union from 2006 and Building Energy Efficiency Certificates (BEECs) in Australia from 2011. Both EPCs and BEECs are mandated so that when commercial office property over a certain area (2000 square metres in Australia) is either sold or leased, an energy performance assessment is required to be displayed on the property (Warren and Huston 2011). The limitation here is that the legislation is restricted to energy performance only, to a restricted sector of the built environment and neither is related to the construction process but to design. Planning legislation in the UK, embodied in Planning Policy Statement 22 (2004) requires a percentage of energy used in new residential, commercial and industrial developments to adopt on-site renewable energy sources. Initial targets of 10 per cent of renewables by 2010 looked unlikely to be achieved as in 2008 only 3 per cent had been delivered (Pitt et al. 2009). Undoubtedly the targets had been affected adversely by the slowdown in the UK economy which occurred as a result of the Global Financial Crisis from 2008 onwards. Table 7.1 summarises the drivers and barriers to sustainable construction which will vary from country to country.

In terms of economic pressures, as stated above, taxes leading to higher construction costs can act as effective incentives and currently many governments globally, in the UK and Australia for example, favour allowing the 'market' to determine what transpires and regrettably the market often places environment behind other factors.

However, realisation is growing that whilst costs need to be minimised, profit on the construction process may be optimised not only through cost saving but by growing the sale value. Although evidence is still patchy (World Green Building Council 2013) a number of studies in the US, Europe, the UK and Australia have drawn conclusions of a value return from some observed correlations between certification of buildings and increased rental values or even in some cases capital value trends (Lorenz et al. 2007; Kok and Jennen 2012; Newell et al. 2013; Fuerst and McAllister 2011a; Fuerst and McAllister 2011b). The previously noted lack of a convincing business case for sustainability in the built environment has been considered a strong barrier to growth (Pitt et al. 2009). The value connection is explored more fully in Chapter 4. If investors and developers see a correlation

Table 7.1 Summary of the drivers and barriers to sustainable construction

Drivers of sustainable construction	Barriers to sustainable construction
• Client awareness	• Lack of client awareness
• Client demand	• Lack of client demand
• Financial incentives	• Lack of business case understanding
• Taxes and levies	• Affordability
• Investment	• Lack of proven technologies
• Planning policy	• Planning policy
• Building regulations and codes	• Building regulations and codes
• Certification / measurement	• Lack of certification / measurement standard

Source: Adapted from Pitt *et al.* (2009)

between provision of certificated buildings and sale price they will be motivated, as will other stakeholders, to invest in these features and this is a positive change in the market.

Research reported in 2009 (Pitt *et al.* 2009) claimed that in the UK the top three barriers to sustainable construction were affordability, lack of client awareness and client demand. Their empirical research concluded that the construction industry:

- Is geared to replacement and not repair (or reuse or recycling).
- Has no common accepted definition of sustainability.
- Is reactive not proactive.
- Finds it difficult to move towards sustainability due to the uniqueness of projects and stakeholders' knowledge, priorities and motivations which make consistency impossible.
- Requires simple national benchmark under building regulations or codes or measurement tools like LEED or BREEAM.
- Requires fiscal intervention to change the cost/affordability balance.

(based on Pitt *et al.* 2009)

However, this was written some six years ago, since then significant progress has been made as economies come out of recession, although recent research (Green Construction Board 2015) indicates that construction is still driven by cost reduction rather than value enhancement and by compliance rather than a culture of 'beyond compliance'. It appears that there are challenges in the construction phase of property development for developers to overcome if sustainability is to be embedded throughout the entire process of development. Whilst some contractors and developers may be able to achieve some degree of sustainability, the majority will struggle. It is incumbent on the leaders within the industry to lead by example and to disseminate best practices to others within the industry.

7.3   Sustainable building construction principles

Attempts to identify a set of principles for sustainable construction is not new. As long ago as 1997, Hill and Bowen proposed a four-headed approach of social, economic, biophysical and technical issues. These can be distilled as follows:

- Reduce resource consumption.
- Reuse resources.
- Use recyclable resources.

- Protect nature.
- Eliminate toxic materials.
- Apply life cycle costing;
- Focus on quality.

In 2013, the UK government issued their own eight principles based on the experiences of the London Olympics as follows:

- Seek a clear and public commitment to sustainability at the highest level of the organisation.
- Prepare thoroughly: early consideration of sustainability.
- Set specific, clear and challenging sustainability targets from the outset.
- Be an intelligent client: get the right people on board, define the project and set the budget.
- Embed sustainability objectives throughout the team and supply chain.
- Identify and use low impact, responsibly sourced products and materials and ensure good supply chain management.
- Create a structure that supports a collaborative approach while maintaining an environment of challenge.
- Organise procurement so services can be shared.

In the context of the principles, resources are considered to be the land or site on which property is developed, the materials, water and energy used in the development and the eco-systems affected by the development (Kibert 2013). Whilst many have posited concepts such as industrial ecology, construction ecology, bio-mimicry, design for the environment and ecological footprint, the principles outlined above serve as a useful checklist for the key concerns developers need to evaluate in their proposed design and construction options.

One means of evaluating sustainability in construction is to use one or more of the measurement tools that are available. However this course of action should be adopted with the knowledge that there has been much criticism of tools. As long ago as 2003, the Sustainable Construction Task Group (2003) called for a consolidation in the number of tools; however, since then the number of measures and tools available has escalated and are an important, if complex, part of sustainable development. Details of sustainability assessment tools are found in Chapter 9. In summary some measurement tools which are available for the construction phase include:

1   Global Reporting Initiative (GRI) Construction and Real Estate Sector Supplement – provides a reporting framework for all companies engaged in the sector including through the construction phase.
2   Environmental Management Systems (EMS) – developed under ISO 14001 provide guidelines on good practices.
3   Building measurement tools – such as BREEAM (UK, Hong Kong), Green Star (Australia) and LEED (US) and Living Building Challenge (US). Some tools cover the design phase and also operational phase.
4   Energy and water rating tools – such as NABERS in Australia and Energy Star in the US that focus on a limited aspect of sustainability.
5   Life cycle analysis LCA) – tends to evaluate aspects of building performance throughout life, such as windows or structure.

6   Eco-labels – used for specific times, for example light bulbs, and are based in prevailing local standards such as EU standards. Eco-labels adopt life cycle analysis techniques assessing pre-production, production, distribution, utilisation and disposal of the item.
7   Eco-points – relate to a limited number of registered specific products and are aligned to ISO 14001.
8   Energy Performance Certificates – measuring asset level energy and carbon performance are required throughout the EU and have to be produced when buildings are let or sold.

This list is not a detailed summary of all measurement tools that exist and some will have greater direct impact than others. Instead it is simply an overview of the main tools that impact on construction methods and decisions with regards to sustainability. The tools are varied in that some relate to a series of buildings, whereas others focus on individual buildings and others still are limited to building components. It is possible to have a high rating in a tool that is focused on a small part of sustainability only. The question is: does this make the development sustainable? Further it is possible to have a building which achieves a high rating using one measure but which performs poorly on another. Clearly it is fraught with complexity and developers need to consider the tools with great care and insight.

Another means of measuring sustainability is industry awards such as those awarded by professional bodies such as the Royal Institution of Chartered Surveyors (RICS), the Royal Institute of British Architects (RIBA) and the Institute of Electrical Engineers (IEE). As with the tools themselves, there is debate about how effective industry awards and benchmarks are in promoting and stimulating sustainability with stakeholders (Zalejska-Jonsson 2013) and clearly they are subjective.

7.4   Sustainable design

Design plays a major part in the sustainability of any property development. It is essential that the briefing process encompasses sustainability both in terms of the design and construction methods. The initial briefing process is where sustainability targets should be established to enable the design team to evaluate a full range of strategies. During the briefing process, the client's needs and user requirements are investigated and assessed in the context of the site. The benefits of sustainability in design include lower life cycle carbon emissions and water consumption, lower embodied carbon, lower transport related carbon, less waste to landfill, healthy buildings, enhancement to ecology and biodiversity. The long-term future of the building or anticipated life cycle also affects sustainability. For example, a short life building should use different materials and designs compared to property intended to last over the long term. It is even more challenging to design buildings in a society where change is accelerating at an ever faster pace. The need for buildings to be flexible to avoid obsolescence was identified by Baum as long ago as 1993 (Baum 1993) but this was not expressed as related to sustainability. However, building flexibility has become a key consideration (Arge 2005; Ellison and Sayce 2007); lack of adaptability may lead to failure (Sayce *et al.* 2004). Frequently this can happen when they were designed for one specific occupier. When that occupier either changes their requirements or wishes to relocate, the costs of adaptation are found to be prohibitive. More recently, research attention has been turning to the need to consider adaptive reuse from the outset of the design process (Langston *et al.* 2008).

7.4.1 Sustainable construction technology and management

Given that 10–15 per cent of all energy used in construction occurs during the building phase and that various sources estimate that 40 per cent of all extracted minerals and natural materials are used in the built environment, the construction industry needs to look closely at these activities to identify where reductions can be targeted to enhance sustainability and slow the pace of environmental degradation. Increasingly, innovative contractors are taking a lead by identifying in the construction phase, alternative methods or systems of construction that have less environmental impact than traditional approaches. Design and build procurement particularly lends itself to contractor innovation of this type.

Cotgrave (in Cotgrave and Riley 2013) states that although less is known of sustainable construction methods compared to sustainable design approaches, the following aspects in sustainable construction methods need to be addressed:

- Reuse materials as much as possible to lower resource consumption.
- Use recyclable and re-usable materials.
- Avoid specification of materials which emit toxins.
- Consider embodied energy or embodied carbon content of materials or systems. For example a system might require considerable amounts of energy to construct compared to another system which might have a higher embodied carbon content of materials but uses processes in construction which result in a lower overall embodied energy content.
- Protect the ecology of the site and surrounding area.
- Whole life costing (WLC) and life cycle analysis (LCA) should be used as the procurement method to evaluate options.
- Occupant health.
- Operational building energy, water and other resource use.

In addition to this list, comprehensive though it might at first appear, is the need to consider also:

- the transport implications of materials, with local materials being preferred and which often have the benefit of a better aesthetic which fits the local vernacular;
- the use of water through the actual construction process, Waylen *et al.* (2011) reported on the numerous ways in which water is wasted on-site and how it can be reduced;
- choice of materials notably the choice between steel and concrete frames, which have different impacts depending on the actual scheme;
- that some sustainability features themselves such as types of green roofs can require additional materials – so a balance needs to be struck.

7.4.2 Integrated design process

It has been argued that the level of communication, interaction and teamwork required to deliver an effective sustainable property development is far higher than a conventional property development (Kibert 2013). This begins at the orientation stage as sustainability is still a comparatively recent innovation and the issues it raises may be new to many stakeholders and therefore all need to be orientated in order that project goals and objectives may be achieved. The orientation stage can serve three purposes which are to:

1   inform project team about project requirements;
2   familiarise the project team with the developer's priorities and,
3   provide an opportunity for team building to familiarise the group with the development, the building programme and the sustainable building and construction issues.

Integrated design process (IDP) is the term that covers the high levels of teamwork and collaboration that differentiate sustainable design and construction from traditional approaches (Cotgrave and Riley 2013). The perceived benefits of IDP are synergy, high performance and lower costs and are achieved when sustainable design principles are integrated into conventional criteria such as building form, function, performance and cost. The catalyst for success is participation of key professionals such as architects, services engineers, landscape architects and interior designers. The premise is that effective collaboration from an early stage can deliver optimal solutions. For example, a mechanical engineer can calculate the energy use and cost to inform the design team of energy use implications of orientation of the building, configuration, fenestration, mechanical systems and lighting options. In integrated design, the team is formed at the schematic design stage rather than after and has an input through the design period. Therefore, the earlier the collaboration commences the greater the benefits in theory, as the costs of any changes to design increase as time progresses. For developers who wish to develop and hold, as opposed to develop and sell, integrated design may have a greater appeal. However, the IDP as set out above still fails to include representation from those who understand occupier needs. Whether the building is to be sold or held within the developer's portfolio, it is vital that there is imput from the user perspective especially as so many post-occupancy surveys (see Chapter 10) point to a performance gap between design and operation, often at least partially as the building is not used in the ways that the designers envisaged. Further, as evidence mounts as to market sensitivity to the sustainability credentials of a building, so it is imperative that consideration of value implications are built into the design process. .

One of the strategies adopted for IDP is the *charrette,* a French term which translates as the attempt to create a plan. *Charettes* are used extensively in the planning consent process but are new within the construction context. Typically a *charrette* requires that: 1) everyone is involved from the start; 2) everyone works concurrently and cross functionally; iii) everyone works in short feedback loops; and, 4), that everyone works in detail. The underlying rationale is that everyone feels ownership having been involved from the beginning and second, working concurrently allows better solutions to emerge. Working in short feedback loops is more creative and enables more alternatives to be generated, for example it would be desirable for all buildings to have photovoltaics, however, it is not possible for all developers to incorporate them into their projects. By working in as much detail as possible enables more thorough problem solving to occur.

7.4.3 *Executing and delivering the project*

Delivering a sustainable property development is unlike a conventional delivery system and the project team needs to be conscious of the differences and where they arise in the design and construction process. As set out above, once the procurement route is finalised and programming and costing is underway, the first steps are to:

1   Establish priorities for the design team.
2   Select and appoint the project team and the contractor.
3   Apply an integrated design process possibly using a *charrette*.

Following these first steps the project can move on to:

4   Implementation (that is schematic design, advanced design, design development, construction documents and documents related to certification if required).
5   Construction including implementing sustainability measures; and,
6   Final commissioning and handover to the developer.

Before undertaking this, however, it is essential that documentation is finalised in a way that will ensure successful delivery. This is now considered.

7.5   Sustainable building documentation requirements

Where certification is the goal, developers and their design team will be required to seek documentation from assessment providers such as BRE for BREEAM or USGBC for LEED and so on. This is covered in Chapter 4 and this section of this chapter considers the documentation required through the design and construction period of property development.

In Chapter 8 we shall consider the choice of procurement route which will depend on a range of factors. The conclusion to that chapter is that any form of contract can be used to promote sustainable practices but that newer forms more specifically address the need to drive sustainable developments.

The procurement route will dictate the nature of the contract documentation in that it will set out the parties and their respectively legal rights and liabilities and their proposed *modus operandi*. It may also include special contract conditions which, as the name suggests, are an extension of the general conditions and apply specifically to the project.

However, the contract, including any special conditions, is only one element of the overall documentation that is needed before work commences. In addition to the contract, the following are required:

*   *Bill of quantities*: Theis is not used for all contracts but it comprises a list of materials, parts and labour (and their costs) that are included in the contract. The bill of quantities is helpful in valuing variations and assists in the preparation of progress claims. It is important that in preparing the bill of quantities that specified products do not get compromised in order to secure cost reductions.
*   *Specification*: The specification sets out the technical requirements of the work and is critical. If less sustainable materials are specified the end result is compromised. Where possible, the professional undertaking the specification writing should have significant sustainability knowledge and they should work closely with the design team and the quantity surveyor to ensure that the overall specification and design work effectively both financially and in sustainability terms.
*   *Drawings:* The architectural and structural plans of the building are critical parts of the documentation and it is in this area that significant changes have taken place in recent years with the widespread adoption of Computer Aided Design (CAD) drawings and, more recently, comprehensive Building Information Modelling (BIM) which is considered below. Drawings will normally have to be signed off by the approving authority and form the basis against which the physical work on the ground is judged.

Other documents may also be required; generally these include technical and pricing schedules as well as the following forms:

- instruction,
- time extension claim,
- request for information,
- preliminary building agreement,
- progress payment certificate,
- practical completion notice,
- defects document,
- contract information statement,
- collateral warranties.

Finally arrangements need to be put in place for site management. In the UK, there is a regulatory requirement (Construction and Design Management Regulations (CDM) 2007) covering site management. These place legal duties on almost all those involved in the construction phase including clients, designers, contractors and site operatives. Introduced originally to ensure better site safety through training, supervision, etc., they have the additional benefit of enhancing communications which should (in turn) help in the delivery of a more sustainable product. Whilst the Löfstedt Review (2011) made a number of recommendations to overhaul the regulations, it did not specifically address the issue of sustainability except insofar as improving site safety is an important social consideration.

It is recommended that all contracting parties endorse complete sets of all contractual documents, and that all documents are kept intact. All contracts, including related plans, specifications and directions, should be retained on file for seven years from the date they were formally adopted in case of any subsequent litigation or building failure.

7.5.1 *Computer aided design (CAD)*

For small projects, hand-drawn hard copy drawings many still be produced but increasingly drawings are CAD generated. Originally developed in the 1980s, CAD was at first resisted within the construction industry on the grounds of cost and skill, meaning that its adoption was initially restricted to large design practices. However, with the growth of trained CAD designers and the increased capacity of computers, CAD has become an integral part of the design process. At first, the technique was aiming at automating only some of the tasks normally undertaken by the designer, notably the modelling of the product.

However, the use and capabilities of CAD have grown significantly so that the software can now be used for most steps within the design process, including integrating with the specified product details. Whilst CAD was first designed as 2-D modelling, it was subsequently enhanced to 3-D which again provides at little extra cost additional valuable information which may be slow and expensive to generate through hand-drawn work.

The use of CAD software speeds up design and hence can increase the productivity of the designer. More importantly, it can help to improve the quality and accuracy of design, speed up communications and provide a means of easy adjustment to design. A key advantage of CAD is that it enables the documentation to be handled digitally: something which is vital as design teams may be physically separated, maybe by many thousands of miles.

7.5.2 *Building information modelling (BIM)*

Building information modelling (BIM) involves the generation and management of digital representations of physical and functional characteristics of a property development; it is therefore a significant step on from CAD. The National Building Information Model Standard Project Committee defines BIM as: 'a digital representation of physical and functional characteristics of a facility. A BIM is a shared knowledge resource for information about a facility forming a reliable basis for decisions during its life cycle; defined as existing from earliest conception to demolition' (National Building Information Model Standard Project Committee,2013). Although first mentioned in 1992, uptake has been slow, even though BIM adoption accelerated amongst UK construction professionals from 13 per cent in 2011 to 39 per cent in 2013. In the US, adoption rates have exceeded 400 per cent since 2007 (AECOM 2013) and globally BIM is predicted to grow from US$1.8 billion in 2012 to US$6.5 billion by 2020. BIM models are shared knowledge resources assisting decision-making about the property from the conceptual stage, through design, construction and operational life and to demolition or deconstruction (Cotgrave and Riley 2013). Adoption of BIM is argued to help fulfil the ambitions of contracting clients. A study undertaken by Stanford University in the US on 32 major construction projects using BIM, found a 40 per cent reduction in unforeseen change orders (variations), an 80 per cent reduction in cost estimating time a 7 per cent reduction in project completion times and a 10 per cent cost savings in projects (AECOM 2014). BIM also enhances stakeholder communication. Overall, there is variation globally in the level and extent of uptake of BIM, Figure 7.3 shows BIM adoption by region in 2012 (AECOM 2013).

Previously most design was predicated on two-dimensional (2-D) drawings such as plans, elevations and sections, although CAD can extend to 3-D. BIM routinely extends this to three dimensions (3-D), augmenting the three primary spatial dimensions (i.e. width, height and depth). Time is the fourth dimension and cost the fifth with further dimensions being explored. Thus BIM covers more than geometry, embracing spatial relationships, light analysis, geographic information and quantities and properties of building components such as manufacturers' details. Significantly it has the possibility of guiding the industry in a more sustainable direction by allowing easier access to the tools to quantify a more sustainable design approach (Krygiel and Nies 2008).

BIM allows a virtual information model to be passed from the design team (i.e. architects, civil, structural and building services engineers) to the contractor and subcontractors and thereafter to the owner, operator and/or facility manager. Each professional contributes

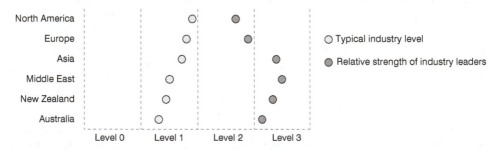

Level 0 – Unmanaged CAD with pdf files as the main form of data exchange.
Level 1 – Managed CAD in 2 or 3D with a collaborative data environment.
Level 2 – Managed 3D environment with proprietary exchange formats. May include 4D program and 5D cost data.
Level 3 – Fully-open process with a single project model and data exchange using Industry Foundation Classes standards.

Figure 7.3 BIM adoption by region
Source: AECOM Blue Book (2013)

data to the shared model and BIM reduces information losses that can occur when new stakeholders take ownership of a development. BIM provides more information to owners of complex developments. A BIM manager manages the processes and is retained from the pre-design phase to develop and to track the BIM against predicted and measured performance goals, supporting multi-disciplinary building information models that drive analysis, schedules, take-off and logistics (Kibert 2013).

A subset of BIM focuses on sustainable building design and operation. Therefore, it is argued, BIM can contribute to the design, construction and commissioning of buildings with lower environmental impacts, in the form of energy efficiency, the reduction of carbon or the better use of fewer materials (Bell in Cotgrave and Riley 2013). For example, drawing in three dimensions allows the cutting of 2-D and 3-D sections in the building design which means that thermal bridging or defective detailing can be resolved prior to construction, leading to better performing and more energy-efficient buildings. Further numerous options and impacts can be modelled to achieve a more integrated design and increasing accuracy and enabling better evaluation (Yezioro *et al.* 2008). BIM can be used for rainwater harvesting evaluation, renewable energy and energy modelling, and the use of sustainable materials (Krygiel and Nies 2008).

BIM can be enriched with additional information, analysis and evaluation tools such as day-lighting and solar studies, materials and product libraries providing a sound basis for building management information for the whole life cycle of a development, including deconstruction; further, it allows for integrated evaluation with building performance evaluation (BPE) and post-occupancy evaluation (POE) analysis and compliance tools allow different design options to be compared (Bell in Cotgrave and Riley 2013). In turn, this leads to informed decision-making at early stages, reducing risks to developers of abortive design and potentially reducing the performance gap.

Although BIM provides the potential for integrated sustainable design and aids transparency, it is an aid to decision-making and theoretically it is possible to link BIM to industry assessment models such as BREEAM and LEED (Azhar *et al.* 2011). It should, however, always be remembered that BIM is an *aid* to decision-making: it is not the decision tool itself.

The key to BIM adoption is access to competitively priced software, to trained and knowledgeable professionals, as well as the compilation and maintenance of up-to-date and reliable libraries and tools. Currently some perceive that BIM can add time and costs to the initial stages of development, though it can be recouped throughout the building life cycle (Bell in Cotgrave and Riley 2013). Although BIM has met with barriers, in much the same way as CAD did two decades ago, the future of BIM is predicted to become increasingly relevant to the construction industry and thus property developers. Industry perceptions are currently that BIM is most useful in the design and construction stages followed by costing and the operational phase of the life cycle as shown in Figure 7.4 (AECOM 2013). Further, industry is required to fully understand the benefits of BIM in the costing and operational phases.

7.6   Construction waste

The concept of waste reduction as a factor of sustainable construction was introduced earlier in this chapter. Although waste elimination and a transfer to a so-called circular economy is fairly recent, waste has long been acknowledged to be a major issue and it is as long ago as 2000 that the UK government first developed a generalised waste strategy

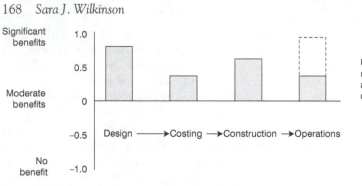

Figure 7.4 Industry perceptions of BIM benefits by asset stage
Source: AECOM Blue Book (2013)

which has since been updated several times, most recently in 2012. However, although this addresses construction waste, it is not focused on construction. El Haggar's work (2010) developed a waste management hierarchy specifically as a framework for contractors to use to create a waste management plan for projects. An integrated approach is advocated with five key steps which are: reduce, reuse, recycle, recover and disposal, which mirrors the UK's current strategy. Various benefits are realised when a structured approach is adopted, particularly reduced costs for the contractor. The benefits were found to be cost savings and profit maximisation, reduced demand for landfill, improved resource management, image improvement and productivity and quality improvement (Bon-Gang and Zong 2011). The study conducted by Bon-Gang and Zong (2011) concluded economic drivers (cost savings and profit maximisation) were driving waste management in Singapore. The ability to manage construction waste is affected by the characteristics of construction projects themselves and as argued earlier, the use of off-site manufacture can be instrumental in reducing waste on-site. Partly this is because there are fewer off-cuts and site security is easier so the possibilities of materials being stolen or pilfered are very significantly reduced.

Although each project is a temporary undertaking to create a unique product, the characteristics can be grouped as follows: size, nature, type, duration and key materials used. Clearly some projects involve more than one type or all types. Different types of project, however, generate different amounts of waste typically. Demolition typically accounts for 53 per cent of waste, followed by renovation at 38 per cent and last, construction at 9 per cent (Bon-Gang and Zong 2011). Project duration is correlated positively to waste production. Finally materials such as concrete and steel are the main materials used in commercial structures. Steel is relatively easy to reuse and recycle whereas concrete is more difficult to recycle and to separate and in this way materials affect the amount of waste that is reused and recycled (Bon-Gang and Zong 2011).

7.7   Current practices in the context of the definitions of sustainability and sustainable development

Given the range of interpretations of the definition of sustainability and sustainable development outlined in Chapter 1 of this text, an empirical analysis was undertaken in 2012 of a) the conceptual understanding of sustainability within the ten leading Australian construction firms and, b) the implication of this level of conceptual understanding with regards to delivering sustainability. The study revealed that there is variance in the conceptual understanding of Australian construction companies; and that sustainability is, as Cook and

Golton (1994) noted; 'an essentially contestable concept'. On a positive note there were encouraging signs that some of the positions advocated by accommodating environmentalism were gaining traction and this reflected a shift from the findings of the UK construction sector study undertaken in the early 1990s (Cook and Golton 1994). To date, none of the companies adopted any ecocentric perspectives and this indicates that we are in a position only to deliver weak sustainability from this sector at this point in time in Australia. Given that Brown (1995) has stated that weak sustainability will not, in itself, provide the solutions to the problem humankind is facing, there are significant issues that the Australian construction industry needs to address. Despite all the green rating tools and schemes, the current level of understanding of sustainability shows we are in imminent danger that we will hit the targets but miss the point. The study has not been replicated outside of Australia but it is indeed possible that similar perceptions are found elsewhere, especially as only two of the ten firms operated in Australia exclusively. Furthermore, the construction companies are a subset of the sector and further work is required to investigate the conceptual understanding of the other stakeholders. If our industry has a limited perspective and understanding of the sustainability concept at present, we should endeavour to ensure that the industry leaders of the future are equipped to make more informed evidence-based decisions.

7.8   Case study Forte Melbourne, Australia

7.8.1 *General description*

Forte is the first Cross Laminated Timber (CLT) building constructed by Lend Lease and is the tallest timber apartment building in the world at nine storeys with 23 apartments. Construction commenced in February 2012 and was completed by October 2012 at a cost of AU$11,000,000. The building is located at 807 Bourke Street in Melbourne's Victoria Harbour, Australia. The aim was to achieve a Five Star Green Star Multi Unit Residential rating by virtue of the choice of materials and the methods used throughout the construction. The construction process differed from that of conventional builds in that the design was completed and sent to the factory for processing, installation sequencing, crane calculations, logistics and delivery planning, namely it was a real example of off-site manufacture. This attention to detail helped to minimise waste as well as reducing on-site decision-making and errors. Sustainable design features included low energy consumption through the specification of LED lighting and passive design, a comprehensive smart metering system and energy-efficient appliances. Future water consumption is likely to be reduced through the installation of efficient fittings in the apartments, whilst rainwater is collected in a tank to feed the toilets and irrigation of the soft landscaping; however, the design fell short of using waterless toilets. To encourage less operation waste recycling facilities are also provided. Furthermore data display panels show home owners how much energy and water they are consuming in an attempt to encourage behaviour change. The design has cross ventilation to enhance occupant health and the materials used are low Volatile Organic Compound (VOC) and no formaldehyde for good internal environmental air quality, IEQ. Good public transport including trams, trains and buses are located nearby, as are bike and car share and cycle way facilities.

7.8.2 *Key issues related to construction methods and materials*

The issues to focus on in this case study are the construction methods and materials which increase environmental sustainability.

Figure 7.5 Elevation Forte apartment Victoria Harbour, Melbourne, Australia

Figure 7.6 Forte apartments under construction, Victoria Harbour, Melbourne, Australia

- Compared to the traditional concrete frame specification the embodied energy in timber is substantially reduced and the carbon footprint of the building is low. Timber reduced CO_2 equivalent emissions by more than 1,400 tonnes compared to steel or concrete, which equates to removing 345 cars from Australian roads.
- Furthermore the concrete specification had a high fly ash content which reduced its environmental impact whilst retaining its strength.
- Construction related water consumption was reduced by 6 per cent compared to concrete and steel construction.
- Construction waste was reduced and health and safety practices were improved with the elimination of manual handling and the use of off-site manufacture.

Overall there was a reduced impact of construction on the local community because the speed of construction shortened the construction time and so social sustainability was enhanced. Forte has other sustainability features which are not discussed here as the focus is construction materials and methods and readers are encouraged to visit www.lendlease.com.au and http://www.ancr.com.au/forte_apartments.pdf to learn more.

7.9   Conclusion

The design and construction stage of property development has a significant impact on the overall sustainability of the project and, therefore, it is imperative that this stage is carefully planned and managed. The most obvious impacts are environmental ones such as energy use, water use, waste and pollution and biodiversity as well as the choice of materials, including transport issues, renewability and their future reuse and recycling. However, construction also has special impacts, notably on those adjoining the construction site, the eventual occupants and the health and safety of operatives during the construction. A holistic approach is required to balance the sustainability of the development design with the sustainability of the construction of the property; in essence a 'sustainable design' which has unsustainable construction processes and procedures undermines the objectives of developing property sustainably. Having appraised the drivers and barriers which are operating in respect of the development it is possible to consider design and construction.

Here the developer has the option of selecting a conventional approach with the consideration of the sustainability issues or, of taking an integrated design process (IDP) approach whereby sustainability is strategically and practicably embedded. As the construction process inevitably is a multi-agency one, often with complex contractual relationships, good communication and clarity of design are essential to underpin the implementation through the build. Therefore it is not just the procurement methods adopted which will have significant impact but the whole suite of documentation, including the contract, the plans and the specifications. In the past, the nature of the documentation has been difficult to work with and changes are often necessitated during the build for a whole range of reasons. However, the shift to digital working is aiding sustainability particularly through the development of BIM which has enabled the implications of many design and construction options to be worked through to aid better decision-making. This is especially the development for owner-occupation as it will enable the facilities management team to both feed into the design process and have more complete data to help them manage the eventual building after handover.

In the recent literature, energy and carbon have been the priority considerations, but more recently the issues of water and waste have gained warranted consideration. Water is a scarce resource which is often wasted during construction; also the choice of materials used affects water consumption in construction. Both steel and concrete require significant quantities of water for their manufacture and shifting to natural materials such as wood can reduce consumption. Similarly, one of the key issues around construction is the amount of waste generated by the process and the adoption of waste management programmes is an effective way of managing the issue. Clearly developments that retain large amounts of existing structures minimise waste creation and maximise retention of embodied energy. Finally a word of caution, whilst great strides have been made in terms of strategies for developers and the development team to adopt delivery of sustainable property, our current conceptual understanding of sustainability could be strengthened by greater understanding of the issues involved.

References

Abidin, N.S. and Pasquire, C.L. (2005) Delivering sustainability through value management: concept and performance overview, *Engineering, Construction and Architectural Management* 12(2):168–180.

Addis, B. and Talbot, R. (2001) *Sustainable Construction Procurement: A Guide to Delivering Environmentally Responsible Projects*, London: Construction Industry Research and Information Association.

AECOM (2013) *The Blue Book 2013. Collaboration: Making Cities Better. Insights on Building, Infrastructure and Construction*, fifteenth edn, Los Angeles, CA: AECOM.

Anderson, J. and Mills, K. (2002) *BRE IP9/02 Part 1: Refurbishment or Redevelopment of Office Buildings? Sustainability Comparison*, Watford: BRE.

Arge, K. (2005) Adaptable office buildings: theory and practice, *Facilities* 23(3/4): 119–127.

Arup (2013) *Low Carbon Routemap for the UK Built Environment,*. Green Construction Board. Retrieved from http://www.greenconstructionboard.org/.

Australian Bureau of Statistics (ABS) (2013a). A statistical overview of the construction industry. Retrieved from http://www.abs.gov.au/AUSSTATS/abs@.nsf/Lookup/1350.0Feature+Article1Oct+2010.

Australian Bureau of Statistics (ABS) (2013b). Waste. Retrieved from http://www.abs.gov.au/AUSSTATS/abs@.nsf/Lookup/4613.0Chapter40Jan+2010.

Azhar, S., Carlton W.A., Olsen, D., and Ahmad, I. (2011) Building information modelling for sustainable design and LEED rating analysis, *Automation in Construction* 20: 217–224.

Better Building Summit (2003) Better Building Summit. Retrieved 13 May 2015 from http://www.hbf.co.uk/policy-activities/news/view/notice-better-building-summit/

Baum, A.E. (1993) Quality, depreciation, and property performance, *Journal of Real Estate Research* 8(4): 541–565.

Bon-Gang, H. and Zong B.Y. (2011) Perception on benefits of construction waste management in the Singapore construction industry, *Engineering Construction and Architectural Management* 18(4): 394–406.

Brown, C.S. (1995) Anthropocentrism and ecocentrism: the quest for a new worldview, *The Midwest Quarterly*, 36(2): 191.

Brownhill, D. and Yates, A. (2001) *BRE IP01/01 Environmental Benchmarking for Property Portfolio Managers*, Watford: BRE.

Building Research Establishment (BRE) (2002) *Managing Sustainable Construction: Profiting from Sustainability*, Watford: BRE.

Cement Concrete and Aggregates Australia (2007) *Use of Recycled Water in Concrete Production*. Retrieved from http://www.concrete.net.au/publications/pdf/RecycledWater.pdf.

Cook, S.J. and Golton, B. (1994) Sustainable development concepts and practice in the built environment. A UK perspective, CIB TG 16, *Proceedings of the Sustainable Construction Conference*, Tampa, FL, 6–9 November 1994.

Cotgrave, A.J. and Riley, M. (eds) (2013) *Total Sustainability in the Built Environment*, Basingstoke, Macmillan.

Department of Environment and Climate Change NSW (2013) *Sustainable Property 17 Guide 2013* Retrieved 24 August 2014 from http://www.environment.nsw.gov.au.htm.

Desai, P. (2009) *One Planet Communities: A Real-life Guide to Sustainable Living*, Chichester: Wiley.

Dong, B., Kennedy, C., and Pressnail, K. (2005) Comparing life cycle implications of building retrofit and replacement options, *Canadian Journal of Civil Engineering* 32(6): 1051–1063.

Edwards, B. (2002) *Rough Guide to Sustainability*, London: RIBA Publications.

Edwards, B.W. and Naboni, E. (2013) *Green Buildings Pay: Design, Productivity and Ecology*, Abingdon: Routledge.

Egbu, C. (1995) Perceived degree of difficulty of management tasks in construction refurbishment work, *Building Research & Information* 23: 340–344.

El Haggar, S. (2010) *Sustainable Industrial Design and Waste Management: Cradle-to-cradle for Sustainable Development*, Sheffield: Academic Press.

Ellison, L. and Sayce, S. (2007) Assessing sustainability in the existing commercial property stock: establishing sustainability criteria relevant for the commercial property investment sector. *Property Management,* 25(3): 287–304.

Environmental Services Association (ESA) (2013) *Going for Growth: A Practical Route to a Circular Economy*, London: ESA. Retrieved from http://www.esauk.org/esa_reports/Circular_Economy_Report_FINAL_High_Res_For_Release.pdf.

European Union (2008) *Directive 2008/98/of the European Parliament and of the Council: The Waste Framework Directive*. Retrieved from http://eur-lex.europa.eu/LexUriServ/LexUriServ.do?uri=OJ:L:2008:312:0003:0030:en:PDF.

Facilities Society (2013) *Value Management and Engineering*. Retrieved from http://www.facilities.ac.uk/j/cpd/61-project-management/106-value-management-and-engineering.

Financial Times (2013) Responsible Investment. Retrieved from http://lexicon.ft.com/Term?term=responsible-investment.

Fuerst, F. and McAllister, P. (2011a) Green noise or green value? Measuring the effects of environmental certification on office values, *Real Estate Economics* 39(1): 45–69.

Fuerst, F. and McAllister, P. (2011b) Eco-labelling in commercial office markets: do LEED and Energy Star offices obtain multiple premiums, *Ecological Economics* 70(6): 1220–1230.

Green Construction Board (2015) Mapping the real estate life cycle for effective policy interventions. Retrieved from http://www.greenconstructionboard.org/images/stories/Valuation_and_Demand/GCB610%20Final%20Report.pdf.

Hawken, P., Lovins, A.B., and Lovins, L.H. (2010) *Natural Capitalism: The Next Industrial Revolution*, London: Earthscan.

Hill, R.C. and Bowen, P.A. (1997) Sustainable construction: principles and a framework for attainment, *Construction Management & Economics* 15(3): 223–239.

Hostetler, M., Allen, W., and Meurk, C. (2011) Conserving urban biodiversity? Creating green infrastructure is only the first step, *Landscape and Urban Planning* 100(4): 369–371.

Kelly, M.J. (2008) Britain's Building Stock. A Carbon Challenge. Retrieved 7 April 2010 from http://www.lcmp.eng.cam.ac.uk/wp-content/uploads/081012_kelly.pdf.

Khalfan, M. and Maqsood, T. (2011) Attitudes towards social and economic aspects of sustainable construction amongst construction contractors, *International Journal of Construction Project Management* 3(3): 243–255.

Kibert, C.J. (2013) *Sustainable Construction. Green Building Design and Delivery*, third edn, Hoboken, NJ: Wiley.

Kok, N. and Jennen, M. (2012) The impact of energy labels and accessibility on office rents, *Energy Policy* 46: 489–497.

Krygiel, E. and Nies, B. (2008) *Green BIM. Successful Sustainable Design with Building Information Modeling*, Hoboken, NJ: Wiley.

Kukadia, V., Upton, S., Brimwood, C. and Yu, C. (2003) *BRE Pollution Control Guide Part 1: Controlling Particles, Vapour and Noise Pollution from Construction Sites*, Watford: British Research Establishment.

Langston, C., Wong, F.K., Hui, E., and Shen, L.Y. (2008) Strategic assessment of building adaptive reuse opportunities in Hong Kong, *Building and Environment* 43(10): 1709–1718.

Lee, H.W., Choi, K., and Gambatese, J.A. (2014) Real options valuation of phased investments in commercial energy retrofits under building performance risks, *Journal of Construction Engineering and Management* 10: 1061/(ASCE)CO.1943-7862.0000844.

Löfstedt, R.E. (2011) *Reclaiming Health and Safety for All: An Independent Review of Health and Safety Legislation*, London: Department of Work and Pensions. Retrieved from https://www.gov.uk/government/uploads/system/uploads/attachment_data/file/66790/lofstedt-report.pdf.

Lorenz, D.P., Trück, S., and Lützkendorf, T. (2007) Exploring the relationship between the sustainability of construction and market value: theoretical basics and initial empirical results from the residential property sector, *Property Management* 25(2): 119–149.

Mathews, J.A. and Tan, H. (2011) Progress toward a circular economy in China, *Journal of Industrial Ecology* 15(3): 435–457.

Medineckiene, M., Turskis Z., and Zavadskas, E.K. (2010) Sustainable construction taking into account the building impact on the environment, *Journal of Environmental Engineering and Landscape Management* 18(2): 118–127.

Miles, J. and Whitehouse, N. (2013) *Offsite Housing Review: A Report for the Construction Industry Council*. Retrieved from http://www.buildoffsite.com/pdf/publications/BoS_offsitehousingreview.pdf.

Naiman, R.J., Decamps, H., and Pollock, M. (1993) The role of riparian corridors in maintaining regional biodiversity, *Ecological Applications* 3(2): 209–212.

National Building Information Model Standard Project Committee (2013). Building Smart Alliance. Retrieved 12 November 2013 from http://www.buildingsmartalliance.org/index.php/nbims/faq/.

Newell, G., MacFarlane, J., and Kok, N. (2013) *Building Better Returns. A Study of the Financial Performance of Green Office Buildings in Australia*. API and PFA. Retrieved from www.api.org.au/assets/media_library/000/000/219/original.pdf.

OECD (Organization for Economic Co-operation and Development) (2006) *Performance Review – UK's Progress Report*, London: HMSO. Retrieved from www.defra.gov.uk/environment/internat/oecd/pdf/epr-ukreport2006.pdf.

OGC (2005) *Achieving Excellence in Construction – Procurement Guide 11: Sustainability*, London: Office of Government Commerce.

ONS (Office for National Statistics) (2013) *Updated Estimates of UK Resource Use Using Raw Material Equivalents*. Retrieved from http://www.ons.gov.uk/ons/rel/environmental/uk-environmental-accounts/2013

Parkin, S. (2000, November) Contexts and drivers for operationalizing sustainable development, *Proceedings of the ICE-Civil Engineering* 138(6): 9–15.

Pitt, M., Tucker, M., Riley, M., and Longden, J. (2009) Towards sustainable construction: promotion and best practices, *Construction Innovation* 9(2): 201–224. Retrieved from www.emeraldinsight.com/1471–4175.htm.

Pivo, G. (2008) Exploring responsible property investing: a survey of American executives, *Corporate Social Responsibility and Environmental Management* 15(4): 235–248.

RICS (2005) *Sustainable Construction (Worldwide)*, Coventry: Royal Institution for Chartered Surveyors. Retrieved from www.rics.org/Builtenvironment/Sustainableconstruction/ (accessed 24 August 2013).

RICS (2006) *RICS Response to UK Energy Review*, Coventry: Royal Institution for Chartered Surveyors.

RICS (2011) *Green Infrastructure in Urban Areas: An Information Paper*, first edn, London: RICS Practice Standards. Retrieved from rics.org/globalstandards rics.org/standards.

RICS (2012) *Methodology to Calculate Embodied Carbon of Materials*, first edn, Information Paper 32/2012. Retrieved from www.rics/standards.

Rogerson, D. (2013) *Letter to Stakeholders Dated 6th November*. London: Department of Environment Food and Rural Affairs (DEFRA).

Sayce, S., Walker, A., and McIntosh, A. (2004) *Building Sustainability in the Balance: Promoting Stakeholder Dialogue*, London: Estates Gazette

Stern, N. (2006) *Stern Review: The Economics of Climate Change*, Vol. 30, London: HM Treasury.

Sustainable Construction Task Force (2006) *Procuring the Future: Sustainable Procurement National Action Plan: Recommendations from the Sustainable Construction Task Force*, London: Department of Environment, Agriculture and Rural Affairs (DEFRA).

Sustainable Construction Task Force(2000) *Reputation, Risk and Reward*. Retrieved from http://projects.bre.co.uk/rrr/RRR.pdf.

Sustainable Construction Task Force(2003) *The UK Construction Industry: Progress Towards more Sustainable Construction 2000–2003*. Retrieved from www.dti.gov.uk/construction/sustain/sctg.pdf.

Tavri, P., Sayce, S., and Hands, V. (2013) Waste reuse and preparing for reuse: the top priority, in F. Castro, C. Vilarinho, J. Carvalho, A. Castro, J. Araujo, and A. Pedro (eds), *Proceedings of the Second International Conference and Exhibition WASTES: Solutions, Treatments and Opportunities*, Portugal: CVR, pp. 465–470.

Taylor, S. (2009) *Offsite Production in the UK Construction Industry: A Brief Overview Report*, Construction Engineering Specialist Team: HSE. Retrieved from http://www.buildoffsite.com/downloads/off-site_production_june09.pdf.

Town and Country Planning Association (2012) *Planning for a Healthy Environment – Good Practice Guidance for Green Infrastructure and Biodiversity*. Retrieved from http://www.tcpa.org.uk/data/files/TCPA_TWT_GI-Biodiversity-Guide.pdf.

Treloar, G., Fay, R., Ilozor, B., and Love, P.E.D. (2001) Building materials selection; greenhouse strategies for built facilities, *Facilities* 19: 139–149.

UK Government (2008) *Strategy for Sustainable Construction*. Retrieved from http://www.bis.gov.uk/files/file46535.pdf.

Vergnes, A., Viol, I.L., and Clergeau, P. (2012) Green corridors in urban landscapes affect the arthropod communities of domestic gardens, *Biological Conservation*, 145(1): 171–178.

Warren, C.M.J. and Huston, S. (2011) Promoting energy efficiency in public sector commercial buildings in Australia. *Proceedings of the RICS Construction and Property Conference COBRA: Construction and Building Research Conference*, 12–13 September 2011, Salford, United Kingdom, pp. 128–134.

Waylen, C., Thornback, J., and Garrett, J. (2011) *Water: An Action Plan for Reducing Water Usage on Construction Sites: A Report for the Strategic Construction Forum*. Retrieved from http://www.strategicforum.org.uk/pdf/SCTG09-WaterActionPlanFinalCopy.pdf.

Weeks, J.L. (2011) Health and safety hazards in the construction industry, in K.S. Ringen and J.L. Weeks (eds), *Health, Prevention and Management Encyclopaedia of Occupational Health and Safety*. Geneva: International Labour Organization.

Wilkinson, S. J., Ghosh, S., and Page, L. (2013) Options for green roof retrofit and urban food production in the Sydney CBD. RICS COBRA, New Delhi, India, 10–12 September 2013.

Williams, N.S., Raynor, J.P., and Raynor, K.J. (2010) Green roofs for a wide brown land: opportunities and barriers for rooftop greening in Australia, *Urban Forestry and Urban Greening* 9(3): 245–251.

World Green Building Council (WGBC) (2013) *The Business Case for Green Buildings*, Toronto: World Green Building Council. Retrieved from http://www.worldgbc.org/files/1513/6608/0674/Business_Case_For_Green_Building_Report_WEB_2013-04-11.pdf.

Yates, A. (2003a) *BRE IP13/03 Part 1: Sustainable Buildings: Benefits for Occupiers*, Watford: BRE Centre for Sustainable Construction.

Yates, A. (2003b) *BRE IP13/03 Part 2: Sustainable Buildings: Benefits for Designers*, Watford: BRE Centre for Sustainable Construction.

Yates, A. (2003c) *BRE IP13/03 Part 3: Sustainable Buildings: Benefits for Investors and Developers,* Watford: BRE Centre for Sustainable Construction.

Yates, A. (2003d), *BRE IP13/03 Part 4 Sustainable Buildings: Benefits for Constructors,* Watford: BRE Centre for Sustainable Construction.

Yezioro, A., Dong, B., and Leite, F. (2008) An applied artificial intelligence approach towards assessing building performance simulation tools, *Energy and Buildings* 40(4): 612.

Zalejska-Jonsson, A. (2013) Impact of energy and environmental factors in the decision to purchase or rent an apartment: the case of Sweden, *Journal of Sustainable Real Estate.* 5(4) 66–85.

Zhang, Z.H., Shen, L.Y., Love, P.E.D., and Treloar, G. (2000) A framework for implementing ISO 14000 in construction, *Environmental Management and Health* 11: 139–148.

8 Procuring the project in a sustainable way

Sara J. Wilkinson and Sarah L. Sayce

8.0 Introduction

The adopted procurement route influences the way the development is delivered and has significant consequences for time, quality, cost and sustainability (Lupton *et al.* 2012). After land acquisition, procurement involves the second biggest financial outlay made by developers (Wilkinson and Reed 2008); in some low-value location, especially where the land being developed suffers from, for example, contamination, the purchase cost may be far less than the building procurement costs. The procurement route selected affects the composition and the size of the professional team; furthermore different methods of procurement may influence the extent to which sustainability criteria are integrated into both the design and construction processes. In this chapter, the latest methods of procurement in use are presented and in each case the potential interaction with sustainability impacts is considered. Over the last decade, many of the large private sector developers and governments have achieved considerable progress in adopting sustainable procurement throughout their purchasing policies, including the procuring of buildings (see for example DEFRA 2006; Walker *et al.* 2012; National Audit Office 2013). Such policies include social, economic and environmental considerations into the processes adopted. New innovations and modifications to existing procurement methods are discussed to show how these can result in greater sustainability in property development. After the initial brief is determined, a schedule of accommodation prepared and general design constraints are agreed, the building contract can be selected for the development.

It has not been the development of an explicit sustainability agenda only, that has driven innovation and change in procurement. For over 20 years, construction has been a high priority among governments who have perceived the industry, and its working methods, as 'backward' (Woudhuysen *et al.* 2004). UK industry-led reports such as those by, for example, Latham (1994) and Egan (1998 and 2002) called for greater collaboration and innovation and led to the setting up of bodies such as Constructing Excellence whose role is to foster and disseminate innovation within the construction industry.

Although every contract will be different as each development is unique, there are many standard forms of contracts or suites of contracts used in many regions. Among the most widely used contracts in Europe, are those published and promoted by JCT (Joint Contracts Tribunal), FIDIC (Fédération Internationale des Ingénieurs-Conseils or International Federation of Consulting Engineers) and NEC, the latter of which is advocated for many public sector contracts. All these contracts include reference to the need to make construction practices more sustainable.

8.1   Sustainable procurement options

An important contribution to sustainable development can be achieved through the adoption of sustainable procurement in the public and private sectors. In the public sector, governments are responsible for immense amounts of spending. The US government for example spent US$6,129.8 billion in 2013 with an estimated US$6,454.7 billion allocated for 2014 (US Government Spending 2013). These figures represent 37.8 per cent and 37.9 per cent of GDP for 2013 and 2014. UK government spending totalled £675 billion in 2013, of this £506 billion was spent by central government, and £169 billion was spent by local authorities (UK Public Spending, 2013). This UK figure is predicted to be £719 billion in 2014 and £729 billion by 2016 (UK Public Spending, 2013). As a percentage of GDP, these figures represent 43 per cent and 44 per cent in 2013 and 2014 respectively, higher than the US. Publicly, through policy and publications (Hartwell in Cotgrave and Riley 2013) the UK government is committed to sustainable development and therefore committed to procuring services and buildings in a sustainable manner. The issue is: how does such a general and laudable ambition translate into practice? In the view of the ISEAL Alliance (2013) the public sector has a unique leadership position which suggests that governments have the capacity to transform markets. However barriers remain, even within the public sector, based on lack of knowledge, resource constraints and in some cases weak frameworks (ISEAL 2013). Further, where a developer is procuring a building using one of the JCT suite of contracts they can specifically refer to the JCT's own sustainability guidance (JCT 2011) which has been prepared in order to assist management teams, design teams, the construction industry and its clients (both public and private sector) in dealing with environmental (though not social) sustainability.

The client base requiring the incorporation of sustainability is growing. In the private sector, some 5,500 companies are now signed up to the Global Reporting Initiative (GRI) and, following the introduction in 2012 of their Construction and Real Estate Sector Supplement (CRESS), have been provided with a framework for reporting which includes building procurement practice. Whilst is it early days to evaluate the influence of GRI CRESS on procurement practice, it is likely to be highly influential as the rate of take up of GRI gathers momentum.

Conventionally three inter-dependent criteria dominate procurement method choice; these are time, cost and quality (see Figure 8.1). Time relates to the priority of completing the development by a certain date or the speed of development. Some projects are very time driven, for example the sports facilities constructed for an Olympic Games had time as a very high priority; similarly retail schemes tend to have high pressure points for sales. Cost is focused on price level or cost certainty and for some developers this is of vital importance. For example, if the profit in a development is marginal and the market is perceived to be turning and property values may decline, a developer would wish to minimise exposure to risk by having more cost certainty. Finally there is quality; which is related to performance and functionality. Again, for some developments, quality is paramount where, for example, high quality residential developments demand the highest quality of workmanship. Similarly, developments commissioned for owner-occupation, such as a prestigious headquarters building, will often be specified for high quality and durability. When the focus is heavily on one, it can be to the detriment of the others (Hartwell in Cotgrave and Riley 2013); too often cost has been dominant at the expense of quality and sustainability (Bradley and Anantatmula 2011).

Hartwell (Cotgrave and Riley 2013) suggests a modification to Figure 8.1 to incorporate sustainability as shown in Figure 8.2. In this approach, developers and their team take into

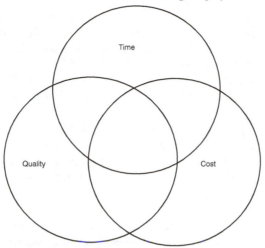

Figure 8.1 Traditional criteria in procurement

account sustainability factors; the development will have environmental and social impacts that need to be balanced and also reconciled economically. Whilst this may be the aim for public sector projects, where sustainable development is mandated, where a development is for sale to the market, the developer needs to be cognisant of investor, funder and occupier sensitivities socially and environmentally that affect the project.

The selection of the form of contract is normally governed by the developer's needs, local market practice and the scale and complexity of the development; whilst it may be simple to balance these, it is actually a complex decision involving many variables (Podvezko *et al.* 2010). Whoever is commissioning the contract must decide the highest priority be it time, quality (building performance) or cost management, as each priority supports different procurement choices. Different kinds of developer and stakeholder attach changing degrees of importance to time, quality and cost and these factors affect the choice of procurement strategy; they may also be heavily influenced by their consultant teams. Indeed Bowen *et al.* (2012) in a South African study found that clients and their consultants held differing

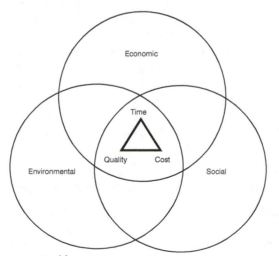

Figure 8.2 Key criteria in sustainable procurement

views in terms of what would be a realistic relationship between the variables. In terms of importance in procurement, owner-occupiers tend to rank quality (45 per cent) over cost (30 per cent) and time (25 per cent). Speculative developers on the other hand, rank time as the highest priority (50 per cent), followed by cost (30 per cent) and quality third (20 per cent). Finally investors have a different set of priorities again and rank quality highest (50 per cent), followed by time (30 per cent) and last cost (20 per cent) (Morledge in Kelly *et al.* 2002).

The core criteria now often include sustainability (Hartwell in Cotgrave and Riley 2013), particularly in the case of public sector commissions (RICS 2013), where consideration of the 'bigger picture' is essential. Considerations of sustainability should be embedded through the evaluation of time, cost and quality; however, this is still problematic in many cases (Hughes and Laryea 2013; ISEAL 2013).

Notably within the public sector, cost is normally perceived in terms of 'best value' rather than lowest cost; sensitive social aspects are evaluated and the environmental impact of the development and the alternative options is deliberated fully. Given the amount of public spending, national governments have the most significant influence on sustainable procurement, followed by corporate occupiers, local government, public opinion and developers and architects (Hartwell in Cotgrave and Riley 2013). When it comes to drivers of sustainable procurement, legislation is most important, followed by brand risk management, supply chain demands and then CSR. Governments are, in many respects, leading the way, with legislation and minimum quality requirements for buildings they occupy and/or commission. For example in Australia the minimum standard for energy in government leased space is 4 Star NABERS and some sectors of the commercial market have redeveloped or retrofitted their stock to achieve this minimum in order that they can accommodate government tenants (Warren and Huston 2011). Similarly in the UK, the government, where they are tenants, requires a certificated building to at least BREEAM Very Good standard; for new builds they now normally require an 'Excellent' certification. This is driving change but the view persists that an increase in sustainability quality leads to cost increase; research findings on this are mixed but cost premiums appear to be declining (World Green Building Council 2013).

Newer forms of procurement are being taken up such as private finance initiatives (PFI) and partnering and with the increasing costs of energy construction, property organisations are operating in an environment where capital costs of construction of the development are not the most important factors in the decisions made. Where there is an ongoing relationship between the commissioning body and the future occupation of the building, operational and life cycle costs are increasingly taken into account and the whole life cycle costing approach may be adopted. This is a framework in which the entire life cycle of the building can be taken into account in decision-making. Within the commercial sector, where building is undertaken speculatively and the developer retains no ongoing interest in the building, initial cost considerations, tempered by legal compliance, still persist (Green Construction Board 2015).

8.2   Life cycle costing (LCC) and whole life cycle costing (WLCC)

The concepts of LCC and WLCC are not new, but have struggled for widespread adoption other than in large-scale owner-occupied and government developments. Using these approaches, the costs of the entire development until life end are taken into account, including land acquisition, design and construction including all consultants' fees, plus operation and maintenance costs. Two terms are used currently: life cycle costing and whole life cycle costing. Life cycle costing (LCC) models the building's performance over its whole life (Kibert 2013), where a cost-benefit analysis is undertaken for each year of the building's estimated life cycle. For Hartwell (Cotgrave and Riley 2013), WLCC considers the whole life cycle costs of acquiring a development including consultants' fees, design, construction, equipment, operating and maintenance costs to disposal. Where appropriate, the costs of developers' internal resources and overheads are included, along with risk allowances and refurbishment costs.

In LCC, the present value of each year's benefits are determined using a discount rate and in turn this is used to calculate the total net present value of a particular feature. For instance, the economic return on a photovoltaic system is ascertained by amortising the systems costs over its lifetime. The value of the energy generated each year is quantified to ascertain the net annual benefit. Developers can use LCC to determine whether the payback for any system meets their criteria. Furthermore, LCC can be used in conjunction with life cycle assessment (LCA) which is covered in Chapter 11. In whole life cycle costing, the costs of sustainability, as well as refurbishment and health and safety compliance, is also considered.

There are two broad schools of thought with regard to costs of developing property sustainably. One is that sustainable property can cost the same as a conventional property (Kibert 2013). In this paradigm, the integrated design process outlined in Chapter 7 is followed to ensure costs are kept in line with standard expectation in the marketplace be it for retail, residential, industrial or commercial developments. The second school of thought is that sustainable developments are more expensive but that this is offset against higher values and less risk over the long term. The World Green Building Council's review of literature and case studies (WGBC 2013) revealed a mixed picture, perhaps not surprising given that a number of variables, including procurement route, influence delivery cost.

Furthermore, using a LCC approach, it can be shown that over the building life cycle, advantages are apparent. For example, sustainable developments may have lower operating costs and reduced maintenance costs, that justify higher capital costs and which will be accepted by the market, except where the benefit and burden are split between different parties. Although a number of studies in Europe, the US and Australia have found a differential in rental values, and sometimes capital values, associated with energy and/or sustainability certified office buildings (Fuerst and McAllister 2011a, 2011b; McFarlane and Newell 2012), there are a number of factors at play in the value equation. It is not universally accepted that there is an equivalent trade-off between costs and added value and it only applies in some sub-markets. Consequently there are still many studies that make the 'business case' for green on soft issues such as reputation and brand. Where value differentiation is seen to be taking place, the markets are valuing the lower operating costs, better working conditions and internal environmental quality associated with sustainable office developments (World Green Building Council 2013).

LCC divides costs into hard and soft costs. Hard costs are fairly easy to quantify and assess and include factors such as utility bills and consumption of energy and water. Soft costs are less tangible and harder to quantify. They include aspects such as improved internal environmental quality (IEQ), worker productivity and employee satisfaction and wellbeing. These aspects are covered in Chapter 10. An LCC using hard costs only typically evaluates alternative strategies including a trade-off of operational costs versus capital costs. However an LCC including soft costs is more difficult to justify as the information cannot be verified with the same amount of rigour as one restricted to hard costs. It is a matter for individual developers and design teams to determine how confident they are in the inclusion of soft costs for an LCC on a proposed development. Factors such as whether the developer intends to hold or sell, or whether the developer is in the residential or commercial market, for example, will affect the decision to include or exclude soft costs. As time goes by, methodologies for the quantification of soft costs will improve and become more sophisticated; when this happens the case for sustainability to be written into procurement contracts will be stronger.

Two of the main issues with both WLCC and LCC are the period assumed for building life and the discount rate adopted (if any) for future costs and benefits. Clearly, predicting the future is difficult and the argument made against taking a long period is the uncertainty that is implicit; however, placing due weight on the future is a fundamental principle of Brundtland's definition of sustainable development. In relation to discount rate, the rate adopted will significantly affect the results; the higher the rate, the less value is attributed to future benefits and the more critical initial costs become. Frequently a life of 50 or 60 years is assumed and the discount rate will often differ between private and public sector. In an extensive European study, Davis Langdon (2007) found that assumed building life varied typically between 25–40 years but could be up to 120 years. Sometimes the building life was assumed to coincide with the length of PFI/PPP arrangements. They also found that where discounting was applied, rates varied from 0 per cent to 10–12 per cent but that typically they were between 3–6 per cent for the public sector. Unless/until greater standardisation of method is adopted, the results are not easily transferable and the case for sustainability may be compromised.

8.3   Sustainable procurement and the supply chain

An effective sustainable procurement policy is predicated on ethical sourcing which supports the early engagement of suppliers throughout the supply chain; it also places requirements on those who are part of the supply chain. It is normal practice now for tenderers to be required to supply their sustainability credentials before they are entitled to bid for public sector and some private sector contracts. A supply chain is defined as the sequence of processes involved in the production and distribution of a commodity, or here, a development. The integrated design process (IDP), discussed in Chapter 7, is a good means of ensuring these issues are taken into account early in the design where the most value gains can be realised in terms of sustainability. Over the last two decades, the use of terms such as 'best value' and 'best practice' have become widespread to reflect the longer-term perspective where short-term economic gains or savings may not be the best or most cost efficient option over the long term or whole life cycle.

Experience has shown that a development specified with less durable but often cheaper materials is likely to cost more to maintain and more to operate and may suffer component failure. Previously developers who held their projects may have had different views from those who sold on completion. However, astute and intelligent investors and buyers are realising that life cycle costs impact greatly on their overheads and parts of the market are changing. Further, as indicated above, a developer wishing their new building to have maximum market appeal is finding that building to a less sustainable standard will restrict not just price but the type of purchaser and hence may restrict their ability to sell. Table 8.1 illustrates factors to consider in construction procurement sustainability and the supply chain.

During the design phase, the developer and the supply team can influence the sustainability performance in several ways, including provision for biodiversity, orientation

Table 8.1 Factors in construction procurement sustainability and the supply chain

- Consider the environmental, social and economic sustainability from initiation.
- Commence planning for procurement early where the greatest impact is possible.
- Adopt performance specifications, where appropriate, better to ensure quality is achieved.
- Engage early with suppliers and screen for sustainability credentials.
- Adopt 'best value' when appraising tenders to avoid selection of lowest tender only using appropriate social and environmental criteria in decision-making

Source: Authors

of the building for natural light and layouts which promote social cohesion. However, often the prime consideration is through the identification of materials that meet established sustainability criteria. These criteria include factors such as embodied carbon content and energy efficiency in use. In the Forte development in Melbourne discussed in Chapter 7, Head of Sustainability for Lend Lease Matt Williams stated:

> The panels were procured from Austria and even with the transport factored in we saved nearly 1,600 tonnes of carbon, which for a building of that size is enough to offset all of the occupants' lifestyle/operational emissions for about 12 years.
>
> (Williams personal communication, January 2014)

Environmental rating tools exist and many developers use these tools as a framework to deliver sustainability. Some tools cover the design period only, whereas others also include the in-use phase of the life cycle. As might be expected, there are differences in the sustainability measures and the value of those measures in the different tools. Where tools are used, careful selection and interpretation is vital for sustainability outcomes. This is especially the case for rating tools which include calibrated scores for a range of different aspects and for which it is possible to skew the resultant grade by emphasising certain aspects over others. This is explored further in Chapter 9.

At the stage before the contract is awarded the commissioning developer and their team must connect with the supply chain and ascertain their knowledge and experience with respect to sustainability. Achievement of, or progress towards, sustainability accreditations such as ISO 14001 (see http://www.iso.org/iso/theiso14000family_2009.pdf) is often required. Typically previous projects are visited or reviewed to determine the scale and scope of experience and knowledge prior to appointment. Questions may be asked as to how innovation has been and about the experience of the workforce. In addition an enthusiasm for, and a commitment to, sustainability is important; and for some companies this may exist in the form of their Corporate Social Responsibility (CSR) strategy.

The building is normally handed over following the issue of a Certificate of Practical Completion and at this stage comprehensive and systematic process is required to inform the building facility manager or owner about the operation of the building management system (BMS). Incorrect operation of a building can lead to less sustainable outcomes. For example, one sustainable building in Melbourne was designed with a system of night purges of heat during the summer months. During the night, the windows were programmed to open and purge the hot air and then shut in the morning and the air-conditioning system then cooled the building but from a lower temperature than had the windows remained shut at night. In the first summer of operation, the system performed well, however, during the winter months, energy consumption increased markedly. At first look, all the systems were functioning as intended. However, on closer examination it was apparent the computer was running on the summer programme. In effect the building lost all its heat each night when the windows opened and then the heating system was required to rapidly heat the whole building from low temperatures to a comfortable working level within two to three hours. Clearly the result was unsustainable winter energy consumption. This is not an isolated example. Bennetts, writing the preface to the Soft Landings Framework argued that: 'as an industry, we have often seemed incapable of learning about the performance of own creations, with the inevitable result that buildings regularly fail to meet their owners' operational expectations or, worse, are demolished less than a generation after their completion' (BSRIA 2009: 5).

The Soft Landings Framework was developed in an attempt to overcome what has come to be known as the 'performance gap' between design and occupational experience. The framework was designed to overcome the identified problems of:

- designers lacking full understanding of occupiers' needs;
- greater use of technology in buildings that requires more knowledge from those charged with commissioning and managing the building;
- over complexity of design leading to increased cost and complications in management.

Under the framework, the design team do not step away from the building on handover but retain involvement until the building is fully evaluated and operating to its specification. Although the framework considers all aspects of delivering developments, the situation with energy is particularly acute with estimates that energy consumption in some cases can be between two and five times the design predictions, which is clearly an unsustainable situation (see http://www.designingbuildings.co.uk/wiki/Performance_gap_between_ building_design_and_operation). The solutions, in addition to the use of Soft Landings, which are advocated include the systematic improvement in collection and modelling of energy data and stronger regulatory and fiscal frameworks (Arup 2013).

8.4   Procurement strategy and options

It has been argued that the 'selection of the procurement method is probably the most important decision' the developer makes (Smith *et al.* 2004). Procurement methods have been categorised as falling into three types: traditional, design and build/manage led and integrated/partnered and each is explored within this chapter. Choosing an appropriate procurement strategy should involve full evaluation of options and selection. Typically consultants advise developers by evaluating the project priorities, including taking account of the client's approach to risk as some procurement routes can pass risk to the contractor; with other forms more remains with the client. Thereafter, the developer should consider all possible procurement options, evaluate them and choose the most suitable. Traditionally the criteria which should be considered include:

- factors outside the control of the professional/project team (such as interest rates, inflation and legislation);
- developer resources;
- project characteristics;
- ability to make changes;
- risk management;

- cost;
- time; and,
- performance and quality.

Most developers use checklists to help determine which procurement route is most suited to their circumstances and help them set priorities (Morledge *et al.* 2006). Where sustainability principles are to be adopted, developers can adopt the UK government's standard for sustainable procurement. Published in 2010, BS 8903 – Principles and Framework for Procuring Sustainably shifts the paradigm for property development by providing additional criteria for the procurer to consider: environmental, social and economic. It is recognised that there may be conflicts between those criteria and the traditional considerations and priorities will need to be set to ensure that the developer retains control over the factors that are most important to them. As stated above, in many cases, standard forms of contract will be used, but variations are often made to accommodate the complexities or individual circumstances of any project.

BS 8903 contains comprehensive guidance for organisations on how to adopt and embed sustainable procurement principles and practices at all stages of procurement. The standard steers supply chain organisations and developers through the tendering, contract options and clauses stages to facilitate sustainable procurement. For example, a developer may choose to specify the way goods are supplied and transported to enhance sustainability. Contract performance clauses, on the other hand, stipulate how the contract should be undertaken. Some examples of this could be the use of reusable containers for components and materials, or, the delivery of concentrated materials to site reducing transport emissions.

The standard allows developers to influence the specification. For example, they can specify that only energy efficiency heating systems or Forestry Stewardship Council timber or reclaimed materials are used. In the selection of tenderers, the criteria adopted normally include financial standing and technical capability to deliver the development as well as environmental performance. The company's CSR policy may be used for this though it must relate directly to performance in the contract.

As far as the award of the contract is concerned, there are two options, lowest price or most economically advantageous tender (MEAT). MEAT is most likely to be adopted and is similar to VFM (value for money) and reflects the inclusion of sustainability criteria. The contract conditions are then used to ensure the contract is undertaken in line with the developer's objectives. For large developments, a contract condition might require the successful contractor to use a certain transport system to deliver materials. The 2012 London Olympics development at Stratford is a good example of this condition. More often, delivery times outside normal working hours are specified for inner city developments to avoid congestion. Another relatively recent phenomenon is relationship management where contractors and developers work co-operatively with each other and their supply chains to promote sustainability. With social and environmental issues, it is best to consider them as early as possible in order to have most impact. Relationship management practice can help to drive sustainability but skill is needed to ensure that it can be delivered as revealed in a comparative practice study between Beijing and Sydney (Ling *at al.* 2014).

If the development includes a service component, such as provided under a design-build-operate contract or a PFI, developers often give responsibility for operational costs, such as energy, to the supply team. In this approach, WLCC (as discussed in section 8.2) is part of the continuous process to deliver value for money and reduce energy related greenhouse gas emissions. Another option is to adopt clauses where parties are incentivised to make operational efficiencies which are known as 'pain-gain' share clauses. Value for money (VFM) is achieved when users or buyers get the quality they require within WLCC. On this basis, the lowest tender is unlikely to fulfil the requirements of VFM and therefore the traditional paradigm is shifted. An example in use is a development where some social engagement is required with the local community, here the contractor has to submit a plan and a strategy outlining what they propose to do and how they will do it. The tender evaluation also requires the design team to consider this component as well as the tender price and programme submitted. In the EU, all public bodies are required to comply with BS 8903; this provides a very good example of how legislation can assist positively in moving property development towards more sustainable practices.

Where the project is for a refurbishment, another aid to help sustainability is the SKA rating system, operated by RICS. SKA provides a range of good practice in which to deal with environmental concerns such as waste and water. SKA is considered in more detail in Chapter 9.

8.5   Procurement options

Developers determine whether the design of the development will be undertaken by their own in-house or commissioned architect and professional team, or the contractor. For instance, if time is critical, the pre-contract period may be reduced by combining the design and construction elements. On the other hand, fast-track methods of construction can deliver early completion. A critical factor is whether the developer would like flexibility to be able to make changes to the design during the contract. Finally the issue of risk is important and the extent to which a developer wishes to transfer risk to the contractor. An additional issue for public sector developers is the desire to achieve value for money to meet public accountability requirements. A further concern will be whether there will be an ongoing relationship between the developer and the building. For example, for many public sector projects, the developer will retain responsibility for maintenance and management for a period of up to 30 years or more. The ultimate occupier may also have a view as to the type of contract to use because of the implications for time, cost and quality. They too may have views depending on their approach to sustainability. The last consideration will be the size and complexity of the development; some standard building contracts have been developed specifically for small schemes; others are designed for large and complex, probably phased, projects.

As introduced above, there are a number of standard forms of building contract which a developer may vary to suit their requirements, provided that it is acceptable to building contractors. However, the advantages in using the forms of contract typically used in the building industry, is that they are tested in use, and the strengths and weaknesses of the contracts are known. Although there are many types of contract possibilities, or procurement methods, they can be categorised into generic categories, each of which has variants. This next section of the chapter considers six commonly used approaches: Design-Bid-Build, Design and Build (also known as Design and Construct), Management Contracting, Construction Management, partnering and Turnkey.

8.5.1   Design-Bid-Build

Design-Bid-Build is widely used in many countries. It owes its origin to a standard form of contract evolved in the UK by the JCT. Typically such a contract, which is often termed conventional or traditional procurement, provides for a main contractor to carry out the construction in accordance with the designs and specifications prepared by the developer's professional consultants and upon whom they must rely for the quality of design, adequate supervision of construction and suitability of the building for the purpose for which it is designed. Design-Bid-Build grew into standard practice in the nineteenth century after general contracting firms emerged and independent consultants became established and it is now used globally (Krygiel and Nies 2008). With this route, a number of contractors, carefully selected for their experience in constructing the type of development, receive copies of the drawings, specification and possibly a Bill of Quantities (BQ) from which they price the project. In essence it is a competition between the contractors to price the project and also submit a programme for the duration of the works. In times of low work opportunities, contractors may bid down their tenders to levels that will compromise their ability to deliver on time and to quality; it therefore can have inherent dangers in terms of delivering sustainable construction.

Under this method, design is separated from construction; therefore to be effective, full documentation, including design detailing, should be complete before contractors tender. The developer contracts with an architect or an engineer to carry out the design and then enters into a separate contract with a contractor who constructs the development. As such, it is the responsibility of the developer's team to determine the scope and extent of sustainability. The appointed architect, engineer or project manager will act as contract administrator (CA). The CA acts as the agent of the developer, provides the design and supervises the construction of the development to ensure completion on time and within cost (RICS 2011).

Sometimes full detailing cannot be achieved by the bid date; in this case the effectiveness of this procurement route is weakened. Projects are then vulnerable to problems of design alterations during the construction period; this adds to cost and can compromise time and quality. When issuing certificates or when undertaking decision-making under the contract, a CA is required to act knowledgably, independently, impartially, truthfully and equitably between the developer and the contractor (RICS 2011). A CA is usually deemed to have a dual role. One is to act as the developer's agent in respect of certain parts of their duties, at the same time acting as an independent and impartial certifier in respect of those duties where the CA is required to apply their professional skills in the decision-making process. The architect, engineer or project manager does not enter into a direct contract with the contractor and has their own appointment with the developer. In executing the work, the contractor directly engages subcontractors and suppliers of services, goods and equipment. This system can seem adversarial between the contractor and the client and if a dispute occurs, both time and cost are compromised. Within the UK, legislation supports a swift adjudication process for some types of disputes but nonetheless it is a concern.

The issue of compliance with and enforceability of the contract can be problematic. Under the legal doctrine of privity of contract, only parties to the contract can enforce it. As there is no direct contractual link between the developer and a contractor's subcontractor, disputes can arise; however, the widespread use of collateral warranties, which extend the warranty for different parts of the works to other parties, resolves some of the associated problems. However, research shows that traditional contracting is more prone to litigation claims than, for example, Design and Build (example Kandil *et al.* 2014).

Under Design-Bid-Build, the contract price is usually a lump sum, subject to adjustment only as a result of variations (change orders in the US). It is frequently based upon a BQ provided by the developer which quantifies all aspects of the works as far as possible. The measurement of the quantities can be based upon a standard method of measurement, of which one of the most widely known and adopted is the RICS's New Rules of Measurement (RICS 2012). An alternative to a BQ is where contractors are required to price the works on the basis of a set of drawings and specification of the works being provided. Also, it is quite common for re-measurement contracts, target cost contracts and cost plus contracts to be used to price the works under Design-Bid-Build. It remains popular with many in the construction industry, perhaps on the basis of its familiarity to developers and contractors.

The perceived advantages of the Design-Bid-Build procurement route and probably why it is so widely used still are:

- the developer maintains responsibility for and control of the design team;
- there is direct reporting by the design team to the developer to ensure that quality control is preserved;
- the developer has an independent professional, the CA, monitoring the project;
- familiarity among contractors and consultants – roles and responsibilities are well known;
- if work is fully designed in advance there is price certainty;
- priced BQs provide a basis for variations to be priced at tendered rates; and finally,
- as all prices are based on the same information:
  - there is no need for contractors to build in risk premiums;
  - it is easier to analyse the prices;
  - the lowest price is usually the best value for money; and,
  - where elements of the building are not fully designed, provisional sums may be used to allow for the later design of those elements.

Further, the constant communication system it involves can help to aid time and quality (Aecom Consult 2005) but, as discussed below, this is not universally accepted. There is debate about whether this is the best delivery method for sustainable property development as it has been predicated on the lowest tenderer usually winning the contract. In particular, sustainability concerns are expressed about the lack of collaborative approach between all stakeholders that is inherent in Design-Bid-Build (Molenaar *et al.* 2010). Once the tenders are submitted, the lowest tender is evaluated by the quantity surveyor or the estimator for mathematical accuracy. The programme is evaluated to see if it is reasonable bearing in mind that a short time scale may not be deliverable. If there are any anomalies in the pricing, the contractor is invited to correct, or to stand by, the sum submitted. At this point, it is sometimes the case that the second lowest tender is then evaluated especially if they are close or there are significant errors in the lowest tender. A tender report is submitted to the project manager or architect, depending on the composition of the design team, for discussion and a decision on the selection of the contractor.

In this procurement method, the contractor plays no part in the building design phase and therefore opportunities to gain from contractor experience of buildability are lost; this can be a concern for the integration of sustainability expertise (Molenaar *et al.* 2010). In this procurement method, it is essential that the design team are experienced to redress the loss of expertise from the contracting side. Given that the contractor does not participate in the design, and has typically won the job on the basis of the lowest possible price there may be little leeway in the budget. Accordingly, if unexpected costs are encountered, the contractor is then looking for ways to reduce losses; consequently either the quality of the materials or workmanship may suffer. Such practices inevitably lead to confrontation and conflict between the parties. Furthermore in times of economic constraint any additional costs can make a marginally profitable project unprofitable for the contractor. In recent times, a number of large Australian building contractors have gone into receivership due to cash flow problems and a tight tendering market. In summary the disadvantages of Design-Bid-Build procurement are:

- the fragmented design and construction process and responsibility can lead to disputes, such as whether construction defects are design or construction defects;
- a contractor may price to win the project rather than providing a price that reflects the work – this may encourage claims if the tender price was too low due to market forces;
- there is potential for over-design and/or over-engineering;
- as the contractor is not involved in design they are not required to buy in to the design;
- to be effective, it requires the project to be more or less fully designed before tendering which can result in extended pre-tender periods;
- the developer maintains responsibility for the design team performance and hence carries risk;
- a fixed lump-sum price is rarely achievable;
- the use of provisional sums and the capacity of the architect, engineer or project manager to issue instructions for additional or varied works can lead to price escalation, and finally;
- the scope and type of sustainability is determined by the developer team without contractor input.

In order to be effective in terms of time, the traditional approach demands the project to be fully designed before tendering and this leads to extended pre-tender periods; if it is not, delays during the on-site period may occur as design runs concurrently. For cost issues, if a priced BQ is used which provides a basis for variations to be priced at tendered rates, contractors may price to *win* the job rather than pricing to *do* the work and seek to make alterations thereafter; this can lead to disputes and claims. With regards to quality, whilst the developer retains responsibility for and control of the design team and there is direct reporting by the design team to the developer to ensure that quality control is maintained, there is potential for over-design and/or over-engineering as the contractor has little input into design.

Given the integrated design process (IDP) discussed in the previous chapter, the Design-Bid-Build procurement route does not lend itself well to this approach and it is perceived that where sustainable property development is the goal, other procurement routes may offer greater benefits (Krygiel and Nies, 2008; Hale *et al.*, 2009).

In some instances, a modification of the Design-Bid-Build can work. In the Lewis and Clark State Office Building in Jefferson City, Missouri, a high level of partnering between the design team and the contractor delivered a high performing sustainable office building (Krygiel and Nies 2008). The level of collaboration and co-operation between the two parties was such that the contractor was able to outperform the goals set by the design team. Other features of this project were adoption of an integrated design process with *charrettes*. Further an analysis of 12 case studies by Mollaoglu-Korkmaz *et al.* (2011) concluded that integration and collaboration could be achieved with Design-Bid-Build, but that it could be difficult.

8.5.2 *Negotiated Guaranteed Maximum Price*

In a Negotiated Guaranteed Maximum Price (GMP) delivery method a maximum price is set for the building and this makes commissioning developers comfortable that a ceiling price has been set. Although if there are changes that are not in the documents guaranteed then increases will occur. The developer separately engages the design team and contractor but the contractor can be hired early in the process to facilitate collaboration in the design stage. The disadvantage is that if the contractor finds costs escalating for which they cannot claim back, then quality reduction will be inevitable as, for example, they seek to substitute cheaper, possibly inferior materials.

8.5.2.1 *Design and Build/Design and Construct*

The second type of contract is called Design and Build in the UK, and Design and Construct in Australia. With this form of contract, the onus for the design, specification and construction rests with the contractor who takes full responsibility for ensuring that the building meets the developer's requirements and is fit for the purpose for which it is designed. In effect, the design team transfer the risk to the contractor, although as UK litigation has established, risks resulting from client-led variation to the scope of work will still reside with the client (*Midland Expressway* v. *Carillion Construction, 2012*). Design and Build has gained in popularity as it binds the designer and contractor into one contract with the developer and its use has been one of the reasons for the growth in multi-disciplinary consultancies, able to provide a 'one-stop' service to the developer client. The market share of Design and Build increased from a 10 per cent share in the 1980s to 35 per cent in the 1990s (Smith *et al.* 2004), mostly at the expense of management contracting. The benefits of close collaboration between the designer and the contractor are realised and, as stated, with sustainable property development a keen understanding of the knock-on effects of one decision upon another aspect of building sustainability is a distinct advantage for optimum decision-making and sustainable outcomes. For this reason, at least within the US, Design and Build is the preferred choice where a 'green 'building is being procured (Xia *et al.* 2013).

Design and Build is a generic description for the form of procurement; there are alternatives depending on the extent to which initial design is included in the developer's requirements and they can be grouped under three main categories:

1   Package deal or turnkey contract: This is where the developer settles on a complete package for design and build, often to some standard specification from a commercial firm. Within this form of contract, the commissioning client plays a completely passive, disengaged role and is entirely dependent on the skill and expertise of the design and contracting team to achieve a satisfactory outcome. This is considered more fully below.
2   Design and Build contract: This is the normal arrangement in which the contractor is responsible for the complete design and construction of the works, although the client may have some engagement in the process.
3   Contractor's design for specific elements only: Under this arrangement, the client retains responsibility for some elements of design; it is typically used where the developer client has specific in-house expertise. Such contracts are essentially not design and build but 'work and materials' contracts which include for limited design provision relating to an identified portion of the work. To guarantee that the developer gets what is sought in respect of a finished development, it is vital that the developer specifies what is

required and checks that this corresponds with what the contractor proposes. Although it is not necessary for full documentation before the contractor tenders for the work, it is important that the developer's brief and requirements are clearly established.

Whatever variant of Design and Build is adopted, the commissioning developer will normally contract with an agent, usually an architect, a quantity surveyor or a project manager, to administer the contract on their behalf. They then enter into a separate contract with a contractor to carry out the design and construction of the development. The agent does not contract with the contractor. In carrying out the work, the contractor often engages subcontractors and suppliers of services, goods and equipment, but the risks in so-doing lie with the contractor.

Privity of contract is relevant and collateral warranties provide a direct contractual link between parties that require such a direct contractual link, for example, between the contractor, subcontractors and a funder. Under Design and Build, the contract price, which is usually a lump-sum price, subject to adjustment as a result of variations, is usually the price for the works provided by a contractor and this is usually based on a set of drawings and a specification of the works. Design and Build procurement is well liked as the liability for the design and the build lies with the contractor, and there is less risk of a liability of a defect falling between design and construction.

There is extensive literature on the advantages and disadvantages of Design and Build procurement (see for example El Wardani *et al.* 2006; Morledge and Smith 2013). Among the most commonly identified advantages are:

- Speed of delivery from concept to completion: Design and Build allows work on-site to begin earlier than under traditional contracting, before the design is fully completed, due to the level of design control given to the contractor. It allows programmes and budgets to be more easily met and the speed of construction is often faster.
- Single point responsibility: The contractor is responsible for the design and the construction so the developer has a single point of responsibility and liability against the contractor. Consequently, there is little chance of claims in respect of the split responsibility of design, and the contractor will be unable to make a claim for late design instructions being issued other than for changes subsequently made by the developer.
- Acceptance of design: As the contractor is responsible for the design and the construction, the contractor and their supply chain are involved in the production of the design to be used, and buy in to that design. The design is likely to be more 'buildable' compared to other methods. There are more opportunities to incorporate sustainability in design and construction methods.
- Novation of design: There is normally the facility for the developer's own designers to be novated to the contractor. Novation is the act of either replacing an obligation to perform with a new obligation; or adding an obligation to perform; or replacing a party to an agreement with a new party. There are several benefits, including: the developer might have used those designers previously and will be happy with the quality of their work; the design team is likely to be more attuned to the developer's requirements; the design team can continue with the contractor where they left off with the developer; and some developers believe that through the novation of their own designers they have an independent voice in respect of the contractor's subsequent design intentions. This can be especially useful if the developer's own designers have specific sustainability

expertise. If this is the case, an additional benefit ensues; that of sharing good practice and disseminating expertise.

- Cost certainty and effectiveness: Under Design and Build the contractor can use their experience and expertise in providing a design that allows them to buy goods and services which offer the best buying margins. Therefore it can be more cost effective and can provide more cost certainty, provided that the developer does not change the brief.
- Less developer management/consultant involvement: The main purpose of using this form of contract is to ensure that responsibility for full delivery rests in one place. Therefore although the client will employ a CA, the client involvement post contract is reduced compared with traditional contracting; this should result in lower management costs and lower consultants' fees.
- A higher duty imposition on the contractor: Unless a contract states otherwise, the law implies a duty of fitness for purpose on a Design and Build contractor. This is more onerous than the normal duty of reasonable skill and care imposed on a design consultant. Often the contract states otherwise, and the contractor's design obligation is limited to a duty of reasonable skill and care. One of the reasons for this is that most professional indemnity insurance policies do not cover for a fitness for purpose obligation.

Although Design and Build has become increasingly popular and is deemed to support sustainability better than traditional procurement (see for example Hale *et al.* 2009) there are known disadvantages. These include:

- Pricing: Given that the contractor is normally absorbing a higher level of risk, the quoted price may be higher to compensate; further post-contract variations can be more expensive as the contract may make lesser allowance for these.
- Control: The developer has less control and influence over design, given that the design is developed by the contractor once the contract is awarded. It is also more difficult to monitor the additional charges raised especially where works are priced on a specification and drawings.
- Lack of flexibility: There is limited scope for the developer to make changes to requirements once the developer's requirements and contractor's proposals have been agreed as the cost consequences may be prohibitive. If the developer does not have a firm and robust set of requirements she/he may be given a design that she/he did not want, or may be required to pay considerably more to obtain the design that she/he did require. Where sustainability is a key consideration, given the ambiguity of the term, great care is required to explain specifically in the brief what aspects of sustainability are required, especially when this goes beyond the commonly accepted interpretation of low energy and water use during the build process.
- Potential contractual conflict: The contract will be awarded based on the documentation setting out the developer's requirements which are interpreted by the contractor to shape their design and specification. Inevitably there is potential for there to be conflicts between the two sets of documentation. In order to avoid this risk, it should be established before contracts are signed which document takes precedence.
- Design quality: It is perceived that contractors are driven by price rather than design standards; therefore, unless a robust specification is included with the developer's requirements Design and Build may be considered inappropriate. This risk is exacerbated

by the lack of control that the developer has over the architect and that the architect acts for the contractor not for the developer.

- Conflicted loyalties of novated architect: There are potentially complex legal issues in relation to novation. In *Blyth & Blyth v. Carillion* – [2001] CILL 1789, a Scottish case with persuasive authority in England and Wales, the court ruled that the novation did not entitle the contractor to recover loss for a failure by the employer's engineer to perform its services with reasonable skill and care prior to the novation. Therefore contractors need to ensure that they are able to pursue claims against the novated consultants for any pre-novation losses they may suffer as a consequence of breaches of duty by the consultant's pre-novation.
- Lack of independence of the architect: If the developer wishes to take independent advice on design issues following the building contract being entered into, or the novation of the design team to the contractor, the developer will have to pay additional fees; otherwise the client is left with a situation in which the designer has prime responsibility (other than under the general contractual terms) to the contractor.

For the reasons given above, Design and Build allows for greater speed of delivery from concept to completion, with a quicker commencement on-site and delivery time than for Design-Bid-Build. This process allows programmes to be more easily met and the speed of construction is quicker. In respect of cost, the eventual contract price may be higher as the contractor may build in a risk premium and post-contract variations can be more expensive. As there is a single point of responsibility between Design and Build, it is less likely claims will be made by the contractor in respect of the relationship between the design and the build function, although this is not guaranteed as litigation demonstrates. Design and Build can also be more cost effective as contractors use their experience and expertise in providing a design that allows them to buy goods and services with the best buying margins. With quality, the design is more likely to be 'buildable' than under other methods. However, the developer has less control and influence over design, and there is inflexibility in respect of design changes to be made. Also, as the architect acts for the contractor and not for the developer, the check on quality at that level is not available to the developer. Therefore if sustainability is a critical consideration, it is essential that it is firmly written into the initial brief and that the commissioned team have a strong, demonstrable track record in sustainable construction in its widest sense.

8.5.2 Lean construction

Another method is known as lean construction (www.leanconstruction.org) which is a production management based approach to project delivery and which originated with car manufacture in Japan. The architect, contractor and developer are all contracted together and not separately. According to Constructing Excellence (www.constructingexcellence.org.uk) the principles of lean construction are to:

- eliminate waste;
- precisely specify value from the perspective of the ultimate customer;
- clearly identify the process that delivers what the customer values (the value stream) and eliminate all non-value adding steps;
- make the remaining value adding steps flow without interruption by managing the interfaces between different steps;

- let the customer pull – do not make anything until it is needed, then make it quickly, and;
- pursue perfection by continuous improvement;(see http://www.constructingexcellence. org.uk/pdf/fact_sheet/lean.pdf).

The characteristics of lean construction are:

- the development and its delivery process are designed together to better reveal and support customer/occupier purposes;
- the work is structured throughout the process to maximise value and to reduce waste at the project delivery level; and,
- the efforts to manage and enhance performance are geared to improving total project performance as that is more important than reducing costs or speeding up the programme.

Although lean construction is, as yet, not widely used, it has been advocated as being able to deliver high quality projects at significantly lower costs (Mossman *et al.* 2011); it is also argued to work well with the principles of Building Information Modelling (BIM) (Sacks *et al.* 2010) (discussed in Chapters 7 and 10). In relation to assisting in sustainable construction, Lapinski *et al.* (2006) found that adopting lean construction in a major US car plant development led to significant waste savings and achievement of a Gold LEED project at a conventional build cost. As lean construction is *principles* based it should be possible for it to be replicable for other projects and adapted for use with other procurement routes.

8.5.3 *Management Contracting*

Management Contracting, based on American methods of construction, is the third type of procurement considered. Since the 1980s, it has been used by some of the larger development companies on complex developments. The professional team is responsible for the design and specification. However, the building work is split into specialised trade contract packages and the management contractor – for a management fee – co-ordinates and supervises the various subcontractors on behalf of the developer. In Management Contracting, the management contractor takes overall management responsibility for delivery, managing the work through works contractors who have contractual liability to the management contractor. The developer or their project manager usually appoints the management contractor early on to take an active role in the development and, as a result, the management contractor is normally an experienced contractor. Therefore the level of expertise of the management contractor in relation to sustainability will be critical for the overall inclusion of sustainability criteria, as long as their remit is not compromised financially.

Whilst the overall design is the responsibility of the developer's design team consultants, the management contractor is usually responsible for defining packages of work and subsequently for managing the work packages through separate trades or works contracts. In this approach, the management contractor is not engaged to carry out the work but to manage the process. All the work is subcontracted to works contractors who are directly engaged by the management contractor. The developer is usually given the chance to approve the terms and conditions of the trades or works contracts before the packages are subcontracted.

A management contract usually comprises a pre-construction and a construction phase. Documentation commences with development drawings, a project specification and a cost plan, and this material is developed into documentation on which competitive tenders are obtained for the work packages. In this approach, the management contractor is responsible for the administration and operation of the works contractors. However, the management contractor is not liable for the consequences of any default by a works contractor so long as the management contractor has complied with the particular requirements of the management contract. Typically management contracting is set up using an industry standard form of contracting.

Some of the advantages of the Management Contracting route, as identified by RICS (2013), are:

- it permits early 'buildability' and programming input from the management contractor acting as a consultant;
- it is predominantly advantageous for fast-track complex projects where minimal design information is available at the commencement of the project;
- there is a single point contractual and payment arrangement for the developer with the management contractor (rather than to all the separate works contractors);
- the preliminaries and management fee can be fixed, allowing for a degree of certainty on price;
- the quality can be controlled by the design team; and finally,
- there is abundant scope for developer-led changes.

Conversely some disadvantages of Management Contracting are:

- Although guaranteed maximum price can be achieved, the process remains essentially prime cost in nature – an approach many contractors favour. The developer does not shed risk to the management contractor as the latter has little responsibility for package contractor defaults, bankruptcy and so on.
- Cost increases can be considerable, and there is often a propensity for the initial cost plan to be amended upwards.
- To counter the cost increases, sustainability features which may be deemed to be expensive are taken out of the specification.

In terms of the time, cost, quality triangle, Management Contracting is beneficial time wise as it can fast-track complex projects where minimal design information exists at commencement and it allows for early programming input from the management contractor. In respect of cost, the preliminaries and management fee can be fixed, allowing for some price certainty, but because changes can be written in, cost increases can be significant, and the initial cost plan tends to be often adjusted upwards. With regard to quality, this can be managed by the design team where there is great scope for developer changes, and the process allows for early 'buildability' input from the management contractor acting as a consultant. However, the quality can be compromised if costs start to escalate and in this case attempts to incorporate sustainability criteria can be compromised.

8.5.4 Construction Management

In the Construction Management procurement approach the construction manager, often a contractor or someone with effective project management skills, manages the work through trade contractors. Although the trade contracts are arranged and administered by the construction manager, contractually they are the developer's risk, and the developer forms direct contractual relationships with the trade contractors. For this to be effective, the construction management appointment and the trade contract for each trade contractor must be compatible. The construction manager is paid a fee as are other consultants to cover staff costs, and overheads. The construction manager is required to co-ordinate the trade contractors. It is a method where overall design is the responsibility of the developer's consultants. Some advantages, identified by RICS (2013), are as follows:

- The developer is more in control of the process through the employment of the construction manager and the direct contracts with the trade contractors. As a result, the developer has better cost and budgetary control, with a higher degree of control due to the project being broken down into trade packages.
- There is a fully integrated design and construction process which should lead to more sustainable outcomes.
- The construction manager acts on the developer's behalf whereas a traditional contractor acts in its own interests.
- The process is flexible and changes to suit the developer are fairly easy to accommodate; and,
- There is a reduced potential for claims.

Conversely the disadvantages of the construction management approach are:

- The project needs to be sufficiently large or complex to be cost effective.
- The process requires the developer to have mechanisms for entering into direct contracts with trade contractors and for making monthly payments to individual contractors.
- The developer needs the necessary experience and internal management ability to operate this procurement process.
- The developer retains the contract risk of non-performance of the trade contractors; and,
- The developer maintains responsibility for design team performance (RICS 2013).

In terms of time, cost and quality, the Construction Management approach integrates design with construction, making the lead-in period before commencement shorter. However, as the process is very flexible, the on-site period may be prolonged due to developer indecision. In respect of cost, the developer retains strong control. However, the developer retains the contract risk of non-performance of the trade contractors and the approach requires the developer to have mechanisms for entering into direct contracts with trade contractors and for making monthly payments to many individual contractors. This is time-consuming and can lead to decisions to pare costs in other areas. As far as quality is concerned, integration of design with construction means that innovative and practical alternatives can be incorporated into the building more easily, and the developer retains control of the design team performance; therefore quality assurance is a good feature which may make this route particularly suited to large projects in which sustainability is a key consideration.

8.5.6 *Partnering*

Partnering has been described as 'perhaps one of the most innovative developments in delivering a project efficiently and reducing construction disputes' (Chan *et al.* 2004). It is argued to provide a sound basis for a 'win-win' climate and synergistic teamwork. Promoted as long ago as 1994 by Latham (Latham 1994) as a means of reducing the level of conflicts and delays which were regarded as prevalent in construction, partnering can be applied to many procurement routes. It is a co-operative relationship between business partners formed to improve performance in the delivery of projects. Partnering is best viewed as a group of collaborative processes which emphasise common goals and raise questions such as how goals are agreed upon, at what level they are specified and how they are expressed. It is used in a project situation known as project partnering or in a long-term relationship known as strategic partnering. Although in principle it is extremely attractive, early attempts led to many challenges (see for example Bresnen and Marshall 2000).

There are two views regarding the role of the contract between the developer and the contractor in the partnering process. The first is that partnering is all about co-operation, dispute avoidance and self-improvement and that a successful project partnering agreement can be independent of the contract, even when the contract contains clauses that do not align with the co-operative principles of partnering. The second view supports the use of the project contract to reinforce the elements of a partnering arrangement. This can be in the form of a traditional standard form contract amended to enforce a partnering agreement or in the form of partnering-type standard contract. Partnering is usually operated in one of three ways (RICS 2012) as follows:

1   A traditional construction contract with a separate partnering charter; or,
2   A two-party contract aligned to partnering. Under this method, the construction contract chosen reflects the principles of the intended collaborative relationship between the parties. This remains a two-party approach and relies on contract conditions covering the partnering aspects. The crucial difference to the first approach is that the parties are contractually bound to working co-operatively; or,
3   A multi-party partnering contract. A major difficulty in the acceptance of such a multi-party contract is the perceived complex legal situation in regard to the responsibilities and liabilities in a multi-party situation.

In partnering negotiation, rather than competitive tendering, is the key. This means that good ongoing communication is critical. Baylis *et al.* (2004) in their case study research reported a successful partnering venture in Hong Kong implemented by MTR Corporation Ltd who undertook the Tseung Kwan rapid transit extension. In this case, the critical factors underpinning the success were attributed to regular monthly partnering review meetings and the use of incentives.

Under partnering arrangements, both parties share risks that are made transparent at the start of the project; risk sharing is based on which party can best bear those risks and/ or insure against those risks. The essence of any partnering agreement involves a duty of good faith, mutual co-operation and trust between all parties involved in the construction process. Among the advantages of partnering put forward are:

*   reduced number of disputes;
*   benefit of early supply chain involvement;

- based on an open book and a win/win culture;
- integration of the design process with the construction process which should lead to greater sustainability outcomes; and,
- the ability to integrate the management of complex multiple projects.

Whereas the disadvantages of partnering are perceived to be:

- The process can be abused be one of the parties.
- The process requires more developer resources to compensate for the less competitive environment, and the process can collapse when one party becomes disadvantaged.
- To be most effective, partnering needs to be practised and learnt over a series of projects and requires early commitment in terms of management resources and direct costs; and,
- There are the direct costs of workshops, of training staff and of the more intensive early involvement of management in establishing the partnering approach.

In terms of time, cost and quality issues, partnering is deemed to satisfy all three. First, due to integration of design and construction the lead-in period prior to commencement can be shorter, although care needs to be taken that the on-site period is not prolonged due to unresolved design issues among the partnering team members. In respect of cost, because partnering is usually based upon an open book and a win/win culture, there are incentives for contractors to pass on savings. However, partnering requires resources to compensate for the less competitive environment, and an early commitment in terms of management resources, workshops and training of staff; so it is not necessarily a cheap option, but it may win on value for money. With regard to quality, integration of design with construction means that innovative and practical alternatives can be incorporated into the building more easily; for this reason, if no others, partnering procurement may well assist in the drive for sustainable development.

8.5.7 Turnkey

A turnkey contract is a business arrangement whereby a project is delivered in a completed state. Rather than contracting with various parties to develop a project in stages, the commissioning developer enters into a contract with one party, usually a developer or a contractor, to undertake the entire project without further developer input; the project is handed over only once it is fully operational. In effect, the developer or contractor is finishing the project and 'turning the key' over to the developer. This arrangement is used for construction projects ranging from single buildings to large-scale developments.

Under a traditional lump-sum contract, the developer agrees to pay the contractor to complete a project that is built to the contractor's specification. The developer is given many opportunities to make decisions throughout the project, and to make changes as needed. In a turnkey contract, the developer is generally left out of the building process entirely as the developer or contractor handles all decisions and problems related to construction. Some advantages of the turnkey approach identified by RICS (2012) are:

- The developer or contractor has responsibility for the project throughout so is motivated to finish the job as quickly and efficiently as possible.
- The commissioning developer does not have to pay until completion; this provides time to seek financing and onward sales before there is any requirement to pay; and,

- The commissioning client does not need to make complex decisions so it is appropriate for even an inexperienced client.

According to RICS (2012), the disadvantages of turnkey procurement are:

- The commissioning client cedes control over both design and construction decisions; it may therefore result in a project which does not meet the clients' needs including their sustainability aspirations; and,
- Where the turnkey contractor will retain an ongoing interest in the project for a specific period of time, the decisions could be driven to advantage the contractor's long-term interests rather than those of the commissioning client. This has long been the criticism of some public sector PFI contracts.

In terms of the time, cost and quality equation, turnkey projects may take longer to set up but, as the contractor/developer will only receive their payment upon completion, there is an incentive to achieve early completion once the deal is struck. Similarly the commissioning client has the financial motivation to see the job completed as quickly and efficiently as possible. The real potential issues with turnkey contracts arise in relation to control and quality, as the client lacks control over design decisions. Whilst this may not be an issue, if the client is a prospective owner-occupier and their requirements alter, they lack the ability to make changes and may take over a building that is not totally suited to their needs when complete. In turn, this could affect the sustainability aspects of the building. If the contractor/ developer has some financial long-term interest in the project this may encourage them to make construction decisions based on the long-term quality needs and life cycle cost aspects of the project. This could be a sustainability argument in favour of the use of a turnkey arrangement as longevity of economic life is a goal. However, if the contractor remains engaged for a limited period only, typically 25–30 years in the case of hospitals and schools, the result could be that the building is designed only for the period over which the contractor retains some liability, and 30 years is hardly a satisfactory sustainability-orientated goal, unless the building is designed specifically for short life using re-usable materials.

8.6   Conclusion

Anyone seeking to procure a development has many options from which to choose. Normally, the choice will be taken based on considerations of cost, time and quality, although other factors such as the skills and experience of the participants and the cultural and legal context will impact. Within countries such as the UK, contracts such as those offered through the JCT have for many years been the industry 'norm' but in the light of hard hitting criticisms of the construction industry in the 1980s and 1990s by, for example, Latham (1994) and Egan (1998 and 2002) respectively, all of which called for greater collaboration and innovation, new standard forms of procurement have emerged, notably based on partnering and with them new forms of standard contracts such as those promoted by FIDIC (Fédération Internationale Des Ingénieurs-Conseils or International Federation of Consulting Engineers) and NEC, the latter of which is advocated for many public sector contracts.

Whilst the conventional view of procurement is that time, cost and quality are the overriding criteria, where the client wishes to achieve a more sustainable development, this needs to be built into the choices made: environmental and social as well as economic considerations should be critical where the client espouses CSR policies. In addition to

CSR being adopted widely in the private sector, it forms a major part of public sector requirements. As public sector spending in the US and UK is around 37–49 per cent of GDP (http://www.heritage.org/index/ranking), the opportunity for enhanced sustainability is significant. Legislation can have a positive effect on the amount of sustainability delivered in projects as BS 8903 and ISO 14001 have demonstrated. Furthermore, adoption of life cycle costing and whole life cycle costing approaches enables the developer to take a wider and longer view of development which inherently is more sustainable.

This chapter has analysed the major procurement methods with respect to key features, advantages and disadvantages and their impact on sustainability. Whatever type of procurement route is chosen, there will be the ability to structure the actual contract such that sustainability criteria can be highlighted. Those commissioning buildings need to consider issues such as their resources, the characteristics of the project, ability to make changes, risk management, cost time and quality. They also need to take into account factors outside of their control, such as interest rates, inflation and legislation which may impact on their development and possibly jeopardise the resultant development. Whichever route is chosen, development is an inherently risky process. Therefore, depending on the developer's level of experience and in-house expertise, consultation with advisers should be sought. Further the adoption of standard contracts may reduce risks, but these alone cannot guarantee that disputes will not arise. Although no two sites or developments are identical and issues of logistics will normally arise in any contract, the use of checklists to assist with decision-making can enhance the process. Similarly examining case studies of previous projects is a useful way of learning with regards to integrating sustainability as new and innovative ways of increasing sustainability in property development are emerging.

References

Aecom Consult (2005) *2005 Design-Build Effectiveness Study: Final Report*, USDOT – Federal Highway Administration. Retrieved from http://www.fhwa.dot.gov/reports/designbuild/designbuild2.htm.

Arup (2013) *The Performance Gap: Causes and Solutions – A Report for the Green Construction Board Buildings Working Group*. Retrieved from http://www.greenconstructionboard.org/index.php/resources/performance-gap.

Baylis, R., Cheung, S-O., Suen, H.C.H., and Wong, S-P. (2004) Effective partnering tools in construction: a case study on MTRC TKE contract 604 in Hong Kong, *International Journal of Project Management* 22(3): 253–263.

Bowen, P. A., Cattel, K.S., Hall, K.A., Edwards, P.J., and Pearl, R.G. (2012) Perceptions of time, cost and quality management on building projects,.*Australasian Journal of Construction Economics and Building* 2(2): 48–56.

Bradley Robichaud, L. and Anantatmula, V. S. (2011)). Greening project management practices for sustainable construction, *Journal of Management in Engineering* 27(1): 48–57. Retrieved from http://ascelibrary.org/.

Bresnen, M. and Marshall, N. (2000) Partnering in construction: a critical review of issues, problems and dilemmas, *Construction Management & Economics* 18(2): 229–237.

BSRIA (2009) *The Soft Landings Framework* available from https://www.bsria.co.uk/services/design/soft-landings/.

Chan, A.P., Chan, D.W., Chiang, Y.H., Tang, B.S., Chan, E.H., and Ho, K.S. (2004) Exploring critical success factors for partnering in construction projects, *Journal of Construction Engineering and Management* 130(2): 188–198.

Cotgrave, A. and Riley, M. (eds) (2013) *Total Sustainability in the Built Environment*, Basingstoke: Palgrave Macmillan.

Davis Langdon (2007) *Life Cycle Costing (LCC) as a Contribution to Sustainable Construction: A Common Methodology: Final Report*. Retrieved from http://ec.europa.eu/enterprise/sectors/construction/files/compet/life_cycle_costing/final_report_en.pdf.

DEFRA (2006) *Procuring the Future*. Retrieved from http://www.defra.gov.uk/publications/files/pb11710-procuring-the-future-060607.pdf.

Egan, J. (1998) *Re-thinking Construction: The Report of the Construction Task Force*, London: The Office of the Deputy Prime Minister. Retrieved from http://www.constructingexcellence.org.uk/pdf/rethinking%20construction/rethinking_construction_report.pdf.

Egan, J. (2002) *Accelerating Change: A Report by the Strategic Forum for Construction*, London; Strategic Forum for Construction. Retrieved from http://www.strategicforum.org.uk/pdf/report_sept02.pdf.

El Wardani, M.A., Messner, J.I., & Horman, M.J. (2006) Comparing procurement methods for design-build projects, *Journal of Construction Engineering and Management* 132(3): 230–238.

FTSE (2013) FTSE4Good Index Series. Retrieved 31 October 2013 from http://www.ftse.com/Indices/FTSE4Good_Index_Series/index.jsp.

Fuerst, F. and McAllister, P. (2011a) Green noise or green value? Measuring the effects of environmental certification on office values, *Real Estate Economics* 39(1): 45–69.

Fuerst, F. and McAllister, P. (2011b) Eco-labelling in commercial office markets: do LEED and Energy Star offices obtain multiple premiums?, *Ecological Economics* 70(6): 1220–1230.

Green Construction Board (2015) Mapping the real estate life cycle for effective policy interventions. Retrieved from http://www.greenconstructionboard.org/images/stories/Valuation_and_Demand/GCB610%20Final%20Report.pdf.

Hale, D.R., Shrestha, P.P., Gibson Jr, G.E., and Migliaccio, G.C. (2009) Empirical comparison of design/build and design/bid/build project delivery methods, *Journal of Construction Engineering and Management* 135(7): 579–587.

Halliday, S. (2008) *Sustainable Construction*, Oxford: Butterworth Heinemann.

Hughes, W. and Laryea, S. (2013) Organizing for sustainable procurement: theories, institutions, and practice, in R. Yao (ed.), *Design and Management of Sustainable Built Environments*, New York: Ebook SpringerLink .

ISEAL Alliance (2013) *Buying for Tomorrow: Sustainable Public Procurement and the Use of Standards as a Mechanism to Scale-up Implementation*. Retrieved from http://www.isealalliance.org/sites/default/files/ISEAL-SPP-Report-Full-Document.pdf.

JCT (2011) *Building a Sustainable Future Together: A Guidance Note*, London: JCT Ltd.

Kandil, A., Hastak, M., and Dunston, P.S. (2014) Comparative Analysis of Design-Bid-Build and Design-Build from the Standpoint of Claims. *Bridges,* 10.

Kelly, J., Morledge, R., and Wilkinson, S. (eds) (2002) *Best Value in Construction*, Coventry: RICS/Blackwell.

Kibert, C.J. (2013) *Sustainable Construction. Green Building Design and Delivery*, Hoboken, NJ: Wiley.

Krygiel, E. and Nies, B. (2008). *Green BIM. Successful Sustainable Design with Building Information Modeling*, Hoboken, NJ: Wiley.

Lapinski, A.R., Horman, M.J., and Riley, D.R. (2006) Lean processes for sustainable project delivery, *Journal of Construction Engineering and Management* 132(10): 1083–1091.

Latham, N (1994) *Constructing the Team – 'The Latham Report': Final Report of the Government/Industry Review of Procurement and Contractual Arrangements in the UK Construction Industry*, London: Department of the Environment.

Ling, F.Y.Y., Ong, S.Y., Ke, Y., Wang, S., and Zou, P. (2014) Drivers and barriers to adopting relational contracting practices in public projects: comparative study of Beijing and Sydney, *International Journal of Project Management* 32(2): 275–285.

Lupton, S., Cox, S., Clamp, H., and Udom, K. (2012) *Which Contract?*, fifth edn, London: RICS Publishing.

Molenaar, K., Korkmaz, S., Swarup, L., Horman, M., Riley, D., Sobin, N., and Gransberg, D. (2010) *Influence of Project Delivery Methods on Achieving Sustainable High Performance Buildings: Report on Case Studies*. Retrieved from http://www.pankowfoundation.org/download. cfm?ID=108.

Mollaoglu-Korkmaz, S., Swarup, L., and Riley, D. (2011) Delivering sustainable, high-performance buildings: influence of project delivery methods on integration and project outcomes, *Journal of Management in Engineering* 29(1): 71–78.

Morledge, R. and Smith, A. (2013) *Building Procurement*, second edn, Oxford: Wiley-Blackwell.

Morledge, R., Smith, A., and Kashiwagi, D.T. (2006) *Building Procurement* Oxford: Wiley-Blackwell.

Mossman, A., Ballard, G., and Pasquire, C. (2011) The growing case for lean construction, *Construction Research and Innovation* 2(4): 30–34.

National Audit Office (2013) *Sustainable Procurement in Government*. Retrieved from http://www.nao. org.uk/wp-content/uploads/2013/03/EAC_briefing_sustainable_procurement_government.pdf.

Newell, G., MacFarlane, J., and Kok, N. (2013) Building better returns. A study of the financial performance of green office buildings in Australia, API and PFA. Retrieved 3 January 2014 from www.api.org.au/assets/media_library/000/000/219/original.pdf.

Podvezko, V., Mitkus, S., and Trinkūniene, E. (2010) Complex evaluation of contracts for construction, *Journal of Civil Engineering and Management* 16(2): 287–297.

RICS (2011) *Contract Administration Guidance Note 69/2011*, London: RICS.

RICS (2012) *RICS New Rules of Measurement: Order of Cost Estimating and Cost Planning for Capital Building works*, London: RICS.

RICS (2013) *Developing a Construction Procurement Strategy and Selecting an Appropriate Route: Guidance Note 109/2013*, London: RICS.

Sacks, R., Koskela, L., Dave, B.A., and Owen, R. (2010) Interaction of lean and building information modeling in construction, *Journal of Construction Engineering and Management* 136(9): 968–980.

Smith, J., O'Keefe, N., Georgiou, J.. and Love, P.E.D., (2004) Procurement of construction facilities: a case study of design management within a design and construct organisation, *Facilities* 2(1): 22–34.

UK Public Spending (2013) Spending Breakdown. Retrieved 31 October 2013 from http://www. ukpublicspending.co.uk/total.

US Government Spending (2013) Government Spending in the US. Retrieved 31 October 2013 from http://www.usgovernmentspending.com/total_spending_2014USbn.

Walker, H., Miemczyk, J., Johnsen, T., and Spencer, R. (2012) Sustainable procurement: past, present and future, *Journal of Purchasing and Supply Management* 18(4): 201–206.

Warren, C.M.J. and Huston, S. (2011) Promoting energy efficiency in public sector commercial buildings in Australia. *Proceedings of RICS Construction and Property Conference, COBRA: Construction and Building Research Conference*, Salford, UK, 12–13 September 2011, pp. 128–134.

Wilkinson, S. and Reed, R. (2008) *Property Development*. fifth edn. London: Taylor and Francis.

Williams, M. (2014) Personal communication.

World Green Building Council (WGBC) (2013) *The Business Case for Green Building: A Review of the Costs and Benefits for Developers, Investors and Occupants*, World Green Building Council. Retrieved from http://www.worldgbc. org/files/1513/6608/0674/Business_Case_For_Green_Building_Report_WEB_2013-14.pdf.

Woudhuysen, J., Abley, I., Muthesius, S., and Glendinning. M. (2004) *Why is Construction so Backward?* Hoboken, NJ: Wiley.

Xia, B., Skitmore, M., Zuo, J., Zhao, Z., and Nepal, M. (2013) *Defining Sustainability Requirements for Design-Build (DB) Contractor Selection in Public Sector Projects*. Retrieved from http://eprints.qut. edu.au/60953/1/60953A.pdf.

Zou, K., Potangaroa, R., Wilkinson, S., and Rotimi, J.O.B. (2009) A project management prospective in achieving a sustainable supply chain for timber procurement, *International Journal of Managing Projects in Business* 2(3): 386–400.

9   Sustainable property reporting and rating tools

Pernille H. Christensen and Sarah L. Sayce

9.0   Introduction

It is now some two and a half decades since the UK's Building Research Establishment (BRE) launched the world's first building sustainability rating tool, BREEAM (Building Research Establishment Environmental Assessment Method) in 1990. That first tool addressed offices only. Since then, not only have BRE widened the scope of BREEAM very significantly, but the property industry has witnessed the conception, introduction and development of a plethora of rating tools aimed at helping stakeholders throughout the real estate cycle develop some 'shorthand' expression of what can be understood by the term 'sustainability' within the property context. However, it is perhaps only over the last decade that rating tools for property have proliferated and gained in widespread usage among both the development and investment communities worldwide.

Originally developed for use at the point of initial design of buildings, the aim was to raise awareness among owners, occupiers, designers and operators of the benefits of taking a sustainability approach and to provide recognition of so doing. However, over time the scope and ambition of the tools and certification schemes have both broadened and deepened and many now address the occupation and investment phase of the life cycle and some deal with portfolios rather than individual buildings.

With the development of many, mainly commercially operated and competing systems, concerns have been expressed about the resultant significant confusion and lack of transparency about what they each represent (see for example Reed and Krajinovic-Bilos 2013); however, despite this, there is evidence that some tools are beginning to have influence on purchase and letting decisions as expressed through the pricing mechanism (Sayce *et al.* 2010; Kok and Jennen 2012; World Green Building Council 2013), although this remains patchy in nature. However, if there is the view that they might impact eventual development values then their criteria may be taken into account at the design stage. Indeed, some academics and industry professionals argue that building design is being driven by the credit point structure of these rating tools but not necessarily creating more sustainable development (Christensen 2012). If this is the case, rating tools are failing in their original goal.

This chapter presents a comparison of the key sustainability reporting and assessment rating tools around the globe which are most applicable to property development. It then assesses critically their contribution to the development of buildings in a sustainable manner. As rating tools, at least potentially, can have an influence on market pricing the discussion is not restricted to those tools which are implemented purely at the design and development stage, although these are the most important and relevant to this book. Taking an objective approach, this chapter asks the question: are we, as a society, collectively and as a development industry, in danger of hitting the targets but missing the point with regards to developing more sustainable buildings with these tools?

9.1   A rationale for the use of rating tools

The aim of this book is to analyse both the state of knowledge in relation to developing property in accordance with sustainability principles and to assess ways in which those engaged with the process can drive change. With these aims in mind, it is critical to understand why a developer in either the public or private sector might wish to adopt any of the rating schemes considered below. Essentially, as discussed in earlier chapters, the aim of development or re-development will depend on who the stakeholders are. If the developer is within the private sector, the chief motivation will be to maximise the profitability of the Scheme; if within the public sector, profit *per se* is not a consideration but fulfilment of social purpose at least cost is likely to be the ultimate consideration. Whoever is the decision maker, they will need a rationale for adopting a rating, particularly as some come as high-cost items in terms of actual assessment fees. In essence there are a number of reasons why a rating system is adopted as part of the development proposition. These may be summarised as follows:

9.1.1   The rating is mandated

In most countries the use of a rating tool is voluntary; however, this is beginning to change and Singapore has mandated the use of a sustainability level, whilst in Europe, the Energy Performance Certificate (EPC) is required for all new buildings before they are let or sold. Whilst generally the level of certification is not specified and may be little, if any, beyond the building regulatory code, within the UK, the proposed introduction of a minimum standard of EPC rating prior to letting can be regarded as an attempt to encourage the adoption of energy standards beyond building codes. Whilst rating tools do not equate to building codes, there is in some cases overlap (see for example analysis by UK government of the relationship between mandatory energy codes and BREEAM (DCLG 2013). As compulsory codes are tightened and individual elemental mandated certificates are introduced and with it greater knowledge of certificates, the incentive for voluntary certification may grow as long as there is clear differentiation between these and the mandated codes. A further aspect to mandatory certification is the link to planning which is outlined below.

9.1.2   A smoother path to consents

Gaining all the consents necessary to start a scheme can be both time-consuming and risky with one of the major risks being concerns from Consultees over the impacts of the development. BREEAM in their literature claim that its use and that of other recognised third-party certification schemes, provide credibility and reassurance to local authorities and stakeholders, thereby enabling applications to move more efficiently and swiftly through the consents process saving time and money for the developer (see http://www.breeam. org/filelibrary/BREEAM%20Communities/KN5321_BREEAM_Communities_FAQs.pdf). This claim has been substantiated in recent research for the Green Construction Board (Green Construction Board 2014). However, whilst submitting a design that can claim sustainability credentials due to a rating scheme may make it more attractive to decision-makers in the planning process, it can present difficulties to developers. Within the UK, it is not uncommon for a requirement to have a rating, for example Code for Sustainable Homes Level 4 or BREEAM Very Good, as a condition of consent. In the commercial field, this may not be too much of an issue, although it could add to cost; however residentially, where most houses are, in effect, factory produced, it is a real issue where the standard production line cannot be easily adapted to the required revised specification. It is therefore critical that all those engaged with the consents process understand the implications of rating schemes before decisions are made to link them to permissions.

9.1.3 A market imperative

For many development schemes involving secondary or small-scale units where the eventual owner and/or occupier is unlikely to be 'sensitised' to sustainability, the use of a rating tool other than one that is mandated is unlikely. This is also likely to be the situation with most private sector housebuilders. However, where the development is to be either sold on to an investor who has recognised the lower risks of obsolescence that might occur or the occupier is either the public sector with a green acquisition policy or a corporate with a strong CSR policy, there is an increasing market imperative to obtain a certificate as evidence of the building's 'credentials' for future saleability/lettability or a statement of corporate values. Whilst the evidence that this is the case is still very mixed and localised within markets and property types, the market push towards certification cannot be overlooked.

9.1.4 An owner-occupier brand

As stated above, the matter of a certification is, for some investors or corporate occupiers, a matter of principle. For owner-occupiers, commissioning a headquarter office or other buildings, such as educational or healthcare establishments that will remain in the same long-term occupation, a requirement to their contracted consultant and design team to ensure that the building being commissioned meets a certain level of certification may help the client be assured that they are acting sustainably. However, as is argued in this chapter, the presence of a certificate granted at the design stage may be no guarantee that the building will perform as anticipated. Nonetheless it does show intent and a belief that the building will perform efficiently and effectively.

9.1.5 A management tool

Within the aim of this book, rating tools developed for use either at the point of construction or at major refurbishment are the principal concern. However, increasingly, as principles of responsible property investing (RPI) gain traction (see for example Pivo and MacNamara 2005) so there is an increasing requirement for benchmarks and tools to assess the ongoing performance of buildings and indeed portfolios of buildings in terms of their sustainability. Tools used for portfolio analysis, such as GRESB and EcoPAS, are recent in origin and have little impact on development, except insofar as they influence the long-term investors' attitudes. Of greater importance at the individual property level are measures such as Energy Certification, which although they are strictly 'in-use' measures are, where mandated, first applied at the point of completion and may impact on lettability. In many countries lease terms are short, any developer who intends to hold over other than the short-term will wish to ensure that the property being developed will remain attractive to occupiers.

The above summarises the practical rationale for the adoption of rating tools which, has been influential in shaping their development, however, there are other, academic arguments about what principles have driven them. Some theoreticians, such as Kats (2003) conclude that the baseline rationale is guided by the principles of the 'triple bottom line' which favours an approach which incorporates and categorises individual characteristics. The linking of rating tools to the three-pillars approach to sustainability can be seen as mirroring the approach to sustainability which is most commonly adopted by corporate entities within their decision-making.

Gibson (2001), conversely, suggests using a principles-based approach to sustainability assessment. In this approach, sustainability principles underpin the sustainability criteria rather than triple bottom line goals, thereby emphasising the interconnections and interdependencies between the 'pillar' areas. Gibson (2001) argues that as a result, a principles-based approach may circumvent some of the intrinsic limitations of the triple bottom line approach to sustainability (for example, the need to quantify and commodify environmental attributes whose primary contributions are social, i.e. a park, or environmental, such as preserving watersheds). George (2001) recognised the limitations of the triple bottom line approach (as applied in the UK) and concluded that a principles-based approach is more appropriate for developing the criteria on which to base metrics. Both George (2001) and Sadler (1999) recommend an approach based upon fundamental principles of sustainability as defined by Agenda 21. Additional support for a principles-based approach comes from Gutíerrez-Espeleta (2007) who argues that whatever approach is adopted it 'must be able to meet the challenge of fully integrating the social, economic, environmental, and institutional aspects of development, in accordance with the main conclusions of the UNCSD in 1997' (2007: 353). It is important to note that Gutíerrez-Espeleta (2007) also includes the fourth 'pillar' of sustainability, as outlined in the principles of responsible investment, institutional governance.

Rating tools, whilst primarily developed to provide transparent information and assist market movement, actually serve different purposes, depending on the motivation of the user. They also offer different levels of complexity which can provide challenges in their use. To the developer they can be a way of differentiating their produce, albeit at a possibly increased cost; to governments they can be encouraged as a means of moving market perceptions; for long-term owners they may represent statements of principles and a tool to assist benchmarking of performance. Last to the transaction markets, they may provide information to assist differential pricing where the demand for a sustainable building exists. However, all these points are dependent on what the tool is measuring and the understanding of the measure by its user.

9.2   Categorising building assessment rating tools

A wide variety of rating tools exists which has led to an accusation of an 'ever-thickening alphabet soup' (UNEP FI 2011: 4). Appendix A provides a listing of rating tools used both in individual countries and across countries. In this section, the main characteristics of some of the leading tools relating to property development are summarised and a commentary on these is included in the conclusion. First it is useful to categorise the tools. One of the first attempts to categorise building rating systems was undertaken by Reijnders and van Roekel (1999) who separated assessment tools into two broad classifications: qualitative tools based on scores and criteria, and quantitative tools using a physical life cycle approach. At that time, many of the measures now in existence were either not yet developed or were significantly different from their current formats. However, most of the recent developments seen in the assessment tools listed in Appendix A fall in the category of the qualitative assessment tools, as described by Reijnders and van Roekel (1999), and are ones that continue to be re-calibrated or otherwise adjusted and re-issued.

Haapio and Viitaniemi (2008) undertook an analysis of several leading systems and characterised them by:

- component or whole building;
- stages of the life cycle (design through to refurbishment);
- building type;
- users of the tool.

Whilst such a categorisation is a helpful starting point, to the developer it may not be the most useful. Lowe and Ponce (2009) conducted an evaluation of current assessment rating tools and developed a different set of key sustainability principles and measures. Each principle was included in at least five of the six building rating tools studied (BREEAM, LEED, Green Star, CASBEE, HQE and Protocollo ITACA). Their key finding was that most of the principal building assessment rating systems are primarily concerned with matters related to environmental issues, and that economic and social issues are under-represented; something that is still the case. Lowe and Ponce (2009) also acknowledged a general shift in building assessment rating tools towards a more holistic, integrated and regenerative assessment structure.

The variety of assessment tools around the globe represents each of these approaches, as well as mixed methods approaches. Qualitative tools are often based on auditing of buildings and assigning scores to each investigated parameter. In contrast, the quantitative group of assessment tools that emerged in the late 1990s used quantitative data from life cycle inventories (LCI) or production data of material or energy flows. These can normally only be established post-construction, whereas most of the measures used for development are, predominantly, pre-construction. For the purposes of this analysis, the following categorisations have been adopted in relation to individual buildings:

9.2.1 Individual criteria or multi-criteria:

Whilst some measures apply only to one characteristic (for example Energy Star for energy use and EPCs for Energy Asset rating) others use a range of primarily environmental criteria but may include scoring systems to included innovation in design or construction, thereby providing an industry educative incentive and social measures such as design for accessibility and neighbourhood coherence. Whilst it is easier to compare buildings based on single criterion ratings and the more convincing economic case applies to their adoption, they have the drawback that, to date, it is only energy and carbon that tends to be subject to individual rating systems. All other environmental factors and social factors only feature as part of multi-criteria certification schemes, such as BREEAM, Green Star and LEED, and the weighting between different elements and indeed the composition of factors varies from scheme to scheme, as detailed in the consideration of schemes below. Due to this, the possibility (and reality) exists of a building achieving a very high rating when, for example, it has a fairly low score against a factor, such as energy efficiency which is normally regarded as key to the concept of a sustainable building; conversely it could be very energy efficient but obtain a lower rating due to poor scores for example on pollution as it was built on a green field site or away from public transport. This situation has led to what has been termed the 'batbox'[1] issue in which a developer may take a cynical point scoring approach to design to incorporate low-cost elements (such as a simple ecology feature like a batbox) in preference to expensive measures such as local materials. Indeed this approach is clearly advocated by some organisations:

> Ecology credits are worth up to 12 per cent of the Code for Sustainable Homes rating, which could mean the difference between achieving Level 2 or 3.
> (Gwent Wildlife Trust, 2014)

The advantage, however, of multi-criteria approaches is that they do provide a platform for discussing and debating early on, both the nature of sustainability and, as applicable, within the context of an individual development, and hence arrive at individualised and supportable decisions tailored to the needs of the site and the client. However, it is vital that they are used and interpreted intelligently.

As the more established building assessment systems (e.g. BREEAM and LEED) have evolved, they have continued to move away from their environmental impact assessment (EIA) and strategic enviromental assessment (SEA) roots, based in environmentalism, towards a more holistic approach considering all the facets of sustainability. This has also allowed these rating tools to integrate broader measurements associated with corporate social responsibility in to their assessment criteria. It should be noted, however, that although each revision of the rating tools moves towards a more holistic approach to assessment – with the goal that, in addition to reducing a building's environmental footprint, buildings will have positive social and economic impacts in their communities – there is still a long way to go before the complex, multi-faceted nature of sustainability is represented in the various building assessment rating systems.

Figure 9.1 reproduced from Berardi (2011) provides an illustration of how some of the leading measures compare in terms of coverage and weighting. From this, it is clear that they are not all measuring the same items. This provides a simple analysis; more detailed and extensive tables of comparison can be found in Reed *et al.* (2009) and Reed and Krajinovic-Bilos (2013).

9.2.2 Life cycle stage

Early rating systems were designed to assist at the 'front' end of the building's conception and design and, indeed, the whole assessment process and issuing of certification in some cases takes place before construction starts. Whilst this provides comfort to the commissioning client and may be the basis on which consent is granted, as has been argued elsewhere, there are often discrepancies between the designed building and the constructed building. For example, materials may be found to be unobtainable and others substituted or cost escalation can cause alterations to the specification. Further, the way in which the building is commissioned, and in the case of a building with a complex building management system, the training given to building and facilities managers, as well as the behaviours of the occupier, may lead to a variation in performance against design. Therefore any rating scheme which relies entirely on design documentation may give a limited assessment of the eventual long-term sustainability success of the asset.

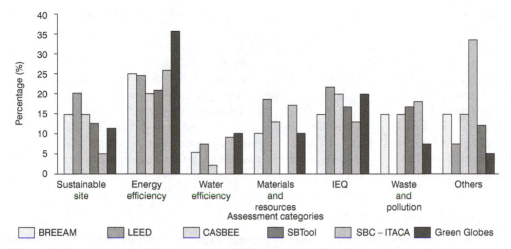

Figure 9.1 A comparison of leading rating tools by coverage and weighting
Source: Beradi (2001)

When sustainability began to become a highlighted concern within the built environment the focus was very much on the supply side of the industry. However, over time, the realisation has grown that within the old industrial economy countries, such as the UK, which has the oldest residential building stock in Europe and probably the world (BPIE 2011), the environmental impact of existing buildings far outweighs that of new builds, even at times of high economic activity. In the light of this growing realisation, there has been a shift towards ratings of existing buildings, with notably, both BREEAM and LEED both now producing 'in-use' certification schemes. Further from 2009, within the EU a process   by which over time, on letting or sales, all existing buildings will have an Energy Performance Certificate (EPC) has been mandated by directive. Whilst these ratings of existing buildings could be argued to be of lesser importance in terms of developments, the ability to gain a certification upon refurbishment can be important and certificated older buildings will increasingly compete for occupiers with new builds.

9.2.3 *Adaptability to different locations/building types*

Most of the major rating systems now recognise that the location and purpose of a building will require different treatment. For example, whilst energy efficiency is perhaps the major sustainability issue in many countries, in areas which have a high supply of naturally occurring renewable sources, such as Iceland, it may be less of an issue. Similarly water conservation will be of greater importance in arid areas. In terms of building use, waste is of greater significance in shopping centres than it is in residential development. For this reason, there is recognition that the weighting of factors in multi-criteria schemes has to be adjusted for both the type of building and the country location. Whilst this is an entirely logical approach it does mean that interpretation and comparison is rendered very complex, as discussed later.

9.2.4 *Commercial or quasi-governmentally owned*

One of the issues surrounding rating systems is a concern that many are being produced by commercial concerns and that the profit motive, rather than the cause of more sustainable buildings, is beginning to drive the agenda. For example within the US, where the use of LEED, which is controlled by the US Green Building Council, and Green Globes, controlled by the Green Building Initiative, are industry focused but essentially non-profit making organisations. BREEAM, however, is owned by the Building Research Establishment, which operates for profit but under the auspices of the BRE Trust, which has an impartial educational mission in which profits generated are funnelled back into education and research. Other systems, such as EPCs, are public sector in both ownership and control. It could be asked why this matters. In most cases it probably does not, but the interface between industry and rating can lead to pressure through lobby groups to ensure either that certain products are rated more highly than others, or that categories of assessment are given more significance than others.

9.2.5 *Mandated or voluntary*

As discussed in the rationale for rating systems, many have grown as voluntary codes aimed at driving greater sustainability through the construction of new buildings or more recently through refurbishment or occupational schemes. However, successive governments across the world have regarded progress as too slow and, in response, mandatory certification schemes are becoming more common, either by requiring a certificate to be obtained or, more stringently, a standard to be met. The UK provides a good example of this shift in emphasis. Since 2008, it has been a requirement for a building to have an EPC issued prior to sale but there has been no mandate as to the level that had to be achieved – it was aimed at awareness raising. However, from 2018, whilst a sale will still be allowed, whatever grade of certificate the building has obtained, a letting will be prohibited. A subtler way of transforming a voluntary scheme into what is in effect a mandated one is by tying it into planning controls. Again, within the UK, it is very common for a condition of a planning consent to be that the development achieves a BREEAM Very Good as a minimum; indeed some local planning authorities are imposing the even higher standard of Excellent.

If, and as, schemes become increasingly mandated and integrated with regulatory codes, so in effect a building previously regarded as 'sustainable' compared to other stock will simply become the norm. However, currently, in most countries this is a long way from the reality, despite claims by some accrediting scheme owners as to the volume of stock now certified.

9.2.6 *Monitored or 'lifetime' award*

The criteria against which a building is judged in terms of sustainability and other aspects of quality has changed very significantly over the years. The rating system designers review their assessment criteria as knowledge develops and new technologies provide more advantageous environmental solutions. Standards that would have been acceptable previously may not be so now. Therefore in interpreting rating systems it is important to appreciate not just the level awarded but when it was awarded. Whilst this may not be an issue in terms of development, it can be for those valuing and managing the asset moving forward.

It is therefore important that all those involved with the development process, particularly when they intend to keep an ongoing interest in the building, recognise:

9.2.7 The time at which the award is made

Different systems work in different ways; some awards are made purely on the building design, at a point before construction is started; others may be issued upon practical building completion and take into account the inevitable compromises that have taken place through the build process, whilst others may be dependent upon the proven performance up to a point at which post-occupancy evaluation is undertaken. Both BREEAM and LEED work on the basis of preliminary assessment prior to building, with the assessor working alongside the design team, but with the requirement for a post-construction (as opposed to post-occupancy) review.

9.2.8 The longevity of the rating

Most rating systems that work on the award of the rating at, or immediately after, construction are lifetime awards and remain until the building is altered or demolished. In the case of a substantial refurbishment, there is a growing tendency to design the work to achieve an 'in-use' rating which provides an audit of a building to enable a company to adjust their management to improve the environmental performance of their portfolios. However, it is not a fixed period award; it is a year-on-year monitoring. Conversely an Energy Performance Certificate is assessed at the point of completion but has a life of only ten years and must be re-assessed thereafter upon a letting or sale, by which time it is possible that the criteria may have changed.

9.3   The major sustainability reporting frameworks schemes

Rating tools can be divided into those which relate to new builds or major refurbishments, those which relate to in-use and management of the asset and those which relate at a multi-building level. To developers, the chief concern will be those intended to influence the design and construction phase. However, given that many buildings are intended for owner-occupation or may be the subject of forward sale to a long-term investor, developers should give consideration to these as well.

9.3.1 Multi-criteria building level schemes

As shown in Appendix A there are many rating schemes and it is outside the scope of this book to detail all of these. Links are provided but below we provide brief introductions to some of the world's leading schemes. It must be emphasised however that versions change and readers are advised to consult the relevant websites and links.

9.3.1.1 British Research Establishment Environmental Assessment (BREEAM)

BREEAM is the oldest rating system and aims both to stimulate the demand for more sustainable buildings and enable buildings to be recognised for their sustainability credentials. BREEAM does not extend to residential buildings but its owners, BRE, have a sister organisation that produces the Code for Sustainable Homes, which is now enshrined in UK policy to be introduced statutorily over the next few years until a point is reached at which all new homes will be designed to be zero carbon in use.

BREEAM was first developed in 1990, and the scheme has been revised many times, most recently in 2011. It claims that some 200,000 buildings have been awarded a BREEAM

Table 9.1 BREEAM rating scheme banding

Rating	%
Pass (P)	30%
Good (G)	45%
Very Good	55%
Excellent	70%
Outstanding	85%

Source: Authors

certificate whilst there are in excess of a million that have been registered (BREEAM brochure). The scheme awards successful applications with one of five grades ranging from Pass to Outstanding. It recognises both the location and type of building and currently BREEAM schemes have been designed separately for categories such as schools, hospitals, retail, etc. Further it has adapted the schemes for a variety of countries depending on their legislative and policy environment and on building technologies and environmental concerns.

Although the schemes are adapted to meet a range of different building types, all BREEAM ratings cover 'a broad range of categories and criteria from energy to ecology. They include aspects related to energy and water use, the internal environment (health and wellbeing), pollution, transport, materials, waste, ecology and management processes' (BRE 2015). For each category a set number of credits are available, with more for some categories than others to reflect BRE's views as to their relative importance. The total is then graded in line with Table 9.1

In arriving at an assessment, which is always carried out by a trained assessor, the process 'uses recognised measures of performance, which are set against established benchmarks, to evaluate a building's specification, design, construction and use' (BRE 2015). The benefit of an overall classification system is that design teams can 'flex' to optimise their points, offsetting higher scores in one area against potentially low scores under other headings. However, whilst recognising that real attempts have been made, it can lead to some potentially arbitrary decisions. For example, whether or not the development is on previously contaminated land will affect the score. Whilst this could be relevant in some old industrial areas to try and encourage re-use of difficult and expensive to develop sites, it is of little importance within a service-based area where encouragement of such sites is not an issue. Also under the management head for which, under the current schools scheme, a potential of 22 points are available, only three relate to having undertaken a life cycle cost (LCC) analysis. As such, analysis is expensive, unless an outstanding score is being targeted; it is likely that this item will be excluded. There is therefore a danger, as with all point scoring systems, that the objective becomes how to achieve the points at minimum cost, rather than how to drive forward on the wider sustainability agenda.

The requirement to have a trained assessor underscores the commitment of BREEAM's owners, BRE, to research and education and the intent behind BREEAM is that it will assist clients, developers, contractors and those who grant consents in their decision-making process. In practice, it is important that the assessor is appointed at an early stage in the design of the building so that they can, in collaboration with the design team, work to ensure that all aspects such as choice of material, arrangements for waste, use of rainwater harvesting or grey water, etc., are all considered early in the design phase. This will prove to be not only cheaper than designing them in later, but also it will be more likely to optimise the score achieved. However, as a downside, there is an inevitable tendency of design teams to then concentrate on matters which will reflect in the score, rather than thinking of the potential needs of the eventual occupier.

There is recognition that BREEAM is assessed only at the point at which the building is complete, although there is the potential to gain additional points for conducting a full monitored post-occupancy evaluation. There is therefore no guarantee that the building will indeed perform to the intended and designed specification. Much of this will depend on the management of the building, leading to a so-called performance gap as explored elsewhere. At the time of writing, BRE Global is in the process of developing a database of 'green buildings' and performance measures so that more research may be done to evaluate the impact of the BREEAM rating systems.

9.3.1.2 *British Research Establishment Environmental Assessment (BREEAM) (in-use, United Kingdom)*

The realisation that management of existing buildings has become as important a sustainability issue as new builds in countries with a large stock of mainly energy and water inefficient existing buildings, such as the UK, BRE developed BREEAM In-Use which they launched in March 2009 with the aim of offering insight into the environmental performance of existing non-residential buildings throughout their entire operational life (BRE 2011a). The in-use system includes tools to assist owners, occupiers and investors in short- to long-term monitoring of the sustainability specifications of their building, assessing management and operational practices related to the building, and helps create action plans for improving the overall sustainability of the both the asset and the occupying organisation(s). As such, it focuses on changing behaviours, reducing running costs, improving staff productivity, demonstrating commitment to CSR, providing certification of proven and maintained sustainability over time, and protecting and enhancing asset value over time.

In an effort to balance the market's need for ease of use with the scientific, evidence-based methodology that is its signature, the 2009 in-use system is an online-only system comprised of 197 'smart' questions to assess the environmental performance of the overall building asset, the operational and client management performance, as well as performance in ten key indicators developed by the International Sustainability Alliance. Questions in the BREEAM In-Use questionnaire are set up as a hierarchical system of questions split between categories and between sub-sections. There are three stages to the BREEAM In-Use assessment: the building (Asset Rating), the operation of the building (Building Management Rating) and how clients are managing their activities with the building (Organisational Rating).

The BREEAM questionnaire allocates credits based on meeting specific performance targets. The credits are then tallied into the standard nine categories (energy, water, materials, pollution, land use and ecology, health and wellbeing, waste, transport and management) and the raw score for each category is multiplied by its weighting factor to determine the number of points achieved in each category. The category points are added to determine the final rating achieved (unclassified, acceptable, pass, good, very good, excellent, or outstanding).

The goal is for the in-use rating to be part of a long-term management process which can aid clients in improving their data collection over time, and as a result their certification rating through the re-assessment process (Christensen 2011). Last, the in-use system is able to evaluate questionnaire responses and propose a range of retrofit opportunities to improve property performance. In addition, in-use offers a 'broad brush' assessment for property portfolios that highlights the strengths and weaknesses of individual assets.

These characteristics are designed not only to assist building users but to help developers considering green retrofit opportunities to determine how they can have the most significant impact on building performance, and to make decisions about where to invest money on larger upgrades that will translate to improved performance and lower operating costs, and to identify lower priced options that together might have a positive impact on building performance. These decisions can translate into improved Energy Performance Certificate (EPC) scores, which may influence tenant lease decisions and negotiations, or in the UK the landlord's ability in the future to re-let. In addition, the ability of the questionnaire to make performance assumptions enables portfolio managers to quickly, and simply, provide basic information on the assets in their property portfolios with the data they currently collect. This enables organisations to improve their data collection process over time, thereby improving the accuracy of the building impact assessment. The incentive for organisations to improve their data collection process is that more building-specific information most often translates into higher EPC and BREEAM ratings. However, it does present an issue for asset managers in that they are required to produce a plethora of information in different types of formats to satisfy different reporting requirements.

The in-use methodology is flexible with how users define the boundaries of assets. The client may define a property as: the whole building, a floor of a building, a room of a building, a wing of a building, or as separately managed tenanted areas. However, an asset cannot include more than one building. This flexibility enables tenants to achieve ratings for retrofit of their space within a building, regardless of whether the overall building has attempted certification. It also enables developers to retrofit and improve their BREEAM rating over time, as tenant leases expire. However, although the BREEAM In-Use rating has achieved significant steps in the environmental sustainability assessment of commercial real estate and provided a more flexible interface for users, there is still a long way to go before it can be considered a truly sustainable measure.

9.3.1.3   *Leadership in environment and energy design (LEED) v4, United States*

LEED is a more recently established system than BREEAM with which it shares many characteristics, being based on a multi-criteria, multi-level approach that is reviewed on a periodic basis. It was originally launched in 1994 but the current version LEED v4, was adopted by its membership in 2013. LEED v4 comprises a series of four different rating systems, each of which focuses on different aspects of construction, adaptation/reuse/restoration of existing buildings. These include the Operations and Maintenance (O+M) and Interior Design and Construction (ID+C) rating systems. To developers, the Design and Construction tool is the most pertinent, and in some US States the adoption of LEED is mandated. However, this is not the case everywhere and some states have prohibited its use in favour either of other systems or none due to criticism that it is too lax in its standards.

LEED has a variety of different schemes for different building types:

- new construction and major renovation;
- core and shell development;
- schools;

- retail;
- data centres;
- warehouses and distribution centres;
- hospitality;
- healthcare.

Each assessment works on a range of five main core assessment categories (sustainable sites, water efficiency, energy and atmosphere, materials and resources, and indoor environmental quality). Within each category there are sub-headings such as site pollution, heat island effect, lighting, air quality and acoustics. A high percentage of the LEED v4 credit changes focus on reducing carbon emissions and increasing energy efficiency in an effort to contain or reverse global climate change. Certified carbon offsets are also included among the credit for the first time. This move is an effort towards greater global alignment with other international rating tools, such as the BREEAM, ESTIDAMA (the Abu Dhabi Urban Planning Council), DGNB (the German Sustainable Building Council), Green Star (Australia) and the Living Building Challenge (US/Canada). It is a characteristic of all these systems that they incorporated some form of life cycle-based product assessment into their material selection requirements, but these are not necessarily ones that have to be achieved to gain a high score. However, unlike BREEAM there is an extensive list of required standards for several items including pollution, water usage and metering and energy standards and metering.

As with BREEAM, the grading system places a heavy weighting on energy, but whilst some matters carry points to contribute to an overall score leading to the eventual categorisation there is an ability to gain a high score in some areas at the expense of other aspects. Over time though there has been a shift in LEED towards a greater emphasis on social aspects (Todd and Kaplan 2014) and LEED v4, through an improved interface, ongoing training for users and a new performance-based approach to indoor environmental quality to ensure occupant comfort, stands testament to this.

Among the notable differences to BREEAM is that LEED operates solely on design modelling, without reference to actual performance (UKGBC 2007); further, there is no absolute requirement to have the assessment carried out by a trained professional assessor, although this is encouraged and rewarded within the points scheme.

The Operations and Maintenance (O+M) rating system is for existing buildings undergoing improvement work but little construction, so it targets minor refurbishments. O+M targets single buildings, whether owner-occupied, multi-tenant, or multiple-building campus projects, and is a whole-building rating system; individual tenant spaces are not eligible. The focus is on operational benefits throughout the life of the building, and recertification is required every five years to ensure performance is being maintained.

The Interior Design and Construction (ID+C) rating system is for complete interior fit-out of buildings and requires at least 60 per cent of the gross floor area to be complete at the time of certification. ID+C targets high-performance green tenant spaces, giving tenants and designers the ability to achieve certification for sustainable choices at the tenant space level, regardless of the performance of the whole-building operations. The focus is on providing healthy, productive places for employees while also decreasing the property's operation and maintenance costs and environmental footprint.

LEED v4 scorecards include up to four Regional Priority Credits to address regional environmental priorities for buildings in different geographic regions, and up to six Innovation in Design or Innovation in Operations Credits to address sustainable building expertise as well as design measures not covered under the five core LEED credit categories In addition, with the aim of aligning LEED v4 more closely with LEED's long-term vision, 'impact categories' were developed to supersede the LEED 2009 aims to limit damage and instead emphasise the potential for projects to have positive impacts in their communities and on the planet. The impact categories are used to assign points to each credit with the goal that projects pursuing higher-point-valued credits and higher certification levels will achieve better environmental, economic and social outcomes. By so doing, the intention is to signal their intent to reward efforts with greater impacts by explicitly weighting points against life cycle assessment performance categories, meaning a given credit's point value will more accurately reflect its potential to either mitigate the negative environmental impacts of a building or promote positive impacts.

9.3.1.4 Green Star, Australia

Within Australia the main whole-building rating systems is Green Star which is owned and operated by the Australian Green Building Council. First launched in 2002, Green Star was developed along the principles adopted by BREEAM and LEED. It has been designed to establish 'individual environmental measurement criteria with particular relevance to the Australian marketplace and environmental context' (GBCA 2014a). It has been designed to cater for different types of building ranging from offices to healthcare.

The emphasis of Green Star has been on ease of use and self-assessment although there is a requirement for validation before a certificate (graded by a one to six star system) is issued. The categories which include management, internal environmental quality, energy, transport, water, emissions, materials, land use and ecology are all similar to those adopted by many other schemes. Again the highest weighting is on energy at 25 per cent, whilst water is only 12 per cent, despite the fact that drought could be a higher risk in Australia than in many jurisdictions. Green Star has two versions for some types of property: designed and as built. However, there are currently plans to undertake a fairly major overhaul of the systems with a move towards a single integrated Design and As Built suite of tools. Under this, most aspects of the scheme, including the scope and weighting system which currently varies from state to state is being reviewed (Lindup 2014).

This review is being undertaken in response to criticisms that the current rating tools are 'expensive, lack[s] clarity, and require[s] too much documentation' with a failure to 'create the right incentives' and an 'assessment process (which) has been seen as pedantic and bureaucratic' (GBCA 2014b). Whilst it could be argued that rating systems, to be rigorous, do require a thorough assessment process, this self-reflection is welcome in an environment in which competition between rating system providers is seemingly increasing.

Green Star does not have an in-use version yet although a pilot is being undertaken. If it is confirmed, it is likely to focus on environmental impacts (including management, indoor environmental quality, energy, transport, water, materials, land use and ecology, emissions and innovation). The intention is that the in-use rating will last for a continually monitored three-year certification after which there is an entitlement to apply for re-assessment and recertification at the end of the certification period.

9.3.1.5 The Living Building Challenge

Most rating tools address sustainability only at the weak level but there is one rating scheme that has been developed that does seek to address stronger level sustainability. The Living

Building Challenge, first conceived in Canada in the mid-1990s and formally launched in 2009, aims to 'produce the most advanced sustainable design project in the world'. Unlike other tools considered in this chapter, the Living Building Challenge is claimed to be 'a philosophy, certification and advocacy tool' which moves projects 'beyond merely being less bad to become truly regenerative' (International Living Future Institute 2014: 4) as shown in Figure 9.2.

Under the scheme, buildings are generally only considered to meet requirements for full accreditation when their performance against each of 20 criteria, which are grouped under seven major headings, or 'Petals' as they call them, has been tested either through audit or in some cases through demonstrable compliance a year into operation, as shown in Table 9.2.

The seven Petals into which the criteria sit are: Place, Water, Energy, Health and Happiness, Materials, Equity and Beauty: a list that is far more holistic, demanding and indeed subjective than the more widely known and adopted rating schemes. For each criterion, the demands are exacting. For example, under Energy, 100 per cent of the building's energy needs on a net annual basis must be supplied by on-site renewable energy and no combustion is allowed. However, stringent though this is, this does not by itself fulfil the energy Petal. To do so the project must also account for total embodied carbon through either a one-time carbon offset in the institute's Living Future Carbon Exchange or an approved carbon offset provider. Whilst the environmental issues are perhaps predictable, if demanding, other criteria are unique to the challenge. For example to meet the Beauty and Spirit criterion lifts the notion of health and wellbeing to a new level with its requirement

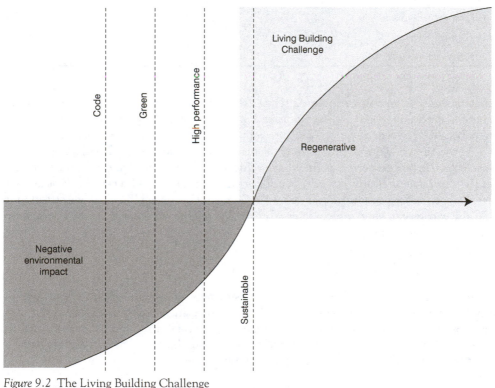

Figure 9.2 The Living Building Challenge
Source: International Living Future Institute (2014 :4)

Table 9.2 The Living Building Challenge criteria for accreditation assessment

Imperative	Preliminary audit	Final audit
01: Limits to growth	✓	
02: Urban agriculture		✓
03: Habitat exchange	✓	
04: Human powered living	✓	
05: Net positive water		✓
06: Net positive energy		✓
07: Civilised environment	✓	
08: Healthy interior environment		✓
09: Biophilic environment	✓	
10: Red list	✓	
11: Embodied carbon footprint	✓	
12: Responsible industry	✓	
13: Living economy sourcing	✓	
14: Net positive waste		✓
15: Human scale + humane places		✓
16: Universal access to nature and place	✓	
17: Equitable investments		✓
18: Just organisations	✓	
19: Beauty + spirit		✓
20: Inspiration + education	✓	

that the project contains features 'intended solely for human delight and celebration of culture, spirit and place' and integrates public art whilst the equitable investment head requires a 0.5 per cent donation of all development costs to a recognised charity.

At the time of writing, the institute claims that there are some 192 projects, primarily residential, in process but few of these have achieved full accreditation. Whilst the ambition of the challenge is clearly beyond most developers currently, it is known that it is at least on the agenda for consideration of some commercial developers. If it does gain traction it has the capacity to alter contemporary thinking in relation to what is meant by the term 'sustainable development'.

9.3.2 Single-criteria schemes

Single-criteria schemes are less common but there are some which warrant a place within this chapter, as they are influential. The advantage of a single criterion scheme is that it is not possible to manipulate in the way that a multi-criteria scheme can be 'flexed' between one criterion and another. It therefore offers transparency, but it can nevertheless be subject to criticism and none are free from implementation issues.

9.3.2.1 Energy Performance Certificates (EPC)

Energy Performances Certificates are mandated by the European Union and apply across all member states under Directive 2010/31 EU (Energy Performance of Buildings Directive). The directive requires an asset rating on all buildings, though member states can interpret the directive in slightly different ways, with the exception of heritage, short-life buildings and other categories. A certificate lasts ten years unless major works are undertaken that trigger the requirement for a new certificate and the hope that the rating will be better.

When introduced in 2008 into the UK and some European countries, the ratings, that range from A (the best) to G (the worst), required evaluation before letting or sale when all heads of terms were agreed or upon building completion. Initially EPCs were not accurate due to poor quality assessments and this led to a culture in which they were seen as a necessity but of no value; a matter of compliance, and Murphy (2014) reported in the Netherlands they had little impact. However, the requirement to make EPCs part of the marketing materials, combined with a proposal under the Energy Act 2011 to link minimum performance standards with an ability to let a property, have heightened awareness and led to a positive market response; however, the criticism of their inaccuracy has not been overcome. Further the requirement upon completion is simply to produce an EPC; even if it is a G, as long as the building is not to be let, it passes the compliance threshold. In Australia a similar system exists. The Mandatory Disclosure Act 2010 requires building owners of space exceeding 2,000 square metres to provide a NABERS Energy rating at the point of sale or leasing. This is explained in more detail in Chapter 11 section 11.5.

9.3.2.2 Display Energy Certificate (DEC)

A DEC is allied to an EPC and measures actual energy used annually. The DEC is required to be displayed in the building to which it applies. However, as it applied to buildings to which the public has access, the potential impact for driving sustainability is less; private and residential buildings are excluded. To developers, it has less relevance as the rating, from A to G, is dependent on the operation of the building. In this respect, the DEC needs careful interpretation, as a building whose use declines year on year can look as though it is becoming more energy efficient whereas in reality it simply represents an inefficient use of space. Conversely many organisations look to reduce space per capita, the energy needs, particularly cooling, and computer usage may increase with a consequent rise in energy use.

9.3.2.3 Energy Star

The Energy Star system is used in the US and Canada and measures energy use for an individual building, calibrated on a 1–100 scale. The calibration takes account of the type of building and its usage (for example the density and hours of use) and scores it against a national median of 50. A score of 75 plus is regarded as a top score. The reliability of Energy Star lies in both the normalisation of the building to reflect its individual use and the reliability of the baseline date. In terms of the former, the efficiency is adjusted to take due consideration of size, location, number of occupants, number of computers and then benchmarks the actual consumption against the amount of energy it would use if it were a top, bottom or median performer to provide a comparison. As such, it is a management guide. The benchmark date itself is obtained from the US Energy Information Administration which conducts a Commercial Building Energy Consumption Survey every four years, see www.eia.gov/consumption/commercial/about.cfm.

The Energy Star rating is, prima facie, a management tool, not a rating aimed at developers. As some of the most extensive research connecting capital value patterns with energy efficiency are based on assessing correlations between observed rents and capital values and Energy Star data, it is not a measure which developers can afford to be unaware of.

9.3.2.4 NABERS

NABERS is an Australian tool that has two versions, one measuring building energy consumption, NABERS Energy, and the other building water usage, NABERS Water. NABERS is government owned and controlled (with the help of a stakeholder group) and is an in-use scheme, in which the actual performance in key environmental areas can be measured for commercial offices, shopping centres, hotels, data centres and homes. As well as running a qualified assessor scheme, NABERS offers a self-assessment tool aimed at awareness raising. It should be noted that, unlike some other schemes, the factors rated vary from property type to property type, although all include energy and water.

NABERS offers the advantage of simplicity as it uses actual quantitative data which can be prepared by the applicant but which is then assessed using a standard calculation method by an assessor. It can apply to the whole or part of a building and can be reviewed annually. Therefore it offers the possibility of addressing occupier behaviours, although the quality of the base build will be a factor in performance and therefore the achieved rating can act as an incentive to developers.

However, there are tensions in having two national competing schemes and it has long been recognised that this can lead to confusion (Mitchell 2010). Consequently, many buildings are now double rated with NABERS and Green Star.

9.3.3 *Portfolio and corporate level ratings*

Portfolio and corporate level ratings are of lesser concern to developers; however, as argued above, they are influential on the thinking of institutional investors; therefore they are matters of which those who are stakeholders in the development process need to be aware. If the final product does not perform well in use, then reputational damage to the whole design and construction team could result.

Within the business community, the process of benchmarking for sustainability is well developed, primarily through the ISO 4001. However, until recently no systems at the portfolio level had been developed which lent themselves to property. That has changed and recently several significant efforts were undertaken to standardise performance data and reporting systems. These include the Investment Property Databank's (IPD) EcoPAS, the Climate Disclosure Standards Board's (CDSB) Climate Change Reporting Framework, the Greenprint Foundation's Greenprint Performance Report, the Global Reporting Initiative's (GRI) G3.1: Sustainability Reporting Guidelines and the GRI's Construction and Real Estate Sector Supplement (CRESS), and the Global Real Estate Sustainability Benchmark (GRESB).

9.3.3.1 *Investment Property Databank: EcoPAS*

EcoPAS (Eco-Portfolio Analysis Service) was launched in 2012 as a colloabarotation between RICS and Investment Property Databank (IPD). Although in essence it is 'a confidential benchmarking service that identifies and highlights the potential environmental risks in a real estate investment portfolio' (IPD, 2014).

IPD/RICS publish the results as a way of seeking to raise further awareness on environmental performance in the sector. The aim of the benchmarking is to enable individual investors to benchmark their portfolios' environmental performance against those of their competitors in order that they can assess the likely risks moving forward.

A further argued benefit of EcoPAS, which was developed collaboratively with fund managers, valuation surveyors and sustainability managers, is that it contains a sustainability inspection checklist that valuers can use within their normal day-to-day work thus helping to supply an evidence base as to the prevalence and impact of sustainability features.

One attempt to overcome the disparity among the existing benchmarking criteria in the real estate investment community was a research project by the Investment Property Forum (IPF) in London. The primary focus of the research was the development of a methodology to create a framework for producing a sustainability index, the Sustainable Property Index (SPI). Whilst to date this index has not been progressed, the property data used to assess the sustainability characteristics of individual assets, based on earlier work by Ellison and Sayce (2006). has been developed further to provide a benchmark. The performance measurement service does not attempt a full triple bottom line approach to sustainability; instead it concentrates only on those matters known to be of concern to institutional investors.

EcoPAS, which is a confidential service, aims to provide subscribers information to help them identify and manage their potential environmental risks within their portfolios, insofar as these will impact on asset and portfolio values; it also provides a risk analysis. Currently it is only a UK-based system developed by IPD with RICS, but launches in both France and Australia are planned (IPD 2014).

9.3.3.2 *Climate Disclosure Project (CDP): Climate Change Reporting Framework*

The Climate Disclosure Project's Climate Change Reporting Framework includes two categories for disclosure: 1) overall strategic analysis (short-term and long-term) and 2) reporting on risk and governance of climate change and greenhouse gas emissions. Several industry-specific and national guidelines are incorporated into the framework. Among the most influential are the GHG Protocol and the ISO 14064-1 specification. The World Council developed the GHG Protocol for Business and Sustainable Development (2001) in response to developing global climate change policy to understand and manage greenhouse gas (GHG) emissions. The GHG Protocol is the most widely applied international accounting tool used to quantify GHG emissions (see www.ghgprotocol.org). ISO 14064-1 (2007) is part of the larger International Standards Organisation (ISO) 14000-series of Environmental Management Systems. It specifies principles and requirements for quantification and reporting of GHG emissions and removals at the facility/organisation level (see www.iso14000-iso14001-environmental-management.com/). The CDP's framework is among the leading environmental reporting frameworks. From a broader sustainability perspective, its weakness is that it includes only minimal acknowledgement of the social and economic impacts of these activities.

9.3.3.3   Greenprint Foundation: Greenprint Performance Report

Like the Carbon Disclosure Project, the Greenprint Foundation focuses on the environmental impact of business activities, specifically, the carbon footprint of the property industry. The Greenprint Foundation, now the ULI Greenprint Centre for Building Performance, is a growing global alliance of real estate owners, investors, financial institutions and practitioners dedicated to reducing the carbon footprint of the built environment. They are committed to testing and evaluating carbon emission alternatives for all property types and to 'leading the global real estate community toward value-enhancing carbon reduction strategies that support the IPCC goals for global greenhouse gas stabilisation by 2030' (Greenprint Foundation 2012). By providing information about successful sustainability programmes and case studies, white papers and research demonstrating the direct link between property values and energy efficiency, the Greenprint Foundation aims to become a catalyst for change in the built environment. The Greenprint Performance Report, Volume 2 (Greenprint Foundation 2010) measures member's relative GHG emissions reduction progress by providing current carbon footprints of individual buildings and compares them with previous emissions. The organisation analysed 1,623 properties (an increase of 170 per cent from the 2009 report) and 31 million square feet of commercial space (an increase of 93 per cent from the 2009 report). Individual buildings or groups of buildings are analysed, and then reported in the aggregate by asset type: office, industrial, retail, multifamily and hotels. This enables members to compare their individual progress with the industry at large. As Greenprint continues to gather data, the ultimate goal is the development of a true performance index (Greenprint Foundation 2010).

9.3.3.4   Global Reporting Initiative's (GRI) G3.1: Sustainability Reporting Guidelines

The Global Reporting Initiative's (GRI) G3.1: Sustainability Reporting Guidelines is currently the most utilised global standard for reporting corporate social responsibility and sustainability (Pivo 2008; GRI 2011). Like the Greenprint Performance Report, the GRI Construction and Real Estate Sector Supplement (CRESS) specifically targets the built environment stakeholders. Launched in September 2011, it provides guidelines for measuring, monitoring and reporting of sustainable business strategies, performance and impacts at all stages of the built environment life cycle. Some of the issues covered in CRESS include management and remediation of contaminated lands, building and materials certification, carbon emissions and sub-contracted labour health and safety issues. CRESS is intended to help real estate investors, managers,and developers

> be more transparent about the impacts their activities and assets have on the environment, economy and society... making sure that companies in the construction and real estate sector have the tools to communicate their impacts is vital if we are to move to a sustainable economy.
>
> (Goodchild 2011: press release)

9.3.3.5   Global Real Estate Sustainability Benchmark (GRESB)

The Global Real Estate Sustainability Benchmark (GRESB) (2012) is an annual science-based evaluation of environmental and social performance in the real estate industry. A survey of property companies and investment funds scores individual metrics to create scorecards for respondents as well as a report for the industry. The GRESB 2012 Report includes responses from more than 35 institutional investors and 450 property companies and funds, worldwide, providing information about 36,000 properties representing approximately $1.32 trillion in global assets under management. The GRESB scorecard identifies areas of investment risk and areas for improvement. The analysis compares a respondent's score with the regional average and the regional leader in each category. The GRESB scoring methodology rewards sustainability actions and attempts to block potential green washing efforts by weighting implementation and measurement more heavily than management and policy. Several key trends are observed in the GRESB 2012 Report. There was an increase of respondents collecting data and reporting on energy consumption (60 per cent as compared to 34 per cent in 2011). Despite an increase in overall energy consumption, the data also indicates a reduction of GHG emissions of approximately 6 per cent on a like-for-like basis (i.e. normalising the results from 2011 to 2012). In addition, green building certifications are becoming increasingly important (with LEED most widely accepted) with 51 per cent including them in their portfolio.

9.4 The evolution of building assessment rating tools: a critique

Early sustainability assessment systems, such as BREEAM, evolved from environmental impact assessment (EIA) systems (see for example Poveda and Lipset 2011). Over time, the concentration on EIA led rise to concerns of perceived limitations of their usefulness as a result of which some practitioners advocated strategic environmental assessment (SEA) rather than project-based schemes (Devuyst 2000; Pope *et al.*, 2004). It should be noted that in some countries project-based EIAs or SEAs have since become a mandatory requirement (see for example Glasson *et al.* 2013); the impacts of this are considered in Chapter 9. Having their 'roots' in environmental assessment resulted in early sustainability assessment systems focusing heavily on the management of environmental indicators. The triple bottom line model of sustainability performance assessment is a more recent development linking environmental and social impacts with their monetary impact. This development explains why early sustainability assessment rating tools were considered to be the 'next generation' of environmental assessment (Sadler 2001).

The construction and property development industries in the past have been criticised for not including a sustainability focus as part of their strategic planning process (Taskforce on Sustainable Construction 2007); however, the advent of rating systems has enabled this to change radically in some countries, notably those where they are tied into planning and building permit systems. Australia, the United States, and some parts of Europe, as well as other countries around the globe, notably some countries in South-East Asia, are increasingly including a variety of environmental and social/wellbeing factors in both new construction and retrofit projects. Similarly, the number of applications for certification is claimed by ratings organisations to be increasing and presents a significant proportion of new stock. For example, the LEED green rating system, since creation in 2000, has been used to certify over 10.7 billion square feet of space, with more than 1.7 million square feet of new and existing buildings being certified worldwide every day (USGBC 2014). However, this does not indicate the number or distribution of spaces certified by LEED. BREEAM, on the other hand, claims to be the foremost assessment method and rating tool, with 250,000 buildings with certified BREEAM assessment ratings and over a million registered for assessment since it was first launched in 1990 (see http://www.breeam.org/).

Much of the research in the LEED/BREEAM assessment literature is related to the LEED-New Construction (LEED-NC) and BREEAM Office and indicates that, for Grade A office stock, there is increasing shift towards certifying buildings which may demonstrate higher levels of some sustainability characteristics than would be required under national building codes, notably in the field of energy efficiency. However, this is not the same as claiming that rated buildings are fully 'sustainable' buildings as this requires consideration across the full triple bottom line which may not apply to every tool. Further, mandatory standards have also changed and a building that would have been rated highly a decade ago might now not even meet compliance. Therefore there needs to be great use in interpreting rating systems. Rating systems vary significantly and what is deemed important in one system is far less so in another.

A major concern to long-term investors in buildings is that many rating systems apply to new builds whereas, as noted in Chapter 1, new construction typically adds only 1–2 per cent to the total building stock per annum. Whilst it took some considerable time for governments and the industry to register that the issue of existing buildings was more important than new build in sustainability terms, the global financial crisis that began in 2007, led to a change. During the recessionary period, the construction sector slowed down and new builds had even less of an impact on the total building stock and the role of existing buildings became clearer. As a result, there was an important shift in the marketplace; the USGBC reports that since the recession began in the United States in 2007, there have been more LEED Existing Building applications than LEED-NC. By December 2011, LEED-certified existing buildings surpassed LEED-certified new constructions by 15 million square feet on a cumulative basis (Katz 2011).

Industry professionals anticipate this trend towards rating buildings to make visible their 'green' or sustainable characteristics, to continue for both new and refurbished buildings. Whilst the notion of certification started in the UK and US, in a survey of 803 property industry firms in 65 countries, the World Green Building Trends Smart Market Report 2013 found that green building is a global trend not confined to a few geographic or economic regions. Between 2012 and 2015, 63 per cent of respondents have plans for new green commercial projects, 45 per cent for new institutional projects and 50 per cent for green retrofit/renovation projects. In total, 51 per cent of property respondents anticipate that more than 60 per cent of their work will be related to green new and retrofit building by 2015, up from 28 per cent in 2012 (McGraw Hill 2013). Whilst this survey, which updated previous findings from 2008, provides an indication of *intent*, it is heavily dependent on the financial and corporate environment. Seldom do organisations actually do what they may opine; further it must also be borne in mind that sample sizes per country were very small. However, despite the limitations, what is revealed by this research is that the role of legislation is a powerful driver towards embedding green construction principles in market practice.

9.5   Current issues with rating tools

The intention in developing environmental benchmarking tools (e.g. Green Star and NABERS in Australia) has been to reduce the environmental impact of property construction and development activities. Whilst some schemes (for example Green Star and LEED) have been initiated by industry led Green Building Councils, others have been developed by quasi-governmental bodies (NABERS). BREEAM is owned by BRE (Building Research

Establishment) which at the time of its initial development was government owned but is now a private company. Other certifications, notably the Energy Performance Certificate have been developed by national governments working to a European Directive. The intention may be shared but the proliferation of initiators and their skills and interests have inevitability led to systems being divergent in many ways. There are also cost implications to certificates and this can affect their take up where they are voluntary.

However, despite the undoubted good intentions of those who develop certificates, the evidence that their use within the construction process results in more sustainable buildings is questionable. For example, LEED accreditation is based on design criteria and whilst this may lead to a building with potentially lower resource use, it will be the occupier's behaviour that will determine the consumption to a large extent. Further, commentators have long pointed to the so-called 'performance gap' in which design standards are simply not achieved (Cohen *et al.* 2001; Bordass *et al.* 2004). A study by Jones Lang LaSalle commissioned by the Better Buildings Partnership (JLL 2012) found that of two prime office buildings in London, the building with the poorer energy rating was more energy efficient in use. As they concluded 'It is imperative … to focus on actual energy performance rather than just 'design intent' (JLL 2012: 13). In an empirical domestic study in Denmark, Kjærbye (2008) found that there was insignificant difference between the consumption of fuel in 'labelled' and 'non-labelled' dwellings leading to the suggestion that the presence of a label does not, *per se*, lead to changed behaviours.

The reasons why a design-based rating may not provide a reliable guide to actual performance were considered by Diamond (2011) who carried out an empirical study of 17 rated buildings. He found that the LEED energy points did not coincide with actual energy use and concluded that design-estimate and actual performance may vary primarily for many reasons which are summarised as follows:

- The building is not constructed in accordance with a modelled design.
- Incompleteness of data on which to base predictions or record actual use.
- The building use may differ in relation to density and equipment use.

Meanwhile, property investors and occupiers require not just asset ratings based on initial concepts but tools which will provide useful information to aid their decision-making when purchasing, leasing or managing property. Occupiers will have a primary objective of measures which will aid in the management of the asset; investors' primary concern is whether the measure will provide comparative data on financial performance as measured through rents and capital value impacts. These two objectives are different: an occupier's prime concern, apart from any fulfilment of CSR credentials, will be to occupy a building whose sustainability credentials will lead to lower costs and higher user satisfaction. An investor's concern will be to make portfolio comparison by the use of benchmarking financial performance.

Although several organisations and many countries have developed benchmarking tools targeting property owners and occupiers, none has emerged as the go-to standard for assessing building performance although GRESB is gaining considerable traction as a multi-national guide to sustainability measurement. An extensive search conducted by the Engineering and Physical Sciences Research Council (EPSRC) identified 700 different assessment tools, each measured at least one sustainability attribute (i.e. social, environmental and/or economic attributes). The EPSRC report (Horner *et al.* 2009) acknowledged that none of the tools identified was capable of measuring all three attributes of sustainability. Since then other measures have been developed but no system has emerged as the global standard for sustainable property development.

With so many tools to choose from, it is understandable that stakeholders, who may not be experts in the technical distinctions between measures, should find it difficult to decide which measure(s) to adopt for their own management and sale/purchase purposes. From an analyst's viewpoint, the multitude of tools, each of which may include different criteria and employ different scaling or weighting techniques has resulted in problems in terms of the collection and reporting of data as well as an inability to compare and monitor performance in the industry and within portfolios (Levy and De Francesco 2008; IPF 2009; Lowe and Ponce 2009; Ellison and Brown 2011; RREEF 2010). Property industry executives aiming to have a positive impact in their community and on the environment admit the resulting complexity can be daunting. They may be prepared to require managers to collect data for submission to data houses for the production of the benchmark tools, but this is a time-consuming and expensive process; they therefore need to be assured that they are not collecting data in different formats for different measures. As Skodowski notes 'the entire mood in the building industry is more about doing the right thing … the difficulty is understanding what the right thing is' (Malin 2010).

Thus the complexity of sustainability, and how to gain a holistic picture of the issues, has been an ongoing issue for researchers seeking to analyse on comparative bases. Of course, many users of rating tools may now wish for, or need, a holistic assessment: for practical purposes they will require individual measures, such as energy efficiency, water use, or in relation to 'softer measures', the impact on wellbeing and sickness records. This is also the case for researchers and perhaps it is no coincidence that the more robust correlations found between building performance and rating assessments have been those studies connected with single-criteria tools such as NABERS, Energy Star and the EPC.

Whilst the above might appear to present a negative picture of rating tools, there has been increasing evidence that within the main investment and corporate communities, sustainability is feeding into decision-making and tools. Though imperfect, rating tools are an important component to their decision strategies and enable their policies to be put into measurement practice. A study by GVA Grimley (2008) emphasised that although investors were the early adopters among property industry stakeholders, occupiers are increasingly emphasising sustainability in their decision-making process (GVA Grimley 2007; Jones Lang LaSalle 2008). However, although occupiers are beginning to include environment, social and corporate governance (ESG) issues in their corporate space leasing decisions and corporate social responsibility (CSR) statements, the lack of standardisation among the performance measures collected and how the measures can best be used to communicate sustainability performance is still problematic. Ellison and Brown (2011) noted that a common set of metrics for sustainability performance is required for the demand side of the property industry to make effective progress in measuring, understanding and improving the sustainability performance of commercial property. In the same year, the Green Property Alliance (2010) set out four recommendations for the improvement in metrics that would be useful for all stakeholders. These were:

- collect under common measurement methods building classifications;
- develop common metrics for energy, carbon, water and waste;
- set boundaries in terms of inclusion (for example carbon can be direct use and through scopes 2 and 3 indirect impacts); and,
- present data using transparent methodologies that will allow like-for-like comparison.

In presenting this report, the Green Property Alliance supports the views that 'an information demand exists which cannot be appropriately satisfied at the moment' (Lowe and Ponce 2009: 20). Similarly, Muldavin (2010) agrees the need for better and more reliable information but ties this requirement to the relationship between rating systems and property's financial performance as measured through rents and occupancy rates, which he maintains are key demand drivers for collecting sustainability-related data at the property level. Muldavin's claims that buildings which are more sustainable, or green, command higher rents and suffer less vacancy have been supported by several empirical studies which found, to varying degrees, that buildings with 'green' certifications (primarily LEED and Energy Star in the US) may command rental rate and effective rental rate premiums, sales price premiums and increased occupancy rates (Miller *et al.* 2008; Eichholtz *et al.* 2010a; Fuerst and McAllister 2010) although this may be very localised and results should be treated with caution (World Green Building Council 2013).

Collecting data at the portfolio level has also been challenging. One of the first attempts is that undertaken by Bernet *et al.* (2014) who collected data across 40 portfolio holdings in European countries. The findings revealed that, with the exception of energy data, which is now being collected fairly systematically, there was a wide variation in both the type of data collected and the method of collection. It also became apparent that the practice of collecting environmental and social data is still in its infancy with few funds having any significant length of run of data.

In turn, if data is not collected, it cannot be analysed and used to support appraisals in any systematic way. Despite growing numbers of individual research projects revealing some empirical data supporting the positive economic impact of developing sustainable property to the user, until recently there was very little evidence that sustainability is reflected in property pricing. In part this was due to a lack of empirical studies (Sayce *et al.* 2010). Whilst there are now more empirical studies (see World Green Building Council 2013 for a review), the majority relate to restricted types and locations of buildings and the evidence of absorption into the wider practices of valuers is still limited. This is discussed in more detail in Chapter 4. However, as metrics increase, large investment stakeholders are incorporating the requirement of specific sustainability performance information, most notably on environmental issues such as energy and flood risk, when making property acquisitions. The challenge for them is incorporating this data into their portfolio management systems.

Confusion and sometimes lack of information has presented issues in the past for investors, with many property companies and investment funds having to develop their own sustainability measures/matrices rather than work together to develop standard benchmarking practices for the industry. Ellison and Brown (2011) indicated two potential negative impacts of this 'go it alone' strategy:

1   Comparing sustainability performance of properties, portfolios, and organisations becomes limited thereby limiting competition, a key driver of industry change.
2   Lack of consistency further complicates decision-making for organisations concerning the best approach to adopt for data collection and monitoring progress towards achieving sustainability benchmarks.

Since then, there have been a number of initiatives aimed at more collaborative working. The introduction by the Global Reporting Initiative (GRI) of its Construction and Real Estate Sector Supplement in 2012 marked a large step forward by providing a consistent platform against which companies could report. Further, GRESB, which provides a benchmark service, has grown significantly over its short history. Most recently UNEP FI's (United Nations Environmental Programme – Finance Initiative) Property Working Group, recognising the major issue that the search for metrics has become, has promoted the notion of metrics being considered at three levels: corporate, portfolio and individual building (UNEP FI Property Working Group 2014).

9.6   Conclusion

The sustainable property reporting and rating tools in this chapter each approach the complex concept of sustainable development differently, and in many cases they report and/ or apply different metrics to measure sustainability performance; indeed they also vary in the stringency of demands that they make. In asking the question whether we, as a society, are in danger of hitting the targets and missing the point with the rating tools, it might be argued that we are making a lot of attempts at hitting the target but have thus far been unsuccessful. One issue in achieving this goal is that sustainability is in a constant state of flux; as new climate data emerges and new technologies develop, the concept of what sustainable property development is continually evolves. It may also be that the complexity of the task at hand is too much for the industry to fully address at this time. However, with each iteration, the reporting and rating tools make advances and get closer to hitting the target. Will we ever be able to hit the target? Perhaps not, but we are likely to continue to further improve our property stock.

As property industry professionals, there is a key role in engaging and leading in this ever changing process and promotion of ever more demanding performance targets in the property which we develop/manage/invest in. We cannot get discouraged by the changing definitions of sustainable development or changing expectations of the market. Instead, we can instead embrace the potential of buildings to become more sustainable as they approach different life cycle stages, from new construction, to adaptation, to retrofit. Although none of the reporting and assessment rating systems discussed in this chapter currently achieve sustainability by its broadest definition, all of them offer guidance for industry professionals looking to take positive steps towards reducing energy and water consumption, improving working conditions for occupants, and reducing waste. Current industry leaders are exceeding the minimum standards set by many of the sustainable property assessment rating tools and are driving the charge towards developing property more sustainably; however, few would claim that they can achieve anything of the level required of the Living Building Challenge. The effort moving forward now is for vanguard organisations to use their experience to help others take up the effort while continuing to push the barriers imposed by those resisting change combined with stronger mandating of standards and codes.

Note

1   A batbox is a nesting box for bats, whose habitat has been seriously depleted. It can be provided at virtually zero cost – yet it will be awarded points.

References

Banuri, T. (1999) *Sustainable Development and Climate Change*, Policy Matters No.4, Newsletter of the World Conservation Union (IUCN) Commission on Environmental, Economic and Social Policy (CEESP), London: CEESP Secretariat/International Institute for Environment and Development (IIED).

Bare, J. (2002) *Developing a Consistent Decision-Making Framework by Using the U.S. EPA's TRACI.* Retrieved October 2012 from http://www.epa.gov/nrmrl/std/sab/traci/aiche2002paper.pdf.

Bebbington, J. (2001) Sustainable development: a review of the international development, business and accounting literature, *Accounting Forum* 25(2): 128–157.

Berardi, U. (2011) Sustainability assessment in the construction sector: rating systems and rated buildings, *Sustainable Development*, Hoboken, NJ: John Wiley and Sons and ERP Environmental. Retrieved from www.academia.edu/1035576/Comparison_of_sustainability_rating_systems_for_buildings_and_evaluation_of_trends.

Bernet, J., Sayce, S., Ledl, R., Vermeulen, M., and Quinn, F. (2014). *The Sustainability Alpha: Market Evidence for Rental Growth Factors in Office Buildings and Shopping Centers across Europe*, Zurich: EURO Institute of Real Estate Management.

Bordass, W., Cohen, R., and Field, J. (2004) Energy efficiency in non-domestic buildings: closing the credibility gap, in *Proceedings of the International Conference on Improving Energy Efficiency in Commercial Buildings*, Frankfurt, Germany, 20–22 April. Retrieved from http:// www.usablebuildings.co.uk.

BPIE (Buildings Performance Institute Europe) (2011) Europe's buildings under the microscope: A country-by-country review of the energy performance of buildings. Retrieved from http://www.institutebe.com/InstituteBE/media/Library/Resources/Existing%20Building%20Retrofits/Europes-Buildings-Under-the-Microscope-BPIE.pdf

BRE (British Research Establishment Global) (2011a) BREEAM in-use: half-day workshop for auditors and clients. Retrieved 1 April 2014 from www.breeam.org.

BRE (British Research Establishment) (2011b) BREEAM In-use and the International Sustainability Alliance. Ecobuild 2011 presentation. Retrieved 1 April 2014 from www.breeam.org.

BRE (British Research Establishment)(2015) BREEAM. Retrieved from https://www.bre.co.uk/page.jsp?id=829

Christensen, P. (2011) 2009 LEED-EB: O&M and BREEAM in-use: implications for commercial real estate, paper presentation, European Real Estate Society Annual Conference Eindhoven, Holland, June 15-18, 2011.

Christensen, P. (2012) Key strategies of sustainable real estate decision-making in the United States: a Delphi study of the stakeholders, *All Dissertations*, Paper 1073. Retrieved May 2013 from http://tigerprints.clemson.edu/cgi/viewcontent.cgi?article=2073&context=all_dissertations.

Cohen, R., Standeven, M., Bordass, B., and Leaman, A. (2001) Assessing building performance in use 1: the Probe process, *Building Research & Information* 29(2): 85–102.

Dalal-Clayton, B. (2010) *What is Sustainable Development?* London: International Institute for Environment and Development (IIED). Retrieved June 2013 from: www.iied.org/.

DCLG (Department of Communities and Local Government) (2013) *Changes to Part L of the Building Regulations 2013: Impact Assessment.* Retrieved from www.gov.uk/government/uploads/system/uploads/attachment_data/file/226965/Part_L_2013_IA.pdf.

Dermisi, S. (2009) Effect of LEED ratings and levels on office property assessed and market values, *Journal of Sustainable Real Estate* 1(1): 23–47.

Diamond, R. (2011) Evaluating the energy performance of the first generation of LEED-certified commercial buildings. Retrieved from scholar.google.co.uk/scholar?hl=en&q=rationale+for+building+sustainability+rating+tools&btnG=&as_sdt=1%2C5&as_sdtp=.

Devuyst, D. (2000) Linking impact assessment and sustainable development at the local level: the introduction of sustainability assessment systems. *Sustainable Development* 8(2): 67–78.

Eichholtz, P., Kok, N., and Quigley, J. (2010) Doing well by doing good? Green office buildings, *American Economic Review* 100(December): 2492–2509.

Ellison, L. and Brown, P. (2011) Sustainability metrics for commercial real estate assets – establishing a common approach, *Journal of European Real Estate Research* 4(2): 113–130.

Ellison, L and Sayce, S (2006) *The Sustainable Property Appraisal Project: Final Report.* London: Kingston University. Available from http://eprints.kingston.ac.uk/1435/1/Sustainable_Property_Appraisal_Project.pdf.

Ellison, L., Sayce, S., and Smith, J. (2007) Socially responsible property investment: quantifying the relationship between sustainability and investment property worth, *Journal of Property Research* 24(3): 191–219.

Fuerst, F. and McAllister, P. (2009) An investigation of the effect of eco-labeling on office occupancy rates, *Journal of Sustainable Real Estate* 1: 49–64.

Fuerst, F. and McAllister, P. (2010) Green noise or green value? Measuring the effects of environmental certification on office values, *Real Estate Economics* 39(1): 45–69.

GBCA (2014a) What is Green Star? Retrieved March 2014 from http://www.gbca.org.au/green-star/what-is-green-star/.

GBCA (2014b) Industry collaborates on new Green Star rules. Retrieved March 2014 from http://www.gbca.org.au/news/industry-collaborates-on-new-green-star-rules/35585.htm).

General Services Administration (GSA) # 10691 (2010) GSA moves to LEED gold for all new federal buildings and major renovations. Press release, October 28. Retrieved January 2014 from www.gsa.gov/portal/content/197325.

George, C. (2001) Sustainability appraisal for sustainable development: Integrating everything from jobs to climate change. *Impact Assess Proj Appraisal* 19(1): 95–106.

Gibson, R. (2001) Specification of sustainability-based environmental assessment decision criteria and implications for determining 'significance' in environmental assessment. Retrieved September 2014 from: www.sustreport.org/downloads/SustainabilityEA.doc.

Glasson, J., Therivel, R., and Chadwick, A. (2013) *Introduction to Environmental Impact Assessment*, Abingdon: Routledge.

Global Reporting Initiative (GRI) (2011) Construction and Real Estate Sector Supplement (CRESS). Retrieved March 2014 from www.globalreporting.org/resourcelibrary/CRESS-Complete.pdf.

GLOBE Alliance (2010) COP-16 call to action. Retrieved March 2014 from www.globealliance.org.

Goodchild, L. (2011) New guidelines to build transparency in construction and real estate sector. Press release: GRI website. Retrieved December 2011 from www.globalreporting.org.

Green Building Alliance (2010) *Establishing the Ground Rules for Property: Industry-wide Sustainability Metrics*. Retrieved from www.ukgbc.org/search/apachesolr_search/sustainability%20metrics.

Green Construction Board (2014) *Mapping the Impacts of Minimum Energy Efficiency Standards for Commercial Real Estate Final Report*. Valuation and Demand Working Group: Project GCB630. Retrieved from http://www.greenconstructionboard.org/images/stories/Valuation_and_Demand/GCB%20630%20final%20report.pdf.

Green Property Alliance (2010) *Establishing the Ground Rules for Property: Industry-wide sustainability metrics*. Retrieved 04 March, 2105 from http://www.betterbuildingspartnership.co.uk/download/gpa-common-metrics-paper.pdf.

Greenprint Foundation (2010) *Greenprint Performance Report: Volume 2*. Retrieved November 2012 from http://www.uli.org/wp-content/uploads/ULI-Documents/GreenprintPerformanceReportVolume2.pdf.

Greenprint Foundation (2012) *Greenprint Performance Report: Volume 4*. Retrieved November 2012 from greenprintfoundation.org/GCI/CarbonIndex.aspx

Gutierrez-Espeleta, E. (2007) Further work needed to develop sustainable development indicators, in T. Hak, B. Moldan, and A.L. Dahl (eds) *Sustainability Indicators: A Scientific Assessment*. Washington, DC: Island Press.

GVA Grimley (2007) *Sustainability: Towards sustainable offices*. London: GVA Grimley, LLP.

GVA Grimley (2008) *From Green to Gold*. London: GVA Grimley, LLP.

Gwent Wildlife Trust (2014) Advice for developers and householders. Retrieved September 2014 from http://www.gwentwildlife.org/what-we-do/planning-and-policy/advice-developers-and-householders.

Haapio, A. and Viitaniemi, P. (2008) A critical review of building environmental assessment tools, *Environmental Impact Assessment Review* 28(7): 469–482.

Horner, R.M.W., Castillo, H., El-Haram, M., and Walton, J.S. (2009) *Metrics, Models and Toolkits for Whole Life Sustainable Urban Development*. Engineering and Physical Sciences Research Council Grant Report. Retrieved 20 April 2014 from http://gow.epsrc.ac.uk/NGBOViewGrant.aspx?GrantRef=EP/C008030/1.

International Living Future Institute (2014) *Living Building Challenge 3.0: A Visionary Path to a Regenerative Future*, Seattle: International Living Future Institute. Retrieved 04 March, 2015 from: https://living-future.org/sites/default/files/reports/FINAL%20LBC%203_0_WebOptimized_low.pdf.

International Union for the Conservation of Nature (IUCN) (1980) *World Conservation Strategy*. Gland: International Union for the Conservation of Nature – United Nations Environment Programme – World Wildlife Fund. Retrieved January 2014 from http://data.iucn.org/dbtw-wpd/edocs/WCS-004.pdf.

IPD (2014) Performance and risk analysis. Retrieved March 2014 from https://www.ipd.com/performance-and-risk-analysis/real-estate-investing/environmental-risk.html.

Investment Property Forum (IPF) Research Programme 2006–2009 (2009, October) *ISPI (UK): Creating a Sustainable Property Investment Index: Methodology and Initial Results*, London: Investment Property Forum.

ISO 26000 (2010) *Guidance on Social Responsibility, draft*. Retrieved February 2014 from www.iso.org/iso/catalogue_detail?csnumber=42546.

Jones Lang LaSalle. (2008) *Global Trends in Sustainable Real Estate*. Retrieved April 2011 from www.joneslanglasalle.com/csr/SiteCollectionDocuments/Global_Sustainability_Feb08.pdf

Jones Lang LaSalle (JLL) (2012) *A Tale of Two Buildings: Are EPCS A True Indicator of Energy Efficiency?* JLL/Better Buildings Partnership. Retrieved from www.betterbuildingspartnership.co.uk/download/bbp-jll---a-tale-of-two-buildings-2012.pdf.

Kats, G. (2003) *Green Building Costs and Financial Benefits*, Boston: Massachusetts Technology Collaborative. Retrieved November 2013 from www.dcaaia.com/images/firm/Kats-Green-Buildings-Cost.pdf.

Katz, A. (2008) *Green Building Returns Outweigh Costs*. Retrieved October 2013 from www.sustainablefacility.com/articles/green-building-returns-outweigh-costs.

Katz, A. (2011) Square footage of LEED-certified existing buildings surpasses new construction. USGBC press release. Retrieved March 2014 from www.usgbc.org/Docs/Archive/General/Docs10712.pdf.

Kjærbye, V.H. (2008) *Does Energy Labeling on Residential Housing cause Energy Savings?* AKF working paper. Also published in *ECEEE 2009 Summer Study*, 527–537.

Kok, N. and Jennen, M. (2012) The impact of energy labels and accessibility on office rents. **Energy Policy** http://dx.doi.org/10.1016/j.enpol.2012.04.01

Lawn, P. (2003) A theoretical foundation to support the Index of Sustainable Economic Welfare (ISEW), Genuine Progress Indicator (GPI), and other related indexes, *Ecological Economics* 44: 105–118.

Lele, S. (1991) Sustainable development: a critical review, *World Development* 19(6): 607–621.

Levine, M and Ürge-Vorsatz, D. (coordinating lead authors) (2007) Residential and commercial buildings, in B. Metz, O.R. Davidson, P.R. Bosch, R. Dave, L.A. Meyer (eds) *Climate Change 2007: Mitigation*. Contribution of Working Group III to the Fourth Assessment Report of the Intergovernmental Panel on Climate Change, Cambridge and New York: Cambridge University Press.

Levy, D. and De Francesco, A. (2008) *The Impact of Sustainability on the Investment Environment: A Case Study of Australia*, London: RICS Research.

Lindup, R. (2014) Green Star design & as built: scoping paper. Retrieved 4 March 2015 from http://www.gbca.org.au/uploads/100/35428/Green%20Star%20Design%20As%20Built%20Scoping%20Paper%20FINAL%20v02_distributed.pdf.

Lowe, C. and Ponce A. (2009) *UNEP FI/SBCI's Financial & Sustainability Metrics Report*. UNEP-Financial Intiative (FI)/Sustainable Buildings and Construction Initiative (SBCI). Retrieved November 2013 from http://www.unepfi.org/fileadmin/documents/metrics_report_01.pdf.

McGraw Hill Construction (2013) World Green Building Trends SmartMarket. Report available from http://www.worldgbc.org/files/8613/6295/6420/World_Green_Building_Trends_SmartMarket_Report_2013.pdf

Malin, N. (2010) Sprouting green leaders: directors of sustainability often have to invent their own job descriptions as they work to transform their organizations, *GreenSource Magazine*. Retrieved November 2013 from greensource.construction.com/features/other/2010/1007_Sprouting-Green-Leaders.asp.

Miller, N., Spivey, J. and Florence, A. (2008) Does Green Pay Off? *Journal of Real Estate Portfolio Management*, (14)4: 385–400.

Miller, N., Pogue, D., Gough, Q., and David, S. (2009) Green buildings and productivity, *Journal of Sustainable Real Estate*, 1: 65–89.

Mitchell, L. M. (2010) Green Star and NABERS: learning from the Australian experience with green building rating tools, in Bose, R.K. (ed.) *Energy Efficient Cities: Assessment Tools and Benchmarking Practices*, Washington, DC: The International Bank for Reconstruction and Development/The World Bank.

Mitlin, D. (1992) Sustainable development: a guide to the literature, *Environment and Urbanization* 4(1): 111–124.

Muldavin, S. 2010 Value beyond cost savings: how to underwrite sustainable properties. Green Building Finance Consortium. Retrieved September 2010 from www.greenbuildingfc.com.

Murphy, L. (2014). The influence of the energy performance certificate: the Dutch case. *Energy Policy* 67: 664–672.

Pivo, G. (2008) Responsible property investment criteria developed using the Delphi method, *Building Research & Information* 36(1): 20–36.

Pivo, G. and MacNamara, P. (2005) Responsible property investing, *International Real Estate Review* 8(1): 128–143.

Pope, J., Annandale, D., and Morrison-Saunders, A. (2004) Conceptualising sustainability assessment. *Environmental Impact Assessment Review* 24: 595–616.

Poveda, C. A., and Lipsett, M. (2011) A review of sustainability assessment and sustainability/environmental rating systems and credit weighting tools. *Journal of Sustainable Development* 4(6): 36.

Pulselli, F. M., Ciampalini, F., Tiezzi, E. and Zappia, C. (2006) The index of sustainable economic welfare (ISEW) for a local authority: a case study in Italy, *Ecological Economics* 60(1): 271–281.

Reed, R. and Krajinovic-Bilos, A. (2013) An examination of international sustainability rating tools: an update. *19th PRRES Pacific Rim Real Estate Society Conference*.

Reed, R., Bilos, A., Wilkinson, S., and Schulte, K-W. (2009) International comparison of sustainable rating tools, *Journal of Sustainable Real Estate* 1(1): 1–22.

Reed, R., Wilkinson, S., Bilos, A., and Schulte, K.W. (2011, January) A comparison of international sustainable building tools – an update. *The 17th Annual Pacific Rim Real Estate Society Conference*, *Gold Coast*, pp. 16–19.

Reijnders L. and van Roekel, A. (1999) Comprehensiveness and adequacy of tools for the environmental improvement of buildings, *Journal of Cleaner Production* 7: 221–225.

Roberts, T. (2010) USGBC, LEED targeted by class-action suit, *GreenSource Magazine*, July. Retrieved March 2014 from greensource.construction.com/news/2010/101022Class-Action_Suit.asp.

RREEF (Rosenberg Real Estate Equity Fund) (2010) *Green Buildings: A Niche Becomes Mainstream*. San Francisco, CA: RREEF.

Sadler, B. (1999) A framework for environmental sustainability assessment and assurance, in J. Petts, (ed.) *Handbook of Environmental Impact Assessments, Vol. 1*. Oxford: Blackwell.

Sadler, B. (2001) A framework approach to strategic environmental assessment: aims, principles and elements of good practice, *Proceedings of International Workshop on Public Participation and Health Aspects in Strategic Environmental Assessment*, Vol. 11, Szentendre: Regional Environmental Centre for Central and Eastern Europe.

Sayce, S., Sundberg, A. ,and Clements, B. (2010) *Is Sustainability Reflected in Commercial Property Prices: An Analysis of the Evidence Base*, London: RICS Research Report. Retrieved January 2010 from http://eprints.kingston.ac.uk/15747/1/Sayce-S-15747.pdf.

Seven Group and Reed, B. (2009) *The Integrative Design Guide to Green Building: Redefining the Practice of Sustainability*, Hoboken, NJ: Wiley.

Social Investment Forum (2010) *2010 Report on Socially Responsible Investing Trends in the United States*, Washington, DC: Social Investment Forum. Retrieved April 2014 from www.socialinvest. org/resources/pubs/trends/.

Stavins, R.N. and Schatzki, T. (2013) An economic perspective on building labeling policies. Retrieved from http://www.analysisgroup.com/uploadedFiles/News_and_Events/News/Stavins_ Schatzki_Building_Labels_Research_March2013.pdf.

Taskforce on Sustainable Construction (2007) *Accelerating the Development of the Sustainable Construction Market in Europe*, Brussels: Taskforce on Sustainable Construction, European Commission.

Todd, J. and Kaplan, S. (2014) USGBC accelerates social equity with new LEED credits. Retrieved 4 March 2015 from: http://www.usgbc.org/articles/usgbc-accelerates-social-equity-new-leed-credits

UK Green Building Council (2007) BREEAM and LEED: how do they compare? Available from http://www.ukgbc.co.uk/leed.php.

UNEP (United Nations Environment Programme) (1972) Declaration of the United Nations Conference on the Human Environment. Retrieved October 2013 from www.unep.org/Documents. multilingual/Default.asp?DocumentID=97&ArticleID=1503.

UNEP FI (United Nations Environment Programme Finance Initiative) (2011) *An Investors' Perspective on Environmental Metrics for Property*. Geneva: UNEP FI. Retrieved from http://www.unepfi.org/ fileadmin/documents/EnvironmentalMetrics.pdf.

UNEP FI Property Working Group (2014) Sustainability metrics: translation and impact on property investment and management. Retrieved 4 March 2015 from http://www.unepfi.org/fileadmin/ documents/UNEPFI_SustainabilityMetrics_Web.pdf.

UNEP/United Nations Commission on Trade and Development (UNCTAD) (1975) *Cocoyoc Declaration*, Symposium on Patterns of Resources Use, Environment and Development Strategies (October 1974, Cocoyoc, Mexico). Retrieved October 2013 from http://www.unep.org/Geo/geo3/ english/045.htm.

UNEP/United Nations Environment Programme – Sustainable Building and Climate Initiative (UNEP-SBCI) (2009) *Buildings and Climate Change, Summary for Decision-Makers*. Retrieved October 2013 from http://www.unep.org/sbci/pdfs/SBCI-BCCSummary.pdf.

United Nations Conference for Environment and Development (UNCED) (1992), *Agenda 21*, New York: United Nations General Assembly. Retrieved October 2013 from http://www.un.org/esa/dsd/ agenda21/.

United Nations World Commission on Environment and Development (UNWCED) (1987) *Our Common Future (Brundtland Report)*, Oxford: Oxford University Press.

United States Green Building Council (USGBC) (2010a) *Why Build Green*. Presentation. Retrieved October 2013 from www.usgbc.org.

United States Green Building Council (USGBC) (2010b) *About USGBC*. Presentation. Retrieved October 2013 from www.usgbc.org.

United States Green Building Council (USGBC) (2010c) *Introduction to the LEED 2009 Credit Weighting Tool*. Retrieved October 2013 from www.usgbc.org.

United States Green Building Council (USGBC) (2014) *Three Billion Square Feet of Green Building Space LEED®-Certified*. Retrieved September 2014 from http://www.usgbc.org/articles/three- billion-square-feet-green-building-space-leed%C2%AE-certified.

Waddock, S. and Graves, S. (1997) The corporate social performance – financial performance link, *Strategic Management Journal* 18(4): 303–319.

Wiley, J.A., Benefield, J.D., and Johnson, K.A. (2008) Green design and the market for commercial office properties, *Journal of Real Estate Finance and Economics*, 41: 228–243.

World Green Building Council (2013) The business case for green buildings: a review of the costs and benefits for developers, investors and occupiers. Retrieved from http://www.worldgbc.org/ files/1513/6608/0674/Business_Case_For_Green_Building_Report_WEB_2013-04-11.pdf.

10 Post-occupancy and building operation issues

Sara J. Wilkinson

10.0 Introduction

Post-occupancy and building operation issues are a key concern. In the past, these tended to be taken into account only when the developer intended to hold the property. However, realisation has grown that, even when the developer plans to sell the development, many astute investors and buyers are well aware of the need to consider building performance especially with regard to energy performance and occupier satisfaction. Consequently more attention is directed to this aspect now. A development which does not perform efficiently or does not meet market expectations will be harder to sell, harder to lease and will depreciate in value at a faster rate than other competing developments (Ellison *et al.* 2007; Lorenz and Lutzendorf 2008). Concurrent with completion is the commissioning of the development.

Commissioning the building is extremely important in sustainable property development; often where rating tools are used. Commissioning forms part of the assessment of a property's sustainability score, so proof is required of performance. The purpose of commissioning is to ensure that the development functions as intended by the design team (Kibert 2013). It is imperative that all services are properly commissioned. Also user studies can be undertaken to evaluate occupants' satisfaction with the building and/or the workplace. For example, as a result of commissioning or surveying users, 'tweaking' of services can result in significant reductions in energy consumption. Furthermore, over the course of time, building users' requirements and technologies and sometimes regulations change; as a result, the original levels of performance of the building may also change. After commissioning, the property is occupied and with the knowledge that occupier satisfaction is an important component of building sustainability, the role of the facility management team, where there is one, is to ensure that property is maintained and adapted to meet changing user needs. This is critical as our collective knowledge and understanding of what sustainability in the built environment is evolves and changes over time. It is also critical given that a significant body of literature points to the failure of buildings in many cases to perform in accordance with design expectations (Bordass *et al.* 2004; Leaman *et al.* 2010; Menezes *et al.* 2012). This chapter sets out the key issues to consider with regard to occupation and operational issues across key land uses for the reader to note.

10.1 Stakeholders in performance

There are three key stakeholder groups who have an interest in building performance in a development. These are:

1   owner-occupiers,
2   tenants, and
3   investors.

It is also arguable that the community are stakeholders too as they can object to planning applications submitted by developers for all land use types; in some jurisdictions they may also be able to apply for consent. Commonly they are consulted. Owner-occupiers have a two-fold interest in the buildings they occupy. First they are interested in the running costs, general usability and satisfaction; second, many use the building as collateral for loans, or they may wish to sell in the future. Over time, its performance may be linked to realisable value as efficient buildings hold their value more so than inefficient ones, and this aspect appeals to owners. Within the domestic environment, in which many dwellings sit within owner-occupation, lenders are beginning in some countries to link the size of loans to an ability to service the debt taking account of not only income and lifestyle but of building cost outgoings.

Occupiers' interests reflect some of the same concerns as owners in that they require buildings which perform more efficiently and have lower operating costs, and most importantly, in the case of office buildings, which have healthy working environments for users (Smith and Pitt 2013). The features associated with sustainable developments which were found to correlate well with productivity were improved ventilation systems which increased air flow and reduced airborne infection, specification of less toxic materials, fixtures and fittings, reduced energy use and improved day-lighting, use of high quality energy efficient lighting to reduce glare, use of natural light to create a natural environment and improved maintenance to reduce build-up of microbial contamination (Kato *et al.* 2009). It should be noted that most research work to date related to post-occupancy has been focused on the office sector and some on residential and educational/health service buildings.

In the past, when long leases were far more common than they are now, investors had little interest in a building's ongoing performance. Once it was let, the responsibility passed to the tenant, often for 25 years. However, short leases have promoted a stronger requirement on investment owners to consider the ongoing attraction of their buildings or that re-letting may become difficult. Further where buildings are multi-let, as is the case with shopping centres and many office blocks, buildings which prove to be inefficient in terms of energy for example, can give rise to service charge disputes or arguments to reduce rents. In the case of a newly constructed building, the investment owner will be dissatisfied if there is a gap between design and actual performance.

10.2   Health and wellbeing in sustainable property developments

Research undertaken in Australia, the UK and US has shown that occupiers in what their authors describe as sustainable buildings, experienced better health and thus less absenteeism and greater productivity (Kato *et al.* 2009; Leaman and Bordass 1999 and 2007; Preiser 2001; Smith and Pitt 2013; RICS 2005; Wilkinson *et al.* 2011). A key negative health aspect in buildings is sick building syndrome (SBS) which emerged from research conducted in the 1980s (Tong and Leaman 1983). SBS flourishes in conditions where mechanical ventilation and air conditioning is specified and a lack of ventilation and a build-up of pollutants occurs. The symptoms can include eye, ear and nose irritation, dry skin, skin rash, fatigue, headaches and airway infections, cough, hoarseness, wheezing, itching, hyper-sensitivity, nausea and dizziness, which generally disappear on leaving the building (Smith and Pitt 2013). Thomas-Mobley *et al.* (2005) defined a Sick Building as one where 20 per cent of occupants experienced similar or acute symptoms. Volatile organic compounds (VOCs) are linked to off gassing of formaldehyde that can cause skin irritation in low concentrations and dry throats. However, in higher concentrations there is a link to cancer (Guo *et al.* 2004). For these reasons, therefore, specifications should ensure such materials are not used in sustainable developments. SBS should not be confused with building related illness (BRI) which is defined as an illness which is caused by the building; for example, Legionnaires' disease occurs when Legionella bacteria grow in cooling towers and then are distributed through the air conditioning system and infect building occupants. It is for these reasons also that indoor air quality features so prominently in environmental rating tools, as discussed in Chapter 9.

10.3   Productivity in commercial sustainable property developments

Empirical research studies have concluded that a range of building features is correlated to occupant productivity (Lee and Brand 2005; Smith and Pitt 2013). These features are:

- privacy;
- personal control;
- personalisation;
- interior planting;
- colour; and,
- windows and lighting.

Studies undertaken in the 1980s and 1990s found user complaints about lack of privacy (Duvall-Early and Benedict 1992; Goodrich 1982; Kupritz 1998) in open-plan offices which may appear to contradict much current research into Activity Based Workplaces (ABW) whereby users move from different workstations in an office environment in order to undertake different tasks. In ABW the design is predicated on findings that many offices are underutilised with occupants being offsite and so on. Therefore, to increase utilisation rates, the concept of having a dedicated workstation or desk is abandoned and users have a locker in which their personal belongings are stored and they occupy whichever workstation is available when they are in the building. It is predicted that less space is required to accommodate the same number of employees with AWB.

ABW design workspace, however, does not necessarily have to compromise on user privacy, as long as careful space planning is exercised. Studies which have examined productivity have concluded that reasonable levels of privacy are correlated with good productivity outcomes. Similarly perceptions of personal control over the immediate environment are also well correlated with productivity (Pinder *et al.* 2003). Here users value the ability to change ventilation, heating, cooling and lighting to suit their individual comfort levels. James' study on interior planting (2007) found that users liked environments with natural planting and that air quality was perceived to be better and productivity higher. Some plants do absorb airborne pollutants and can improve indoor air quality (IAQ) (Smith and Pitt 2011). The positive emotional state which arises from proximity to nature and plants is known as the biophilia effect (Wilkinson *et al.* 2013a). Sustainable property developments often use features such as internal and external green walls and green roofs, as well as atria, where natural planting is used to promote this proximity to nature and enhance occupant wellbeing and productivity (Smith and Pitt 2013).

One of the issues connected with any open-plan office arrangement concerns levels of noise. Various Scandinavian studies show that productivity may be reduced (see for example Jahncke *et al.* 2011) and sickness rates rise where open-plan offices lead to increased noise levels (Pejterson *et al.* 2011; Clausen *et al.* 2013). The only way to counter this is by having strict codes of behaviour and break out spaces, unless occupants are allowed to wear noise excluding headphones.

Colour has been found to influence the number of mistakes made by building occupants. In a study occupants were set tasks in white and red coloured environments and it was found that more mistakes occurred in the white environment though occupants preferred the white coloured workspace (Stone and English 1998). Although it is likely that these preferences may vary from sector to sector and country to country, it is nevertheless a factor that some property developers and their design and FM team will take into account. Furthermore colour may affect people's perception of thermal comfort; for example feeling cooler in blue coloured environments and in this way colour may indirectly affect occupant productivity and performance (Smith and Pitt 2103).

Access to windows is a strong preference for users though the Stone and Irvine study (1994) found no correlation between proximity to windows and higher performance and that some occupants complain of glare and solar heat gain when located close to windows. Goodrich (1982) claimed the benefit of being close to a window was the feeling of mental freedom, a chance to gain a new insight and lower feelings of stress and fatigue. These are factors which designers and facility managers should take into account when initially designing the development and for subsequent alterations and adaptations. These features are rewarded by inclusion into many of the environmental rating tools covered in Chapter 9.

When occupants of sustainable developments were surveyed, it was found that user perception differed from those in traditional non-sustainable developments (Smith and Pitt 2013). Baird and Oosterhof's study (2008) of properties in 11 countries concluded that users believed the sustainable buildings were healthier and that they were more productive as a result. Similar findings are noted in Leaman and Bordass' (2007) UK study of 177 buildings although it is contended that users are more tolerant of conditions within sustainable buildings (Smith and Pitt 2013). Singh *et al.* (2010) quantified this productivity gain in their study and claimed an additional 38.98 work hours per person was achieved per annum (Smith and Pitt 2013) which makes a good argument for sustainable commercial property developments.

10.4   Value and sustainable property developments

The link between sustainability and value has been explored in other chapters (notably Chapter 4) but is summarised here for the sake of completeness. An increasing number of theoretical and empirical studies have developed a range of links between sustainability (notably energy efficiency in use), building performance and differential values over time. Most of this evidence is concentrated on rental evidence of prime office buildings in US city centres but some studies have been undertaken elsewhere (Reed and Wilkinson 2005; GVA Grimley 2010; Jones Lang LaSalle 2008; Lorenz and Lutzendorf 2008; Fuerst and McAllister 2011a, 2011b; Newell *et al.* 2013). More comprehensive analyses of the value arguments undertaken by Sayce *et al.* 2010 and World Green Building Council 2013, point to value evidence being concentrated in sub-sectors such that drawing overall conclusions can be misleading. However, conclusive or inconclusive, the studies, collectively point to energy efficiency and sometimes other aspects of sustainability being on the agenda of tenants of prime buildings and their investor owners; particularly institutional investors. This acceptance broke one of the links in the purported 'circle of blame' theory posited by Cadman (2000) in a study which examined the perception that the property industry was not convinced about the need for sustainability. The study found a circle of blame existed between developers, investors, occupiers and constructors and was predicated on the premise that developers were not requesting sustainable developments as investors were not looking to buy sustainable developments. The investors' perspective was that occupiers were not demanding sustainable development, therefore there was no investment value in sustainability. The occupiers, on the other hand, found that even for those who wanted to occupy sustainable space there was no supply in the market. Finally the constructors were of the view that they could build sustainable property if requested. Since 2000, the market has evolved and more occupiers request sustainable developments. Constructors have more experience in building sustainable developments and developers are more inclined to request sustainable development because they know the market demand exists and that premiums can be achieved.

By the mid-2000s, Sayce *et al.* (2007) stated that European investors were seeing sustainable developments as a means of creating a positive environmental image, adopting a CSR approach to investment, reducing their risk by avoiding fiscal regulations and penalties and last, enhancing the capital value of their investments. In Australia, Ang and Wilkinson (2008) had found that Melbourne commercial property developers were convinced of the environmental and social arguments for sustainability but remained to be convinced of the economic arguments for sustainable property development. In summary, since the early 2000s, acceptance of the need for sustainability in property has gained momentum within all three key stakeholder groups in key UK, US, European and Asian markets.

10.5   Green leases

The Australian Department of Environment and Water Resources (DEWR) first introduced the green lease in 2006 (Kirsten in Cotgrave and Riley 2013) and this initiative has led to increased sustainability in commercial developments. In Australia, important tenants such as government departments will only lease and occupy property which meets minimum 4.5 star NABERS in respect of energy and water consumption (GBCA 2014). In 2007, this notion was taken up in the UK and, following work commissioned by the Investment Property Forum (2009), a set of green lease clauses was established. This idea evolved in to the Green Lease Toolkit first published in 2009 that set out a series of model clauses that could be included in standard commercial leases (see http://www.betterbuildingspartnership. co.uk/download/bbp-gltk-2013.pdf).

The goal of the Toolkit is to improve the environmental conditions at the property, for example, through energy-saving initiatives. There is flexibility as the green lease can be attached to an original lease in the form of a schedule or as a memorandum of understanding (MOU). However, take up in the UK is still limited. It was found (Sayce *et al.* 2009) that relationships between landlords and tenants often lacked the trust needed to promote greener leases. This reflects the findings of Hinnells *et al.* (2008) that the conventional relationship between landlord and tenant continues to largely neglect environmental considerations. Whilst it is thought significant progress has been made since then, with major investors/corporates in relation to new stock, the principles have still not penetrated throughout the markets.

Where green leases have been introduced, they may be categorised in three forms: light, mid and dark green. The light green lease is the least onerous of the three and typically includes clauses with regard to communications between landlord and tenant. It is not likely to be legally binding and is used to encourage a more sustainable approach to the operation and occupation of the property. The light green lease will consider any CSR objectives and/or business goals and may set goals for environmental improvements to the development. This form of lease is becoming more commonly adopted where the building sits within a large institutional holding. The mid-green leases include more conditions such as setting out some targets and environmental improvements to the development, however, there are unlikely to be penalties attached to the clauses for non-compliance of the targets. Best practice requires that an action plan should be included with a programme for execution of objectives, setting out the responsibilities of the landlord and tenant, along with deadlines and monitoring of actions. Finally the dark green lease can be designed as a lease, rather than a schedule or MOU, and is legally binding. In the dark green lease, there are penalties for non-compliance with targets, as such a high level of commitment is needed from both parties. For example, waste and energy targets may form part of the lease to improve ratings. Improved energy asset performance can lead to an increased EPC rating in the UK or the BEEC rating in Australia. Access to dispute resolution is a requisite of this lease because of the presence of the binding targets and penalties.

The typical clauses found in light, mid and dark green leases, as set out in the Toolkit, include:

1   duties of the landlord and tenant regarding the use of the property and landlord's improvements;
2   rent review including energy efficiency measures;
3   obligations for assigning and subletting so that assignees or subtenants will comply with landlord's environmental policy;
4   duties on tenant fit-out and alterations including works to meet energy efficiency goals and standards;
5   adjustments, provision for service charges or penalties for tenants who have not met specified targets;
6   landlord's obligations to maintain the property in good working order;
7   building management provisions;
8   waste and recycling targets;
9   green transport policy;
10 cleaning provision.

Before committing to a green lease, both parties need to consider the implications of implementation for the development. Some clauses will not suit some developments, for example city centre office developments are unlikely to offer large amounts of on-site parking, whereas in out-of-town office developments no public transport system may exist, and a different approach to transport is necessary. The benefits to landlords or owners of green leases are shown in Table 10.1. For the tenant the benefits are shown in Table 10.2.

Given their recent introduction into the market, there are some concerns with regard to costs associated with green leases for both parties. For example, some perceive that the restrictive clauses may impact on marketability for the tenant and reduction in rental value of the landlord (Sayce *et al.* 2009). Another perception is that the investment risk profile is

Table 10.1 Benefits to landlords or owners of green leases

Better control over environmental management which is likely to enhance energy efficiency.
Clearer definition of environmental liabilities with costs and duties outlined.
Reduced environmental risk, as the landlord is aware of the way the tenant will use the property.
Improved building performance and ratings.
Improved landlord and tenant communication offering benefits to both parties.
Increased tenant satisfaction; by working together the quality of the working environment can improve.

Source: Sayce et al. (2009)

Table 10.2 Benefits to tenants of green leases

Potential flexibility at lease renewal stage and an ability to negotiate on covenants of value to tenants. For instance restrictive user covenants may be traded against improved environmental covenants.
More control over works programmes, with greater awareness of what works are needed and when.
Increased communication with the landlord.
Greater opportunities to discuss lease issues.
Enhanced CSR and image which can appeal to both parties.
Recognition for environmental improvements which links to enhanced environmental performance of workplace and corporate image.

Source: Sayce et al. (2009)

increased due to the restrictions in the lease and a lack of understanding of green liability. Other costs include higher rents due to the improved standards in the development, though this may be offset by lower services charges. Though there is substantial evidence currently of these costs the possibility is an important factor for landlords and tenants (Kirsten in Cotgrave and Riley 2013). As more landlords and tenants gain direct experience of green leases over time, the issues may be resolved and the concerns will diminish. With carbon reduction targets set by urban authorities around the world, initiatives are being established with a view to assisting owners and occupiers to lower building related carbon emissions (Wilkinson 2013b). However, green leases should go beyond the notion of carbon reduction and provide a framework for a constructive dialogue between the stakeholders to improve the ongoing management of the building.

10.6 Occupation and performance – commissioning

It has been the case that most carbon emissions are associated with the operational phase of the building life cycle through heating, ventilation, lighting and cooling (Meir et al. 2009; Wilkinson 2013a). With the slow advent of technologies which allow for buildings (if properly managed) to be carbon neutral in use, the emphasis is beginning slowly to shift to the amounts of embodied carbon within properties. However, it remains that currently most developments have their largest carbon emission impact in use. One way of managing and reducing that impact is through good commissioning of the building. Commissioning needs to be considered from the initial stages of development to provide a means of checking that the building design is performing. The commissioning process is undertaken by an independent party who tests that the services installations are working as designed, and if necessary, modifications are made to ensure the services are running to optimum levels.

The energy systems design is reviewed at this stage, along with the creation of a building management system and manual, so that the occupiers understand how to operate the building. These building management systems and manuals are computerised and can be linked to the BIM (Building Information Modelling) which is designed to make subsequent management of the building more efficient. Typically the services are rechecked and retested after ten months of operations to ascertain whether any further adjustments are needed, of course this can also coincide with the 12-month building defects liability period for mechanical and electrical services established under the building contract. Importantly it is this process of checking and testing that enables claims for sustainability to be validated (Kibert 2013).

With the adoption of sustainability rating tools, commissioning is even more important, so much so that a new profession of commissioning agents (US terminology) has evolved to meet market needs. Although commissioning adds additional costs to the development, it provides a product in which the market can feel confident and which may ultimately be reflected in slower rates of building obsolescence. According to Kibert (2013), whole building commissioning costs approximately 0.5 per cent to 1.5 per cent of the whole building cost, whereas commissioning of heating, ventilation and air conditioning (HVAC) and control systems costs around 1.5 per cent to 2.5 per cent of the mechanical systems costs. Commissioning of the electrical systems costs approximately 1.0 per cent to 1.5 per cent of the electrical system cost. Typically 10 per cent energy savings are attributed to commissioning which is a considerable amount over a building life cycle. Therefore developers who occupy, and for incoming tenants, sustainable property developments which are commissioned are attractive.

Other associated benefits include lower maintenance costs through the specification of more durable materials in the construction. For instance, fluorescent lighting systems with long-life 10,000 hour life cycles as an alternative to incandescent bulbs with 1,000 hour lives lower maintenance requirements. The specification of LED lighting with 50,000 hour life cycles offers even greater reductions. Other examples are the specification of long-life polished concrete floor finishes compared to carpeted finishes which require cleaning and replacement every 15 years or so. Low emission paints are another example of a more durable more sustainable product which reduces building maintenance liability. Some potential owners and tenants can see the benefits of lower life cycle costs and are willing to pay a premium in purchase costs or rental levels to offset these maintenance related savings.

Many buildings are still constructed with HVAC systems. Not only are these expensive both to install and commission, good design may well obviate their use by use of displacement ventilation combined with renewable energy sources, such as photovoltaics. Further there is now a body of developing knowledge which shows that air-conditioned offices are among those which are most expensive and difficult to retrofit for energy efficiency; this in turn can lead to faster obsolescence (Green Construction Board 2014).

Aligned to lower maintenance is the notion of repair-ability, that is the selection of products and components which are easily repaired or replaced. For example, in the design the specification of carpet tiles rather than carpet, in theory allows for easy replacement of worn or damaged tiles. However, in reality, it is sometimes the case that the tile design is no longer available or that the colour match is uneven where tiles have faded over time. Other costs which can be reduced for the occupation phase of a development include:

1   Designing with areas for recycling to reduce waste disposal costs.
2   Sustainable landscaping which reduces the need for irrigation, insecticides, herbicides and fertilisers.
3   Designing natural ventilation systems.
4   Using renewable energy sources.
5   Use of reuseable materials (wood, aluminium) and components (designing for reusable partitioning or deconstruction).
6   Designing in grey water systems.
7   Stormwater management systems which use wetlands in the place of sewers.

Gradually data is being gathered on the financial savings that can be achieved through the adoption of such specifications to present a more robust empirical case to developers and the design team.

10.7   Building Information Modelling (BIM)

BIM is a virtual colour representation of a building in three dimensions (3D) and is discussed in the context of the construction phase of development in Chapter 7. In the operational phase of the building life cycle, BIM has an increasingly important role, especially where sustainability is a concern. At completion a set of as built drawings are provided to the facility manager (FM).

The BIM model shows how the property was assembled and constructed and therefore for maintenance and repair it is a very useful tool for the FM and the team. Furthermore, because the data is provided in the BIM model the FM can source manufacturer's information about components from a computer rather than physically checking the building (Fennimore 2014). BIM can also act as a database of building information where the Construction Operations Building Information Exchange (COBie) is a standard which enables different equipment manufacturers to provide data about their products for inclusion into a BIM file. The BIM data is available for review to check for its ability to meet sustainability criteria and future maintenance needs. The AECOM practitioner survey of 2013 found that currently BIM is not fully embedded in the operational life cycle of developments but that this is likely to change over time (AECOM 2013) especially where its use is mandated, as will be the case for UK government commissioned buildings from 2015.

10.8   Life Cycle Analysis (LCA)

Life cycle analysis (LCA) is a method for assessing the environmental and resource impacts of products and materials or buildings over their life cycles and is also covered in Chapter 7. All energy, water and materials resources, as well as all emissions to air, water and land are measured over the life cycle. The life cycle can be either the construction or the operational phase. LCA is an important, comprehensive method of examining all impacts as opposed to an item's performance within a building. LCA is growing in significance as it facilitates the quantification of the environmental impact of buildings over their entire life cycle. Previously LCA was used to compare products and building assemblies which assisted decision making but did not cover the operational phase of the building life cycle.

Some sustainable building rating tools such as the German DGNB assess the environmental performance of the whole building including materials, construction, operation, demolition and disposal and transportation issues, and this allows comparisons to be drawn with other specifications, designs or buildings. This allows developers to consider a wide range of options before determining which is best suited to their purposes. The Green Star tool in Australia considers energy in terms of CO_2 equivalents rather than energy units so focusing on the impact of climate change. In LEED in the US, LCA is included as a pilot credit though it is not yet known whether this has become a permanent fixture of the next iteration of LEED. Where the development involves the partial retention of existing structures, LCA is a useful tool with which to examine and evaluate sustainability issues. In summary, LCA enables developers and their design team to evaluate different energy strategies over the entire life cycle.

10.9   Post-occupancy evaluation (POE)

Since the early 1980s, a body of research has grown around the topic of user satisfaction and post-occupancy evaluation (POE) (Preiser 2003; Preiser and Nasar 2007; Meir *et al.* 2009). The aim of this research is to determine the characteristics with which users are least, and most, satisfied with in their environments. POE is defined as 'examination of the effectiveness of human users of occupied design environments' (Zimring and Reizenstein, in Turpin-Brooks and Viccars 2006). Where possible, steps can be taken to address issues which impact on user satisfaction (Meir *et al.* 2009) and typically the criteria for judgement are the fulfilment of functional and occupant needs. With a growing awareness of sick building syndrome and building related illness and the negative impact on a developments capital and rental value, owners and developers have become very aware of the need to demonstrate to potential investors and occupiers that the building is healthy and meets user needs (Wilkinson and Reed 2008; Smith and Pitt 2013).

POE is now a formal part of best practice in architectural design, where the architect and design team ascertain feedback from the users on the building design, which originated in the 1960s (Turpin-Brooks and Viccars 2006). The POE is 'a platform for the systematic study of buildings once occupied, so that lessons may be learned that will improve their current condition and guide the design of future building' (Meir *et al.* 2009). The goal is to rate actual performance against design performance and to learn which aspects work well and those which are problematic so that in future designs mistakes are not repeated. Information is collected through a number of ways such as interviews, surveys, observations, photography and archival research (Kato *et al.* 2009).

Typically a POE will focus on nine areas which are health, safety and security being the most important, followed by function, efficiency and work flow and finally, psychological, social and cultural performance. POEs are categorised in to three types:

1   diagnostic
2   investigative, and;
3   indicative.

A diagnostic POE is the most detailed and in-depth and shares similarities with focused research on aspects such as ambient lighting and signage. A diagnostic POE will explain what remedial work is required to redress inadequacies in design and performance. The second type is called an investigative POE which is less detailed than the diagnostic type above. An indicative POE is the least onerous POE and the quickest to execute. It is often used to determine the scope of an investigative or diagnostic POE. The POE uses data drawn from quantitative and qualitative sources (Meir *et al.* 2009) which range from measurements and monitoring and this is where a computerised Building Management System (BMS) and/ or BIM is useful. Some issues which are monitored include air movement, air temperature, relative humidity, light intensity, noise levels, presence of pollutants and pathogens, volatile organic compounds (VOCs), gases such as carbon and carbon dioxide and electromagnetic fields and radiation (including radon gas). Qualitative methods include walk throughs and observations, user satisfaction questionnaire surveys, interviews and focus groups (Preiser 1999). Whichever approach is taken, effective POEs need to:

- avoid intruding on users' time and patience;
- provide value in terms of quality and content;
- be relevant to the situation;
- provide results which are easy to compare with other property developments;
- be reliable (that is if replicated similar results will be produced);
- address issues which relate to user needs, activities and goals (Turpin-Brooks and Viccars 2006).

POE can provide benefits in the short, medium and long term. In the short term, user feedback allows issues to be remedied, whereas in the medium term the lessons learned are fed-forward into the next development cycle. The long-term benefits lie in the creation of databases which facilitate the updating and upgrading and generation of best practice guides in planning, design and construction. There is a tangible benefit to developers who are committed to increasing standards in design and construction over time as their developments will be highly regarded in the market for quality and long-term performance (Meir *et al.* 2009). Developers can also evaluate the project on the basis of value for money invested. Those developers who are reluctant to undertake POE may be wary of finding out that the building is not performing at best; and is breaching legal requirements at worst.

As for developing property sustainably, Smith and Pitt (2013) stated property development and construction involves the creation of waste, energy use, recycling and reuse of materials, pollution and biodiversity; the environmental impact on society. Socially, the impact of property development lies in the way society uses the developments which affects peoples' lives and work (Turpin-Brooks and Viccars 2006; Smith and Pitt 2013). The third sustainability impact is economic and the property development industry contributes here by creating employment and where commercial development is concerned, creates workplaces where economically sustainable growth can occur and socially responsible investment can be made (Smith and Pitt 2013). The arguments for sustainability and POE are strong, however, Meir *et al.* (2009) note the potential conflict of interests with regards to sustainability where POE is concerned. The conflict arises with the desire to lower carbon emissions and decrease energy use which has to be balanced with user comfort. As environmental targets increase, so does the challenge of delivering the environmental targets and maintaining or enhancing user comfort levels. Developers need to be aware and mindful of this issue. As far as the other stakeholders are concerned, POE can help the FM in reducing energy use and maintenance costs. Investors and potential users can see through the POE whether a building is affected by sick building syndrome (SBS) or building related illness (BRI) which might impact on occupant health and absenteeism or productivity (Smith and Pitt 2013). Although each stakeholder will have a different perspective in the POE, each finds value. It is not always undertaken and where it is, as discussed above, it may reveal significant issues in terms of a performance gap.

10.10 Sustainable property management

The responsibility for managing the development on a day-to-day basis often rests with the property manager (PM) or facility manager (FM). However, in reality, many building occupiers do not have a management team. Where they are employed, the PM/FM is able to exert a considerable influence on the sustainability of a building and where undertaken, the POE is a useful tool during the first few years of occupation (Meir *et al.* 2009). Professionally qualified property and facility managers will have access to education as well as the latest developments and innovations with regard to sustainability during the building life cycle. Ideally, the property manager will be committed to implementing and applying knowledge of best practices in sustainability. Many organisations have developed CSR strategies and policies through which sustainability goals are identified and targets set. The organisation then measures and benchmarks itself against these criteria, for example, the amount of materials which are recycled. The goal is to increase the targets over time to achieve ever greater levels of sustainability.

It has been said that overall the property sector and property managers have lagged behind other built environment professionals (Kirsten in Cotgrave and Riley 2013). However, there are patches of activity and engagement. As with most sectors, there are some organisations which embrace change and innovation; within this sector notably some institutional investors and major corporate and public sector owner-occupiers are striving to lead. Furthermore, the uptake and acceptance of sustainability varies from country to country and city to city. For example, Seattle has long held a reputation for embracing sustainable practices in legislation and policy making in the US compared to other American cities. Within markets too, some sectors will embrace sustainability more readily than others, especially where there is a perception of increased capital and/or rental values. Since the mid-2000s sustainability has been taken up in the commercial office market within some Australian cities, mostly Sydney and Melbourne and mostly in the city centres in the better quality stock (Ang and Wilkinson 2008; Reed and Wilkinson 2005). During this period, US and Australian studies have confirmed that more sustainable and energy efficient office developments may command higher rents, have lower vacancies and experience higher capital growth compared to non-sustainable counterparts (Newell *et al.* 2013), although this is not universal (World Green Building Council 2013).

What has driven this change? The main change agents are held to be legislation and fiscal measures, the political climate and agenda, the two-tier investment market and the risk reduction in the investment, CSR and improved sustainability education from early years to completion of professional qualifications (Kirsten in Cotgrave and Riley 2013).

During the late 2000s, a number of governments in developed countries enacted legislation to promote the uptake of sustainability in the built environment. For example, in the EU and UK a large number of directives and guidance on climate change was produced such as the UK Energy White Paper 2003, UK Building Regulations update in 2005 and 2010, UK Sustainable Development Strategy 'Securing the Future' 2005, EU Green Paper – UK Energy Review Report 2006, the Climate Change Act 2008, Energy Performance Certificates (EPCs) in Europe introduced in 2009, the Energy Act 2010, the Carbon Reduction Commitment Energy Efficiency Scheme 2010 and the Energy Act 2011 (Kirsten in Cotgrave and Riley 2013). Much legislation is focused on the construction phase of property development, and on compliance, payment and penalty or reducing energy consumption through the building rating systems such as BREEAM using EPCs, or Green Star using NABERS. However, of importance also has been the work of the United Nations Environment Programme Finance

Initiative, who track first leader behaviour (see http://www.unepfi.org/fileadmin/documents/responsible_property_investing_01.pdf) and the Global Reporting Initiative who have produced a Construction and Real Estate Supplement (https://www.globalreporting.org/resourcelibrary/CRESS-Summary-Document.pdf) to support better reporting on sustainability.

This period of increasing sustainability legislation and acceptance in the business community of its impact and contribution to environmental degradation coincided with economic growth and increasing prosperity especially among the wealthiest sectors in developed countries. Since the Global Financial Crisis in 2008 and the austerity measures which have been put in place as a means of managing the economic problems, there has been a drawing back from this position of acceptance of anthropocentric climate change and a number of measures have been reduced in scope or withdrawn. For example, the Abbott Liberal coalition government elected in 2013 in Australia rescinded the Carbon Tax legislated by the Gillard Labour government in 2012. Furthermore the Abbott government has, for the first time since 1931, removed the position of Minister for Science in the cabinet, thereby undermining the significance and importance of science in contemporary political debate in Australia (Lamberts and Grant 2013). The importance of climate change and sustainability is currently receding at the Federal level. However, in the UK although a Labour administration was replaced by a Conservative/Liberal coalition in 2010, there has been no reduction in the drive for greater building sustainability with the legislative and regulatory framework continuing to tighten.

10.11 Emerging trends in POE and principal contractor involvement

It is often contended that contractors perpetuate the mistakes they make in a building contract because they are not involved with the building following handover. Therefore they do not get the opportunity to learn how the building works in practice and build on this learning for subsequent building commissions. Where a process known as 'soft landing' is incorporated, in which the main contractor remains engaged until building performance meets the design specification levels, such learning deficits can be addressed. In a study on principal contractor involvement in POE in the UK construction industry, Williams *et al.* (2013) noted that involvement in POE is one of several areas where contractors can improve the knowledge and understanding that will deliver better buildings and better sustainable property developments. Using questionnaire surveys and semi-structured interviews Williams *et al.* (2013) asked stakeholders and found a lack of contractor involvement in POE as well as insufficient knowledge about how to conduct a POE. Given the changes in procurement options noted above and an increase in Design and Build whereby contractors take on responsibility for design of developments this situation needs to change. Some of the barriers that exist are a perception that POEs are time-consuming and that the information generated is hard to interpret and understand. Design facilities management professionals in particular should be interested in these findings and endeavour to bridge this gap in knowledge which will undoubtedly result in some buildings being less efficient than they would otherwise be.

10.12 Conclusions

This chapter has shown that astute developers globally are cognisant of the need to ensure developments have operational and life cycle sustainability included in both design and construction. Even when the developer intends to sell the development, some investors and occupiers are placing greater insistence on demonstrable levels of sustainability in both design and operation. Evidence from markets in Europe and North America and Australia supports this change and the link between energy efficient buildings and rents in some locations (Lorenz and Lutzendorf 2008; Fuerst and McAllister 2011a; Newell *et al.* 2013). It is important for developers to understand the key stakeholders influencing their markets and their drivers, be they legislators, investors or occupiers in order that they can determine which physical attributes to include in their developments. Furthermore, initiatives such as green leases offer another mechanism to recognise operational sustainability for tenants and landlords. The issue of commissioning is extremely important in sustainable property development to ensure the operational targets established in the design are realised, and where rating tools are used, that certification is possible. This process of commissioning and providing evidence for rating tool certification is made easier where developments have a BIM. During the building life cycle, LCA is a comprehensive method which can be used to assess environmental and resource impacts of products and materials and which is now incorporated into some rating tools. Another tool that can be applied in the operational phase of property development is POE which can assist with ensuring users are satisfied with their environments. There are varying degrees of POE which developers can employ depending on the development type, market and occupier. The POE can inform the strategies and policies adopted by the PM or FM during the building life cycle to ensure optimum operation in respect of sustainability measures. Developments which are designed and constructed with a view to the building life cycle and inevitable adaptation will embody the most sustainability of all.

References

AECOM (2013), *Blue Book 2013 – Collaboration: Making Cities Better*, Sydney: AECOM.

Ang, S.L. and Wilkinson, S.J. (2008) Property developers and sustainability: the Melbourne experience, *Journal of Property Management* 5(26) 331–343.

Baird, G. and Oosterhof, H. (2008) Users' perceptions of health in sustainable buildings worldwide, Healthy and Creative Facilities, *Proceeding of the CIB W70 Conference in Facilities Management*, Edinburgh 16–18 June, pp 649–656.

Bordass, W., Cohen, R., and Field, J. (2004) Energy efficiency in non-domestic buildings: closing the credibility gap, in *Proceedings of the International Conference on Improving Energy Efficiency in Commercial Buildings*, Frankfurt, Germany, 20–2. Retrieved from http:// www.usablebuildings. co.uk.

Cadman, D. (2000) The vicious circle of blame, *Upstream*. Retrieved 17 September 2006, from http:// www.upstreamstrategies.co.uk.

Clausen, T., Kristiansen, J., Hansen, J.V., Pejtersen, J.H., and Burr, H. (2013) Exposure to disturbing noise and risk of long-term sickness absence among office workers: a prospective analysis of register-based outcomes, *International Archives of Occupational and Environmental Health* 86(7): 729–734.

Cotgrave, A. and Riley, M. (eds) (2013) *Total Sustainability in the Built Environment*, Basingstoke: Palgrave Macmillan.

Duvall-Early, K. and Benedict, J. (1992) The relationship between privacy and different components of job satisfaction, *Environment and Behaviour* 24(5): 670–679.

Ellison, L., Sayce, S., and Smith, J. (2007) Socially responsible property investment: quantifying the relationship between sustainability and investment property worth, *Journal of Property Research* 24(3): 191–219.

Fennimore., J. (2014) *Sustainable Facility Management: Operational Strategies for Today*, Boston, MA: Pearson.

Finch, E. (1999) Empathetic design and post-occupancy evaluation, *Facilities* 17(11): 421–435.

FTSE (2013) FTSE4 good index series. Retrieved 31 October 201 from http://www.ftse.com/Indices/FTSE4Good_Index_Series/index.jsp.

Fuerst, F. and McAllister, P. (2011a) Green noise or green value? Measuring the effects of environmental certification on office values, *Real Estate Economics* 39(1): 45–69.

Fuerst, F. and McAllister, P. (2011b) Eco-labelling in commercial office markets: do LEED and energy Star offices obtain multiple premiums, *Ecological Economics* 70(6): 1220–1230.

GBCA (Green Building Council of Australia) (2014) Leadership by example. Energy efficiency in government operations. Retrieved 9 January 2014 from http://www.gbca.org.au/advocacy/federal/2--leadership-by-example/1938.htm.

Goodrich, R. (1982) The perceived office: the office environment as experienced by its users, in J. Wineman (ed.), *Behavioural Issues in Office Design*, New York: Van Nostrand Reinhold, pp. 109–133.

Green Construction Board (2014) *Mapping the Impacts of Minimum Energy Efficiency Standards for Commercial Real Estate Executive Summary Report*. Retrieved from http://www.greenconstructionboard.org/images/stories/Valuation_and_Demand/GCB630%20Executive%20Summary.pdf.

Guo, H., Lee, S.C., Chan, L.Y., and Li, W.M. (2004) Risk assessment of exposure to volatile organic compounds in different indoor environments, *Environmental Research* 94(1): pp. 57–66.

GVA Grimley (2010) *From Green to Gold 2010 – Key Findings*, London: GVA Grimley.

Halliday, S. (2008) *Sustainable construction*, Oxford: Butterworth Heinemann.

Hinnells, M., Bright, S., Langley, A., Woodford, L., Schiellerup, P., and Bosteels, T. (2008) The greening of commercial leases, *Journal of Property Investment & Finance* 26(6): 541–551.

Investment Property Forum (2009) *Greening Leases: The Landlord and Tenant Relationship as a Driver of Sustainability. A Report Undertaken by Kingston University*, London: IPF.

Jahncke, H., Hygge, S., Halin, N., Green, A.M., and Dimberg, K. (2011) Open-plan office noise: cognitive performance and restoration, *Journal of Environmental Psychology* 31(4): 373–382.

James, P. (2007) Indoor green space influences your health, paper presented at the Senses, Brain and Space Workshop, University of Salford, UK, 8–9 March. Retrieved 13 June 2012 from www.rgc.salford.ac.uk/peterbarratt/p?s=10&pid=6.

Jones Lang LaSalle (2008) *Global Trends in Sustainable Real Estate: An Occupier's Perspective*, London: JLL.

Kato, H., Too, L., and Rask, A. (2009) Occupier perceptions of green workplace environment: the Australian experience, *Journal of Corporate Real Estate* 11(1): 183–195.

Kibert, C.J. (2013) *Sustainable Construction. Green Building Design and Delivery*, third edn, Hoboken, NJ: Wiley.

Kupritz, V. (1998) Privacy in the workplace: the impact of building design, *Journal of Environmental Pyschology* 18(4): 341–356.

Lamberts, R. and Grant, W.J. (2013) An invisible, odourless, weightless science minister for Australia. Retrieved 9 January 2014 from https://theconversation.com/an-invisible-odourless-weightless-science-minister-for-australia-18250.

Leaman, A. and Bordass, B. (1999) Productivity in buildings: the killer variables, *Building Research & Information* 27: pp 4–19.

Leaman, A. and Bordass, B. (2007) Are users more tolerant of green buildings?, *Building Research & Information* 35(6): 662–673.

Leaman, A., Stevenson, F., and Bordass, B. (2010) Building evaluation: practice and principles, *Building Research & Information* 38(5): 564–577.

Lee, S.Y., and Brand, J.L. (2005) Effects of control over office workspace on perceptions of the work environment and work outcomes, *Journal of Environmental Psychology* 25(3): 23.

Lorenz, D. and Lutzendorf, T. (2008) Sustainability in property valuation: theory and practice, *Journal of Property Investment & Finance* 26(6): 482–521.

Meir, I.A., Garb, Y., Jiao, D., and Cicelsky, A. (2009) Post occupancy evaluation: an inevitable step toward to sustainability, *Advances in Building Energy Research* 3: 189–220.

Menezes, A.C., Cripps, A., Bouchlaghem, D., and Buswell, R. (2012) Predicted vs. actual energy performance of non-domestic buildings: using post-occupancy evaluation data to reduce the performance gap, *Applied Energy* 97: 355–364.

Newell, G., MacFarlane, J., and Kok, N. (2013) *Building Better Returns. A Study of the Financial Performance of Green Office Buildings in Australia. API and PFA.* Retrieved 3 January 2014 from www.api.org.au/assets/media_library/000/000/219/original.pdf.

Pejtersen, J.H., Feveile, H., Christensen, K.B., and Burr, H. (2011) Sickness absence associated with shared and open-plan offices – a national cross sectional questionnaire survey, *Scandinavian Journal of Work, Environment & Health*, 86(7): 376–382.

Pinder, J., Price, I., Wilkinson, S.J., Demack, S. (2003) A method for evaluating workplace utility, *Journal of Property Management* 21(4): 218–229.

Preiser, W. (1999) Feedback, feed forward and control: post-occupancy evaluation to the rescue, *Building Research & Information* 29(6): 456.

Preiser, W. (2001) The evolution of post occupancy evaluation: toward building performance and universal design evaluation, in Federal Facilities Council (ed.), *Learning from our Buildings*, Washington, DC: National Academy Press, pp. 9–22.

Preiser, W. (2003) *Improving Building Performance*, Washington, DC: National Council of Architectural Registration Boards, pp. 1–26.

Preiser, W. and Nasar, J. (2007) Assessing building performance: its evolution from post occupancy evaluation, *Archinet IJAR International Journal of Architectural Research* 2(1): 84-99.

Reed, R.G. and Wilkinson, S.J. (2005) The increasing importance of sustainability for building ownership, *Journal of Corporate Real Estate* 4(7): 339–350.

Reed, R. and Wilkinson, S. (2007) Office buildings and the environment – the increasing role of facility managers. Facilities Management Association of Australia (FMA) Conference, May 2007, Sydney.

RICS (2005) *Green Value: Green Buildings, Growing Asset*, London: RICS. Retrieved from www.rics.org/greenvalue.

RICS Professional Information, UK (2012) IP 32/2012. Methodology to calculate embodied carbon of materials, first edn information paper. Retrieved 15 January 2014 from www.rics.org/standards.

RICS Professional Information, UK (2013) GN 105/2013. Sustainability: improving performance in existing buildings, first edn guidance note. Retrieved 25 January from www.rics.org/standards.

Sawyer, L., de Wilde, P., and Turpin-Brooks, S. (2006) Energy performance and occupancy satisfaction. A comparison of two closely related buildings, *Facilities* 26(13/14): 542–551.

Sayce, S., Ellison, L., and Parnell, P. (2007) Understanding investment drivers for UK sustainable property, *Building Research & Information* 35(6): 629–643.

Sayce, S., Sundberg, A., Parnell, P., and Cowling, E. (2009) Greening leases: do tenants in the United Kingdom want green leases and quest, *Journal of Retail & Leisure Property* 8(4): 273–284.

Sayce, S., Sundberg, A., and Clements, B. (2010) Is sustainability reflected in commercial property prices? An analysis of the evidence base, London: RICS Research. Retrieved from http://www.planbatimentdurable.fr/IMG/pdf/Sayce-S-15747.pdf.

Singh, A., Syal, M., Grady, S.C., and Korkmaz, S. (2010) Effects of green building on employee health and productivity, *American Journal of Public Health* 100(9): 1665–1668.

Smith, A. and Pitt, M. (2011) Healthy workplaces: plantscaping for indoor environment quality, *Facilities* 29(3/4): 169–187.

Smith, A. and Pitt, M. (2013) Sustainable workplaces and building user comfort and satisfaction, *Journal of Corporate Real Estate* 13(3): 144–156.

Smith, J., O'Keefe, N., Georgiou, J., and Love, P.E.D. (2004) Procurement of construction facilities: a case study of design management within a design and construct organisation, *Facilities* 2(1): 22–34.

Stone, N.J. and Irvine, J.M. (1994) Direct or indirect window access, task type, and performance, *Journal of Environmental Psychology* 14(1): 57–63.

Stone, N. J. & English, A. J. (1998) Task type, posters, and workspace color on mood, satisfaction, and performance, *Journal of Environmental Psychology* 18(2): 175.

Thomas-Mobley, L., Roper, K.O., and Oberle, R. (2005) A proactive assessment of sick building syndrome, *Facilities* 23(1/2): 6–15.

Tong, D. and Leaman, A. (1983) Sick Building Syndrome: strategies and tactics for managers, *Facilities* 11(4): 19–23.

Turpin-Brooks, S. and Viccars, G. (2006) The development of robust methods of post occupancy evaluation, *Facilities* 24(5/6): 177–196.

UK Public Spending (2013). Public spending totals. Retrieved 31 October from http://www.ukpublicspending.co.uk/total.

US Government Spending (2013) Government spending in the US. Retrieved 31 October from http://www.usgovernmentspending.com/total_spending_2014USbn.

Warren, C.M.J. and Huston, S. (2011) Promoting energy efficiency in public sector commercial buildings in Australia, in *Proceedings of RICS Construction and Property Conference*. COBRA: Construction and Building Research Conference, Salford, UK, 12–13 September 2011, pp. 128–134.

Wilkinson, S.J. (2013a) Are sustainable building retrofits delivering sustainable outcomes? *Pacific Rim Property Research Journal* 19(2) 211–222.

Wilkinson, S.J. (2013b) The preliminary assessment of adaptation potential in existing office buildings. *International Journal of Strategic Property Management* 17(4) 77–87.

Wilkinson, S.J. and Reed, R. (2008) *Property Development*, fifth edn, London: Taylor and Francis.

Wilkinson S.J., Reed, R., and Jailani J. (2011) Tenant satisfaction in sustainable buildings. Pacific Rim Real Estate Conference, 16–19 January, Gold Coast, Australia.

Wilkinson, S.J., Ghosh, S., and Page, L. (2013a) Options for green roof retrofit and urban food production in the Sydney CBD, RICS COBRA New Delhi,10–12 September 2013. Retrieved from www.rics.org.

Wilkinson, S.J., Van Der Kallen, P., and Leong Phui, K. (2013b) The relationship between occupation of green buildings, and pro-environmental behaviour and beliefs, *Journal of Sustainable Real Estate* 5(1): 1–22.

Williams, T., Bouchlaghern, D., and Loveday D. (2012) Principal contractor involvement in post-occupancy evaluation in the UK construction industry, *Facilities* 30(12): 39–55.

Williams, N.S.G., Rayner, J.P., and Raynor, K.J (2013) Green roofs for a wide brown land: opportunities and barriers for rooftop greening in Australia, *Urban Forestry & Urban Greening* 9(3): 245–56.

World Green Building Council (2013) The business case for green buildings. Retrieved from http://www.worldgbc.org/files/1513/6608/0674/Business_Case_For_Green_Building_Report_WEB_2013-04-11.pdf.

Zou, K., Potangaroa, R., Wilkinson, S., and Rotimi, J.O.B. (2009) A project management prospective in achieving a sustainable supply chain for timber procurement, *International Journal of Managing Projects in Business* 2(3): 386–400.

11 New build or adaptation

Sara J. Wilkinson

11.0 Introduction

The real challenge in delivering more sustainable buildings is to address the existing stock of buildings (Newton and Bai 2008; Carbon Trust 2009). With only 1–2 per cent added to the total building stock annually in developed countries, even in periods of high activity, most of the stock that will be in existence in 2050 is already here (Kelly 2010), by which time, within the EU region, there is a firm legal target to reduce carbon emissions by 80 per cent from 1990 levels. Furthermore most of that existing stock has been designed and constructed within regulatory regimes that did not place matters such as energy in use or water consumption high on the agenda. This chapter explores the critical factors required for informed decision-making as to whether redevelopment or adaptation/refurbishment is the better solution in order to promote sustainability. The drivers for and against new build and adaptation are examined in the context of sustainability and the factors that may determine the decision are discussed. The different types of adaptation both within and across land uses are explained. Finally the chapter uses case study exemplars to demonstrate current practice. Environmental sustainability for commercial buildings is now legislated in the building codes or regulations in most jurisdictions worldwide, with minimum standards for energy efficiency applied to new build and some adaptation projects. However, such codes are constantly being upgraded, such that a building constructed only around five years ago may already be non-compliant by current code standards, unless a conscious decision was taken originally to go 'beyond compliance'.

To give an idea of the scale of the contribution of this stock, in 2005–2006 commercial buildings were responsible for 53 per cent of all greenhouse gas emissions in the Melbourne CBD. This figure can be reduced when developing property sustainably. Sustainable development can be viewed as a process; and Harding (2005) noted that sustainable development is 'the path or framework to achieve sustainability'. To Harding sustainable property development is seen as a process, others take the view that unless a property is designed such that it encourages good behaviour, it is not sustainable. The focus of this chapter is sustainable property development in the built environment in the broader sense and in particular on sustainable property development in cities of developed countries. Within this definition consideration is given to the influence that the design of the property has upon subsequent use: a well-designed property that encompasses sustainability features, should make it easier for the occupier to operate it in a sustainable way.

11.1   Defining adaptation

The term adaptation has been broadly interpreted and defined (Mansfield 2002; Douglas 2006; Bullen 2007) and derives from the Latin *ad* (to) *aptare* (to fit). Typically, the definitions refer to 'change of use', maximum 'retention' of the original structure and fabric of a building, as well as extending the 'useful life' of a property (Ball 2002; Douglas 2006; Bullen 2007). Frequently, terms such as retrofit, renovation, adaptive reuse, refurbishment, remodelling, reinstatement, retrofitting, conversion, rehabilitation, re-lifing, modernisation, restoration and recycling of buildings are used or incorporated into definitions. These terms have slightly different meanings, for example 'refurbishment' comes from the word refurbish which means to 're' do again and 'furbish' polish or rub up. On the other hand, 'conversion' literally means to convert or change from one use to another for example a barn converted to a residential property. Some 30 years ago, Markus (1979) noted the terms existed in 'unhappy confusion'; it is an unhappy confusion that still exists today. The implications of what is proposed may or may not, have both environmental and social consequences, as well as economic ones; often they also have legislative or regulatory implications. For example a change of use may, or may not, require specific consents; significant building alterations almost certainly will require permission but remodelling, renovation and restoration may not; and if there is no regulatory control the energy implications may be large but unrecognised.

Building adaptation can occur 'within use' and 'across use'; that is, an office can undergo adaptation and still be used as an office (i.e. within use adaptation) or it may change use to residential and be an example of 'across use' adaptation (Ellison *et al.* 2007). Thus across use adaptation is synonymous with conversion (Wilkinson 2011). Adaptation of existing buildings therefore can encompass some or all of the terms noted above (Wilkinson 2011). Furthermore there are various degrees of adaptation from minor to major. This chapter adopts a broad definition that includes all forms of building adaptation, with the exception of minor day-to-day repair and maintenance work. The definition of building adaptation is:

> any work to a building over and above maintenance to change its capacity, function or performance, in other words, any intervention to adjust, reuse, or upgrade a building to suit new conditions or requirements.
>
> (Douglas 2006: 4)

A definition for sustainable building adaptation is:

> any work to a building over and above maintenance to change its capacity, function or performance, in other words, any intervention to adjust, reuse, or upgrade a building to suit new conditions or requirements which reduces its ecological footprint and or environmental operating footprint.
>
> (Wilkinson 2013)

Even this definition is problematic, in that any such adaptation work will have energy, carbon and materials use costs, and such 'embodied' carbon should be accounted for when taking the decision to undertake capital adaptation works. Further, the definition does not take into account any implications that may arise in relation to health and well-being, or external factors such as changes in transport, pattern of land use and dominance patterns within an urban area. As an example of this, within the UK, there has been a recent tendency to see offices being converted to flats resulting in less local employment opportunities and a shift in social character as the residential stock shifts from houses towards apartment development, with community impact. Similarly whole neighbourhoods of older houses have been converted into flats, which have had a profound effect on the social mix, sometimes positively, and sometimes negatively.

11.2 Building life cycle theory

The concept of any life cycle is that there is a beginning, middle and an end; all living organisms experience life cycles of varying lengths and buildings are the same in this respect, except that, unlike most living organisms, the ability to adapt can prolong the cycle almost indefinitely. Further it is not normally a building's physical failure which leads to its demolition, but economic, social and environmental factors, which collectively lead to value depreciation and a decision to redevelop (for a full discussion on depreciation see Baum 1991).

In terms of predicting building life cycle, the theory is applied to costs, and in relation particularly to commercial developments that are to be held long-term, allows practitioners to evaluate the total costs associated with building construction and operation over an expected life cycle term. The relationship between the total costs for a building over time examines three factors: structure, services and the space plan (i.e. furniture and fit-out). Brand (1994) identified seven layers of change over time; to the site, structure, skin (building envelope), services, space plan (interior layout), stuff (furniture and equipment) and souls (people). There is a sliding scale in terms of the time frames before change occurs. Whilst the site is normally permanent[1], the structure lasts from 30–300 years, the skin 20 plus years, services 7–20 years, the space plan five to seven years, stuff less than three years and the souls change daily (Brand 1994). This makes any reliance on predictions as at best difficult, at worst, meaningless.

Estimates of the time changes vary between countries and over time because of varying conditions and expectations in different property markets and due to structural design. For example, in the Norwegian office market, commercial building structures are estimated to have a typical life cycle of 50 years (Arge 2005), whereas in the UK, many of the estimates of the Building Research Establishment are based on a nominal 60 year life, although evidence would show that in high value areas, such as central London, for offices, this can reduce to 20–30 years. A study by Crosby *et al.* (2012) found that average deprecation rates over the period 1993–2009 were 0.8 per cent p.a. for offices, 0.5 per cent for industrials and 0.3 per cent for standard shops (but not shopping centres). Offices have tended to be the most susceptible to value depreciation of the 'bulk' asset classes due to changes in working patterns, including open plan and the introduction of social breakout spaces and, hence, design considerations. Further changes in IT requirements have placed design requirements in terms of the services required for them.

Typically, within the structural timeframe, the building's services will need to be replaced and upgraded (due to improvements in technology and increases in user expectations) three times over the typical 60 year-timespan. However, for offices, the space plan element will be changed typically every five to seven years, though often less, particularly in markets where occupation periods may be less. For example, in the UK, whereas 20 years ago commercial leases were commonly up to 25 years in duration, they fell to less than ten years during the early 2000s (IPD, 2012) and most recently have fallen to below five years (BPF 2013). Shorter leases do not necessarily lead to tenants leaving at the end of the term, though it is estimated that upon lease expiry many tenants will vacate (Strutt and Parker 2011).

Whenever tenant turnover takes place there is increased potential for significant waste as new tenants refit premises (Forsythe and Wilkinson 2015). It is often stated that owner occupier developers will pay higher construction costs to deliver lower operational and maintenance costs during the whole life cycle, whereas developers who are committed to sell upon completion have no such incentive, although long-term investment owners are increasingly demanding that buildings that they purchase are designed to maintain tenant appeal over time. Furthermore studies found owner-occupied property as easier to adapt on account of more flexible design and better build quality (Arge 2005).

Initially, total building costs are proportioned fairly evenly with the structure tending to cost slightly more than the services and space plan. However, this equation does not hold true across all building types and economic conditions and specifications. A logistics 'shed' for example, will have few services and no space plan; in contrast a high specification city-centre air-conditioned office will tend to be expensive in terms of services provision. This represents the traditional view of buildings costs that takes account of only the initial costs and does not consider the ongoing or life cycle costs of buildings. However, over time, the expenditure on the services and the space plan mean that at the 50-year point the total costs are highest for the space plan followed by the services (Duffy and Henney in Brand 1997). The building structure costs are significantly lower at this point in time. Arge (2005) used the analogy of theatre to describe the notion that a building needs to have adaptability designed in so that it can be altered easily for future changes to the services and space plan factors. In theatres, buildings are required to adapt to the needs of current productions and over time theatres remain little changed, while the sets and arrangements change regularly to accommodate the plays (Arge 2005). The question arises; is this approach more sustainable? Sayce *et al.* (2004) argued that 'loose fit' is a key characteristic required of any building claiming to be sustainable so that it can accommodate both change within and across uses.

Change occurs within building life cycles and Douglas (2006) proposed a five-stage cycle, each having a distinct phase. The first stage was labelled 'birth' when a new activity is housed by the building and a new user is accommodated. Stage two is 'expansion' where new requirements are accommodated, new services are introduced and the internal layout is adapted. In addition, with this stage there is a strain placed on the building fabric, where possible extension may occur and changes in function or spatial performance may result. 'Maturity' is the classification stage three, where either uses continue to fit the building and periodic maintenance and minor adjustments are made or current needs exceed capacity and new space is taken elsewhere. Stage four is 'redundancy' due to changes in sources of power, societal cultural values, market needs, technology and or catchment areas: here the building is partially or totally obsolete, and may be partly or totally vacant. At this point, the property lacks social and economic sustainability. The building might be subject to vandalism, or it may be occupied by squatters. It may be mothballed or partially or totally demolished. The final stage is 'rebirth' or 'demolition' where thought will be given to reuse and the building restored, refurbished or demolished. At this point, the building can be made more sustainable or a new building may be provided after demolition. Consideration of embodied carbon or energy, embodied water and other environmental issues should be major decision factors for environmental sustainability here. This concept of life cycles is shown in Figure 11.1 where adaptation can take place at every stage after 'birth' (Douglas 2006). It should be noted that the level or type of adaptation can, and does, change according to the stage within the building life cycle. Minor adaptations initially give way to more major adaptations as time passes and the building meets the needs of users and the market to a lesser extent. It can be said there is a creeping environmental footprint over the life cycle.

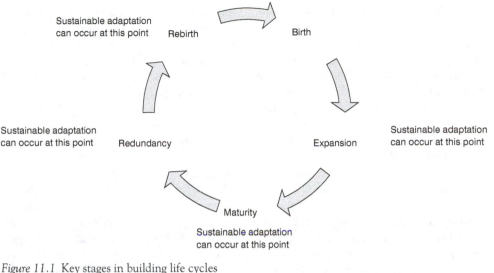

Figure 11.1 Key stages in building life cycles
Source: adapted from Douglas (2006)

Whilst these five points appear from the diagram (Figure 11.1) to be continuous and equally spaced, they are not; incremental changes appropriately positioned during the life cycle are capable of lengthening life significantly, if not indefinitely. Where interventions are appropriate and timely, possibly only through enhanced maintenance programmes, usability will be prolonged. Where maintenance does not take place, or the building suffers functional obsolescence, the life cycle will become truncated.

An interesting observation is that as governments around the world push ever harder with building codes to drive down energy and carbon use through construction, there is far less intervention during the maturity stage to encourage or mandate sustainable behaviours (Green Construction Board, 2015). Yet without interventions to encourage or mandate better behaviours, long-term carbon targets will be missed.

Figure 11.1, like most other depictions of the building life cycle, places emphasis on the *physical* points of change of a building and tends to give over-dominance on the construction/demolition/major refurbishment points. However, these tend to be spread over a long period of time and, the more sustainable the building, the longer the period until major physical interventions are required is likely to be. Certainly buildings with short life spans tend to be less sustainable in carbon terms as the carbon used in construction is amortised over shorter periods.

11.3 Conversion drivers

In conversion, the land and/or building use changes from one use to another. For example, industrial land use becomes residential land use or a redundant school building is converted to retail land use (Remøy and Wilkinson 2012). The drivers for conversion of offices to other uses such as housing are social, economic and environmental, but primarily economic, prompted by social and technological change. Put simply, where another use will yield a higher capital value, allowing for costs of achieving the change the incentive exists and, subject to consents and resolving any tenure issues such as leasehold arrangements, it is likely to happen. One social driver is the renewed appeal for city-centre living and planning policies that reinforce this interest (Heath 2001); another is the long-term oversupply in some cities of offices due to changes in employment patterns or simply that the original use is no longer economically tenable. Adaptation can deliver sustainable urban development policy goals of urban intensification, with the retention of embodied energy whilst encouraging the use of public transport. Furthermore, some authorities allow developers to obtain greater densities in their developments when identified sustainability measures are part of the development, for example, the provision of a green roof in the city of Toronto, Canada.

However, as argued above, changes of use can lead to social issues, such as the loss of local employment and the need for longer commutes. Indeed, part of the issue is that it has perhaps been too easy to argue that conversion of offices to residential is always the right answer in sustainability terms (Remøy and Wilkinson 2012). In the UK for example, planning policy changes brought in to counter high office and shop vacancy rates have allowed greater flexibility for just such changes, but have met resistance from many local authorities as they go against the nature of suburbs (Vaughan and Griffiths 2013). They argue that their town centres, which used to have a vibrant cross section of uses including office and retail are increasingly destined to be dormitories for the locations which have become 'top stack' to use Atkinson's nomenclature, placing additional pressures on transport systems to transfer people longer distances to centres of employment and degrading social communities and further degrading economic activity. Instead, they argue that better protection to ensure reuse will provide better economic and social stimulus to regeneration of their centres. This is acknowledged to be a difficult dilemma but does clearly illustrate that true sustainability is about far more than environmental issues. Indeed, within the UK it has triggered off a series of major reviews into how to retain town centre vitality in the face of such social and economic change (Findlay and Sparks 2014).

In developed countries, building adaptation is a vital part of sustainable urban development that allows a glimpse of the past with references to local history, whilst imparting character and identity to precincts (Department of Environment, Water, Heritage and Arts 2008). There are issues where cities face periods where obsolete buildings blight areas socially (Bryson 1997); recently this has happened on a large scale in Detroit in the US with the collapse of the car manufacturing industry. Proactive and innovative policies are required to regenerate the area socially, economically and environmentally. Adaptation can increase value. A Hong Kong study of the impact of refurbishment on high density residential property showed a 9.8 per cent increase in value compared to identical un-refurbished property (Chau et al. 2003). In Amsterdam, adaptation has been driven by surplus office stock where older buildings are vacated for new ones, and vacancy is concentrated in the older stock where obsolescence occurs. Sayce et al (2004) through a series of case study analyses found that the very fact that a building was located in a low value area could act as a 'protection' against demolition as the economics of development rendered redevelopment unviable; when conditions changed, the building could then find a 'new life'.

Obsolescence is perceived as a problem of economic and social decay; often it is triggered by technology change (for example, the introduction of computers changed social patterns and ways of working), or by infrastructure changes (for example, the construction of mass transit systems changes the viability of travel, both to work and for pleasure). Uncertainty and social insecurity are manifested as vandalism and graffiti, break-ins and illegal occupancy. Investors can spread the risk of obsolescence by building a diverse portfolio and only face the issue of depreciation when selling; however, owners of long-term vacant office buildings suffer a lack of income and the costs of maintaining and protecting the property. In some jurisdictions, they may also pay tax on vacant property (for example in the UK, business rates or council tax is levied on empty property); in some other jurisdictions, a land tax is payable based on a 'higher and best use' regardless of whether or not the land is developed and occupied. In both these cases, the aim is to stimulate the optimal use of a scarce resource (i.e. land).

High vacancy rates hit investors indirectly due to the negative influence on the market, although investors tend to see the problem as someone else's predicament (Remøy and van der Voordt 2007). The investment market is stratified: with new offices procured mostly by institutional investors who sell off older properties, where vacancy concentrates, to smaller or private investors. Such movement is an example of Atkinson's sinking stack theory in action (Langston 2007). Atkinson's sinking stack theory states that new stock occupies the top tier of the stack with higher occupancy while ageing less well-appointed stock gradually sinking to the bottom of the stack as its quality diminishes over time. In sustainability terms this can mean that properties that most need investment to bring them to a good standard of, for example energy efficiency, may be clustered in the hands of those least able to pay for improvement, or where such improvements, if made, will not yield financial return in terms of increased rental and/or capital values.

Office vacancy rates worldwide rose following the 2008 global financial crisis and this led the Dutch government, for example, to acknowledge that long-term vacancy is an issue in that property market. Whilst new office buildings increase the urban footprint, older properties remain vacant, occupying scarce land (Remøy 2010). Adaptation of existing offices is a sustainable way of addressing vacancy; either through residential conversion or within use adaptation. There is a twofold benefit with office conversions that lower vacancy rates and enhance the sustainability of the built environment by reducing embodied energy in converted residential stock.

Where commercial building vacancy rates are low, however, say around 6–8 per cent (Colliers International 2010a, b; Knight Frank 2011), the driver for adaptation is to increase returns. Developers and their advisors carefully examine market forecasts looking for increases in net effective rental levels in the short to medium term and for good overall tenant demand (Knight Frank 2011). The conversion of offices into other land uses is unlikely to occur on a large scale in this market situation. However, buildings that do not suit the needs of current and future office users may be converted if the new use increases the returns (Wilkinson 2012a). Table 11.1 summarises the multiple environmental, social and economic drivers for conversion adaptations.

11.4   Decision-making in sustainable property development

Building adaptation decision-making is complex (Blakstad 2001; Douglas 2006). First, there are many stakeholders involved, each representing a different perspective (see Chapter 2). Decision-makers are investors, producers, developers, regulators, occupants/users and marketeers (Kincaid 2002). In these areas, it is also important not to underestimate the role played by planning regulators and fiscal measures which can be powerful drivers. Another layer of complexity previously described is that stakeholders make decisions at different stages in the process and each has different degrees of influence. Generally decisions made at the early stages of the process have an ongoing impact throughout the project. For example, the decision to change the use affects all decisions that follow. Conversion of offices to residential tends to be a one-way conversion because of the very different

Table 11.1 Drivers for conversion

Lack of demand for existing use
Renewed appeal for city-centre living
Redundancy of original use through social or technology change
Sustainable urban policies for urban intensification or changes in use
Retention of embodied energy
Encouraging the use of public transport
Imparts character and identity to precincts
Increase in capital and rental values
Reverse social and economic obsolescence
Reduce vandalism and squatting and break-ins
Reduce vacancy rates

Source: Wilkinson (2012a)

requirements in respect of building services and the high numbers of owners that may be created, where units may then be sold off for owner-occupation, thus making future redevelopment problematic. The capacity of stakeholders to influence decisions is direct or indirect (Wilkinson in Wilkinson *et al.* 2014). Another layer is added where a stakeholder intends to be an occupier or user, in which case the decisions have a daily impact on their ongoing business operations. The motivations of the stakeholders influencing decision-making in respect of adaptation vary. For example, a developer who intends to sell the property post-adaptation experiences different drivers than if the intention is to retain the property within the owners' property portfolio. In summary, stakeholders are multiple decision-makers for individual buildings and exert their influence to different degrees at different stages that impacts on sustainability. However, too often the stakeholders with decision-making powers are restricted to those with a legal and financial interest in the building, whereas external stakeholders (local residents, office occupiers, shoppers and indeed the community) are impacted by the decisions (Sayce *et al.* 2004). Unless they make representations if the scheme requires planning or the building is listed or otherwise protected, their voices are not heard.

The arguments for and against building adaptation are often categorised as 'social', 'economic' and 'environmental' factors. Within the factors there are sub-sets. For example, within economic drivers the availability of government incentives or risk factors can have an effect. In addition there are regulatory and legal, location and site, and physical building factors which affect adaptation. Figure 11.2 shows a model of the factors that have been identified as influencing the decision to undertake adaptation. All factors in the model have a direct relationship with adaptation and impact on sustainability; however, some factors also have links with other factors (shown as the dotted line in Figure 11.2).

A further aspect is the range of decision options available to stakeholders (Kincaid 2002; Wilkinson *et al.* 2014). The first option is to change the use with minimum intervention because of the inherent 'flexibility' of the building as found. Option two is for adaptation with minor change, whilst option three requires a higher degree of intervention and is typically referred to as 'refurbishment' or 'retrofitting'. Option four involves selected demolition, whereas option five is the extension of the facility. Finally, option six is demolition and redevelopment and is selected when the social, economic, environmental,

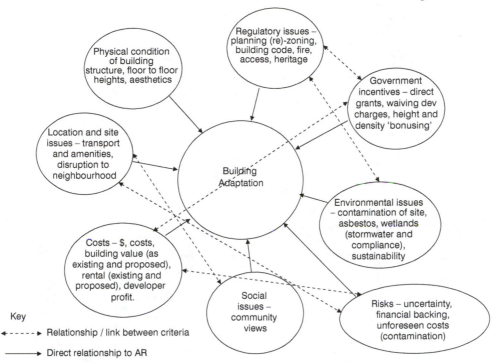

Figure 11.2 Decision-making factors in building adaptation
Source: Wilkinson (2011)

regulatory and physical conditions are such that the building is said to be at the end of the life cycle and lacking in utility (Bottom 1999). Effective decision-making demands the consideration of issues such as framing the issue properly, identifying and evaluating the respective advantages and disadvantages of the alternatives and selecting the best option (Wilkinson *et al.* 2014; Turban *et al.* 2005; Luecke 2006). Another way of illustrating how the factors all relate to the various levels or types of adaptation is shown in Figure 11.3.

11.5   Enabling policy and legislative frameworks for sustainable property development

Measures to encourage building upgrades and retrofit to higher sustainability levels are far less developed in general than the measures which control new building. Enabling frameworks can take several forms:

- requirements to do something – even if this is not in-cycle;
- financial incentives to upgrade by way of a tax for no action or a grant for action; and,
- awareness raising and behavioural 'nudges'.

In most countries, a mixture of these methods is used to stimulate the rate at which upgrades take place. In Australia, using Melbourne as an example; the 1200 Buildings Program was launched in 2008 as a key strategy to deliver carbon neutrality by 2020. The programme encourages sustainable adaptation and provides financial support through a

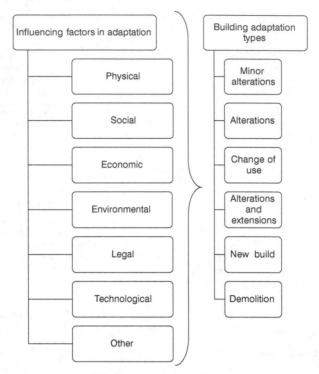

Figure 11.3 Relationship between adaptation factors and adaptation types
Source: Adapted from Wilkinson (2011)

partnership between the city of Melbourne and Sustainable Melbourne Fund (SMF). SMF administers the programme's environmental upgrade finance mechanism, the Environmental Upgrade Agreements (EUAs) above (see Chapter 5). SMF manages the development and the operational delivery of the finance mechanism, whereas the city of Melbourne implements the programme as a whole.

With 7.7 million square metres of office space and around 1,800 commercial office buildings in the city centre, a target to adapt 5.2 million square metres has been set. It is estimated per adaptation that an average performance improvement of around 38 per cent is required (City of Melbourne 2008). The targets are based on the National Australian Built Environment Rating System (NABERS) rating standard of 4.5 stars out of a possible six stars though in 2012 the city of Melbourne stated that it intended to raise the target to five-star NABERS. This is a good example of how standards in respect of sustainable property development are continuously changing and with long lead in times this can be a challenge for developers. The NABERS rating is either a base building energy rating or whole building energy rating. A base building rating covers the performance of central services and common areas, which the owner usually manages, whereas a whole building rating covers tenanted space. These ratings are disclosed when there is inadequate metering to obtain a base building rating.

Under the *Building Energy Efficiency Disclosure Act 2010*, there are mandatory obligations applicable to many commercial buildings. The Act, implemented through the Commercial Building Disclosure programme, forms part of a package of measures to encourage building energy efficiency developed by the Australian government. The Commercial Building

Disclosure is a national programme to improve the energy efficiency of office buildings and is managed by the Department of Climate Change and Energy Efficiency. The scheme shares similarities with the EU Energy Performance Certificates (Warren and Huston 2011). Most sellers or lessors of office space of 2,000 square metres or more are required to obtain and disclose a Building Energy Efficiency Certificate (BEEC). A BEEC comprises a NABERS Energy star rating for the building, an assessment of tenancy lighting in the area of the building that is being sold or leased and general energy efficiency guidance. BEECs are valid for 12 months and must be publicly accessible on the online Building Energy Efficiency Register. From 1 November 2011 a full BEEC has to be disclosed. Mandatory Disclosure requires minimum standards of energy efficiency and the aim is to encourage the market to take up greater energy efficiency (Warren and Huston 2011). Analysis of the Melbourne commercial building adaptation market from 2009 to 2011 shows greater levels of energy efficiency and that this policy appears to be delivering on its aims (Wilkinson 2012a), although whether this is sufficient to meet the target is debatable. Together, the Building Energy Efficiency Disclosure, NABERS and the 1200 Buildings Program create an environment in which sustainable adaptation is incentivised in Melbourne.

Within Europe, there has been increasing interest in the performance of existing stock, though very little legislation has been driven through yet to support this. The major initiative has been the *Energy Performance of Buildings Directive (Directive 2010/31/ EC, EPBD)*. First published in 2002, and updated in 2010, the Directive requires all EU countries to enhance their building regulations and to introduce energy certification schemes for buildings. All countries were also required to have inspections of boilers and air-conditioners. The intent of the certification scheme, which requires the production of an Energy Performance Certificate (EPC), was that purchasers and tenants would adjust their behaviours and stimulate demand for more energy efficient buildings in turn stimulating upgrading. The actual implementation and detailing of EPCs has been for each member state to determine, hence the experiences vary. In some countries it has been a very positive move; in others less so (for a full report see Bio Intelligence Service *et al*. 2013). In the UK, the EPC, which is based on an asset rating, not on energy use, has met with significant scepticism and initially had very little market impact, despite some research (e.g. Fuerst and McAllister 2011) indicating that EPCs can sometimes be associated with higher levels of value. Where it is not, the case to owners is very weak, a point that was not lost on Chegut *et al*. (2011) who argued that the cost implications of upgrade are not well known or understood.

However, within the UK, a sea change is beginning to be observable consequent on legislation (Energy Act 2011) that will introduce minimum energy standards (MEPS) almost certainly predicated on EPC ratings for any lettings post 2018. Whilst arrangements are being put in place to run a finance system alongside (the so-called Green Deal) the very announcements that this is coming in has, anecdotally as yet, focused minds on the issue of energy in existing stock. However, whilst well intentioned, it is very far from clear how this will work out in practice. It is likely that some stock will simply prove uneconomic to improve – even with the Green Deal – and will therefore be allowed to remain unimproved whilst other stock will be demolished. For a fuller discussion of this, see Green Construction Board (2014). Perhaps an equally potent measure to incentivise improvements is that empty proprieties attract occupation tax in the UK, and as demand for 'greener' stock gradually emerges, so investors will be put in a position to upgrade or demolish.

There is no equivalence for owner-occupied buildings, many of which have no EPCs, as they have not transacted since the scheme commenced. However, among owner-occupied stock, there is a greater incentive to improve, simply because the owner also pays the bills. The subject of EPCs and other measures to promote sustainability adaptation of existing buildings, such as the Carbon Reduction Commitment and Display Energy Certificates are discussed in Chapter 9 but it is perhaps the case that the moves towards mandating or even encouraging upgrades are muted to date. Where it is taking place it is concentrated in the commercial investment sectors and there is an implicit assumption that owner-occupiers will be incentivised through the pricing mechanism or their own corporate sustainability ambitions.

Whilst this is but a snapshot of two countries (Australia and UK) at one moment in time, it does illustrate that the decision to adapt properties to improve their sustainability credentials is complex and rests on a mixture of economic (including fiscal and risk) and social reputational issues. Further each sub-mark will operate differently depending on its context.

11.6   Existing office buildings and sustainability

It is within the office stock that the issue of upgrading for sustainability has had most attention. This is not surprising given that they suffer more from depreciation than any other asset class (Crosby *et al.* 2014) although a study in the US pointed to depreciation also being a strong feature of residential apartment blocks (Bokhari and Geltner 2014). Refurbishment can help a building regain both value and increased sustainability performance; however, there is a natural cycle to this (see Figure 11.4).

There are various office building typologies and energy profiles (Table 11.2). Buildings are evaluated in terms of likely energy consumption patterns on the basis of size, configuration, methods of ventilation and the presence of air conditioning. However, it also the case that Premium grade buildings in Australia (type 4 in Table 11.2) have the largest energy

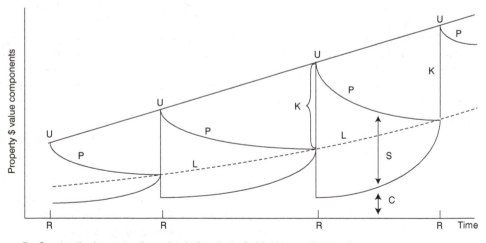

R – Construction/reconstruction points in time (typically 30–100 years between)
U – Usage value at highest and best use at time of reconstruction
P – Property value
S – Structure value
L – Land appraisal value (legal value)
C – Land redevelopment call option value (economic value)
K – Construction (redevelopment) cost excluding acquisition cost

Figure 11.4   The dynamics of refurbishment
Source: Bokhari and Geltner (2014)

Table 11.2 Office typologies and energy profiles

Office typology	Size (m²)	Configuration	Ventilation	Energy consumption
1 Naturally ventilated	100–3,000	Cellular	Natural	Lowest
2 Naturally ventilated	500–4,000	Open plan	Natural	
3 Air conditioned (standard)	2,000–8,000		Air contioned	
4 Air conditioned (prestige)	4,000–20,000		Air contioned	Highest (3 × lowest)

Source: Wilkinson (2013b)

Table 11.3 Responsibilities for energy in office buildings

Energy use for building managers	Energy use for occupiers
Heating and hot water (gas or heating oil)	Office equipment
Cooling (chillers, air-conditioning plant, condensers and cooling towers)	Catering
Fans, pumps and controls	Other electricity (print rooms)
Humidification	Computer communication rooms
Lighting	Personal behaviours; policy of user hours and out of hours lighting

Source: Wilkinson (2013b)

consumption and emissions but on a per metre squared basis lower grade offices, B grade, have higher emissions (PCA 2008). On this basis, the premium quality stock is less energy efficient and has poorer thermal performance and this highlights the individuality of each building in sustainable property development.

When considering energy use within office buildings, heating, hot water and cooling are the largest consumers of energy across all typologies and are at the centre of efforts to reduce emissions. Energy use varies for tenants and managers and this creates some issues in respect of motivations for sustainable adaptation previously described. The respective responsibilities are outlined in Table 11.3.

Clearly property developers have an opportunity to make significant energy savings. The savings that may be achieved can be as high as 70 per cent but are typically 30 to 50 per cent (City of Melbourne 2008). An adaptation that takes building performance from average practice; that is three-star NABERS to best practice, five-star NABERS, represents a 38 per cent improvement in performance (City of Melbourne 2008). The typical measures are shown in Table 11.4.

11.7 Adaptation issues

With economic, environmental and social characteristics of adaptation covered above, this section focuses on location and land use, physical and legal factors (Langston 2007). Physical characteristics determine whether adaptation is possible and desirable. Some

Table 11.4 Typical retrofit measures for office buildings

Measure	Improvements
Air conditioning	Attend to running times, volumetric capacity and operating pressure
Office appliances	Use more efficient equipment and reduce standby losses
Insulation	Improve thermal performance
Heating and ventilation	Use building energy management system (BMS), use heat recovery and perimeter heating for preheating
Lighting	Use energy efficient fittings, timers, linear fluorescent lights for interior, exterior and parking lighting
Water heating	Use efficient systems and technologies such as solar

Source: Wilkinson (2013b)

buildings feature construction forms and materials making adaptation more expensive or challenging. Height, construction type and frame condition was important with steel frames being more adaptable because of the ease of cutting into beams. Floor size was significant in London adaptations where buildings with unusual floor plates or sizes were more difficult to adapt and suited a limited range of users (Kincaid 2002). In addition, the location of the services core is significant in affecting the ability to sub-divide space. For example, a central location gives greater scope for sub-division whilst minimising corridor and circulation space. Whether a building is detached or attached affects the ease or desirability for adaptation. With less attachment, contractors work faster and cause less disruption to users. Access or, the number of entry and exit points, affects retrofit potential across a range of property types.

Recent research (Green Construction Board 2014) has established that, within the UK, the economics of refurbishment will vary considerably depending on the age and type of building. As a rule, air-conditioned office buildings dating from the 1980s are particularly hard to treat; they are therefore more likely to face demolition. This supports the findings of Bokhari and Geltner (2014) in the US that life cycles will vary considerably but that younger buildings may suffer greater rates of depreciation than those that are over 50 years old.

Location, considered in terms of proximity to public transport, is an environmental positive. Where little or no public transport is available the amount of on-site parking may be significant (Douglas 2006). Swallow (1997) concluded that adaptation is affected by tenure because it affects the funds the party is willing to invest. For example, an owner has an interest in perpetuity whereas a lessee's interest lasts for the lease term. Institutional owners invest to maximise the return on investment and probably use professional consultants to advise on adaptation (Swallow 1997). Private owners may or may not use professional consultants and may reside overseas. They may hold property for many reasons, such as future development or for rental income or capital growth and may engage in less adaptation; though this is unknown.

Adaptation is affected by occupation. With single tenants, when leases expire, there is opportunity for adaptation; however, with multiple tenants, unless a deliberate strategy has been developed in relation to upgrades, it is unlikely all leases expire simultaneously and the building may be partly empty (and not income earning) before adaptation can occur. Alternatively adaptation occurs with tenants in situ, which requires careful management and may restrict the nature of the work that is possible. Historic listing protects architecturally or socially significant buildings for society (Ball 2002) but heritage adaptation can be more costly because of the expense of using traditional materials, techniques and craftspeople

(Wilkinson 2012a). Snyder's (2005) study found benefit in proactive policies and legislation in building adaptation and Bromley *et al.* (2005) found proactive policy and legislation enhanced the retention of existing stock. Hostile factors for developers to overcome in adaptation include noise and asbestos that created social and economic barriers which drive up costs (Bullen 2007).

The scope and extent of sustainable adaptation has increased and will continue to do so as there is a growing realisation that to prolong the life of the building has advantages in terms of embedded energy and in protecting a sense of place. There is therefore an overlap with social, economic and location aspects, as detailed above. Whilst retrofitting and adaptation decisions are often taken on an *ad hoc* basis as possibilities arise, the decision to redevelop is increasingly less likely to be taken lightly. However, there are calls to improve decision-making in a more systematic way (Ibn-Mohammed *et al.* 2014).

11.8   Sustainable adaptation case studies

This section illustrates current practice regarding sustainable commercial adaptation to gain a deeper understanding of contemporary practices with regard to sustainable adaptation. Sustainable adaptation involves an extensive team of individuals including financiers, investors, regulators, owners, project managers, designers, engineers and sometimes occupiers. Although two Australian cases are presented, similiar building design and specifications are found in many cities globally. These case studies are illustrative of what can be achieved in practice.

11.8.1   *500 Collins Street, Melbourne, Australia*

Five hundred Collins Street illustrates an extensive adaptation to achieve energy and water efficiencies maintaining high tenancy levels during the works. Completed in the 1970s, 500 Collins Street was renowned for its quality of construction, reflecting modern building standards and services. A consequence of which was that it attracted a high tenancy profile. By 2002, the building had declined to a low B-grade standard through obsolescence and ageing (Wilkinson 2013a). Despite this decline, the building had retained its tenants. This was due to building size and configuration, an excellent location, good design and sound building management. It was these attributes that led the building's owner to determine that it was suitable for a substantial adaptation. Prior to retrofit, the building comprised a total of 23,500 m² of office space, five retail shops and 140 car parking spaces. The adaptation project began in mid-2003 and was completed in early 2011. The project was divided into three stages to allow for the almost fully occupied building to operate while the sustainable adaptation was undertaken (Wilkinson 2013a). Stage one was to replace and upgrade plant, and renovate the façade. The second stage was to maximise retail space and reconfigure the car park, whilst stage three comprised the office floor upgrades.

The works were rolled out progressively as the leases expired. The work included stripping out of each floor and replacing them with new finishes and chilled beam air conditioning. The floor-by-floor upgrade required much planning and could only be realised when tenants vacated space; generally this was achieved three floors at a time. It also meant, as much as possible, minimising the impact of the building construction on the tenants (Wilkinson 2013a). This was achieved by having several lifts dedicated to the builders. Demolition work was completed out of hours and old carpets were laid on the concrete floors to deaden the noise for the tenants.

A chilled beam solution was chosen for the HVAC. The façade was upgraded by replacing glazed spandrel panels with aluminium wall panelling, repairing and refurbishing vertical columns, and repainting. Changes in the floor structure resulted in an increase in net tenantable area to approximately 24,400 m² with eight additional shops, a small decrease in car spaces, and the addition of secure bicycle racks, changing rooms with shower facilities and disabled access and amenities. Foyer entries and public areas were upgraded. Level three was extended onto the podium of level two to create external meeting space and recreational landscaped areas.

The HVAC systems included the installation of new energy efficient chillers with variable speed drives and more water efficient cooling towers and new gas fired boilers for heating, replacing oil fired ones. As each floor became vacant, a chilled beam air-conditioning system was installed. This is a combined system – with active chilled beams that use fans to diffuse cool air around the building's perimeter where solar loads are high and passive in the interior spaces. The original central ducting was reused in the perimeter zones (Wilkinson 2013a). The new system reduced the number of fans for all air conditioning, which decreases energy consumption. As the building was occupied, it was necessary to maintain the old system while the new one was installed.

Energy load was reduced by installing solar panels on the roof for hot water (supplying 25 per cent of domestic hot water), fitting low energy T5 light fittings in all public and tenanted areas, installing variable speed drives on major plant and equipment, and using chilled beam air conditioning.

Water consumption was reduced by installing, waterless urinals, three- and six-litre dual flush cisterns, flow restricting devices on all fixtures, rain water and condensate capture for landscape irrigation using large tanks in the basement parking area to store water and finally baffles on the cooling tower preventing aerosol spray. Waste was addressed through on-site recycling bins and around 80 per cent of construction waste was recycled.

General environmental improvements included minimising embodied energy of the building, using PVC-free materials where possible, using low volatile organic compound materials, a preference for materials with a high-recycled content, selecting materials for durability and from sustainable sources, encouraging the use of bicycles by providing a secure bike compound for 82 bicycles, plus shower and changing room facilities, improving the indoor environment quality by increasing fresh air by 50 per cent, radiant cooling (chilled beams), low VOC materials and reduction in indoor ambient noise levels.

The building controls system was completely renewed. The commissioning of this control system was an ongoing process as each floor was completed. The main electrical switchboard was replaced, and tenancy sub-metering provided to enable effective energy monitoring. The commissioning of plant and equipment is critical in this process so that building management understands how the building functions and is controlled for efficient operation (Wilkinson 2013a). The adaptation objectives were:

a. Achieve a Property Council of Australia (PCA) A-grade building standard.
b. Attain a high degree of environmental efficiency, both during the upgrade works and post-upgrade operations (set before NABERS and Green Star ratings were in place).
c. Maximise tenant retention during the upgrade to maintain optimum cash flow and provide a potential pool of long-term tenants.
d. Elevate tenancy profile by increasing the average size of tenancy, length of tenure and quality of tenant, achieve a commercially justifiable return on investment (Wilkinson 2013a).

Figure 11.5 Front elevation 500 Collins Street, Melbourne (© Ruskin Black)

The adaptation features were:

- energy efficient variable speed drive chillers;
- gas fired boilers;
- chilled beams (passive and active);
- solar panels servicing 25 per cent hot water requirements;
- T5 light fittings;
- water tanks collecting rainwater and condensate for landscape irrigation;
- waterless urinals and dual flush cisterns;
- flow restricting devices on all fixtures (Wilkinson 2013a).

11.8.1.1 Challenges and outcomes

The key challenges with this project were adapting with tenants in situ. Furthermore the approach necessitated the continued operation of existing service whilst new installations were being fitted. The outcomes were as follows:

1 Energy was modelled to achieve a 30 per cent reduction in air conditioning, 50 per cent reduction in lighting and 15 per cent reduction in hot water usage.
2 Water was modelled to achieve 40–50 per cent savings.

3   Sustainability Victoria and the building owner conducted a productivity study in 2007–2008. The study found a 39 per cent reduction in average sick days per employee per month, 44 per cent reduction in the average cost of sick leave, 9 per cent improvement on average typing speeds and significant accuracy improvement of secretarial staff, 7 per cent increase in billings ratio, despite a decline in average monthly hours worked, 7–20 per cent reduction in headaches, 21–24 per cent reduction in colds and flu, 16–26 per cent reduction in fatigue. It is believed these results are due to improved air quality and building amenity.

4   Reduced maintenance costs are due to reduction in plant and equipment, as well as more efficient plant, and better monitoring of plant through the BMS.

5   The rental value of the refurbished space has increased considerably.

6   Over the project, the team maintained ongoing support of tenants with an occupancy rate not falling below 70 per cent. The building now has fewer tenants, meaning the number of larger tenants has increased.

7   The building gained a 5 Star Green Star Office Design v1 rating.

8   The first and principal lesson from this project was the importance of communicating with tenants. Second, strong project management leadership, meant that the team understood the sustainability objectives of the project and worked to assess all elements against the sustainability criteria. The third lesson was the careful management and control of noise and temporary service shut downs. Fourth, was to engage a sustainability consultant, who advocated for the sustainability principles in the project team. Finally the engagement of an independent commissioning agent whose role was to specify commissioning and tuning criteria and timing of the project (Wilkinson 2013a).

11.8.2   115 Batman Street, Melbourne, Australia

This project exemplifies a newly constructed building that uses a range of energy efficient techniques and technologies to achieve an excellent NABERS Energy rating. The building at 115 Batman Street was originally a machinery factory built in the 1920s and had been derelict since the late 1980s. The factory was gutted, leaving only the brick wall façade. The new building was constructed in this space, combining the new and the old. The basement car park and two of the floors sit within the original walls of the factory, and two new floors sit above. The new area above the original brick walls consists of vitrapanel clad with heavily insulated walls and a new pitched, corrugated and heavily insulated roof. The two lower floors utilise the original space in the brick façade for the windows. The free standing building faces north, with very little shade provided by surrounding buildings.

The adaptation objectives were:

a.   introduce state of the art engineering services with very low levels of energy consumption;

b.   provide a comfortable working environment to enhance productivity; and,

c.   achieve five-star Green Star and five-star NABERS Energy ratings (Wilkinson 2013a).

The adaptation features were:

- complete reconstruction within existing façade;
- cighly insulated building shell,
- chilled beams in the ground, first and second levels;

Figure 11.6 Front elevation 115 Batman Street, Melbourne (© Ruskin Black)

- variable air volume (VAV) economy cycle on third level;
- high-efficiency gas boiler for heating;
- high-efficiency luminaries;
- 15,000-litre rain water tank;
- solar panels for water heating (Wilkinson 2013a).

The outcomes were:

1 The chilled beams coped well with the heatwave in Melbourne in March 2009. They responded well to the changes in ambient conditions and were found superior to the third floor VAV system.
2 The lighting of base building consumes less than 2 watts per m² per 100 Lux.
3 The building is performing better than five-stars NABERS Energy. The NABERS rating benchmark for five stars is 101 kilograms/m²/year; 115 Batman Street performed at 89–91 kilograms/m² /year.
4 Socially there is very positive feedback from the staff about the work environment.
5 The system is simple and plant is accessible and this makes maintenance straightforward.
6 Total building outgoings are less than $60/m² which compares well with most commercial office buildings in the city and near-city locations where the outgoings range from $70 to $90/m² (Wilkinson 2013a).

11.8.3 Discussion of sustainability measures

The sustainability measures delivered above can be categorised as environmental and social measures. Many of the environmental measures were implemented because of the potential economic benefit which confirms Swallow's study (1997). Most measures related to the building services and to energy efficiency reflect the importance of energy efficiency in NABERS and Green Star ratings as well as the aims of the 1200 Buildings Program (Wilkinson 2013a). Furthermore the extent of energy efficiency confirmed Douglas' (2006) observation that energy is the most significant sustainability issue and is indicative of poor energy performance in existing stock.

Water economy measures featured less highly. The reasons could be that water economy is not as important as energy, or more likely, that due to stringent water restrictions imposed during the 10-year drought in the early 2000s many Melbourne buildings operate efficiently in terms of water. Again this is an example of the variability of importance of different sustainability measures in different markets globally. Environmental outcomes were achieved and in some cases NABERS ratings exceeded targets. Energy and water use was reduced.

Measures to the building fabric were associated with energy efficiency. Opportunities for building fabric measures occurred less frequently, and involved access challenges and disruption to occupants, as well as being expensive, confirming Bullen's findings (2007). However, once undertaken, these measures offer a more long-term solution than upgraded services which require maintenance and will be replaced typically within a 20-year period. Physical issues were not related to fabric performance though it was acknowledged as important that the costs of adapting fabric are higher. This reflects the current economic climate and timeframe for returns on investment (Wilkinson 2013a). Other physical factors of note were hostile factors such as noise generated by the construction works disrupting tenants in situ. Noise issues identified by Bullen (2007) as hostile were challenges in some projects.

Economic objectives were met in many cases with energy and water costs reduced. Maintenance costs were reduced, higher rents recorded and yields achieved. Economic issues such as yields and returns on investments (Bullen 2007; Ball 2002) were important critical success factors in 500 Collins Street.

Overall social sustainability had a lower profile within the adaptations but its outcomes were highly valued by users (Wilkinson 2013a). Social outcomes are positive with higher productivity and improved IEQ measured in one post-occupancy evaluation. Staff were also noted to be 'happier' in the post-adaptation buildings and productivity increased.

Management issues that arose during the adaptations were the need for strong project management, the need for advocates to promote sustainability and the need for independent commissioning agents to verify data. Retention of tenants was also positive in the cases (Wilkinson 2013a). In some projects, the aim to increase occupancy was achieved and the level of vacancy rates changed pre- and post-adaptation (Swallow 1997).

More general findings were that different drivers motivated owners. Significantly Snyder's (2005) finding that there is a relationship between proactive legislation and change in the adaptation market was supported in these cases; here the realisation is buildings with enhanced sustainability.

11.9 Conclusion

This chapter has presented a definition of adaptation and proposed a new definition of 'sustainable adaptation'. Through the understanding of life cycle theory, the chapter has shown that buildings decline in utility over time to a point where action is required. Physical deterioration, functional obsolescence and technology and social change combine to trigger depreciation in values which triggers the evaluation of adaptation or new build options for property owners and their advisory teams and may lead to proactive interventions by developers.

The drivers for within use and across use adaptations are complex and interact, collectively affecting decision-making in this aspect of development. The many stakeholders who impact on the decision to different degrees at different times further complicate decision-making. However, these stakeholders are primarily those with financial interests in the building, rather than those in the communities affected by the decision. The barriers to sustainable property development were described in order to comprehend the various factors that serve to undermine or compromise sustainable property development. Whether adaptation takes place was seen also to be a function of the legal and planning environment, with some jurisdictions positively encouraging change of use as a way of finding new life for redundant stock. The use of grants, incentives and tax can be levers also, used to encourage owner behaviours towards retrofitting and adaptation. However, it was noted that the framework to encourage or mandate improvements to existing stock lacks the rigour and reach of those relating to new building. This is something that may well change over time and indeed will be essential if carbon targets are to be met.

The final section of the chapter sets out two case study examples of commercial office sustainable adaptation to illustrate the gains which can be achieved when property is redeveloped sustainably. Overall the argument for adaptation as opposed to new build is found to be strong in the context of sustainability because of the benefits of retained embodied energy, the ability to reduce operating carbon emissions and water consumption, the ability to improve the internal environmental quality of the spaces to enhance user comfort and the opportunity to improve the envelopes thermal performance to name a few. Each of these measures as well as other sustainability measures has to be evaluated on its merits and in the context of construction costs, capital values, rental returns, absorption rates, vacancy rates and market supply and demand. Property developers are required to model the costs and returns and to evaluate project risk factors before deciding on the optimum measures which can be implemented. As yet, none of the sustainability rating tools offsets embodied carbon in existing buildings as part of the rating; when this is achieved it will be easier for developers to compare new build versus adaptation.

Note

1 Even this may not be the case in land liable to flood, earthquake or other topographical phenomena or where reclamation works take place.

References

Arge, K. (2005) Adaptable office buildings: theory and practice. *Facilities* 23(3): 119–127.

Ball, R.M. (2002). Re use potential and vacant industrial premises: revisiting the regeneration issue in Stoke on Trent, *Journal of Property Research*. 19: 93–110.

Baum, A (1991) *Property Investment Depreciation and Obsolescence*, London: Cengage Learning.

Bio Intelligence Service, Lyons, R., and IEEP (2013) *Energy Performance Certificates in Buildings and their Impact on Transaction Prices and Rents in Selected EU Countries: Final Report for the European Commission*. Brussels: European Commisson.

Blakstad, S.H. (2001). A strategic approach to adaptability in office buildings. Faculty of Architecture, Planning & Fine Arts, Norwegian University of Science & Technology.

Bokhari, S. and Geltner, D. (2014) Characteristics of depreciation in commercial and multi-family property: an investment perspective. Manuscript, MIT Center for Real Estate.

Bottom, C.W., McGreal, W.S., and Heaney, G. (1999). Appraising the functional performance attributes of office buildings, *Journal of Property Research* 16(4): 339-358.

BPF (British Property Federation) (2013) *Property Data Report*. Retrieved from http://www.bpf.org. uk/en/files/reita_files/property_data/BPF_Property_Data_booklet_2013_spreads_web.pdf.

Brand, Stewart (1995) *How Buildings Learn: What Happens After They're Built*. Harmondsworth: Penguin.

Bromley R.D.F., Tallon, A.R., and Thomas, C.J. (2005). City centre regeneration through residential development: Contributing to sustainability, *Urban Studies* 42(13): 24072429.

Brounen, D. and Kok, N. (2011) On the economics of energy labels in the housing market, *Journal of Environmental Economics and Management* 62(2): 166–179.

Bryson, J.R. (1997) Obsolescence and the process of creative deconstruction, *Urban Studies* 34(9): 1439–1459.

Bullen, P.A. (2007) Adaptive reuse and sustainability of commercial buildings, *Facilities* 25: 20–31.

Carbon Trust (2009) *Building the Future, Today: Transforming the Economic and Carbon Performance of the Buildings We Work In*. Retrieved from https://www.carbontrust.com/media/77252/ctc765_building_the_future__today.pdf.

Chau, K.W., Leung, A.Y.T., Yui, C.Y., and Wong, S.K. (2003) Estimating the value enhancement effects of refurbishment, *Facilities* 21(1): 13–19.

Chegut, A., Eichholtz, P., and Kok, N. (2011) The Value of Green Buildings: New Evidence from the United Kingdom. Working Paper. Retrieved from http://immobilierdurable.umapresence. com/images/2128_uploads/Chegut_Eichholtz_Kok_green_value_in_the_uk.pdf.

Colliers International (2010a) *Office Research and Forecast Report: First Half 2009*. Retrieved on 13 May 2015 from http://www.colliers.com.au/Search#?Keywords=melbourne%20cbd%20office%20market%20report.

Colliers International (2010b) *Office Research and Forecast Report: Second Half 2009*. Retrieved on 13 May 2015 from http://www.colliers.com.au/Search#?Keywords=melbourne%20cbd%20office%20market%20report.

Crosby, N., Devaney, S., and Law, V. (2012) Rental depreciation and capital expenditure in the UK commercial real estate market, 1993–2009, *Journal of Property Research* 29(3): 227–246.

Crosby, N., Devaney, S., and Nanda, A. (2014) Which factors drive rental depreciation rates for office and industrial properties?. Retrieved from http://papers.ssrn.com/sol3/papers.cfm?abstract_id=2421343

Douglas, J. (2006*) Building Adaptation*, London: Butterworth Heinemann.

Department of the Environment, Water, Heritage & Arts (2008) Mandatory Disclosure of Office Energy Efficiency, Consultation Regulation Document.

Ellison, L., Sayce, S., and Smith, J. (2007) Socially responsible property investment: quantifying the relationship between sustainability and investment property worth, *Journal of Property Research* 24(3): 191–219.

Findlay, A. and Sparks, L. (2014) *The Retail Planning Knowledge Base Briefing Paper Town Centre and High Street Reviews*. Retrieved from http://www.nrpf.org.uk/PDF/nrpftopic16_reviews.pdf.

Forsythe, P. and Wilkinson, S. (2015) Measuring office fit-out changes to determine recurring embodied energy in building life cycle assessment, *Facilities* 33(1/2) 262–274.

Fuerst, F. and McAllister, P. (2011) Green noise or green value? Measuring the effects of environmental certification on office values. *Real Estate Economics* 39(1): 45–69.

Green Construction Board (2014) *Valuation and Demand Working Group Project GCB630 – Mapping the Impacts of Minimum Energy Efficiency Standards for Commercial Real Estate Final Report.* Retrieved from http://www.greenconstructionboard.org/images/stories/Valuation_and_Demand/GCB%20630%20final%20report.pdf.

Green Construction Board (2015) Mapping the real estate life cycle for effective policy interventions. Retrieved from http://www.greenconstructionboard.org/images/stories/Valuation_and_Demand/GCB610%20Final%20Report.pdf.

Harding, R. (ed.) (2005) *Environmental Decision-Making,* Sydney: The Federation Press.

Heath, T. (2001) Adaptive reuse of offices for residential use, *Cities* 18(3): 173–184.

Ibn-Mohammed, T., Greenough, R., Taylor, S., Ozawa-Meida, L., and Acquaye, A. (2014) Integrating economic considerations with operational and embodied emissions into a decision support system for the optimal ranking of building retrofit options, *Building and Environment* 72: 82–101.

Investment Property Databank (IPD) (2012) *BPF / IPD Annual Lease Review 2012,* New York: MSCI.

Kelly, M.J. (2010) Energy efficiency, resilience to future climates and long-term sustainability: the role of the built environment, *Philosophical Transactions of the Royal Society A: Mathematical, Physical and Engineering Sciences* 368(1914): 1083–1089.

Kincaid, D. (2002). *Adapting Buildings for Changing Uses: Guidelines for Change of Use Refurbishment.,*London: Spon Press.

Knight Frank (2011) Melbourne CBD Office Market Overview October 2011. Retrieved 2 February 2012 from www.knight.com.au.

Langston, C. (2007) Application of the adaptive reuse potential model in Hong Kong: a case study of Lui Seng Chun, *International Journal of Strategic Property Management* 11: 193–207.

Luecke, R. (2006). *Decision-making: Five Steps to Better Results.* Boston, MA: Harvard Business School Press.

Mansfield, J. (2002) What's in a name? Complexities in the definition of 'refurbishment', *Property Management* 20(1): 23–30.

Markus, T.A. (1979) *Building Conversion and Rehabilitation: Designing for change in Building Use,* London: Butterworth Group.

Miller, E. and Buys, L. (2008) Retrofitting commercial office buildings for sustainability: tenants perspectives, *Journal of Property Investment & Finance* 26(6): 552–561.

Newton, P. and Bai, X. (2008) Transitioning to sustainable urban development: *Transitions: Pathways Towards Sustainable Urban Development in Australia,* Collingwood: Springer.

PCA (Property Council of Australia) (2008), *The Office Market Report,* Sydney: Property Council of Australia.

Remøy, H.T. (Ed.). (2010) *Out of Office: A Study on the Cause of Office Vacancy and Transformation as a Means to Cope and Prevent,* Amsterdam: IOS Press.

Remøy, H.T. and van der Voordt, T.J.M. (2007) A new life: conversion of vacant office buildings into housing. *Facilities* 25(3/4): 88–103.

Remøy, H.T. and Wilkinson, S.J. (2012) Office building conversion and sustainable adaptation: a comparative study, *Journal of Property Management* 3(30): 218–231.

Sanders, M.D. (2014) Ready to retrofit: the process of project team selection, building benchmarking, and financing commercial building energy retrofit projects. Retrieved from http://escholarship.org/uc/item/30p4w0tn.

Sayce, S., Walker, A., and Macintosh, A. (2004) *Building Sustainability in the Balance: Promoting Stakeholder Dialogue,* London: Estates Gazette Ltd.

Snyder, G.H. (2005), Sustainability through adaptive reuse: the conversion of industrial buildings. Master of Architecture thesis, College of Design, Architecture and Planning, University of Cincinnati.

Strutt and Parker (2011) *The Strutt and Parker IPD Lease Events Review 2011,* London: Strutt and Parker.

Swallow, P. (1997) Managing unoccupied buildings and sites, *Structural Survey* 15(2): 74–79.

Turban, E., J. and Aronson, E. (2005). *Decision Support Systems and Intelligent Systems*, Hoboken, NJ: Pearson Education Inc.

Vaughan, L.S. and Griffiths, S. (2013) A suburb is not a tree, *Urban Design*, 125(Winter): 17–19.

Warren, C.M.J. and Huston, S. (2011) Promoting energy efficiency in public sector commercial buildings in Australia. RICS COBRA, University of Salford, Manchester, 12–13 September 2011.

Wilkinson, S.J. (2011) The relationship between building adaptation and property attributes. PhD thesis. Retrieved 13 June 2013 from http://hdl.handle.net/10536/DRO/DU:30036710.

Wilkinson, S.J. (2012a) Back to the future: heritage buildings, sustainability and adaptation in the Melbourne Central Business District, *Historic Environment* 24(2): 7–13.

Wilkinson, S.J. (2012b) Analysing sustainable retrofit potential in premium office buildings, *Structural Survey January 2012–July 2012* 30(5): 398–410.

Wilkinson, S.J. (2012c) Adaptation patterns in premium office buildings over time in the Melbourne CBD, *Journal of Corporate Real Estate* 14(3): 157–170.

Wilkinson, S.J. (2013a) Sustainable urban retrofit evaluation. RICS Research Trust Report. February 2013. Retrieved 4 July 2013 from http://www.rics.org/uk/knowledge/research/research-reports/sustainable-urban-retrofit-evaluation/.

Wilkinson, S.J. (2013b) Are sustainable building retrofits delivering sustainable outcomes?, *Pacific Rim Property Research Journal* 19(2): 211–222.

Wilkinson, S. J., (2013). *Sustainable Urban Retrofit Evaluation*, RICS Research Trust Report, London: RICS. http://www.rics.org/uk/knowledge/research/research-reports/sustainable-urban-retrofit-evaluation/

Wilkinson, S.J., Remøy, H.T., and Langston, C. (2014) *Sustainable Building Adaptation: Innovations in Decision-making*, Oxford: Wiley-Blackwell.

World Green Building Council (2013) *The Business Case for Green Building: A Review of the Costs and Benefits for Developers, Investors and Occupants.* Retrieved from http://www.worldgbc.org/files/1513/6608/0674/Business_Case_For_Green_Building_Report_WEB_2013-04-11.pdf.

Postscript

Sara J. Wilkinson and Sarah L. Sayce

Developing Property Sustainably: Definitions and progress

Our current awareness of the anthropogenic actions that have led to predicted climate changes largely stems from Farman *et al.*'s (2003) research undertaken in the Antarctic which discovered the hole in the ozone layer. The discovery of the Antarctic ozone hole, as reported in *Nature* 30 years ago, was one of the most dramatic scientific findings of modern times. Since then, the science has moved on to a point at which the Intergovernmental Panel on Climate Change (IPCC) have high levels of statistical confidence that 'total anthropogenic GHG emissions have continued to increase over 1970 to 2010 with larger absolute decadal increases towards the end of this period' (IPCC 2014: 6).

Despite the strength of this rigorous scientific research finding, scepticism remains in some quarters and the IPCC consider that the behavioural responses to the challenge of climate change are such that mitigation alone is no longer a viable possibility. In summary, the impact of man on the planet has been such that adaptation to the results of climate change is inevitable. This means that legislation and regulation which so far has been largely focused towards nudging people and organisations towards 'good behaviours' is likely to shift towards mandatory measures. Given the general agreement in principle, if not in terms of exact details, that buildings are a major source of carbon emissions and hence linked to preventable carbon emissions rise, buildings and their development will be targets for intervention.

Since Farman's discovery the United Nations has acknowledged the concept of 'sustainable development' with a landmark definition which established two concepts, intra- and intergenerational equity (WCED 1987). Intergenerational equity is a concept that says that humans 'hold the natural and cultural environment of the Earth in common both with other members of the present generation and with other generations, past and future' (Weiss 1990: 8). Intra-generational equity is concerned with equity between people of the same generation. This is separate from intergenerational equity, which is about equity between present and future generations. Intra-generational equity includes considerations of distribution of resources and justice between nations. It also includes considerations of what is fair for people within any one nation.

Over the last 30 years, the response of the construction and property industry has been mixed. Many definitional attempts have been made to try and understand just what the term 'sustainable' development means in the context of buildings and their specification. In this time, building designs and actual buildings have been labelled as green buildings, greener buildings, ecologic buildings, ecological buildings, eco-buildings, Gaian buildings, natural buildings, environmental friendly buildings, environmental sensitive buildings, and of course, sustainable buildings. These terms have given rise to questions raised by many professionals, including these authors, such as do these terms mean the same? Or are they different? If there are difference, what are the differences, and are they significant?

The answer then, as now, was yes; they are different and yes, it is very important. In short, there is a spectrum of sustainability from very weak to very strong (Cook and Golton 1994; Wilkinson 2013). Weak sustainability pays lip service to the significant issues we face as a species, and will not deliver the changes we need to avoid catastrophic climate change. Very strong sustainability is not without philosophical and moral dilemmas but is practised by so few, that they cannot deliver the changes we need to avoid catastrophic climate change. So the next question must be: what *has* happened in those three decades? Well, certainly the built environment generally, and in particular the property and construction industry, has undergone a change of viewpoint from one of initial denial and ignorance, to a grudging acceptance and acknowledgement and, more recently over the last decade, to an enthusiastic embracing of 'sustainability' and sustainable property development. Much of this change has been driven by the investment and development communities, who have, at the top level, tried to exert real leadership (see for example UNEP FI 2007); other actions have come from governments. However, is current progress towards truly sustainable building stock enough?

Whilst there are those who would say we are making good progress and we are doing enough, prompting some backsliding in regulation in Australia and easing of controls in the UK, it is our view that overall we are making sufficient inroads, but we are not doing enough and time is running out. New building is certainly not the solution. The carbon impact of existing buildings is far greater than the contribution of new buildings, but new buildings *are* significant.

So, is the situation simply impossible due to ignorance or inertia or a lack of preparedness to take steps which may prove expensive? If Stern (2006) is to be believed, the longer the delay in taking action, the more costly the action will be when it is finally taken. Since Stern's review, there has been a more widespread public discourse about sustainability throughout the world. But despite real endeavours by many people, at an international level, governments are still struggling to change rhetoric into action. Indeed, whilst the New York Climate Summit in September 2014 attended by some 100 heads of state succeeded in agreeing that climate change is a 'defining issue' and that 'bold action is needed today to reduce emissions and build resilience', the talk is still of *future* action. Such action they consider should be on five fronts: cutting emissions, mobilising money and markets, pricing carbon, strengthening resilience, and mobilising new coalitions (http://www.un.org/climatechange/summit/2014/09/2014-climate-change-summary-chairs-summary/). All of these have implications for the built environment; for the buildings we build, where they are placed and how they are operated.

Most of the measures proposed go no further than notions of weak sustainability, as introduced in Chapter 1. If we want to take the debate further, ambitions need to be focused further, on to the possibility of moving towards stronger sustainability and to raise the debate in order that we can balance mitigation and adaptation in ways that will at least avoid the most calamitous and irreversible climate change.

Why is it that we hold this view? Just by looking at a few examples we show why we have come to think this way. The State of the Australian Cities Report 2013 (Department of Infrastructure and Regional Development 2013) concluded that all the efficiencies in energy savings made in technologies had been lost in increased per capita consumption. In

September 2014, scientists comprising the Global Carbon Project Team found that annual carbon dioxide emissions rose by 2.5 per cent on the previous year's levels, meaning that irreversible change in temperatures is likely within one generation (http://www.earth-syst-sci-data-discuss.net/7/521/2014/essdd-7-521-2014.html). Whilst buildings can be made to *adapt* for use in higher temperatures, the ability of the Earth to produce food is brought into question and major catastrophic climate events such as drought and floods become inevitable and more frequent.

So, given the plethora of measures undertaken, why have emissions, which were falling and at the individual building level continue to fall in the wake of tighter building codes, started to rise again? The answer is multi-faceted.

Undoubtedly, part of the answer lies in the Jevons paradox. William Jevons, in the nineteenth century, observed that an increase in the efficiency of using coal to produce energy *increased* consumption, rather than reduced it. Jevons argued that the cheaper price of coal-produced energy encouraged people to find innovative new ways to consume energy. Jevons paradox, as currently stated by Alcott (2008) and Owen (2012) and others, is really an extreme statement about an effect economists observe known as the 'rebound effect': some of the gains from energy efficiency are lost because people's consumption rises in response to lower prices. For instance the BedZed development in London is an example of zero-carbon residential development. A research study examined the carbon footprint of the residents and found, when compared to a local social non-sustainable housing estate, the BedZed residents had a much lower carbon footprint. However, when the total carbon footprint of both communities was calculated and included all the overseas travel the BedZed residents' carbon footprint far exceeded that of the residents in the traditional housing.

The Jevons paradox, asserts that, over the long-term, the rebound effect can exceed the original gains from energy efficiency. Consider lighting, which has become cheaper per unit as the world has moved from lamp oil to tallow candles to incandescent bulbs to fluorescent bulbs and now to LED lights. Yet we now use more resources for lighting than ever, since we put lights almost everywhere. This argument can apply to any resource. Consider food production, if we are to feed a further 2.3 billion people by 2050 and provide for increases in meat and dairy consumption from the rising middle class in India and China, we will need to double food production. If we are to avoid ploughing over the Earth's remaining natural forests and grasslands to achieve this target; we need to grow food more efficiently. However, Jevons paradox suggests that in making agriculture more efficient, we will increase total food consumption. To some, this reasoning is flawed. Efficiency is perceived as an unqualified good, a necessary first step towards a more sustainable society. If energy efficiency is the free lunch one is paid to eat, the reality is that environmentalists have only been partially successful at getting people to eat that lunch: there's still a lot of food rotting on the table. If environmentalists have had only partial success at promoting energy efficiency, what are the prospects of fighting for an even more fundamental change in our society's relationship to resources?

Jevons is not the only economist with views on the rebound issue. The so-called Khazzoom–Brookes postulate, based on more modern observations in the US found similar impacts (Saunders 2000). However, whilst it is easy to blame rising carbon on rebound, this is far too simplistic. As Chakravarty *et al.* (2013) argue, the impact varies across sectors and wealth levels and across countries with simply too little being known about the situation in developing countries.

However, whatever the total impact of rebound, which is still discussable territory and can only be addressed through fundamental lifestyle changes, innovations to reduce carbon use are still required. Energy use by itself is not a bad thing: anyone would view the life of hundreds of millions of people living without electricity, as extreme deprivation. Light brings comfort, safety and the ability to be economically active in hours of darkness. With food it is even clearer, as access to enough food is a basic human right which around a billion people are denied. The issue is not *consumption* of a resource, but the environmental costs of satisfying demand. In other words, focus on limiting greenhouse-gas pollution or erosion, not on limiting energy or agricultural production. This means the way the energy is produced triggers a requirement to switch to renewables far more quickly than has been the case up to now.

Therefore we would argue that the rebound paradox suggests a false choice to policy-makers: either make energy production and consumption more efficient, or do something more fundamental. The next few decades are crucial as we strive to meet the resource demands of more than 10 billion people, many of them aspiring to live as resource-intense a life as people in developed countries. We will struggle to protect or restore nature and the benefits it supplies. Efficiency gains buy us time to make our whole economy more sustainable, but not if it leads to complacency and a reason not to make fundamental changes. The arguments surrounding the use of fracking do not lie within the scope of this book, but could be said to encapsulate the arguments in relation to the trade-off between buying time and recognising the need for change.

So is rebound an excuse to do nothing? Why should governments promote efficiency, when the implication exists that the effort is wasted? Not at all, it is like being on a sinking boat which, when the boat takes on water, do you do nothing but enjoy the time left or start bailing and put on a life jacket. Let us not be distracted from putting on the life jackets and building a lifeboat.

But it is not just rebound that leads to increased consumption. As wealth increases, so household sizes fall, so whereas one house might previously have been home to a family of eight or more, that same property is now probably occupied by just two or three people, leading to the need for more dwellings. Conversely with offices, density of use has increased, and with it the need to provide comfort cooling in many cases so that space efficiency may improve at the expense of energy per square metre.

In respect of the built environment one issue is that our political systems are based on short-term perspectives with election cycles every four to five years in most developed countries. Sustainability on the other hand, requires us to take a long-term viewpoint. For example in Australia a Labour government passed a Carbon Tax in 2012 to reduce emissions. However, a new Liberal–National coalition government elected in 2013, immediately repealed the legislation with effect from 1 July 2014 on the premise that 'This will lower costs for Australian businesses and ease cost of living pressures for households' (Department of Environment 2014 http://www.environment.gov.au/climate-change/repealing-carbon-tax, accessed 4 August 2014). Such short termism ensured that the scheme never had the chance to make the difference it could have done and indeed was already so doing.

So, an important step is for pressure to be placed on governments by the built environment professionals not to backslide: the industry can and will accommodate mandated changes in building practice and management: that much is proven. Further in moving practices forward, many of those involved with buildings have become advocates for driving the sustainability agenda. However, developers need certainty so what is required is a clear pathway towards low carbon. The UK government, through its Green Construction Board, which has strong industry backing and engagement, is attempting to do that with the publication of its route map (Green Construction Board 2013) and associated work.

But it isn't just carbon ...

Climate change has been highlighted as a, if not the, major issue facing society. The evidence is that man has been a key influencer and therefore, unsurprisingly, the response has been to seek to reduce the release of carbon into the atmosphere. Therefore the response has been to prioritise efforts into slowing down the rate by which carbon is being released into the atmosphere, primarily through efficiency in energy use and by changes in the type of energy production towards low- and zero-carbon sources.

However, this strategy is not enough. The reality of climate change is here and the effects are already being felt in terms of less predictable weather patterns. So much so that there is recognition that man will have to adapt rather than mitigate. This has already meant that buildings will have to be constructed away from flood zones, or protected against floods; similarly the standard of resilience to storms may impact on, for example, specification of roofs and structural design. All this is possible, and can be accommodated, albeit possibly at increased cost.

However, whilst man can change his environment, they are the only animals who can. Consider this saying by Grasskamp, quoted in Pivo and UNEP FI (2007):

> Man really is the only animal that builds his terrarium around him as he goes and real estate is really the business of building that terrarium. So we have a tremendous ethical content, a tremendous social purpose.

This implies that built environment professionals have a responsibility for protection of other species. Indeed, not only has man this responsibility: it is in his enlightened self-interest for, as WWF (2014) argue 'Ecosystems sustain societies that create economies. It does not work any other way round'. Unfortunately, that same report provides the evidence that this 'tremendous' responsibility, is not working. WWF reports that, out of more than 10,000 representative populations of mammals, birds, reptiles, amphibians and fish, populations have declined by 52 per cent over the 40 years since 1970. This loss of species, they attribute to several causes with climate change standing at 7 per cent and loss or degradation of habitat, largely as a result of developments, to 44 per cent. The report further finds that the greatest species loss is in developing worlds due to two main factors. First, environmental degradation in the developed countries largely occurred *prior* to 1970, which formed the start date for the time series and second by the developed nations effectively 'outsourcing' their impact on biodiversity by importation of the goods and materials that have destroyed natural habitats.

This report stands testament to inadequate action to protect species and the natural capital of the planet. It is now over half a century since Carson's ground-breaking work, *Silent Spring* (Carson 1962), predicting the decline in biodiversity due to chemicals in agricultural practices, first alerted the world to the possibility of a world without birdsong. Regretfully, despite significant improvements in many practices, the decline continues.

Whilst the scope of the problem is not exclusively a built environment issue, it is still extremely relevant and lies within the power of developers and other professionals to improve the situation. First the 'outsourcing' of the problem can be reduced by a shift in specifications towards the use of local materials, the avoidance of products made from materials which harm biodiversity and the encouragement for reuse of materials rather than requiring new ones. Further, whilst biodiversity may feature in many rating tools, such as LEED and BREEAM, the scores afforded to it are low by comparison with other factors rated. Even if the only action were to review the weightings to increase the importance of taking full account of species conservation, it would be a major step in the right direction.

If the ecosystems are to be protected, there needs to be far stronger recognition backed up by positive enforcement that development is not sustainable unless it meets not only the needs and aspirations of people, but equally protects nature.

A further development from that of protection of ecosystems is the notion of ecosystems analysis and payments for environmental systems protection, as discussed in Chapter 4. If the true costs of the externalities imposed by a development are taken into account, the balance of values shifts and there is greater likelihood that biodiversity and environmental protection will be factored in to major decision processes. One of the first steps to allow this to gain traction is for valuers and appraisers to have greater knowledge of ecosystems analysis and for landowners and investors to have awareness of the external costs their investments contain and to require such costs to be reflected within appraisal processes.

However, currently, this does not happen. Indeed, the leg of the three-legged stool of the economy, the environment and society that is exercising most influence globally is the economy. Despite a plethora of recent, and not so recent, economic thinking that calls for a reshaping of economies to steady state or no growth, the main economies are still run on the basic ambition that increases in consumer spending and gross domestic product are desirable, or indeed, necessary, goals. A reduction in consumption is considered undesirable. Yet, with increased consumption comes increases waste, both domestic and commercial, which as indicated in several places in this book is not only an increasing cost of development, due to levies on waste, but represents yet more carbon and yet more planetary pressure. In many countries, as has been noted, waste to landfill has been reduced and recycling is now much more prevalent. However, to these authors at least, the success of recycling represents an opportunity for complacency when the real driver should be more towards lessening of consumption, reducing obsolescence and to reuse rather than recycle. Within construction, there has been real progress. After all, less material consumed pays economic dividends; however, building life is often dictated by economic change and therein still lies waste.

Perhaps we have to acknowledge that no development is ever 'truly' sustainable: but the challenge is to produce buildings that come as close to that as possible. It has been suggested (Sayce *et al.* 2004) that the tests of sustainability of a building are that it should achieve:

- Longevity – as a building in which materials are amortised over short periods of time is not only environmentally poor; it does not add to a sense of place.
- Low environmental impact – in terms of energy, waste and water, not only through its construction but through the life cycle.
- Loose fit – as a building which is essentially flexible in its design is more likely to achieve longevity and be fit for purpose, or alternative uses, for longer.
- Locationally appropriate – too many buildings simply do not fit the context in which they sit. If a building is sufficiently iconic it can create its own sense of space and place but if it is not it needs to fit. Increasingly, a well-located building means one that has good accessibility to multi-modes of transport, and is accessible to a range of occupiers.
- Likeable – in that it not only meets the functionality needs of its occupiers or intended occupiers but works well for them and is a healthy place in which people *like* to be.

How close are we to this intent? Within the new build sector, which is the prime interest of this book, great strides have been made in terms of genuine desire to move along the curve which in turn in most jurisdictions is moving in the right direction. However, the need to contain costs means that however good the intent, going 'beyond compliance' is still difficult for most developers, except where they are aiming their product at a specific 'sensitised' sub-sector of the market. Further, notions of compliance are changing. The rhetoric of 'mitigation' is beginning to shift towards 'adaptation' as new evidence comes forward that it is already too late to prevent significant and possibly devastating climate change. As it does, so building standards can be expected to change, with the emphasis turning from energy efficient buildings, designed to reduce 'in-use' consumption, to those which are capable of resilience to tempest and flooding. Already techniques for buildings able to 'float' in times of flood are in use within domestic environments in the Netherlands and the UK; more such designs will follow.

The cost of fully resilient buildings, however, may involve greater carbon in construction, if the rafts are concrete, so it is not a zero sum gain in environmental terms and this complexity of implications of design choice often leads to conservatism and 'what the market demands'; in turn this tends to be well-proven technologies and conventional design – hardly a recipe for the radical change that might be needed in the future.

In terms of market sensitisation to environmental and social concerns, evidence is emerging that some sub-sectors, notably in the office and shopping centre sector, are now displaying a strong demand for energy efficient buildings, with some evidence that it is permeating to residential. However, as yet, there is very limited evidence that the sustainability agenda has penetrated more deeply or that the matter of cost differential in construction can always be justified. There remains a very long way yet to go and, in our view, this will require strong and decisive action from governments to mandate change. Even then, the further challenge is then to design the building such that it performs as per its design and that the management arrangements incentivise good sustainability practices.

But we will only know we have arrived when there is a shift in normative behaviours and thinking and doing sustainably is just, the way we do things round here, no questions asked. Is such a situation a pipedream? We hope not, or the changes so far will have proved to be an exercise in moving deckchairs around the *Titanic*, not in steering away from the iceberg.

References

Alcott, B. (2008) Historical overview of the Jevons Paradox in the literature, in J.M. Polimari, K. Mayumi, M. Giampietro, and B. Alcott, *The Jevons Paradox and the Myth of Resource Efficiency Improvements*, London: Earthscan.

Carson, R. (1994 [1962]). *Silent Spring*, New York: Houghton Mifflin.

Chakravarty, D., Dasgupta, S., and Roy, J. (2013) Rebound effect: how much to worry?, *Current Opinion in Environmental Sustainability* 5(2): 216–228.

Cook, S.J. and Golton, B. (1994) Sustainable development concepts and practice in the built environment: a UK perspective. CIB TG 16. Sustainable Construction, Tampa, FL, 6–9 November 1994.

Department of Infrastructure and Regional Development (2013) State of Australian Cities Report 2011. Retrieved on 13 May 13 2015 from http://www.infrastructure.gov.au/infrastructure/pab/soac/.

Farman, J.C., Gardiner, B.G., and Shanklin, J.D. (2003) Large losses of total ozone in Antarctica reveal seasonal ClO_x/NO_x interaction, in L. Garwin and T. Lincoln (eds) *A Century of Nature: Twenty-One Discoveries that Changed Science and the World*. Chicago, IL: University of Chicago Press

Green Construction Board (2013) *The Low Carbon Routemap for the Built Environment*. Retrieved from http://www.greenconstructionboard.org/images/folder/GCB_Carbon_ROUTEMAP.pdf.

IPCC (2014) *Summary for Policy Makers*. Retrieved from http://report.mitigation2014.org/spm/ipcc_wg3_ar5_summary-for-policymakers_approved.pdf.

Owen, D. (2012) *The Conundrum*, London: Penguin.

Pivo, G. and UN Environment Programme Finance Initiative Property Working Group (2008) Responsible property investing: what the leaders are doing, *Journal of Property Investment & Finance* 26(6): 562–576.

Saunders, H.D. (2000) A view from the macro side: rebound, backfire, and Khazzoom–Brookes, *Energy Policy* 28(6): 439–449.

Sayce, S., Walker, A., and McIntosh, A. (2004). *Building Sustainability in the Balance: Promoting Stakeholder Dialogue*, London: Estates Gazette.

Stern, N. (2006) *The Stern Review: The Economics of Climate Change*, Vol. 30, London: HM Treasury.

UNEP FI (2007) Responsible property investing: what the leaders are doing. Retrieved from http://www.unepfi.org/fileadmin/documents/responsible_property_investing_01.pdf.

WCED (World Commission on Environment and Development) (1987) *Our Common Future*. Retrieved from http://www.un-documents.net/our-common-future.pdf.

Weiss, E.B. (1990). Our rights and obligations to future generations for the environment. *American Journal of International Law* 84(1): 198-207.

Wilkinson, S.J. (2013) Conceptual understanding of sustainability in Australian property organisations, *Journal of Property Management* 31(3): 522–540.

WWF (2014) *Living Planet Report 2014:Species and Spaces, People and Places*. Retrieved from https://www.wwf.or.jp/activities/lib/lpr/WWF_LPR_2014.pdf.

Appendix A
Rating tools

Existing international rating tools

Continent	Rating tool	Country	Launch date/ most recent version	Website
Africa (1)	Green Star SA	South Africa	2008/2008	http://www.gbcsa.org.za/greenstar/greenstar.php
Asia (17)	GBAS	China	2006	http://www.cngbn.com/; https://docs.google.com/Doc?id=ddfqxmx9_29hs74dhgv
	HK-BEAM Plus	Hong Kong	1996/2010	http://www.beamsociety.org.hk/general/home.php
	GRIHA	India	2009	http://www.grihaindia.org/index.php?option=com_content&task=view&id=13
	LEED India	India	2007	http://www.igbc.in/site/igbc/index.jsp; http://www.igbc.in/site/igbc/publication.jsp
	IGBC Green SEZ	India	2010 Pilot	http://www.igbc.in/site/igbc/publication.jsp
	CEPAS	International	2006	http://www.bd.gov.hk/english/documents/index_CEPAS.html
	CASBEE	Japan	2002/2008	http://www.ibec.or.jp/CASBEE/english/index.htm
	GBI(M)	Malaysia	2009	http://www.greenbuildingindex.org; http://www.greenbuildingindex.org/how-GBI-works2.html#RatingTools
	QSAS	Qatar	2009/2010	http://qsas.org
	BREEAM Gulf	Qatar	2008	http://www.breeam.org/page.jsp?id=196
	Green Mark	Singapore	2005/2010	http://www.greenmark.sg; http://bca.gov.sg/GreenMark/green_mark_criteria.html
	KGBCC	South Korea	2002/2006	http://greenbuilding.or.kr/eng/html/main.jsp

Continent	Rating tool	Country	Launch date/ most recent version	Website
	ABRI EEWH	Taiwan	1999/2003	http://gsp.stsipa.gov.tw/eng/main03_2.html; http://www.taiwangbc.org.tw/english/index.php
	LOTUS	Vietnam	2010	http://vgbc.org.vn
	Estidama Pearl	UAE	2010	http://estidama.org
	LEED Emirates	UAE	2011	http://www.emiratesgbc.org/egbc
	BREEAM Gulf	UAE	2008	http://www.breeam.org/page.jsp?id=196
Australia (3)	Green Star	Australia	2003/2008 (2010)	http://www.gbca.org.au/green-star
	NABERS	Australia	2000/2005	http://www.nabers.com.au
	Green Star NZ	New Zealand	2007/2008	http://www.nzgbc.org.nz/main/greenstar
Europe (13)	PromisE	Finland	2004/ under development	http://virtual.vtt.fi/virtual/proj6/environ/ympluok_e.html; www.promiseweb.net
	HQE	France	2005/2008	http://www.certivea.com/uk
	DGNB	Germany	2009	http://www.dgnb.de/_en/index.php
	Living Building Challenge	Ireland	2010	http://ilbi.org/countries/ireland
	Protocollo ITACA	Italy	1996, 2011	http://www.itaca.org
	BREEAM Netherlands	Netherlands	2010	http://www.breeam.nl/breeam/breeam-nl_english
	LIDER A	Portugal	2005/2009	http://www.lidera.info/?p=index&RegionId=3&Culture=en
	Verde	Spain	2009	http://www.gbce.es/en
	MINERGIE	Switzerland	2008	http://www.minergie.com
	BREEAM	UK	1990/2011	http://www.breeam.org

Continent	Rating tool	Country	Launch date/ most recent version	Website
	LEnSE	EU	2008	http://www.lensebuildings.com
	GreenBuilding Programme	EU	2005/2009	http://www.eu-greenbuilding.org
	Energy Performance Certification	EU	2007/2009	http://www.buildup.eu DIRECTIVE 2002/91/EC: http://eur-lex.europa.eu/ LexUriServ/LexUriServ.do?uri=OJ:L:2003:001:0065:0071:EN:PDF
North America (9)	LEED	USA	1998/2012	http://www.usgbc.org
	Green Globes US	USA	2004	http://www.thegbi.org/green-globes
	Energy Star	USA	1995	http://www.energystar.gov
	Living Building Challenge	USA	1996/2010	http://ilbi.org/countries/united-states
	LEED Canada	Canada	2002/2011	http://www.cagbc.org
	Living Building Challenge	Canada	2009	http://ilbi.org/countries/canada
	ATHENA Environmental Impact Estimator	Canada	2002	http://www.athenasmi.org/our-software-data/impact-estimator/
	LEED Mexico/ SICES	Mexico	2006	http://www.mexicogbc.org
	Living Building Challenge	Mexico	2009	http://ilbi.org/countries/mexico
South America (4)	LEED Brazil	Brazil	2008	http://www.gbcbrasil.org.br/in/index.php
	AQUA	Brazil	2008	http://vanzolini.org.br/conteudo-aqua.asp?cod_site=104&id_menu=760
	LEED Chile	Chile	2008	http://www.chilegbc.cl/chilegbc/www/admintools/index.asp
	LEED Colombia	Columbia	2009	http://www.cccs.org.co

Continent	Rating tool	Country	Launch date/ most recent version	Website
International (6)	BREEAM Global	International	2011	www.breeam.org
	SB Tool (GB Tool)	International	2007/2010 (1998/2005)	http://www.iisbe.org/sbtool; http://www.iisbe.org/iisbe/gbc2k5/gbc2k5-start.htm
	LEED International	International	2011	http://www.usgbc.org/DisplayPage.aspx?CMSPageID=2346
	CEN/TC350	International Standard	2010/2011/ 2012/2013	http://www.cen.eu/cen/Sectors/Sectors/Construction/ SustainableConstruction/ Pages/CEN_TC350.aspx
	ISO 14000 Series	International	2004	http://www.iso.org/iso/iso_14000_essentials
	ISO/TC59/SC17 (ISO 21931)	International Standard	2006/2007/ 2008/2010	http://www.iso.org/iso/standards_development/technical_committees/ list_of_iso_technical_committees/iso_technical_committee. htm?commid=322621

Index

Page numbers in *italics* indicate figures; page numbers in **bold** indicate tables